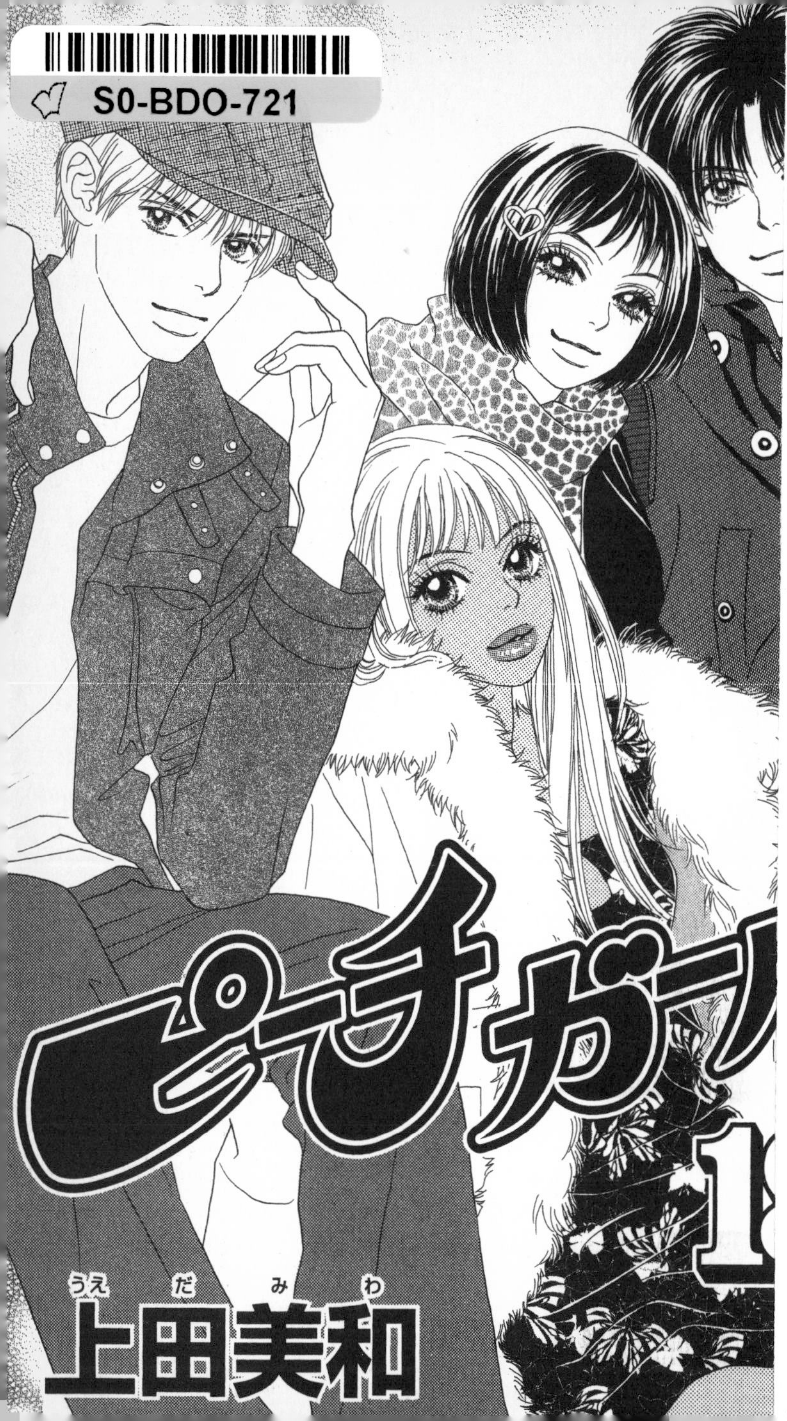
ピーチガー
うえだみわ
上田美和

Peach Girl: Change of Heart Vol. 10
created by Miwa Ueda

Translation - Roy Yoshimoto
English Adaptation - Jodi Bryson
Retouch and Lettering - Keith Olson
Production Artist - James Dashiell
Cover Design - Anna Kernbaum

Editor - Lillian Diaz-Przybyl
Digital Imaging Manager - Chris Buford
Pre-Press Manager - Antonio DePietro
Production Managers - Jennifer Miller and Mutsumi Miyazaki
Art Director - Matt Alford
Managing Editor - Jill Freshney
VP of Production - Ron Klamert
President and C.O.O. - John Parker
Publisher and C.E.O. - Stuart Levy

A  Manga

TOKYOPOP Inc.
5900 Wilshire Blvd. Suite 2000
Los Angeles, CA 90036

E-mail: info@TOKYOPOP.com
Come visit us online at www.TOKYOPOP.com

©1999 Miwa Ueda
st published in Japan in 1999 by Kodansha Ltd., Tokyo.
glish Publication rights arranged through Kodansha Ltd.
English text copyright © 2004 TOKYOPOP Inc.

ISBN: 1-59182-499-0

First TOKYOPOP printing: November 2004
10 9 8 7 6 5 4 3 2 1
Printed in the USA

Peach Girl™
Change of Heart

by Miwa Ueda

10

TOKYOPOP®

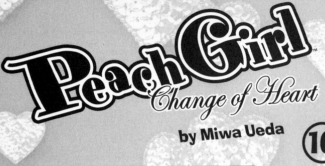

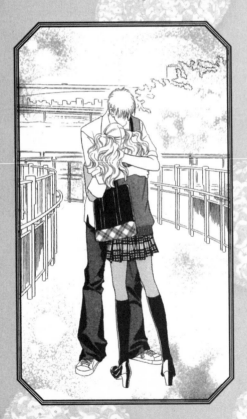

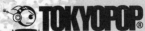

HAMBURG // LONDON // LOS ANGELES // TOKYO

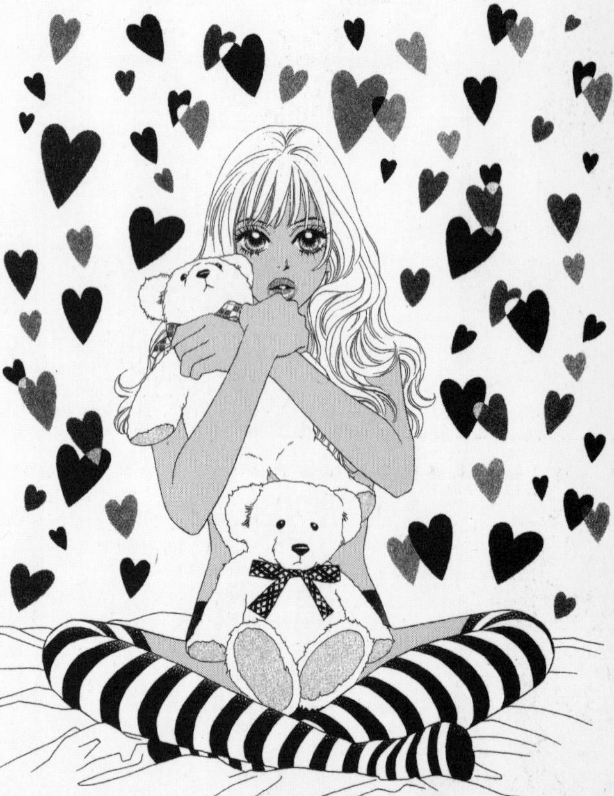
ピーチガール

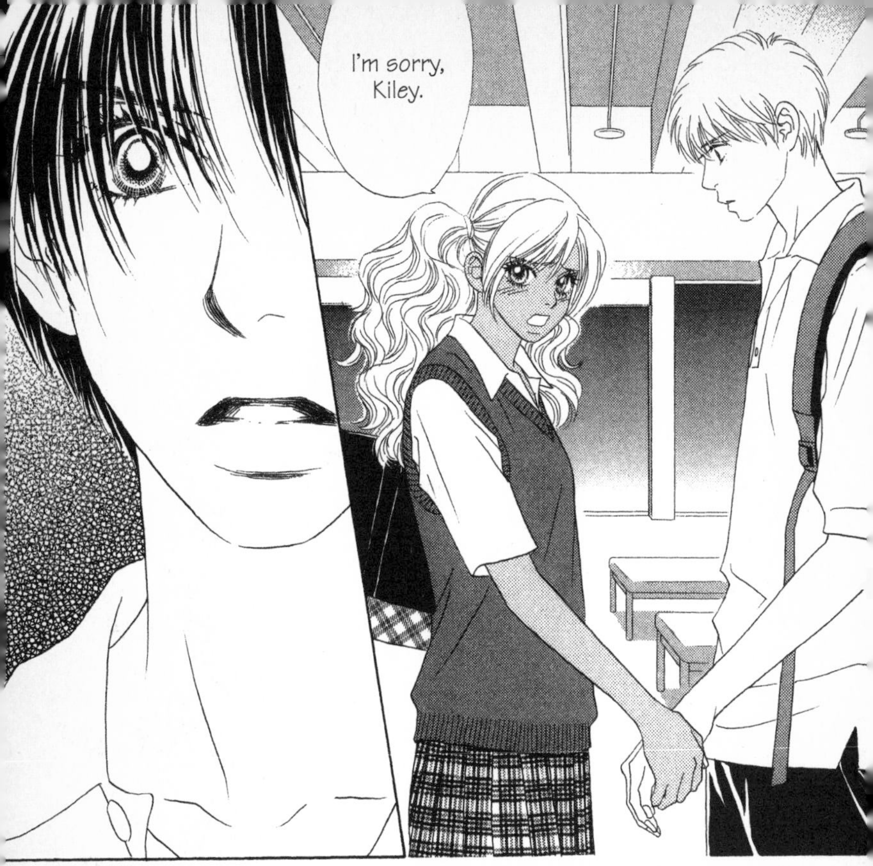
I'm sorry, Kiley.

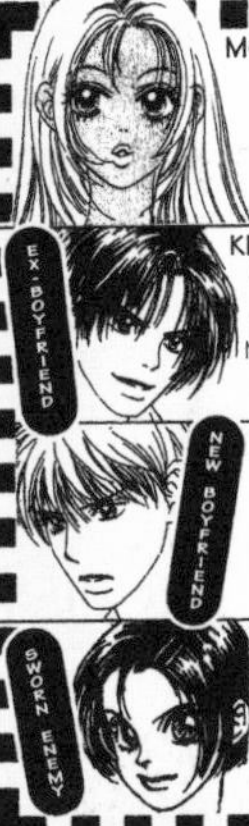
EX-BOYFRIEND
NEW BOYFRIEND
SWORN ENEMY

MOMO ADACHI: Her romance with Kiley apparently over...will she start over with Toji?!

KILEY OKAYASU: He declares his love for Misao, but is rebuffed. Now he still pines for Momo.

TOJI TOJIKAMORI: He and Momo make love at Shiranami, and now they're dating again!!

SAE KASHIWAGI: Obsessed with Ryo, she deludes herself into thinking she's pregnant with his child.

MOMO'S LOVE IS ALWAYS STORMY!! WHY?!

Sae engineers Momo and Toji's breakup. Momo eventually bounces back when she falls in love with Kiley. But she is badly shocked to find out that Kiley's true love is Misao!! Kiley takes a soul-searching trip, and realizes how important Momo is to him. But then Kiley breaks a promise to Momo, who ends up getting together with Toji. Kiley is unable to give up, and tells Momo that he loves her more than ever. Meanwhile, Sae declares that she's pregnant with Ryo's child. Everyone is freaked, but then they find out that Sae was faking! When Momo, Toji and Kiley find themselves in the same room, Toji senses that Momo is confused, and confronts her to choose him or Kiley. Momo's answer is...

Everything you need to know!

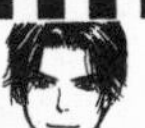

RYO OKAYASU: Kiley's older brother. Shady businessman. Dumped by Misao over Sae's pregnancy situation.

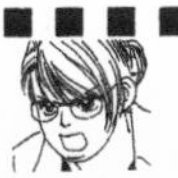

MISAO: The school nurse. Formerly Kiley's tutor who always harbored a crush on Ryo...

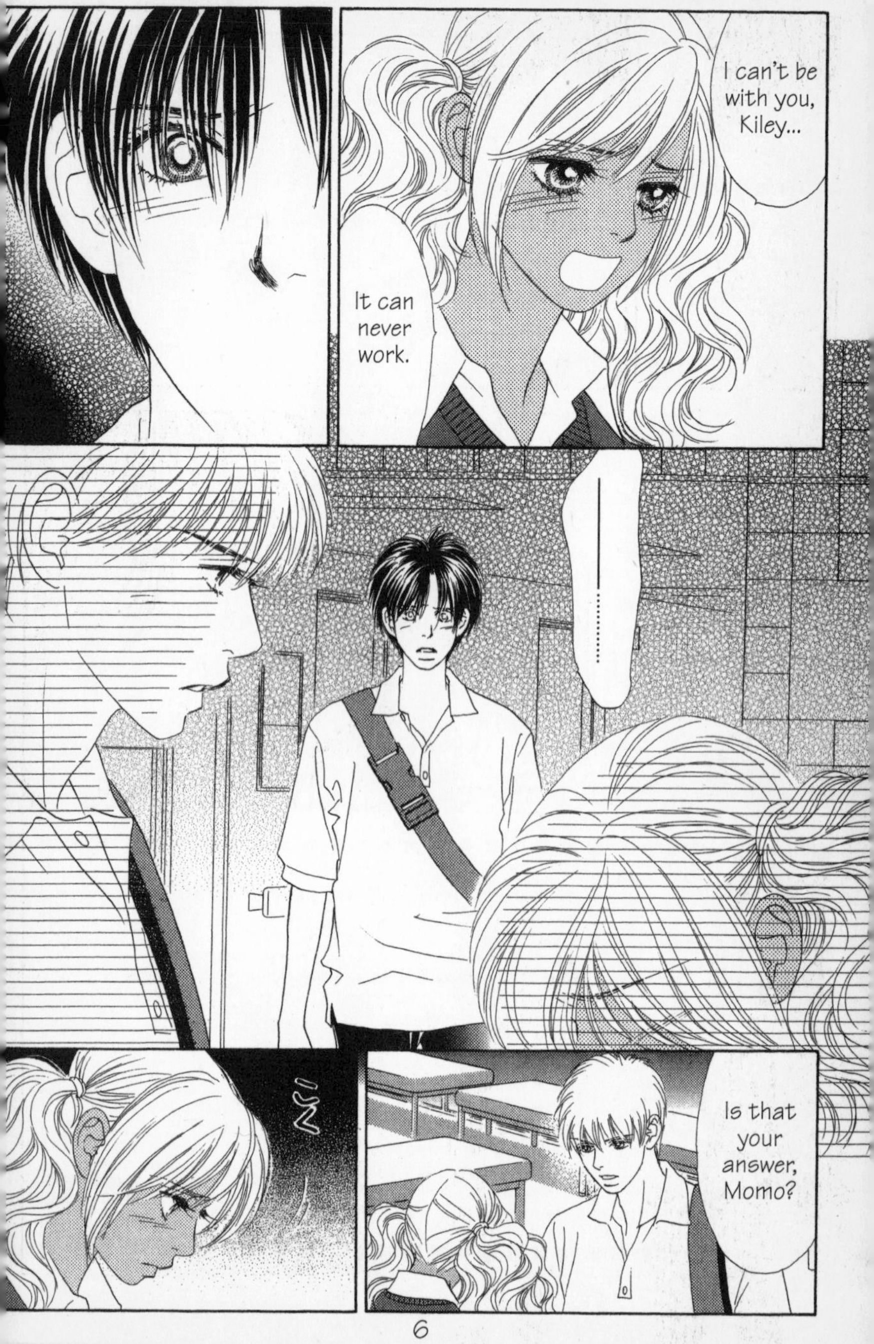
I can't be with you, Kiley...
It can never work.
Is that your answer, Momo?

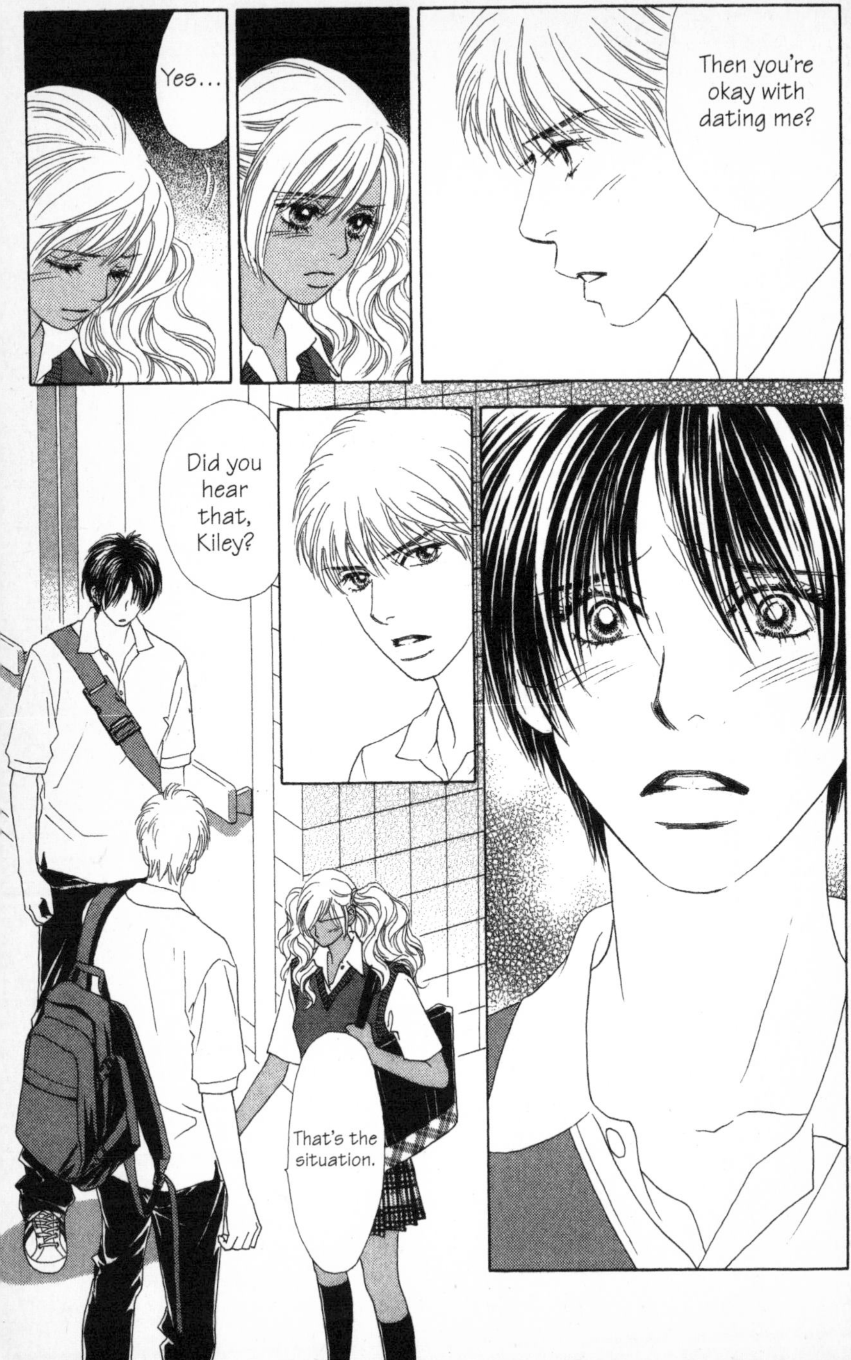
Then you're okay with dating me?
Yes…
Did you hear that, Kiley?
That's the situation.

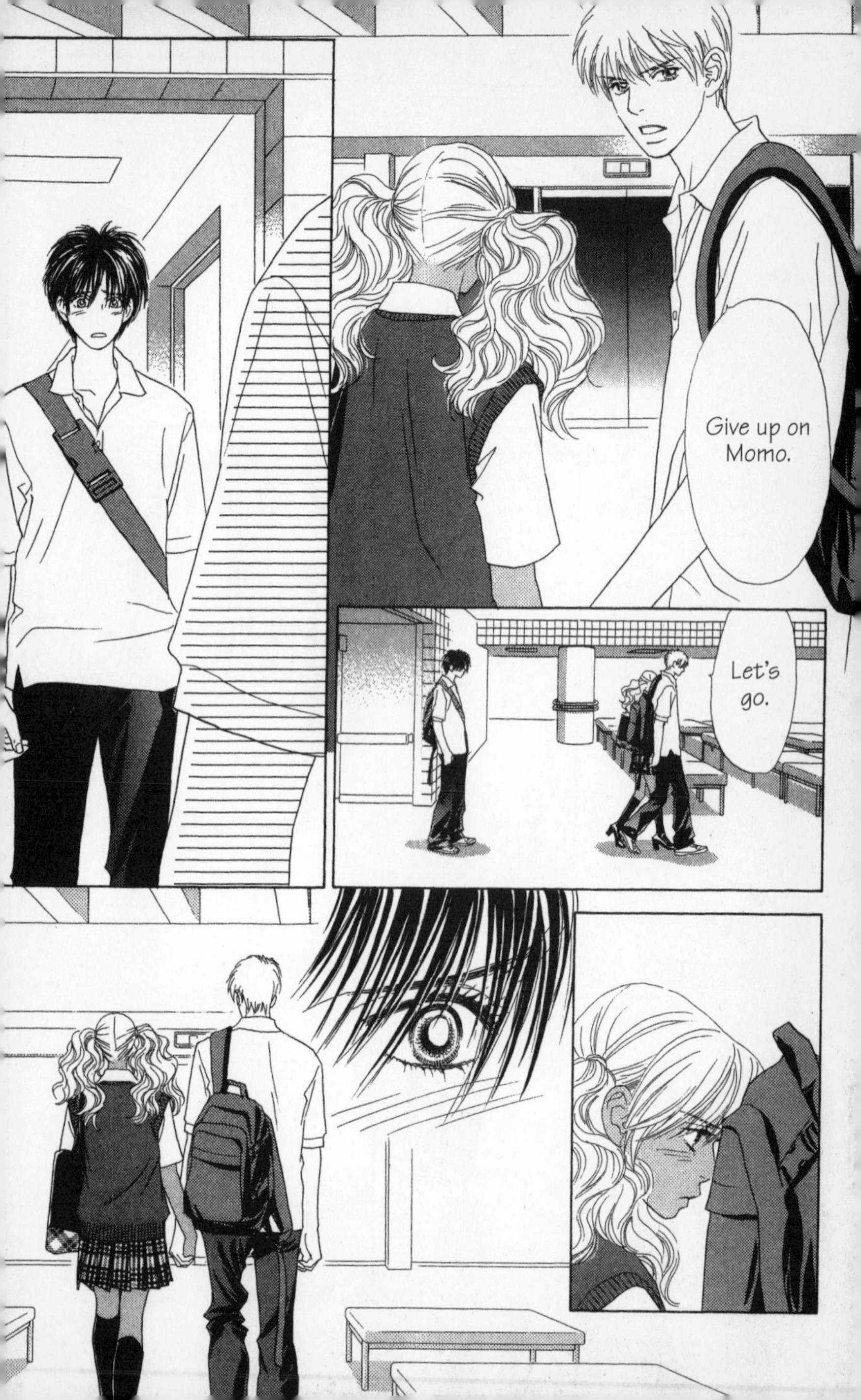
Give up on Momo.
Let's go.

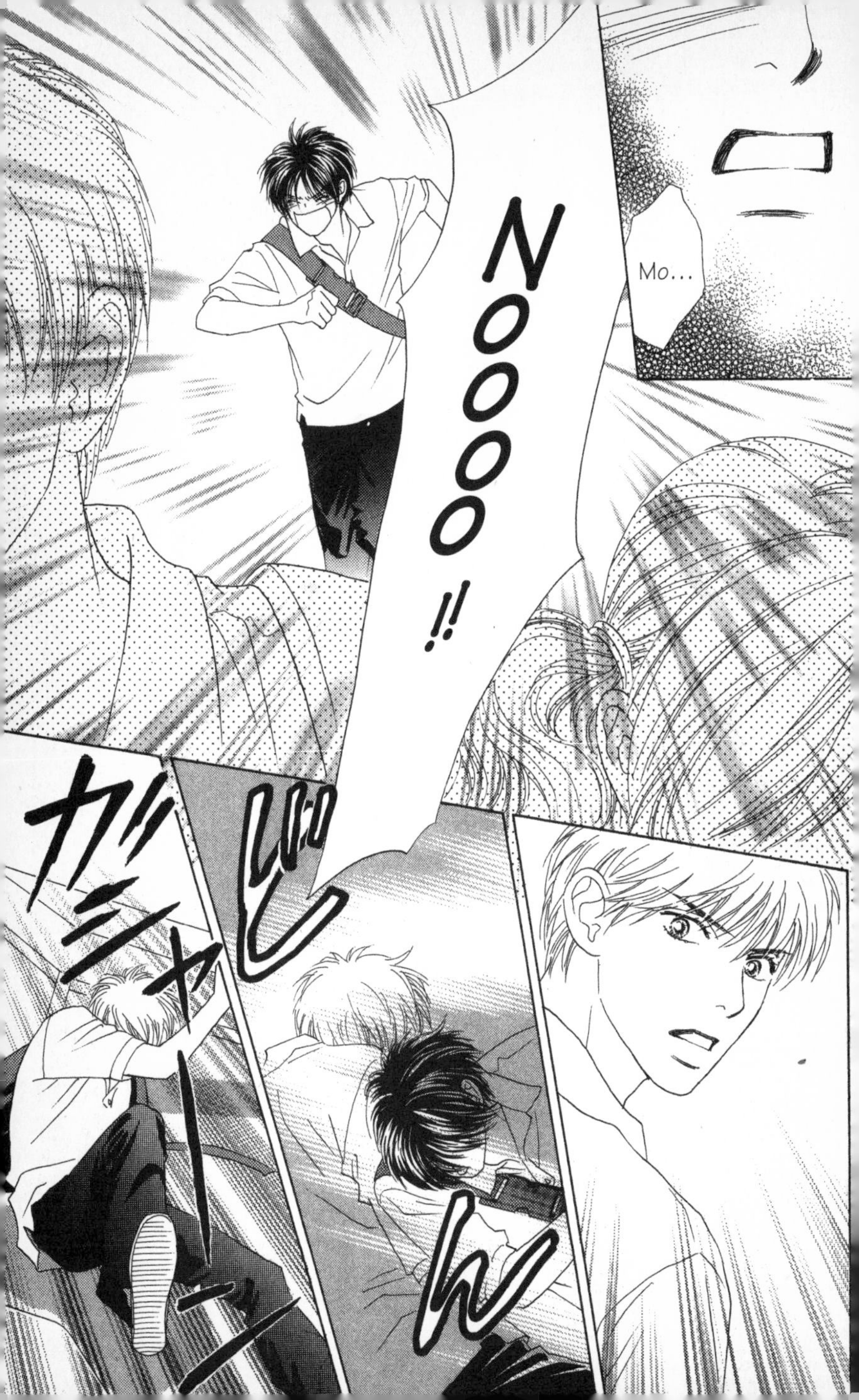
Mo...
NOOOOO!!
どしん
ガシャーン

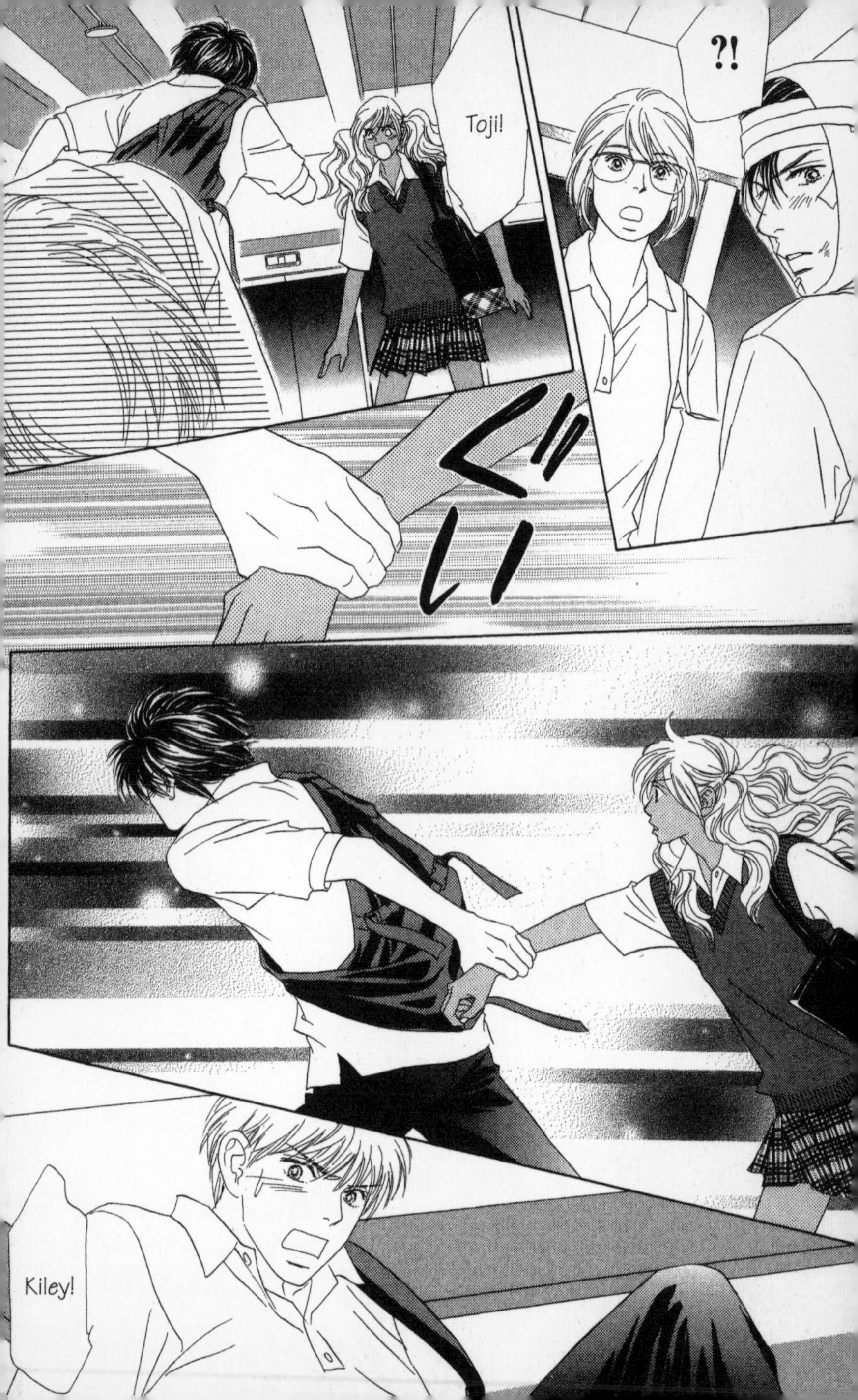
?!
Toji!
ぐい
Kiley!

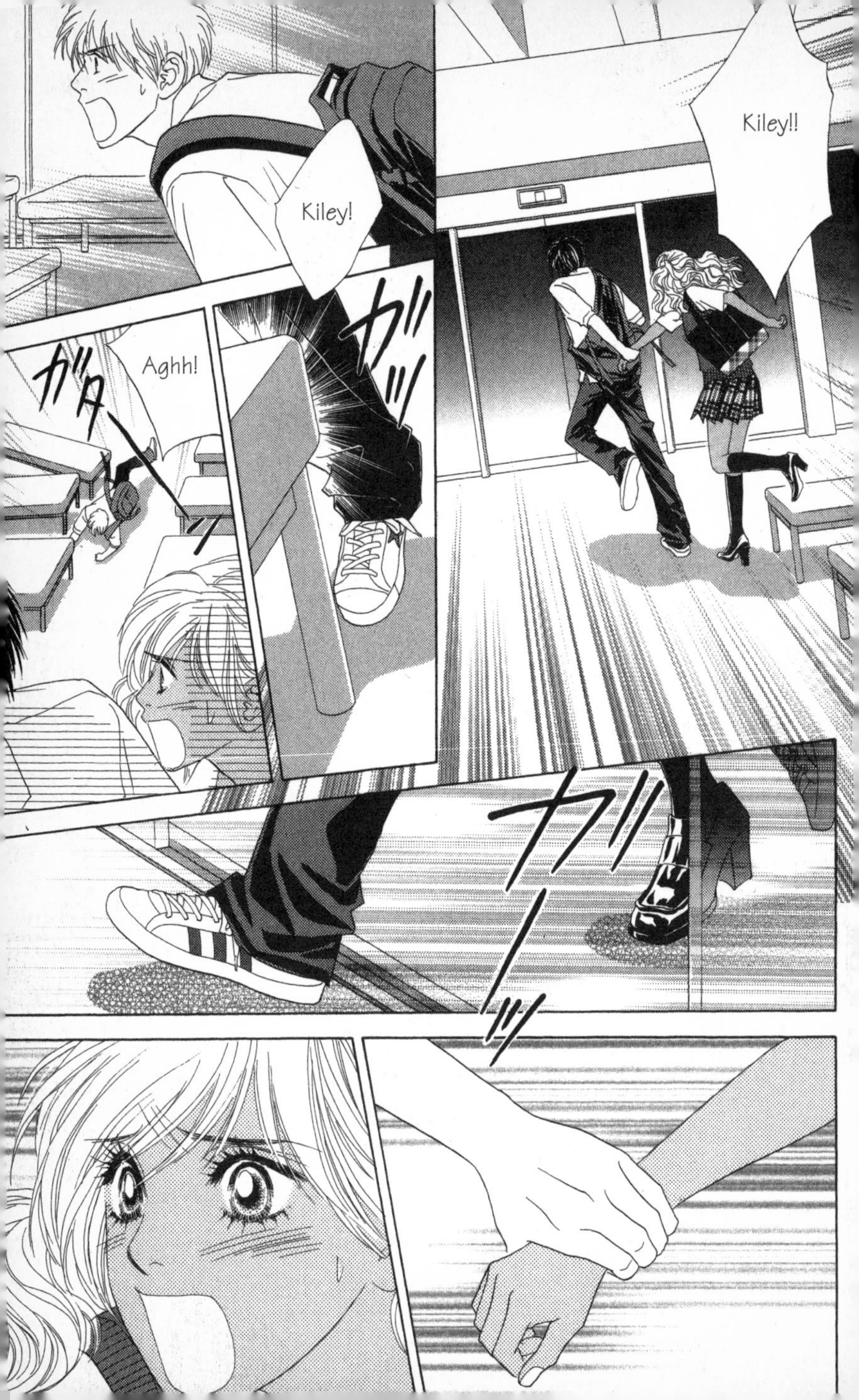
Kiley!!
Kiley!
ガッ
Aghh!
ガタ
ガッ

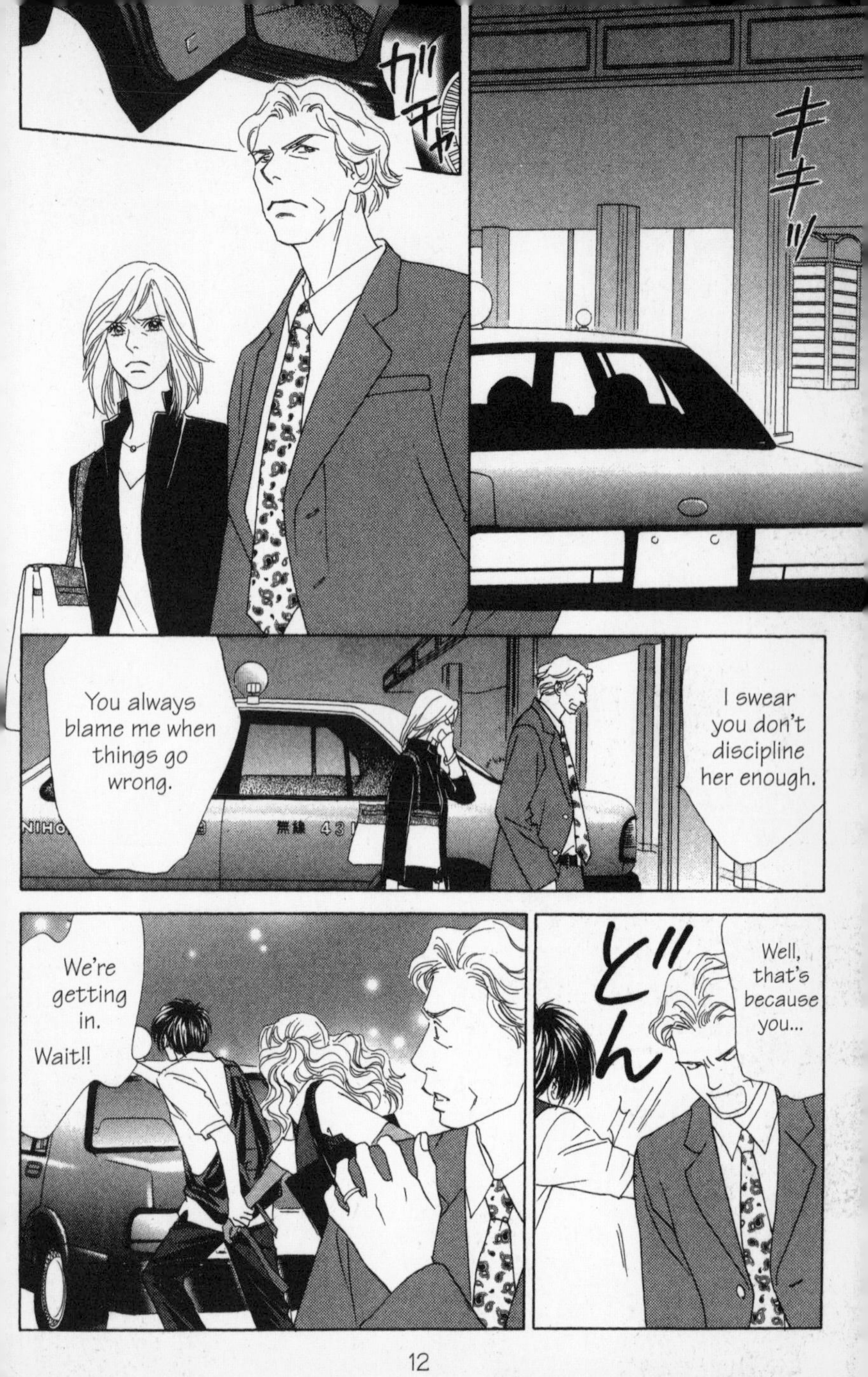
キキッ
ガチャ
I swear you don't discipline her enough.
You always blame me when things go wrong.
Well, that's because you...
どん
We're getting in.
Wait!!

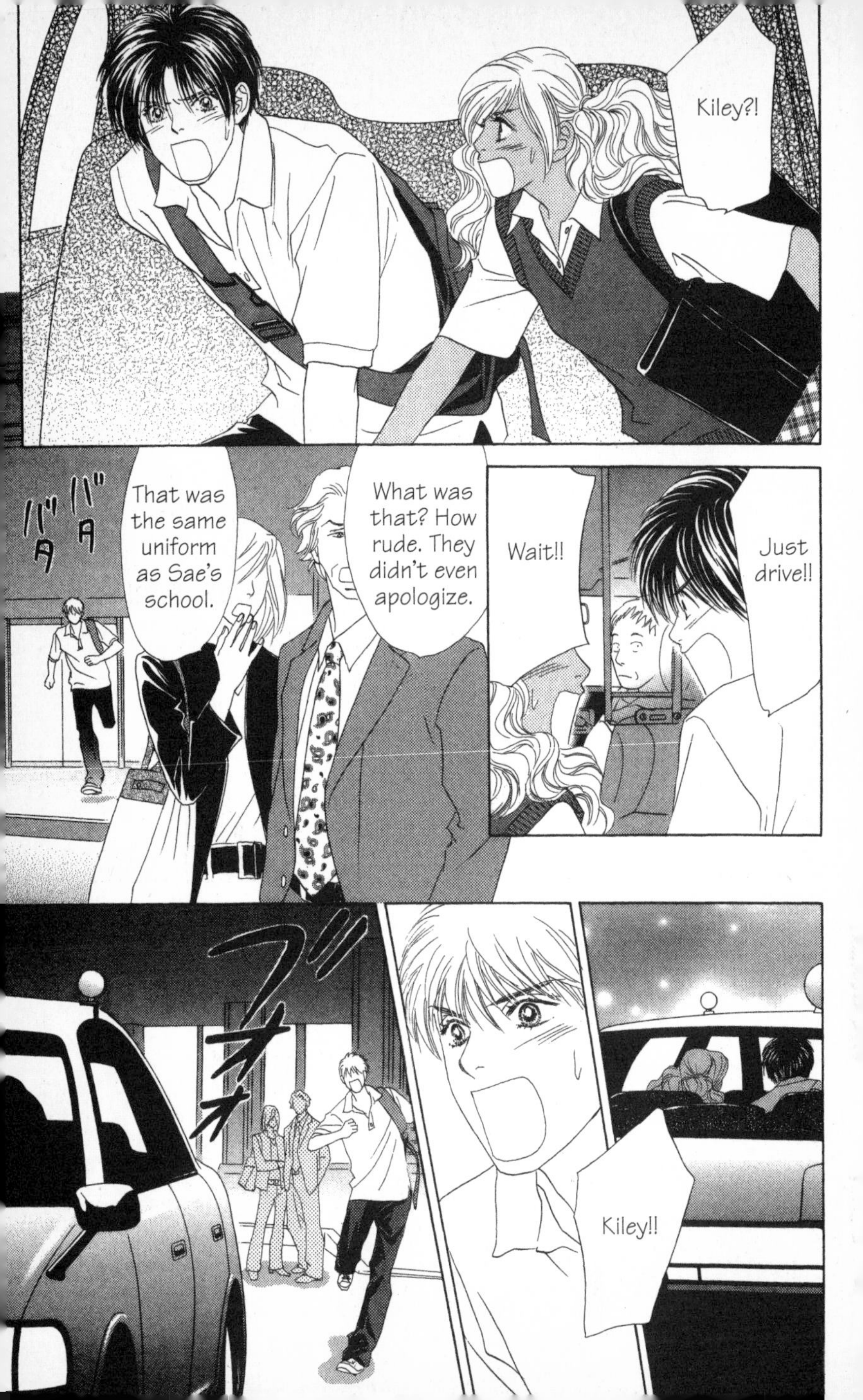
Kiley?!
Just drive!!
Wait!!
What was that? How rude. They didn't even apologize.
That was the same uniform as Sae's school.
バタバタ
Kiley!!

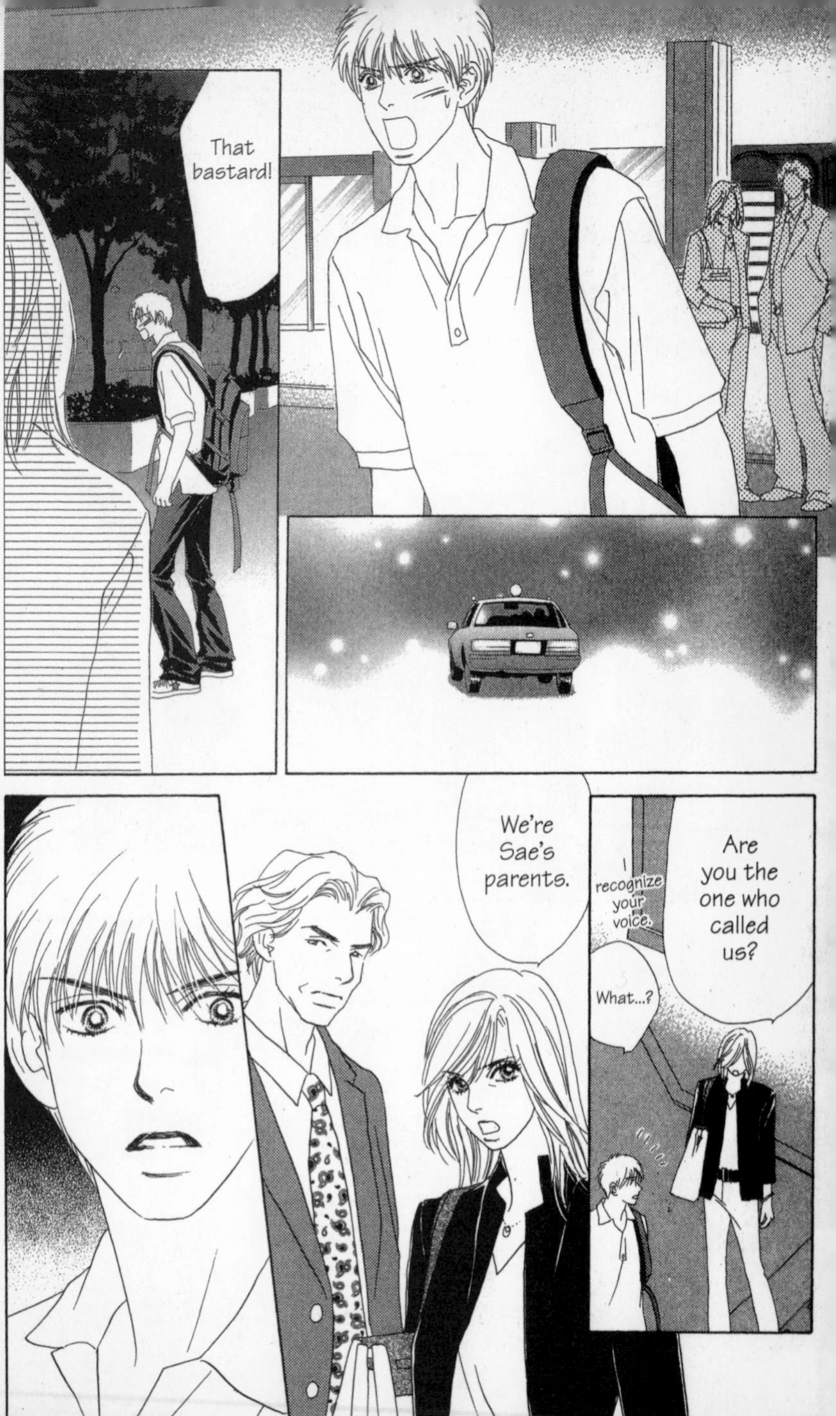
That bastard!
Are you the one who called us?
I recognize your voice.
What...?
We're Sae's parents.

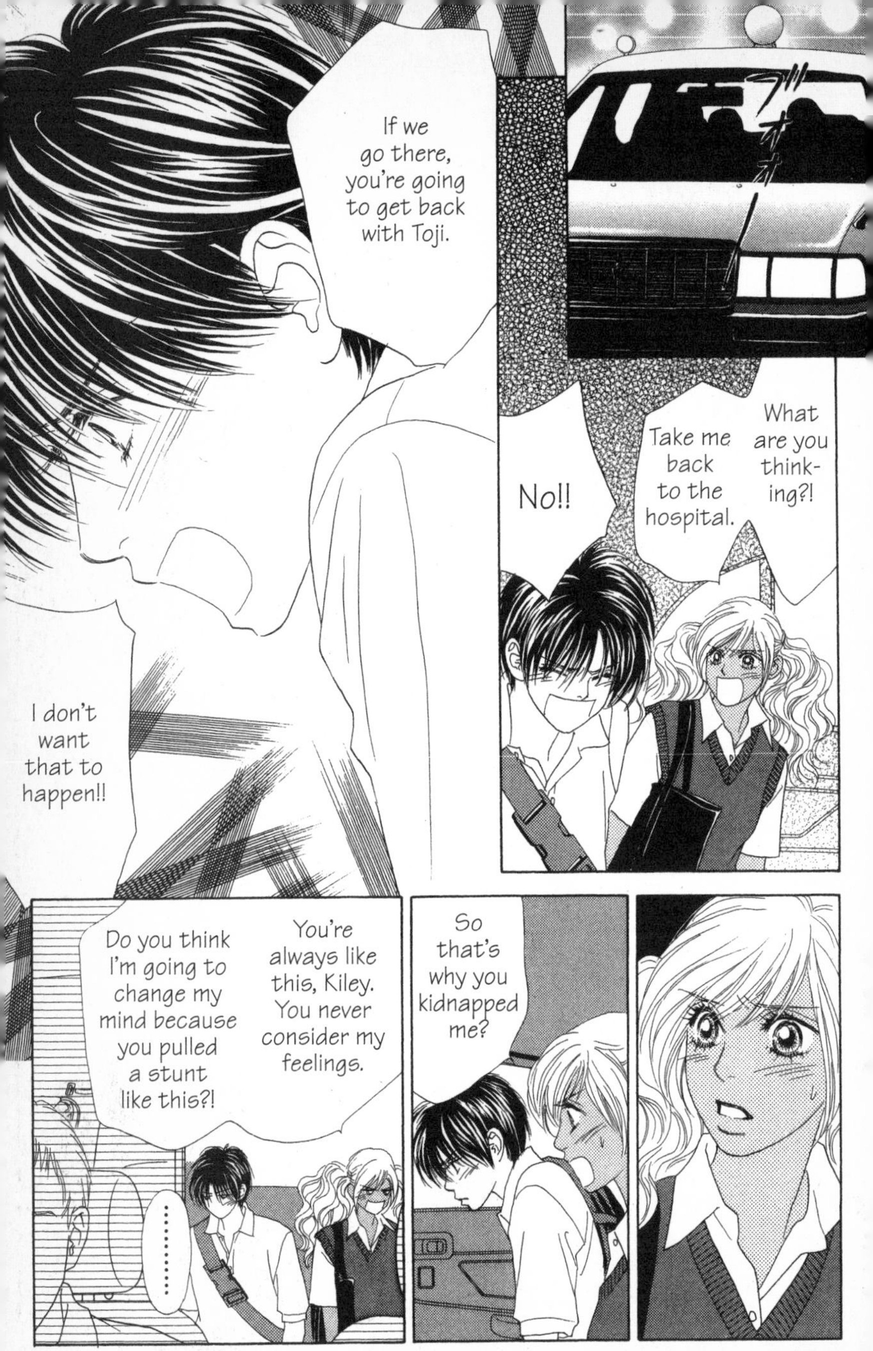
What are you think-ing?!
Take me back to the hospital.
No!!
If we go there, you're going to get back with Toji.
I don't want that to happen!!
So that's why you kidnapped me?
You're always like this, Kiley. You never consider my feelings.
Do you think I'm going to change my mind because you pulled a stunt like this?!
……

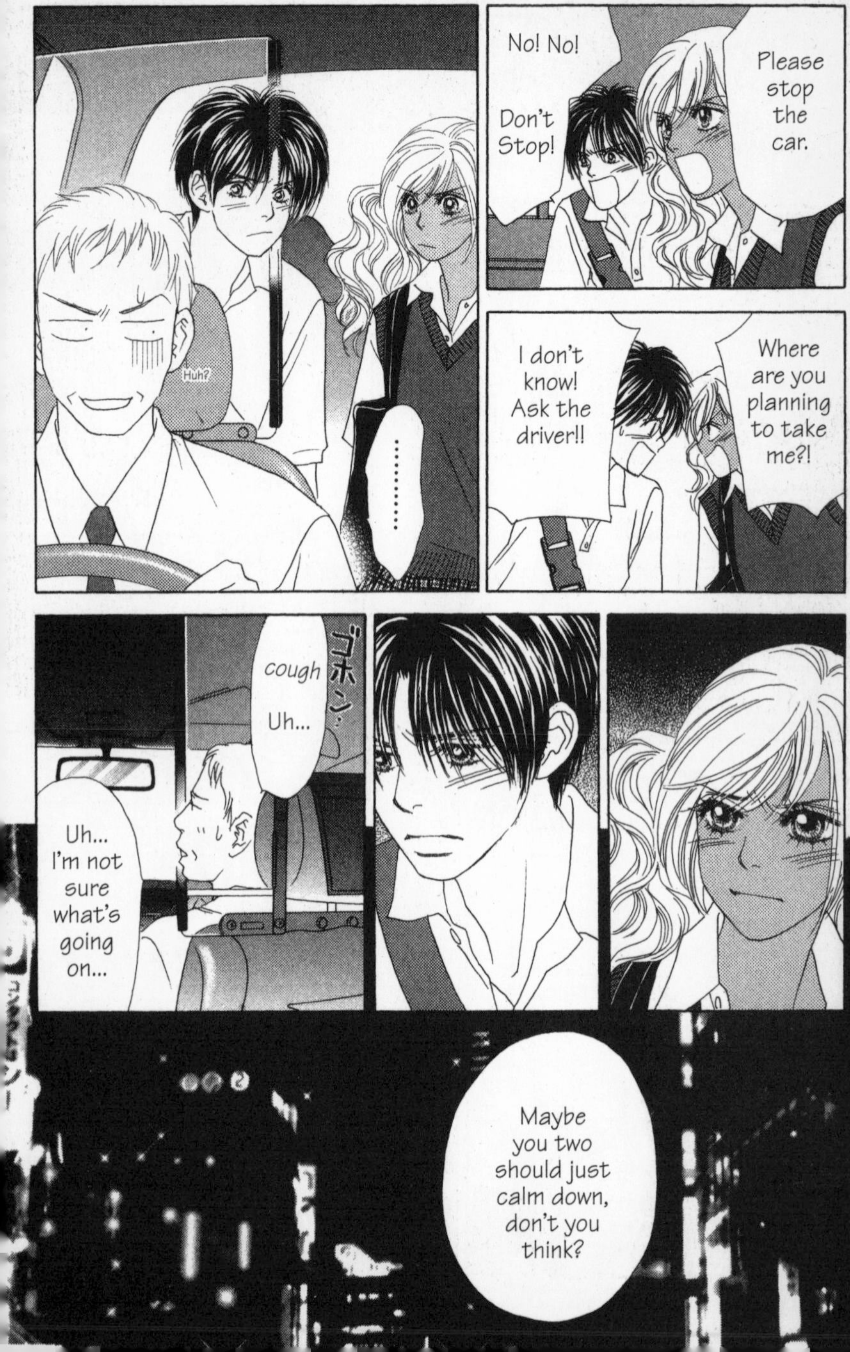
Please stop the car.
No! No!
Don't Stop!
Where are you planning to take me?!
I don't know! Ask the driver!!
Huh?
....
ゴホン
cough
Uh...
Uh... I'm not sure what's going on...
Maybe you two should just calm down, don't you think?

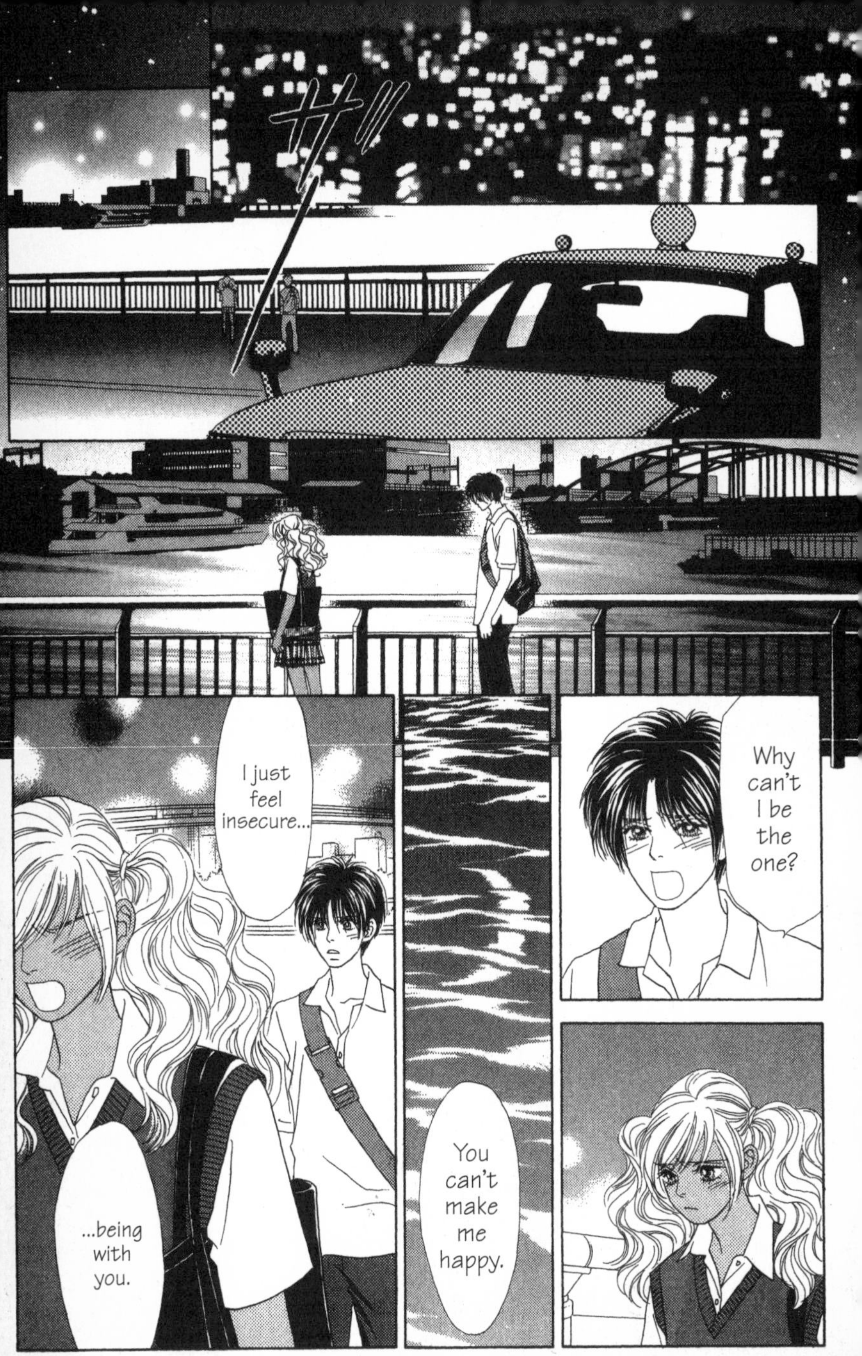
Why can't I be the one?
You can't make me happy.
I just feel insecure...
...being with you.

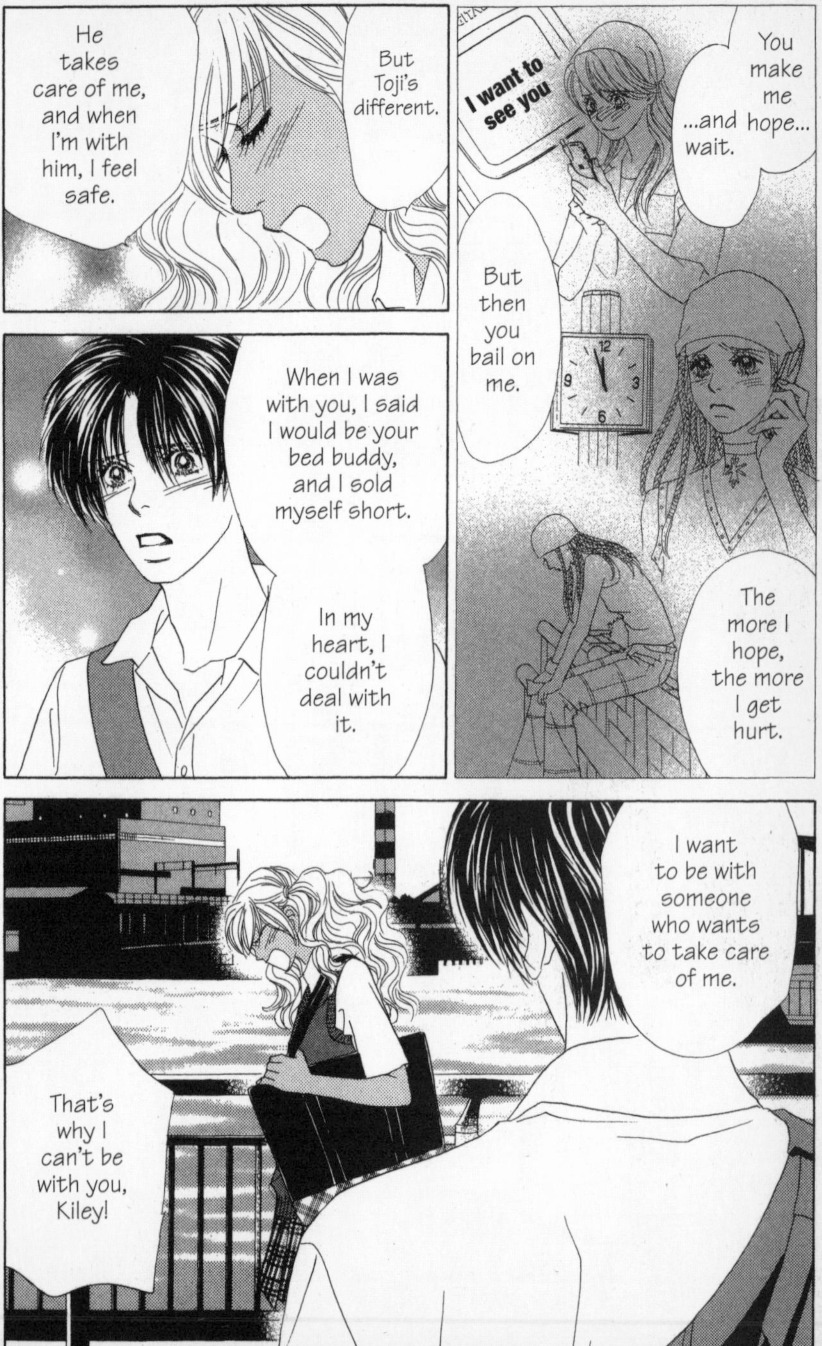
I want to see you
You make me hope... ...and wait.
But then you bail on me.
The more I hope, the more I get hurt.
He takes care of me, and when I'm with him, I feel safe.
But Toji's different.
When I was with you, I said I would be your bed buddy, and I sold myself short.
In my heart, I couldn't deal with it.
I want to be with someone who wants to take care of me.
That's why I can't be with you, Kiley!

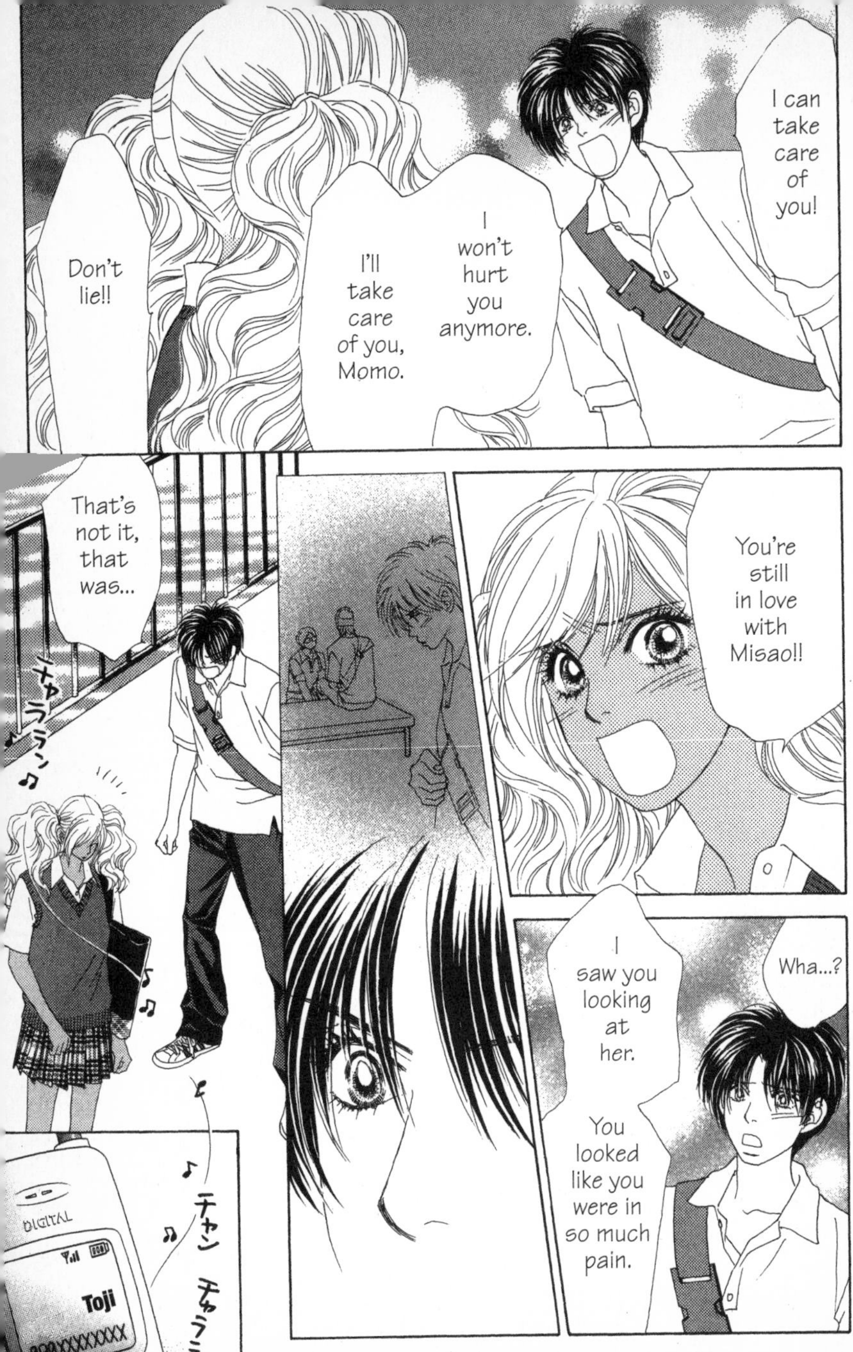

I can take care of you!
I won't hurt you anymore. I'll take care of you, Momo.
Don't lie!!
You're still in love with Misao!!
Wha...?
I saw you looking at her.
You looked like you were in so much pain.
That's not it, that was...
DIGITAL
Toji
090XXXXXXXX
チャン
チャララ

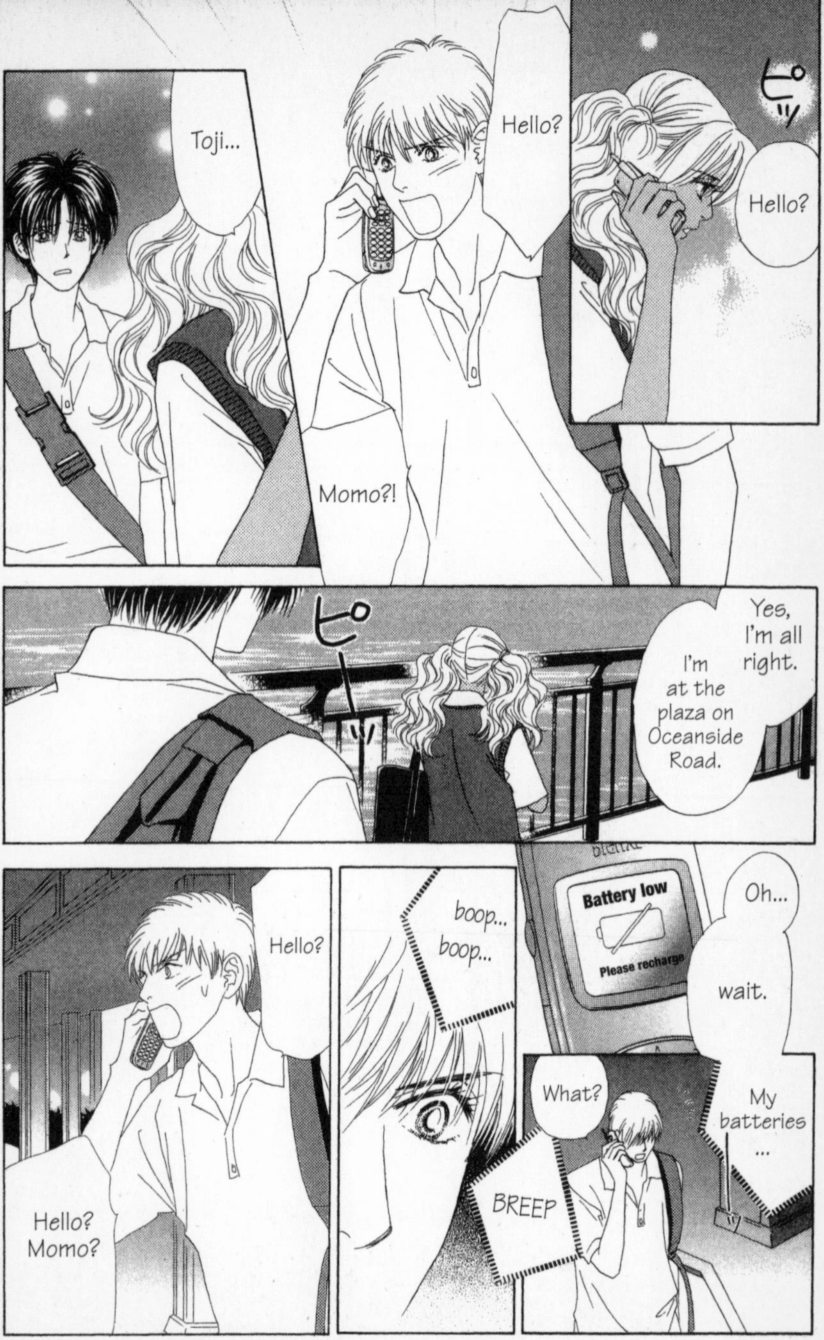
ピッ
Hello?
Hello?
Momo?!
Toji...
ピーッ
Yes, I'm all right.
I'm at the plaza on Oceanside Road.
Battery low
Please recharge
Oh...
wait.
My batteries ...
What?
BREEP
boop... boop...
Hello?
Hello? Momo?

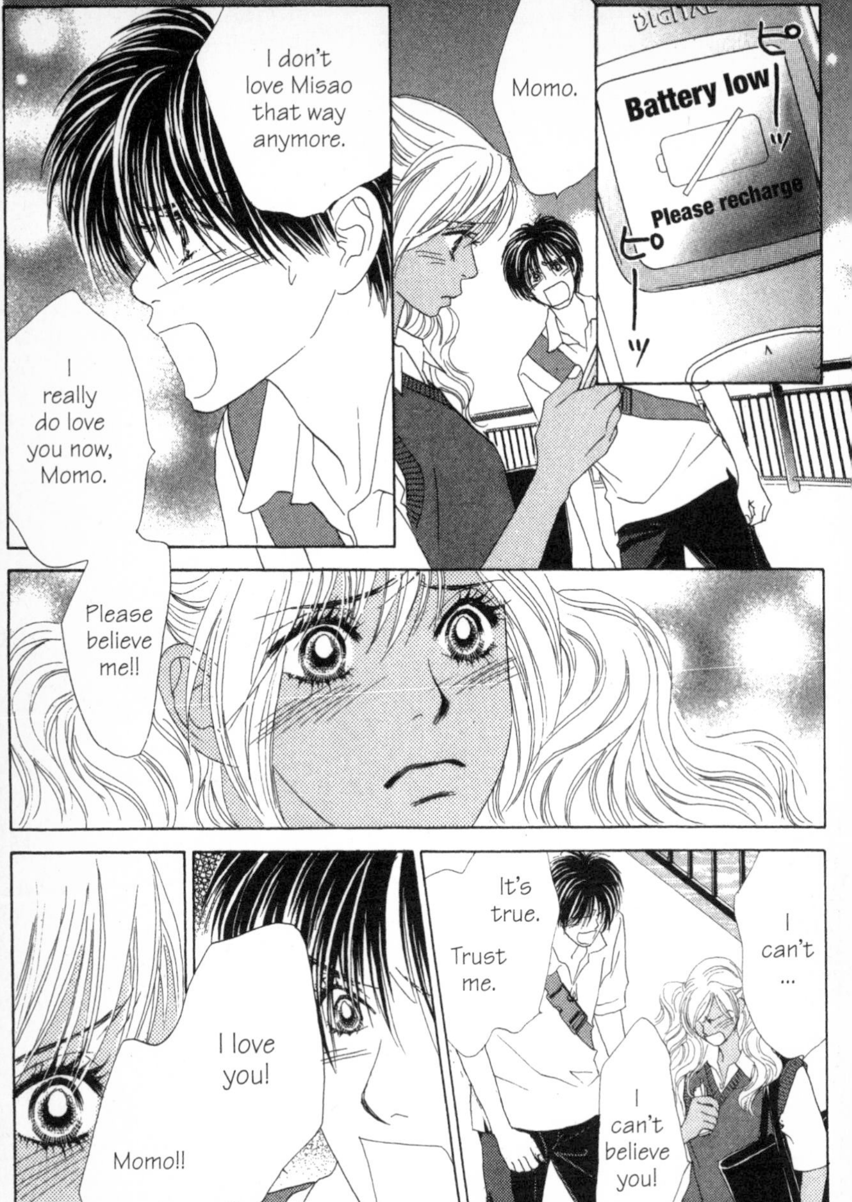
Battery low
Please recharge
ピーッ
ピーッ
Momo.
I don't love Misao that way anymore.
I really do love you now, Momo.
Please believe me!!
I can't ...
It's true.
Trust me.
I can't believe you!
I love you!
Momo!!

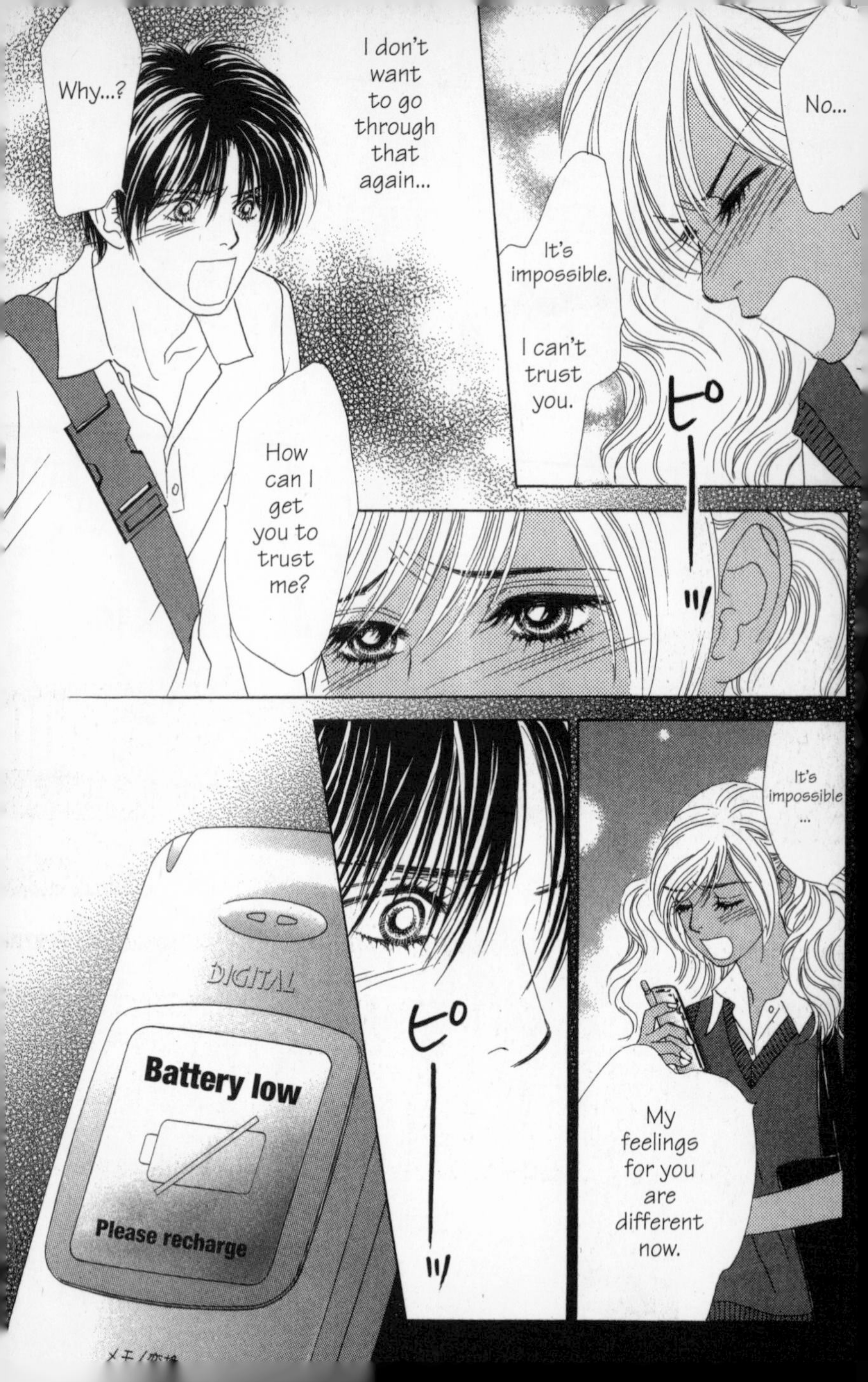
No...
It's impossible.
I can't trust you.
I don't want to go through that again...
ピーーッ
Why...?
How can I get you to trust me?
It's impossible...
My feelings for you are different now.
ピーーッ
DIGITAL
Battery low
Please recharge

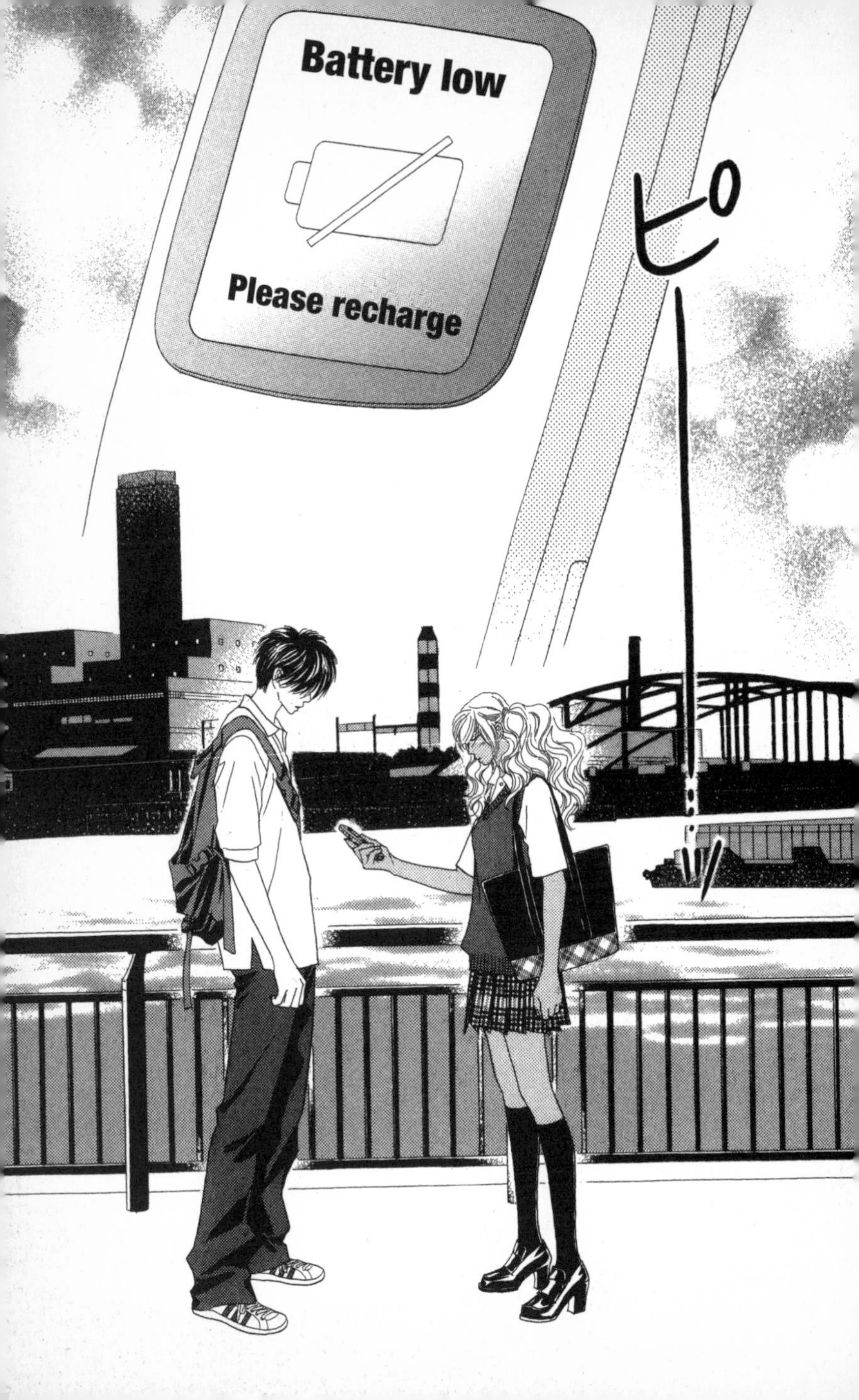

Battery low
Please recharge
ピッ

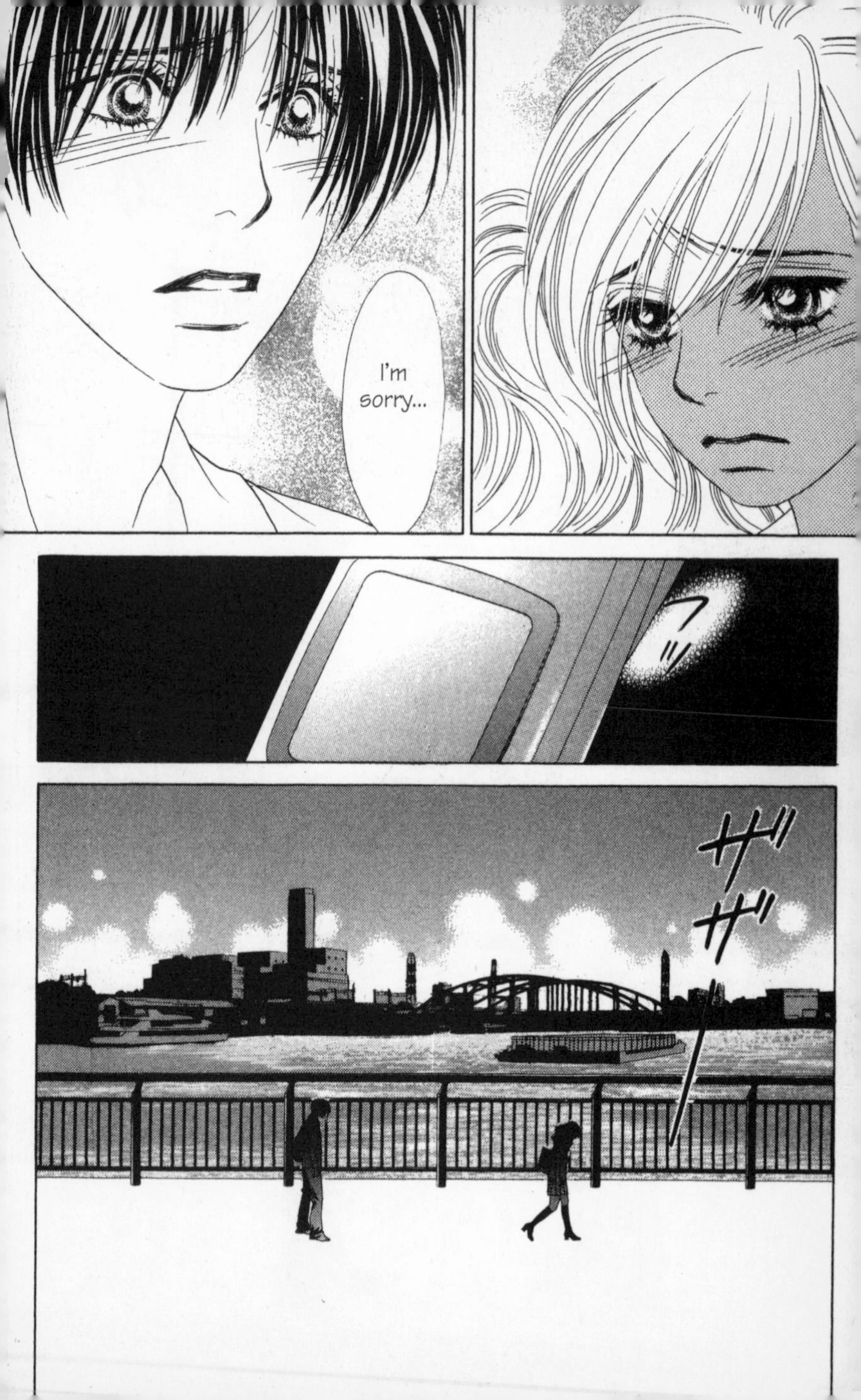
I'm sorry...
ザザ

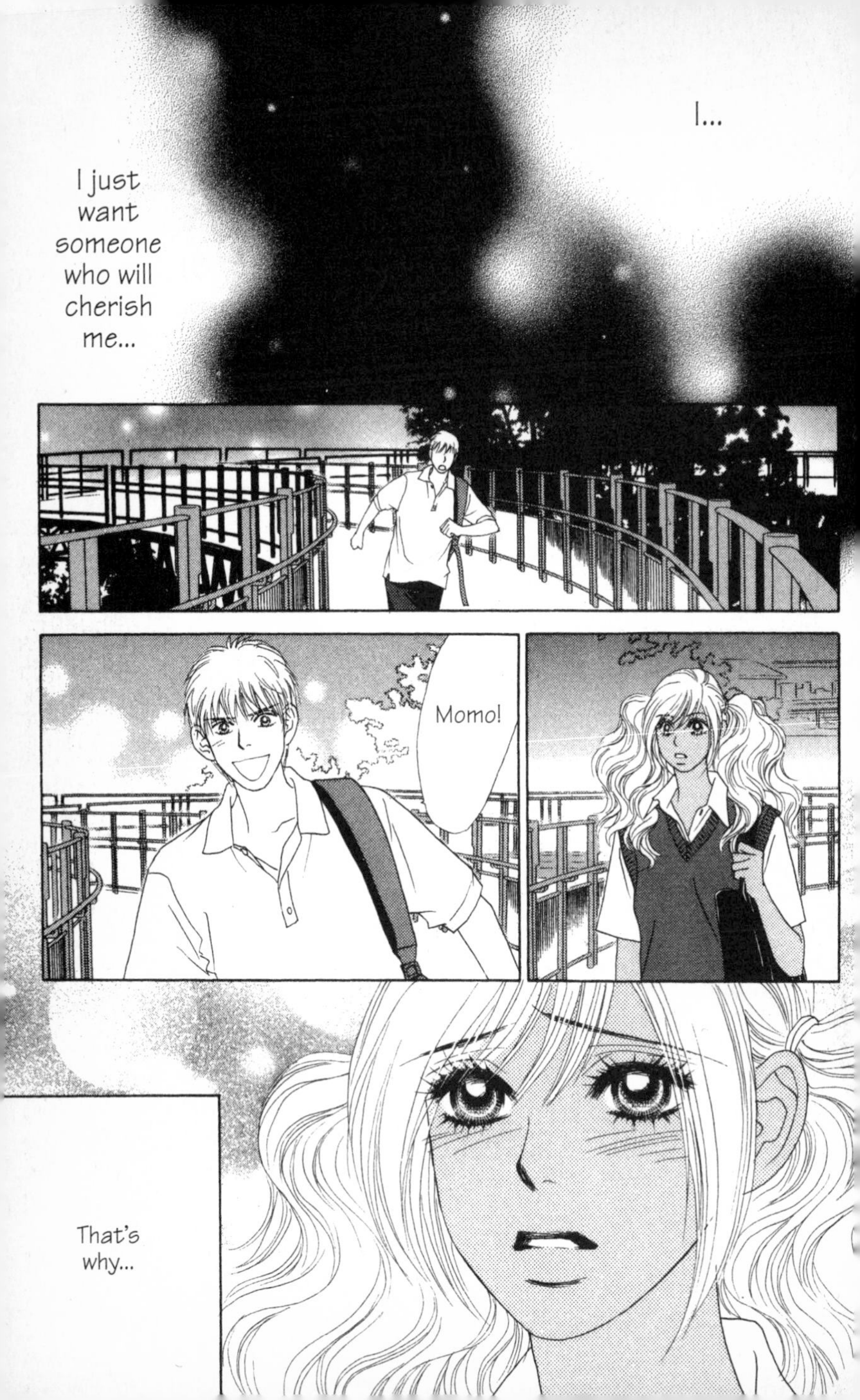
I...
I just want someone who will cherish me...
Momo!
That's why...

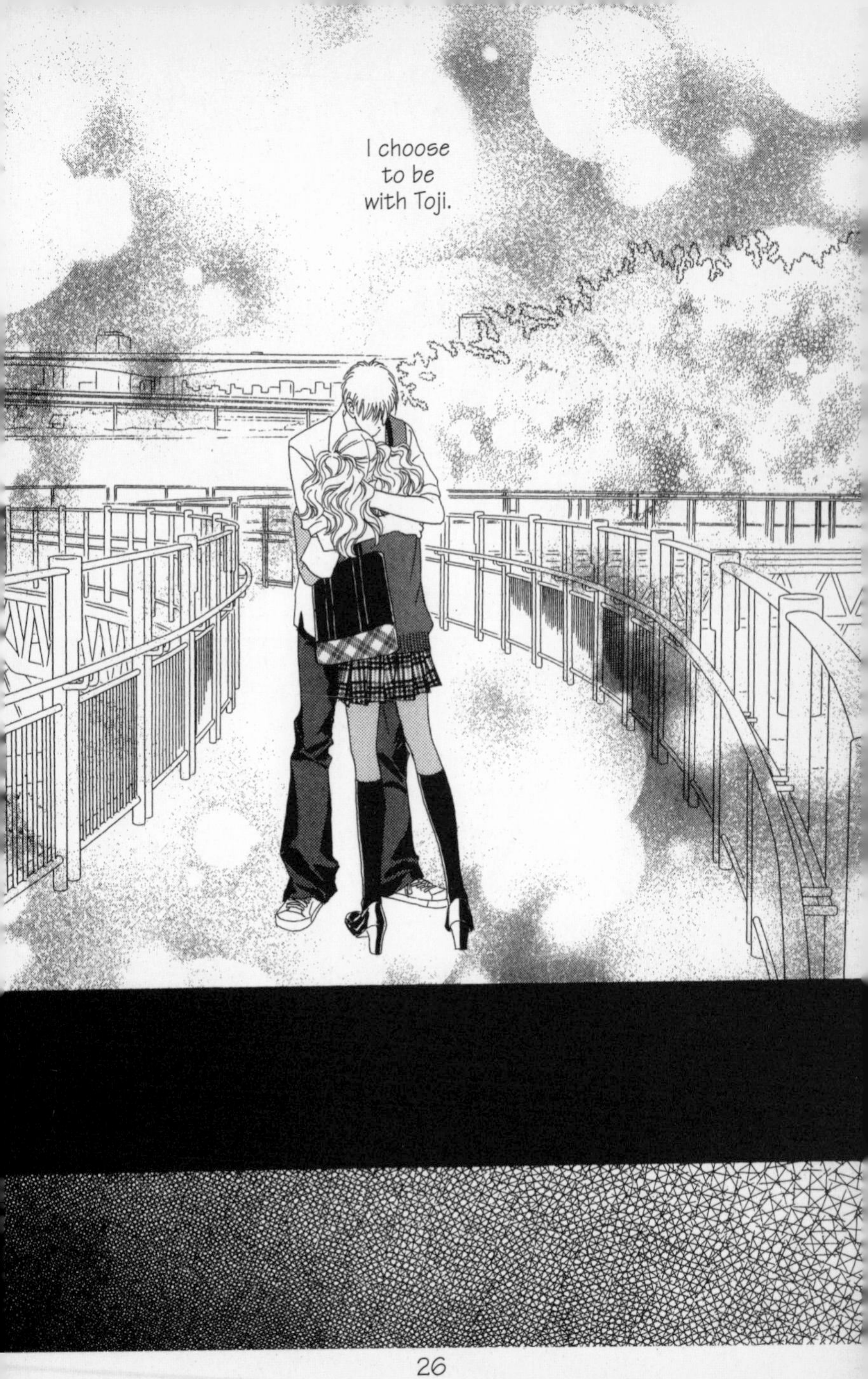
I choose to be with Toji.

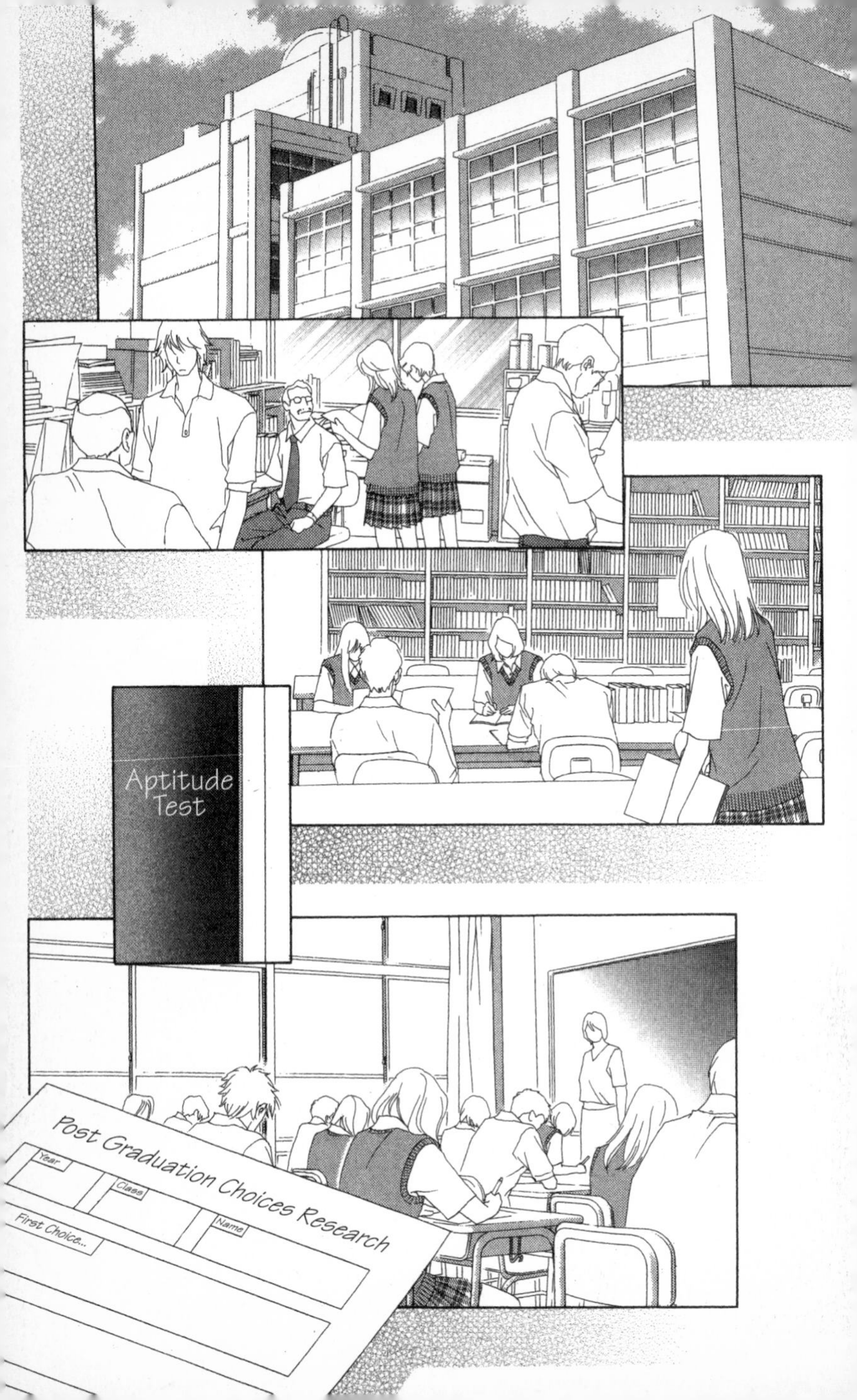
Aptitude Test
Post Graduation Choices Research
Year
Class
Name
First Choice...

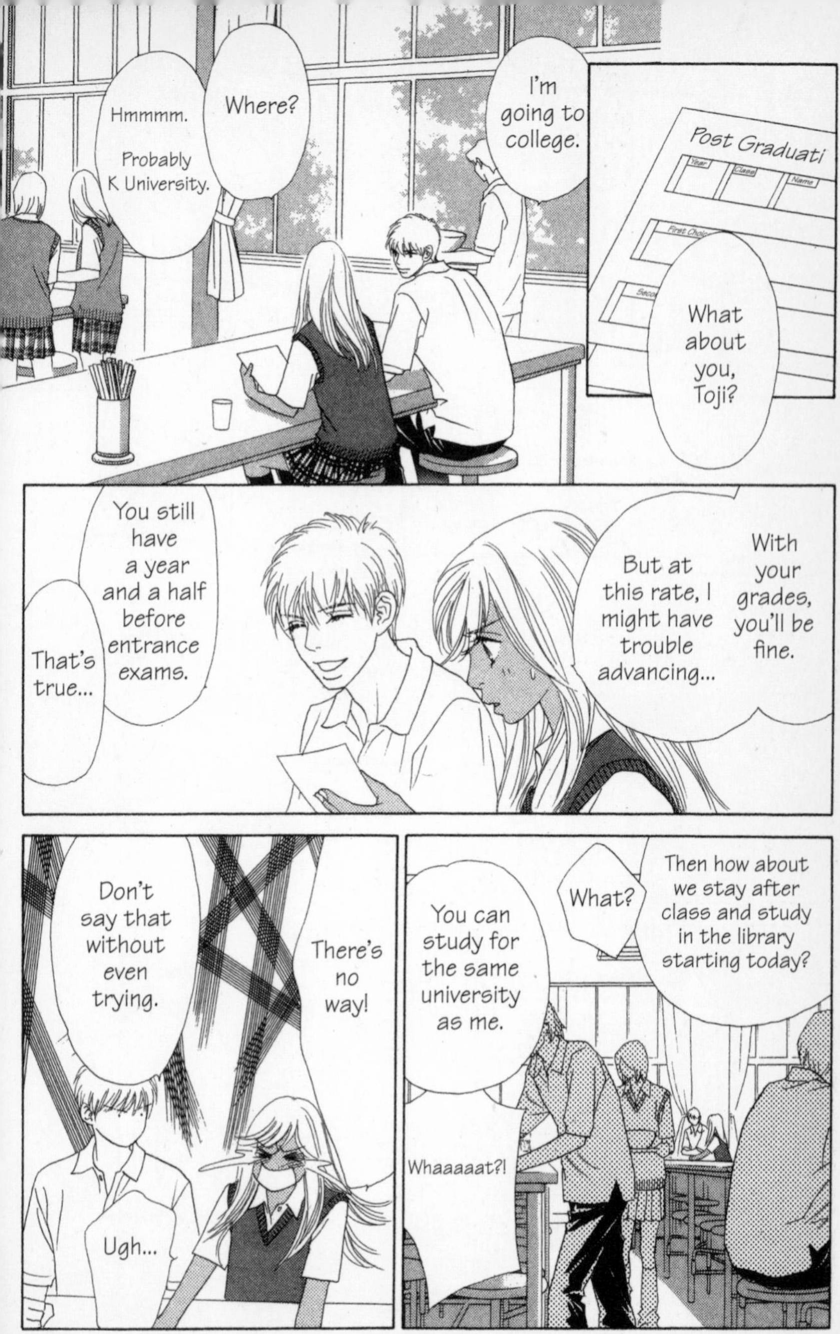
Post Graduati
Year
Class
Name
What about you, Toji?
I'm going to college.
Where?
Hmmmm. Probably K University.
With your grades, you'll be fine.
But at this rate, I might have trouble advancing...
You still have a year and a half before entrance exams.
That's true...
Then how about we stay after class and study in the library starting today?
What?
You can study for the same university as me.
Whaaaaat?!
There's no way!
Don't say that without even trying.
Ugh...

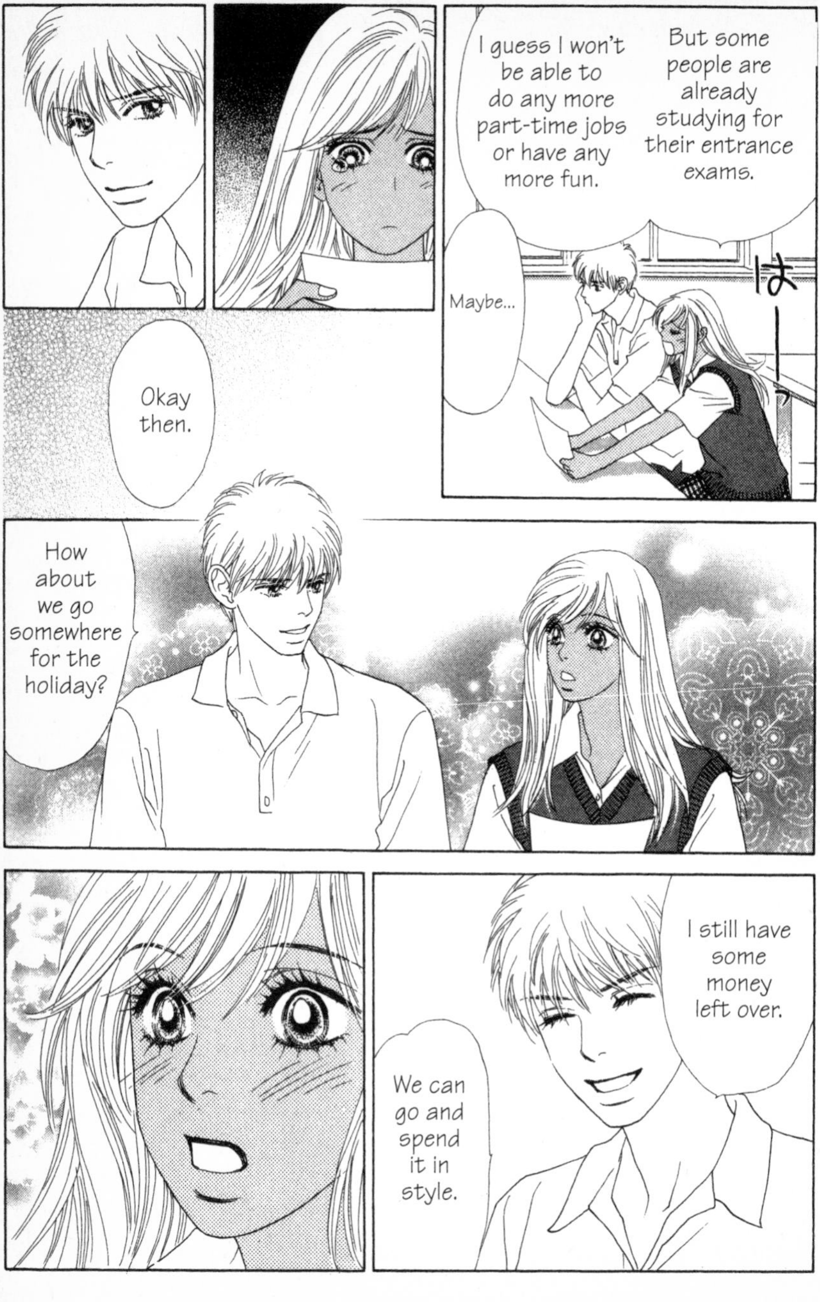
But some people are already studying for their entrance exams.
I guess I won't be able to do any more part-time jobs or have any more fun.
はーっ
Maybe...
Okay then.
How about we go somewhere for the holiday?
I still have some money left over.
We can go and spend it in style.

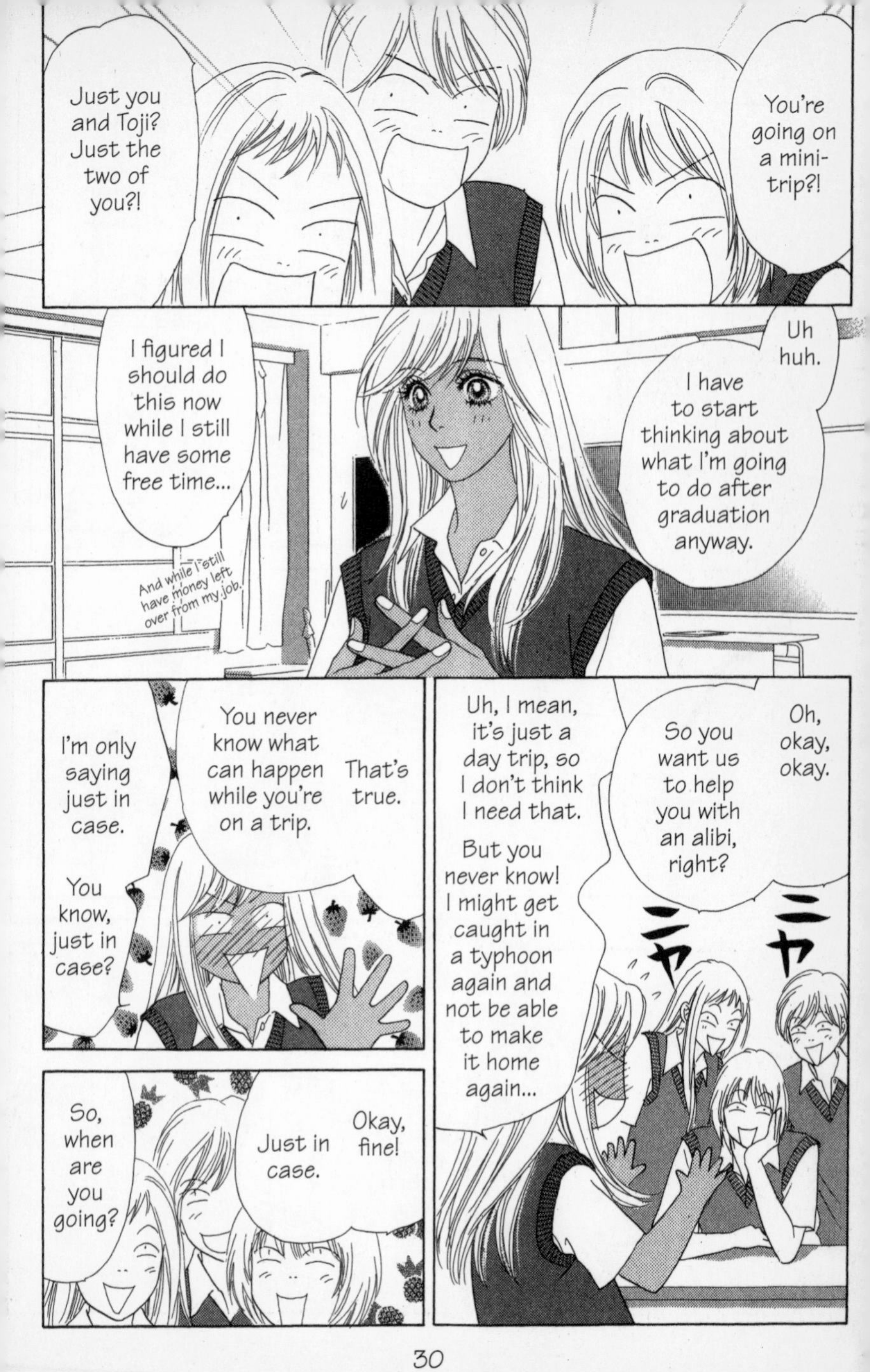
You're going on a mini-trip?!
Just you and Toji? Just the two of you?!
Uh huh.
I have to start thinking about what I'm going to do after graduation anyway.
I figured I should do this now while I still have some free time...
And while I still have money left over from my job.
Oh, okay, okay.
So you want us to help you with an alibi, right?
ニヤ
ニヤ
Uh, I mean, it's just a day trip, so I don't think I need that.
But you never know! I might get caught in a typhoon again and not be able to make it home again...
That's true.
You never know what can happen while you're on a trip.
I'm only saying just in case.
You know, just in case?
Okay, fine!
Just in case.
So, when are you going?

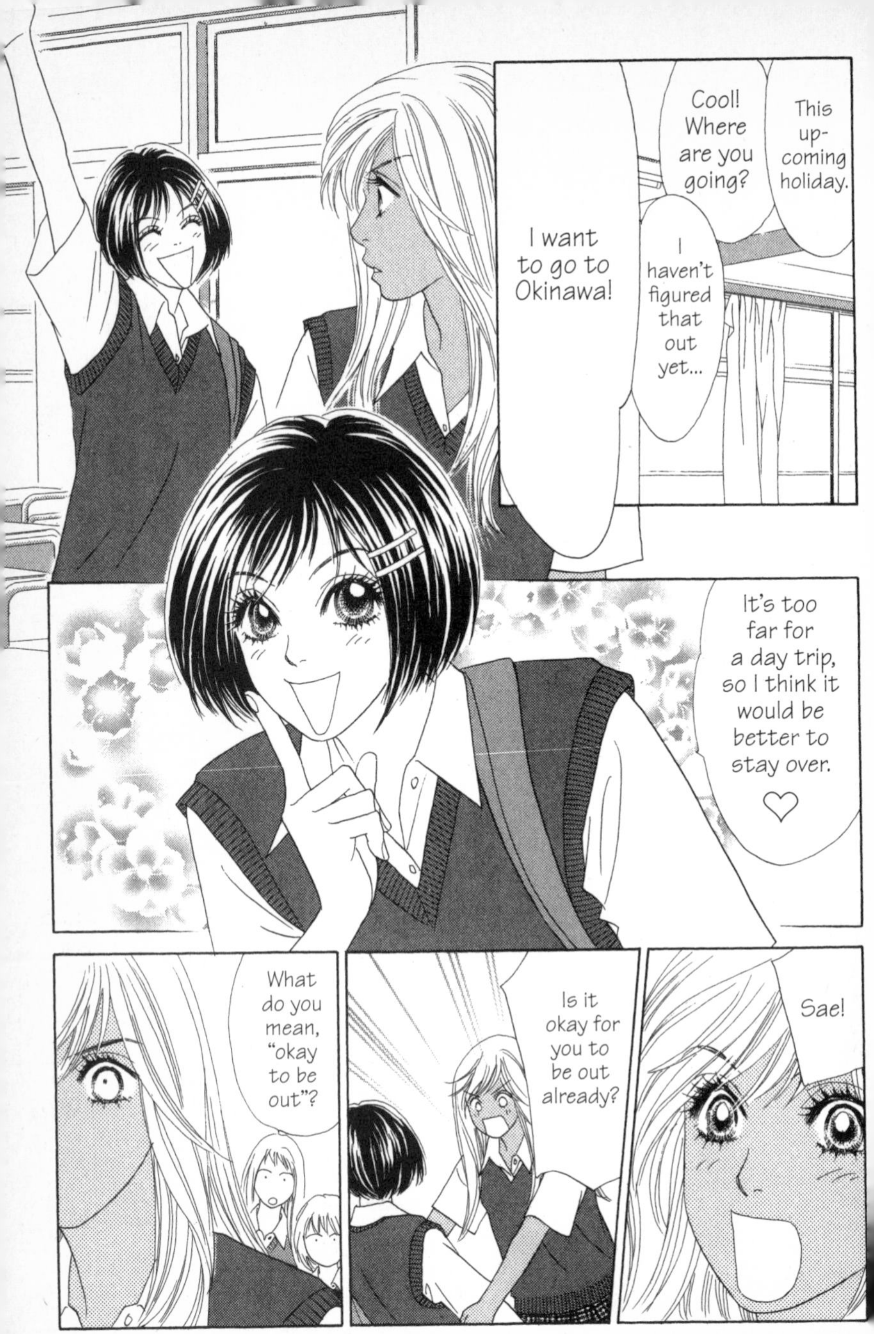
This upcoming holiday.
Cool! Where are you going?
I haven't figured that out yet...
I want to go to Okinawa!
It's too far for a day trip, so I think it would be better to stay over. ♡
Sae!
Is it okay for you to be out already?
What do you mean, "okay to be out"?

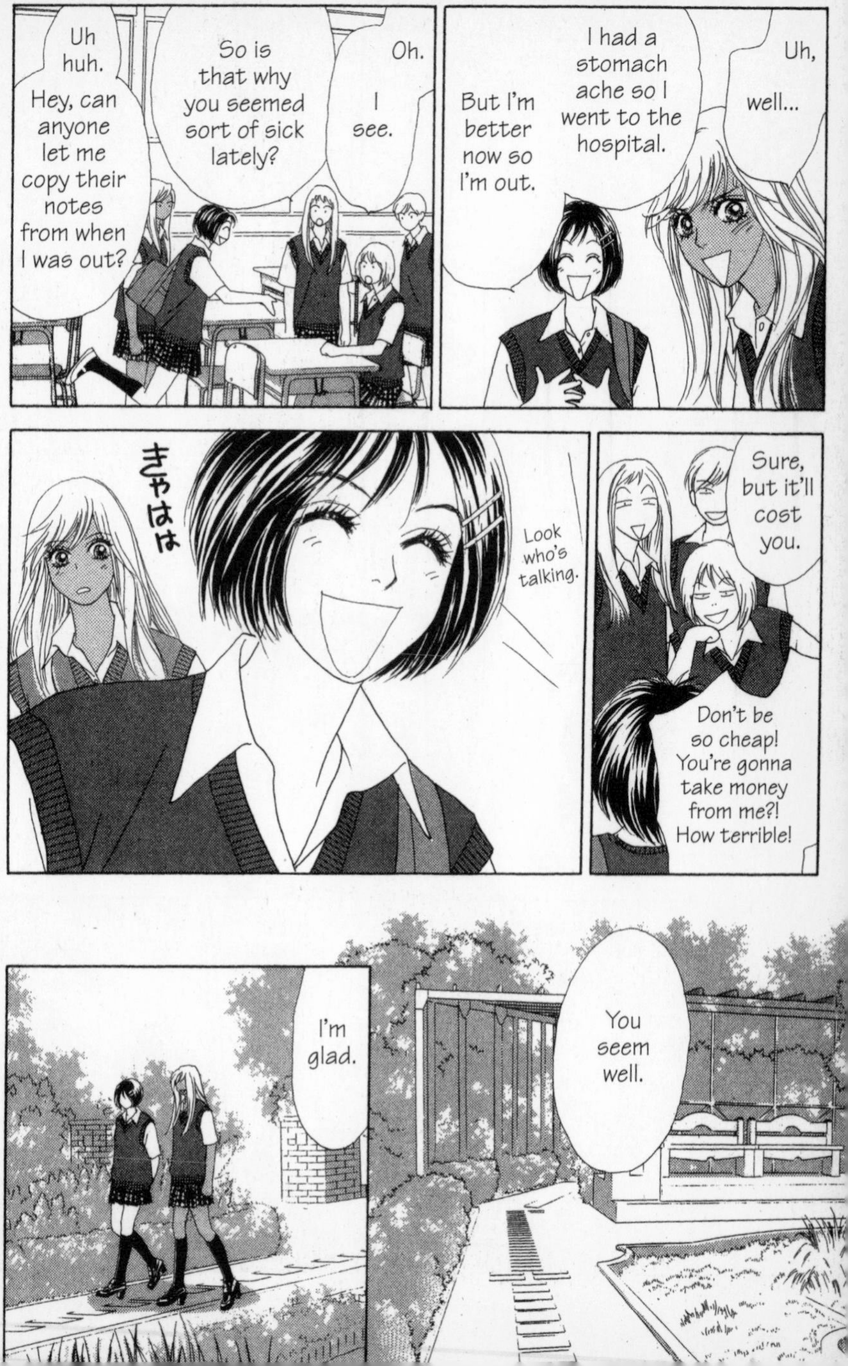
Uh, well...
I had a stomach ache so I went to the hospital.
But I'm better now so I'm out.
Oh. I see.
So is that why you seemed sort of sick lately?
Uh huh. Hey, can anyone let me copy their notes from when I was out?
Sure, but it'll cost you.
Don't be so cheap! You're gonna take money from me?! How terrible!
Look who's talking.
きゃはは
You seem well.
I'm glad.

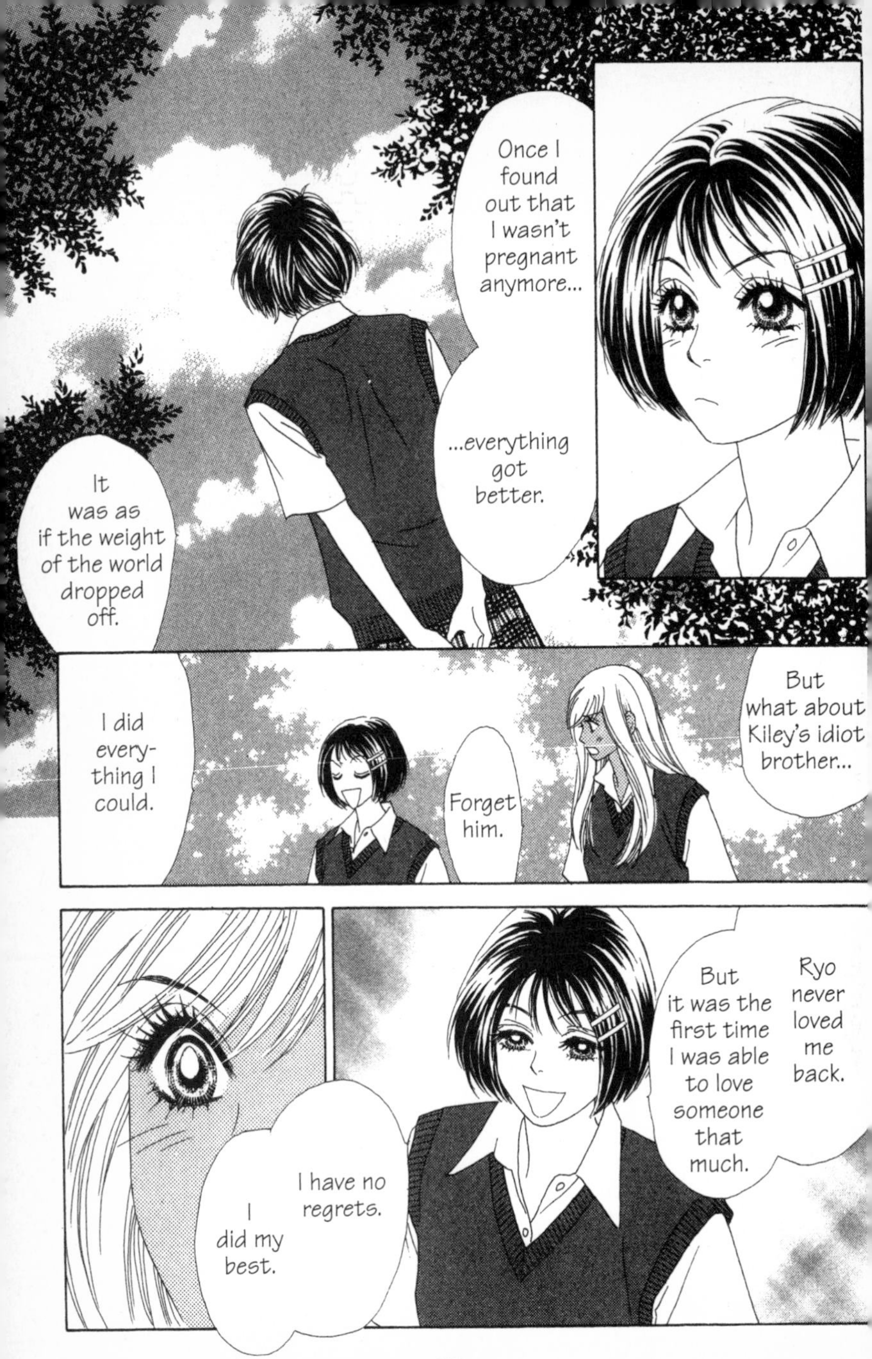
Once I found out that I wasn't pregnant anymore...
...everything got better.
It was as if the weight of the world dropped off.
But what about Kiley's idiot brother...
Forget him.
I did every-thing I could.
Ryo never loved me back.
But it was the first time I was able to love someone that much.
I have no regrets.
I did my best.

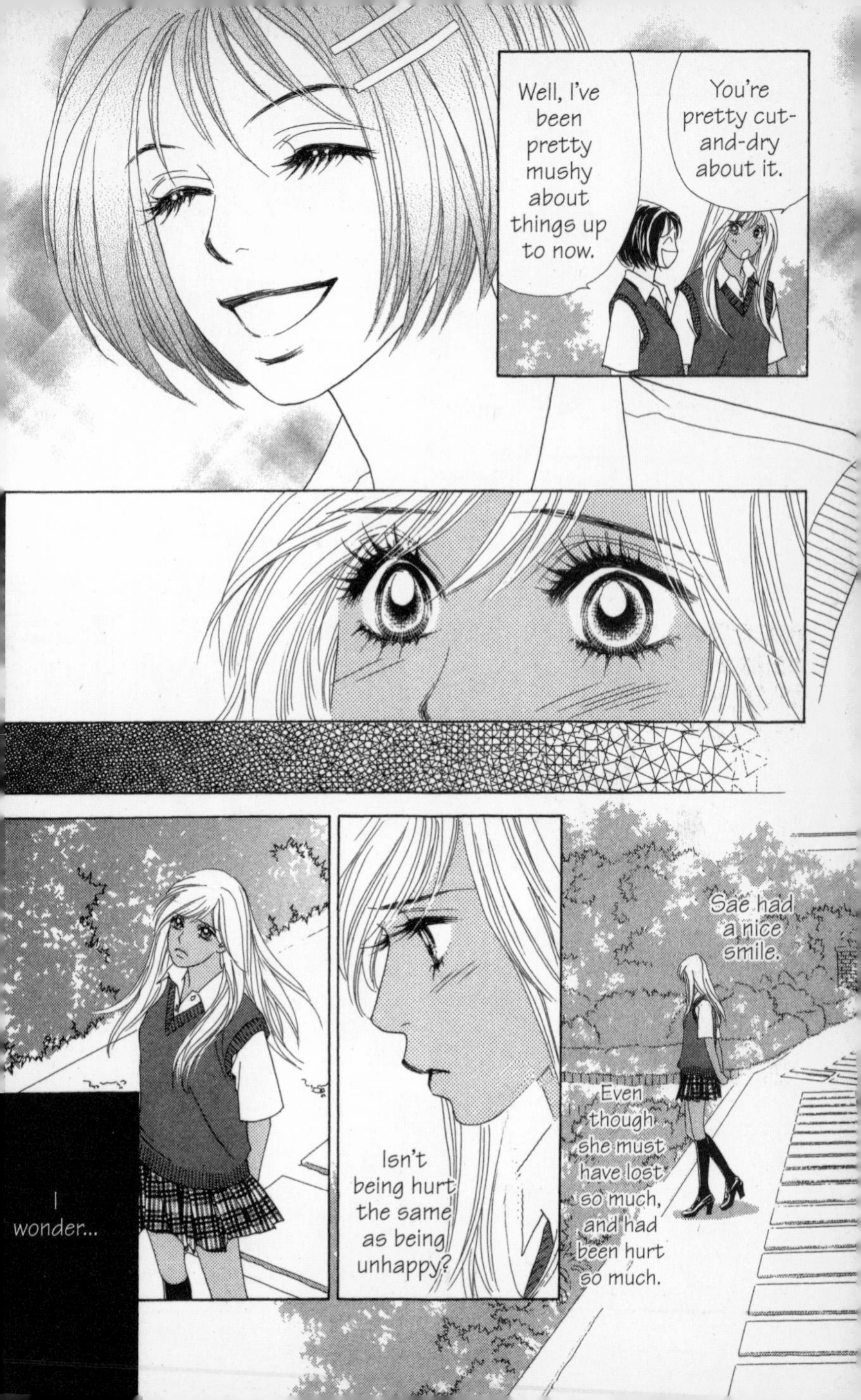
You're pretty cut-and-dry about it.
Well, I've been pretty mushy about things up to now.
Sae had a nice smile.
Even though she must have lost so much, and had been hurt so much.
Isn't being hurt the same as being unhappy?
I wonder...

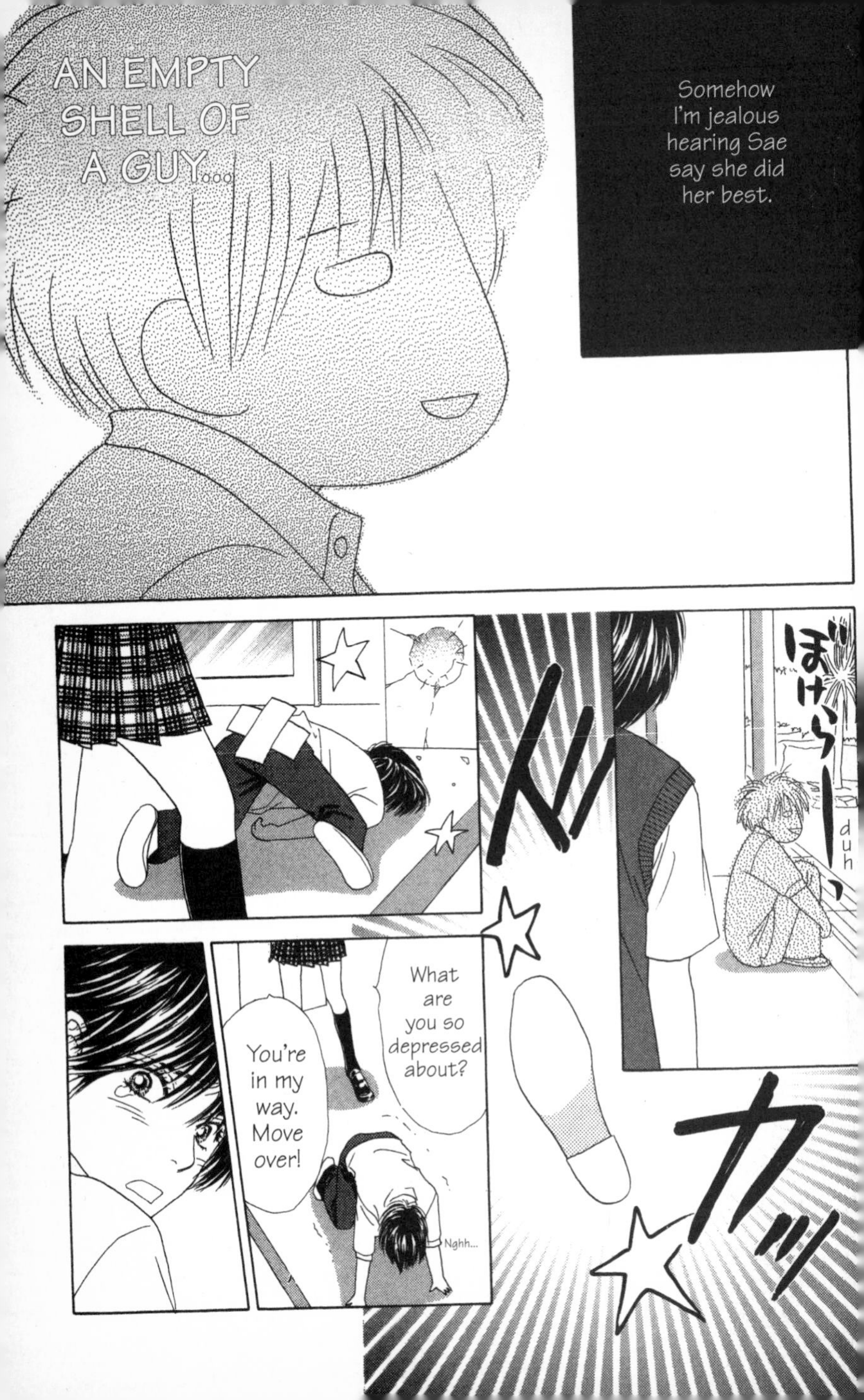
Somehow I'm jealous hearing Sae say she did her best.
AN EMPTY SHELL OF A GUY...
ぼけらー
duh
カッ
What are you so depressed about?
You're in my way. Move over!
Nghh...

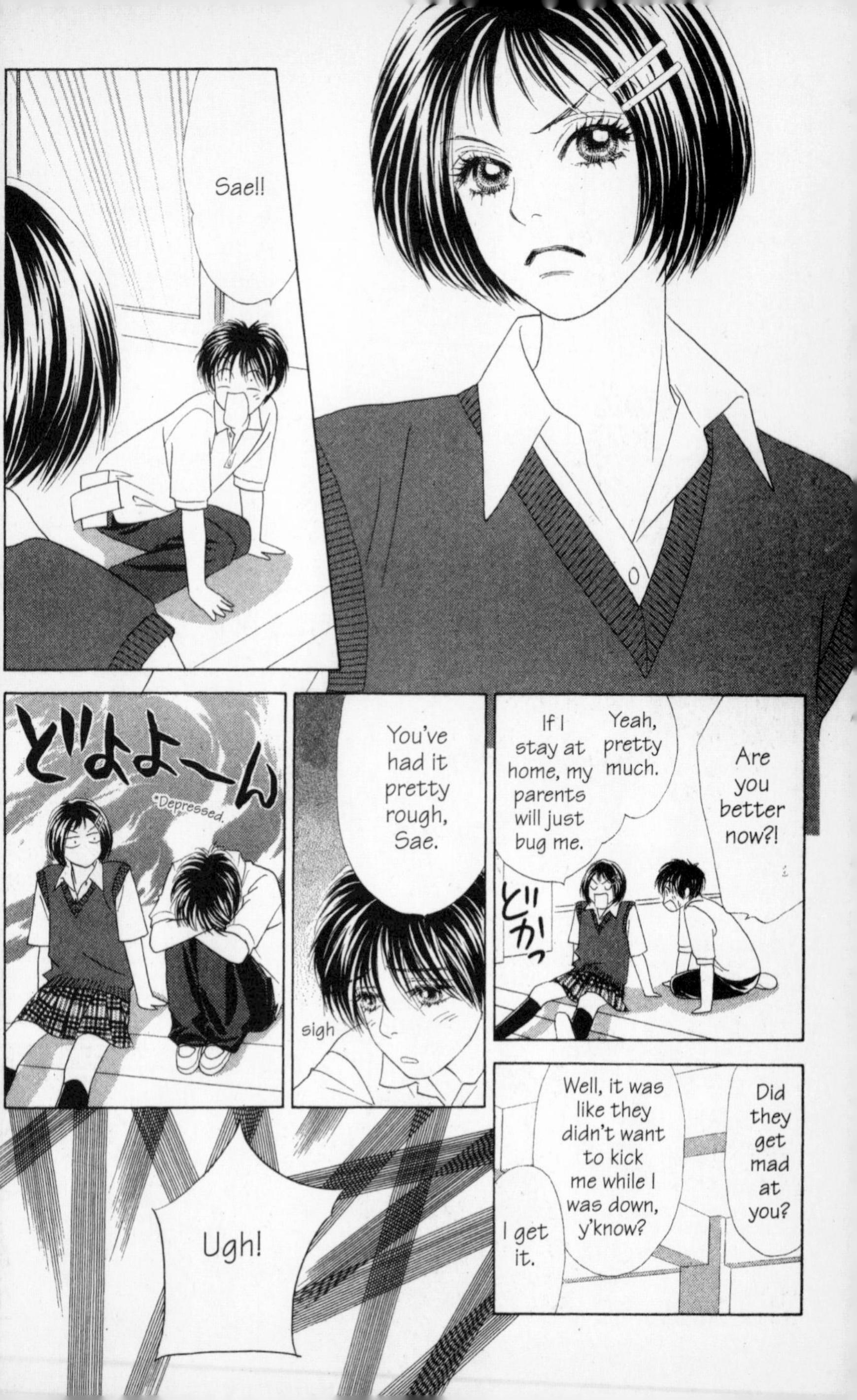
Sae!!
Are you better now?!
Yeah, pretty much.
If I stay at home, my parents will just bug me.
どかっ
You've had it pretty rough, Sae.
sigh
どよよ～ん
*Depressed.
Did they get mad at you?
Well, it was like they didn't want to kick me while I was down, y'know?
I get it.
Ugh!

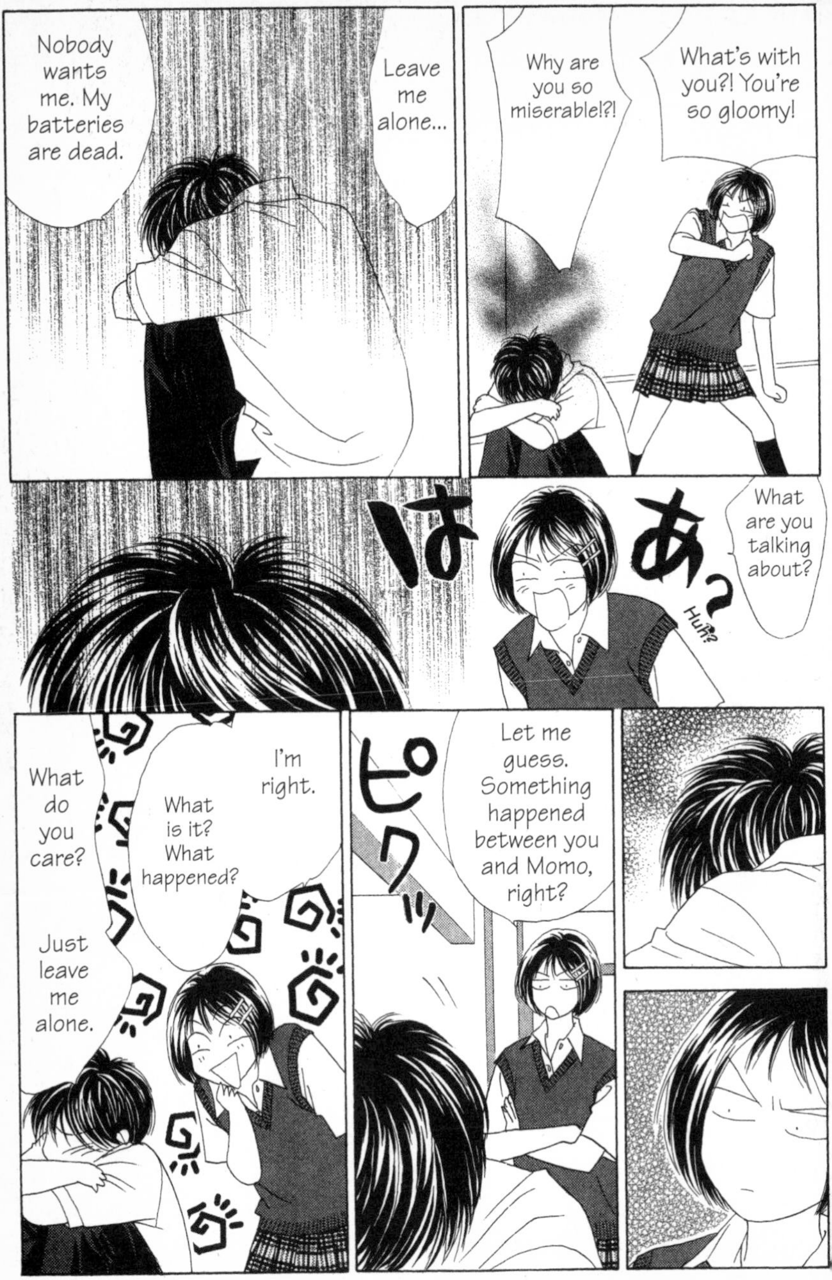
What's with you?! You're so gloomy!
Why are you so miserable!?!
Leave me alone...
Nobody wants me. My batteries are dead.
What are you talking about?
はあ？
Huh?
Let me guess. Something happened between you and Momo, right?
ピクッ
I'm right.
What is it? What happened?
What do you care?
Just leave me alone.

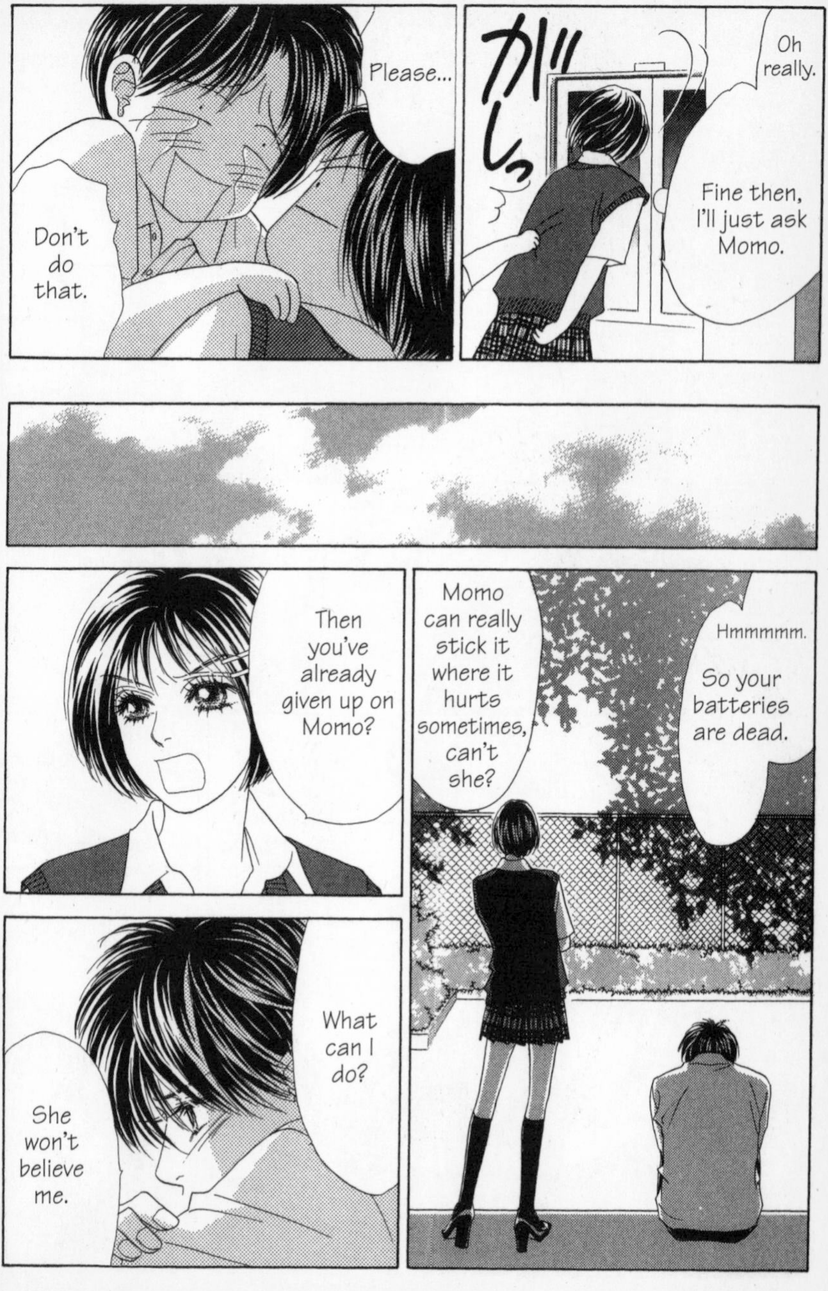
Oh really.
Fine then, I'll just ask Momo.
がしっ
Please...
Don't do that.
Hmmmmm.
So your batteries are dead.
Momo can really stick it where it hurts sometimes, can't she?
Then you've already given up on Momo?
What can I do?
She won't believe me.

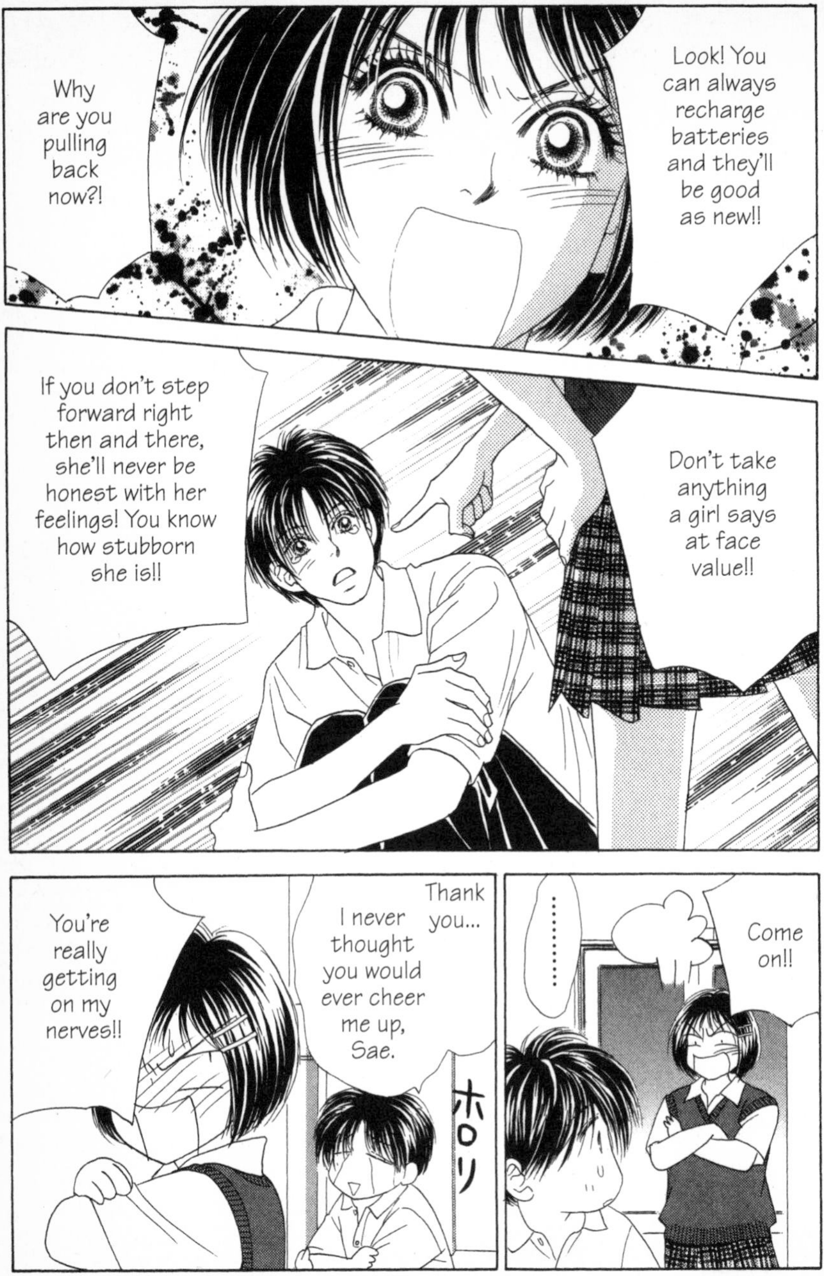
Look! You can always recharge batteries and they'll be good as new!!
Why are you pulling back now?!
Don't take anything a girl says at face value!!
If you don't step forward right then and there, she'll never be honest with her feelings! You know how stubborn she is!!
Come on!!
....
Thank you...
I never thought you would ever cheer me up, Sae.
ホロリ
You're really getting on my nerves!!

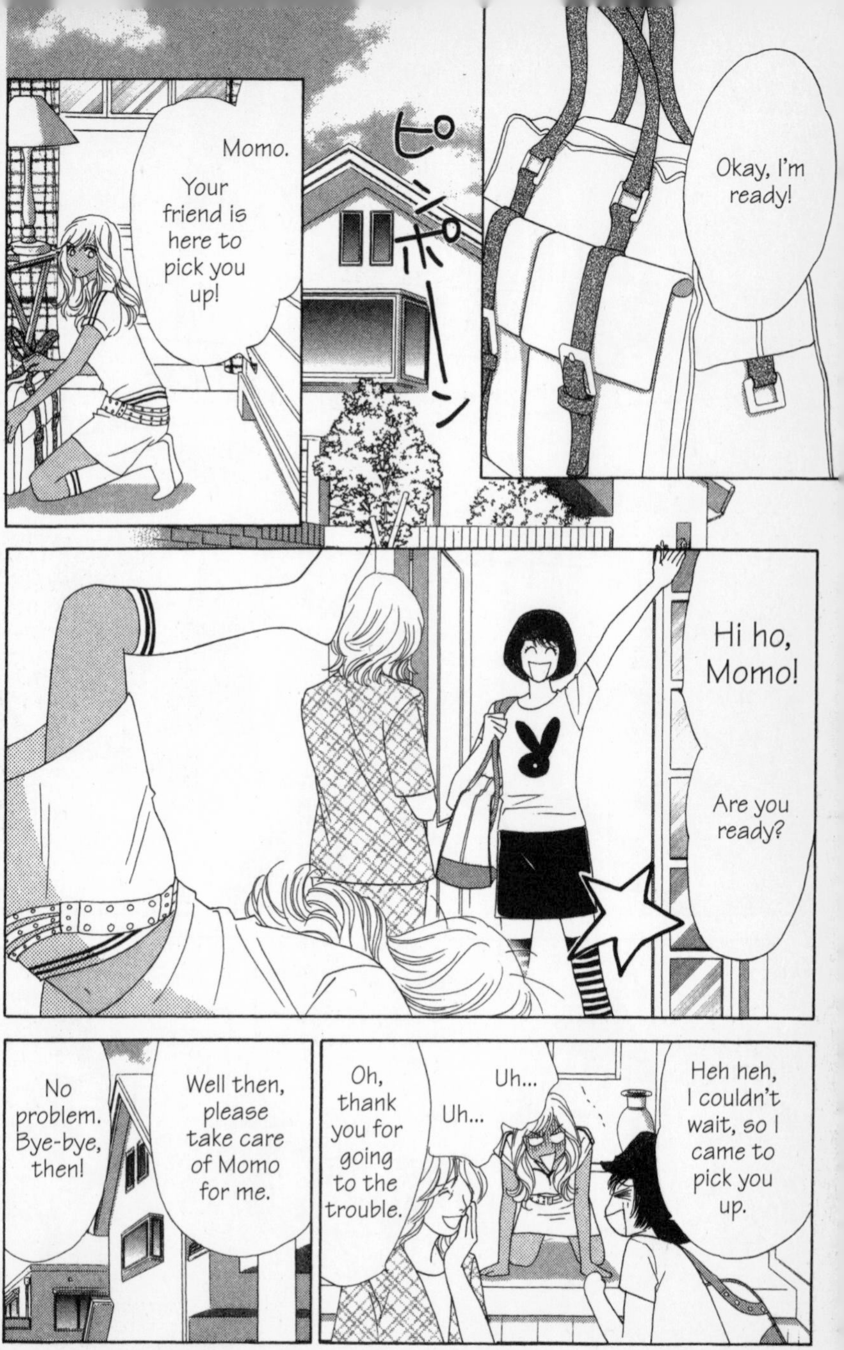
Okay, I'm ready!
ピンポーン
Momo.
Your friend is here to pick you up!
Hi ho, Momo!
Are you ready?
Heh heh, I couldn't wait, so I came to pick you up.
Uh...
Uh...
Oh, thank you for going to the trouble.
Well then, please take care of Momo for me.
No problem. Bye-bye, then!

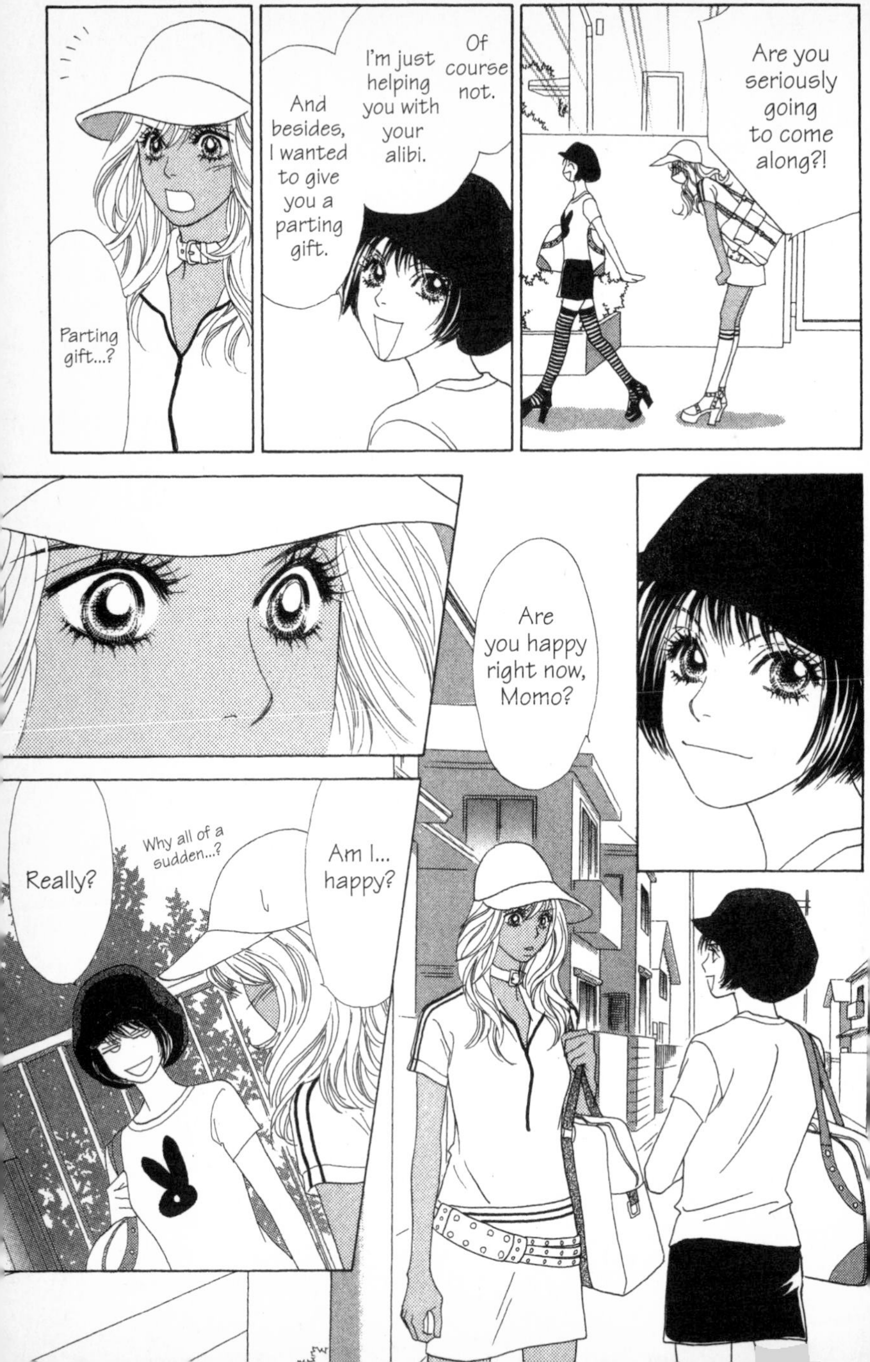

Are you seriously going to come along?!
Of course not.
I'm just helping you with your alibi.
And besides, I wanted to give you a parting gift.
Parting gift...?
Are you happy right now, Momo?
Am I... happy?
Why all of a sudden...?
Really?

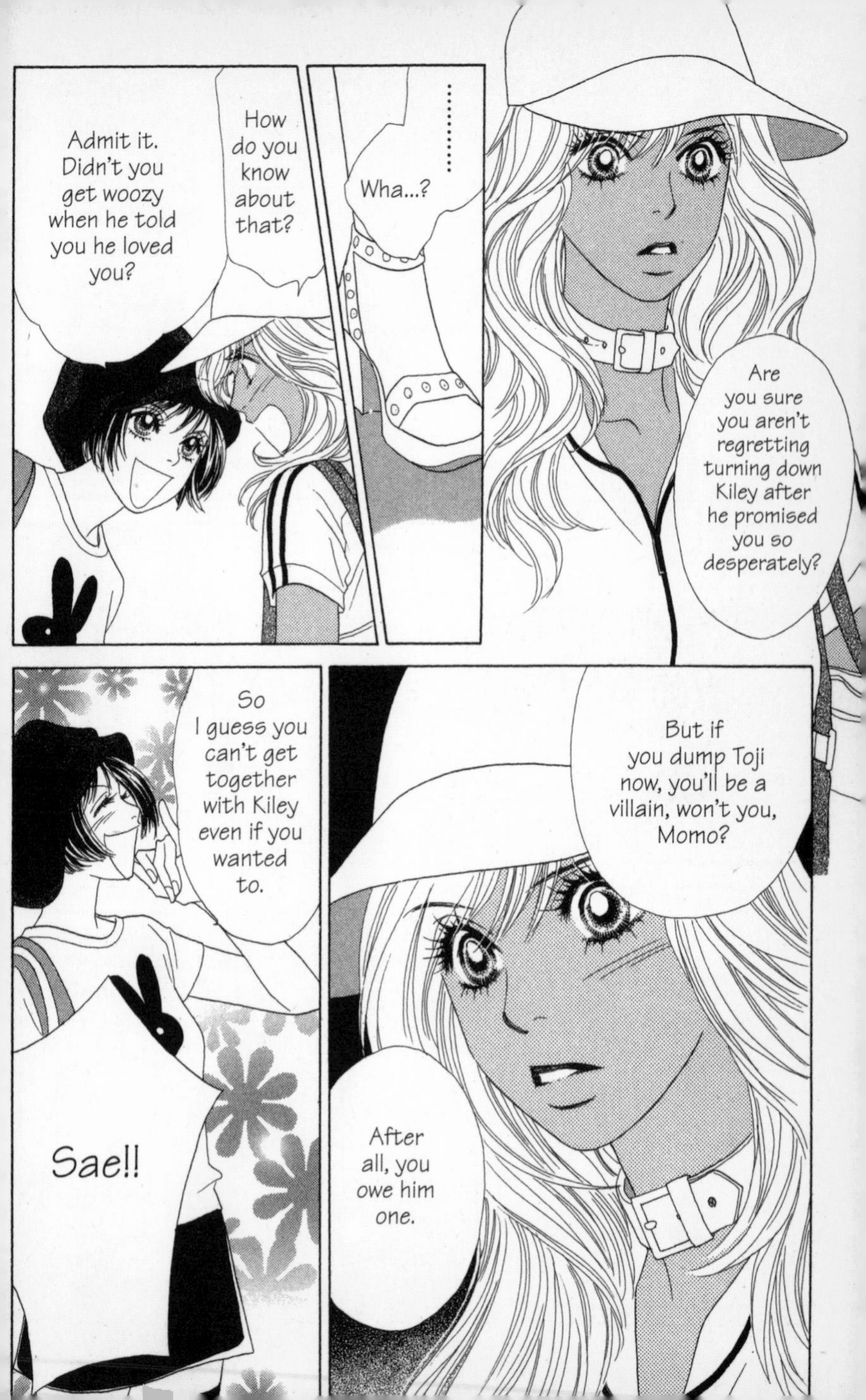
Are you sure you aren't regretting turning down Kiley after he promised you so desperately?
......
Wha...?
Admit it. Didn't you get woozy when he told you he loved you?
How do you know about that?
But if you dump Toji now, you'll be a villain, won't you, Momo?
After all, you owe him one.
So I guess you can't get together with Kiley even if you wanted to.
Sae!!

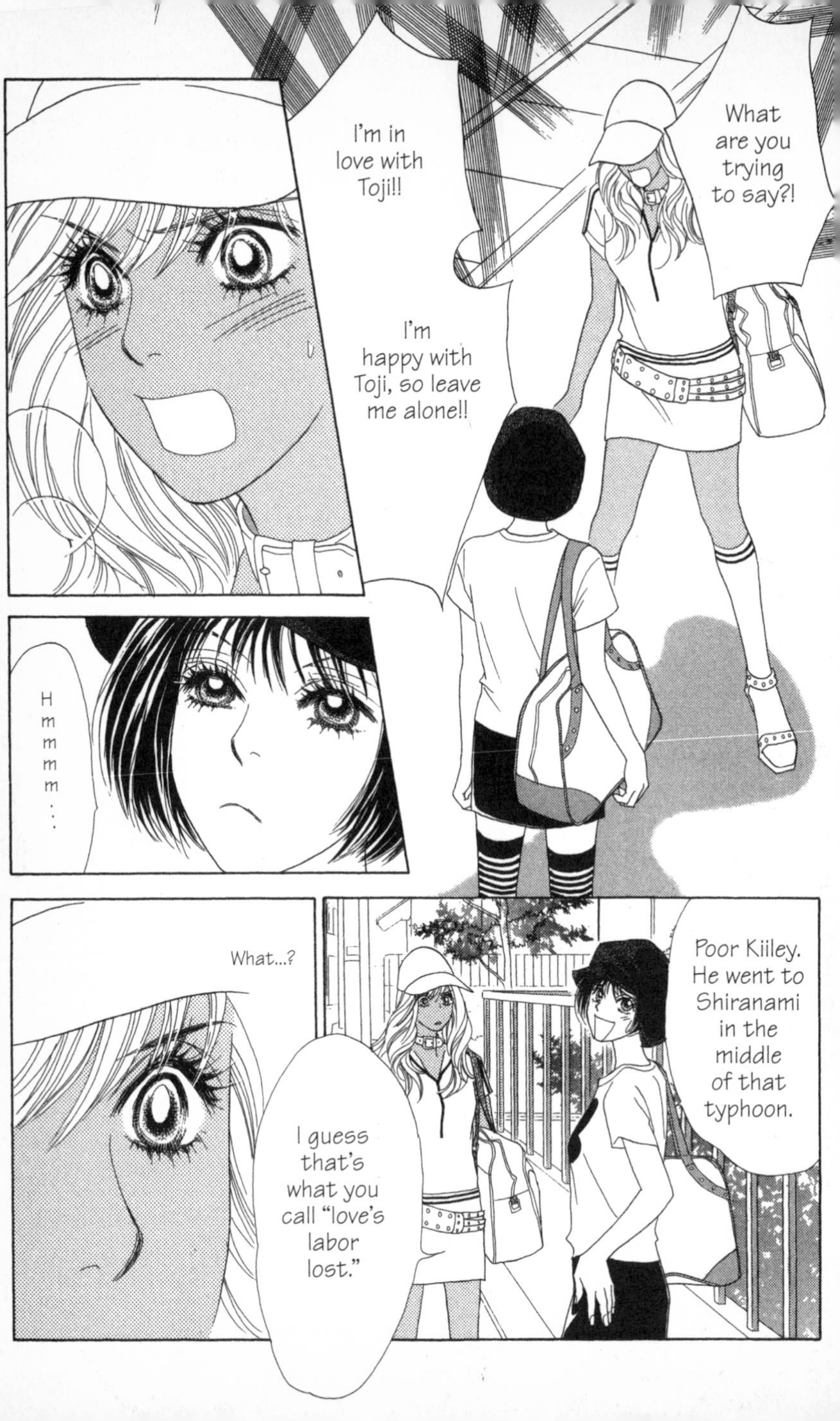
What are you trying to say?!
I'm in love with Toji!!
I'm happy with Toji, so leave me alone!!
Hmmmm...
Poor Kiiley. He went to Shiranami in the middle of that typhoon.
I guess that's what you call "love's labor lost."
What...?

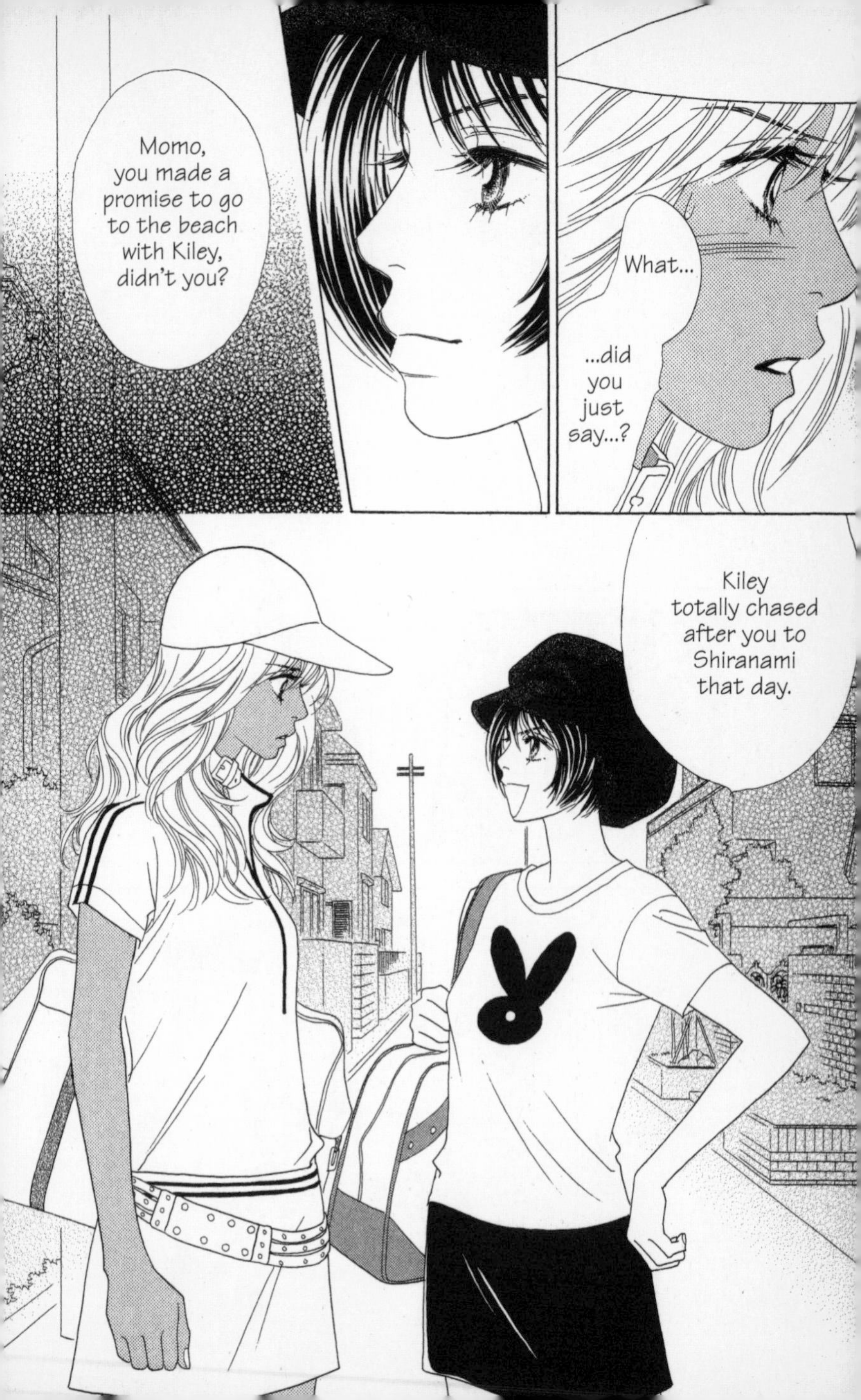
What...
...did you just say...?
Momo, you made a promise to go to the beach with Kiley, didn't you?
Kiley totally chased after you to Shiranami that day.

ピーチガール

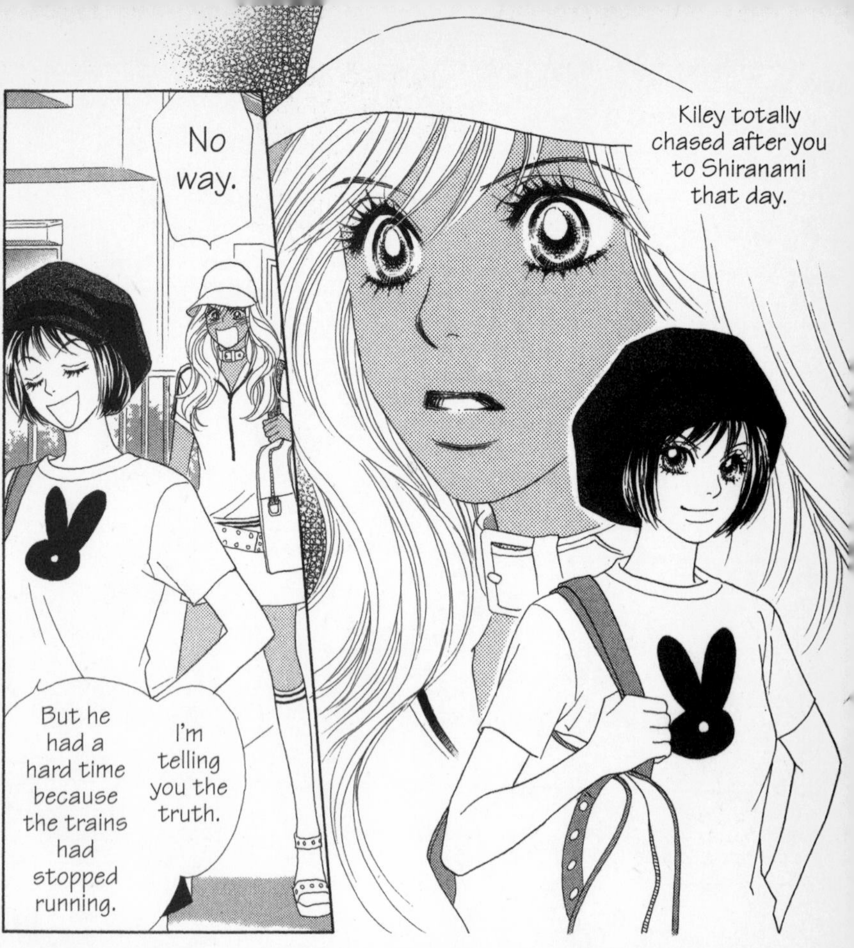
Kiley totally chased after you to Shiranami that day.
No way.
I'm telling you the truth.
But he had a hard time because the trains had stopped running.

PEACH CLUB

Hello, this is Miwa. This is the last volume of *Peach Girl.* I'm not sure this is the ending that everyone was expecting or even hoping for, but thank you all for sticking around until the end. After this is over, I'm planning to put out a special edition as well. I hope you'll read that one, too. Now then, in commemoration of six years of publication, and finally wrapping up the last episode, I've made a decision: as thanks for all my faithful readers, I'm going to put on a special "Peach Festival" in *Bessatsu Friend,* with special bonus gifts like clearfiles. And as part of this special promotion, I've included an interview with one of my favorite celebs, Sonin. I was happy to have heard that Sonin was a reader of *Peach Girl,* but I never thought the day would come when I could interview her! I've always heard that when you meet celebrities in person, you'd find out that their faces are really small, or that they're smaller or bigger than you'd expect, but it's true! Sonin's face is so small! And her hair is so silky smooth! And her skin is so translucent and beautiful! She was so cute! To be continued. -Miwa

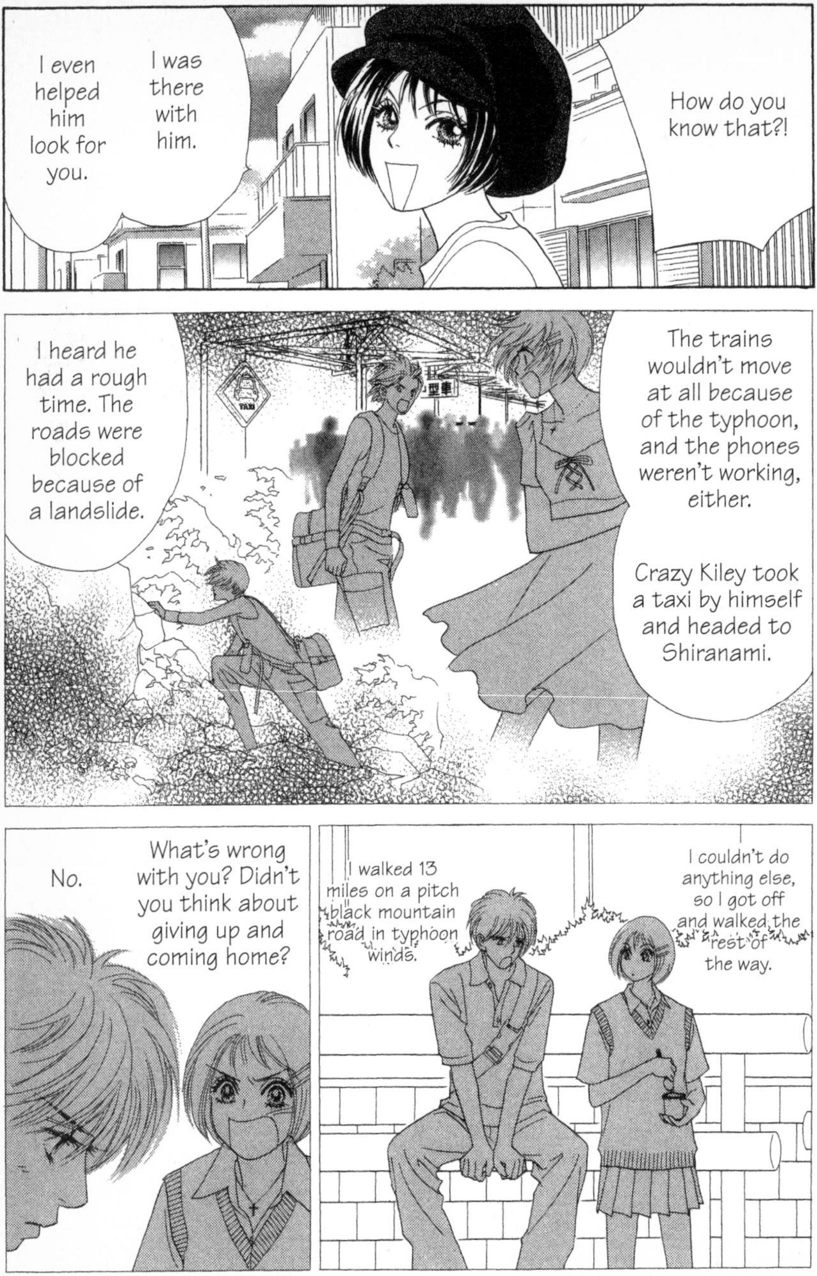
How do you know that?!
I was there with him.
I even helped him look for you.
The trains wouldn't move at all because of the typhoon, and the phones weren't working, either.
Crazy Kiley took a taxi by himself and headed to Shiranami.
I heard he had a rough time. The roads were blocked because of a landslide.
I couldn't do anything else, so I got off and walked the rest of the way.
I walked 13 miles on a pitch black mountain road in typhoon winds.
What's wrong with you? Didn't you think about giving up and coming home?
No.

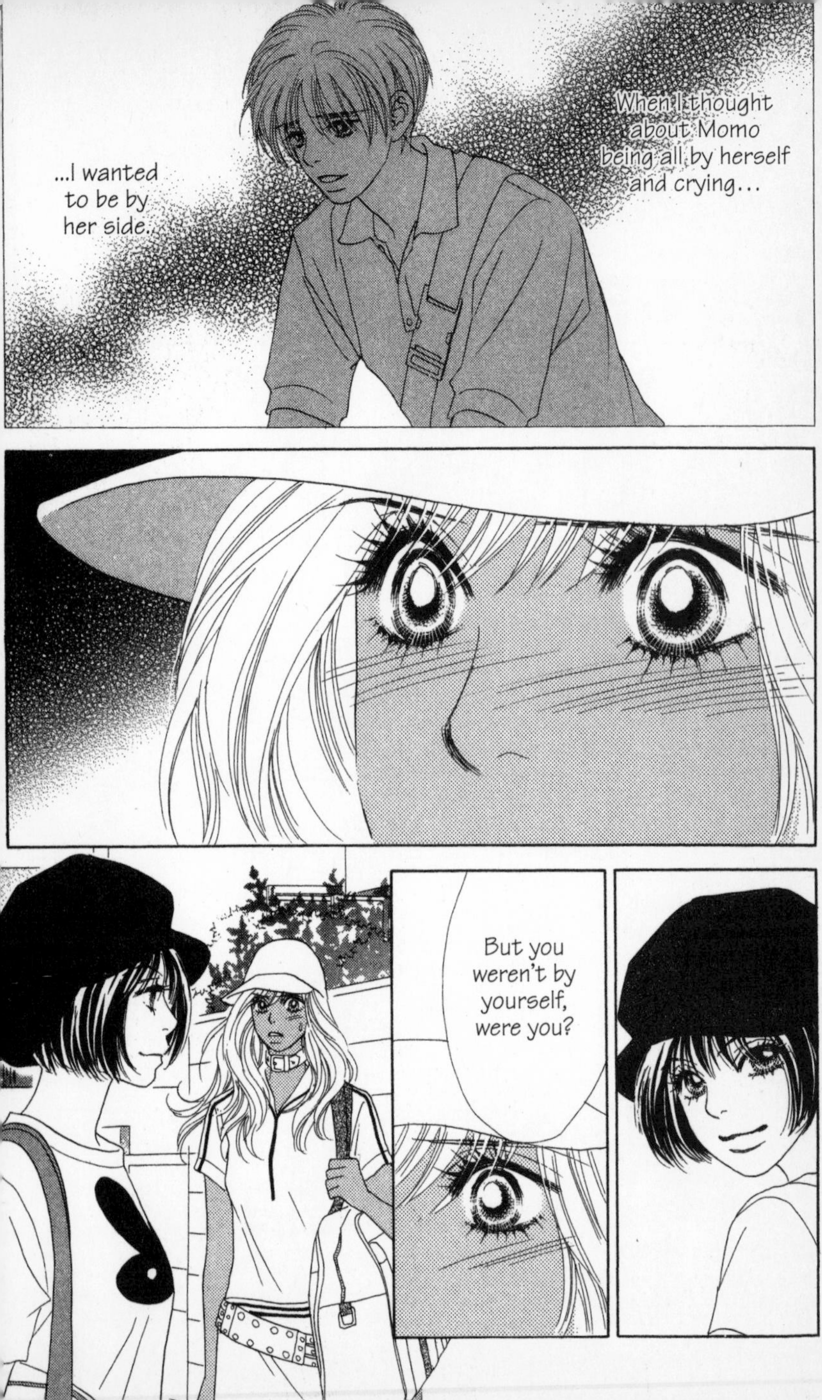
When I thought about Momo being all by herself and crying...
...I wanted to be by her side.
But you weren't by yourself, were you?

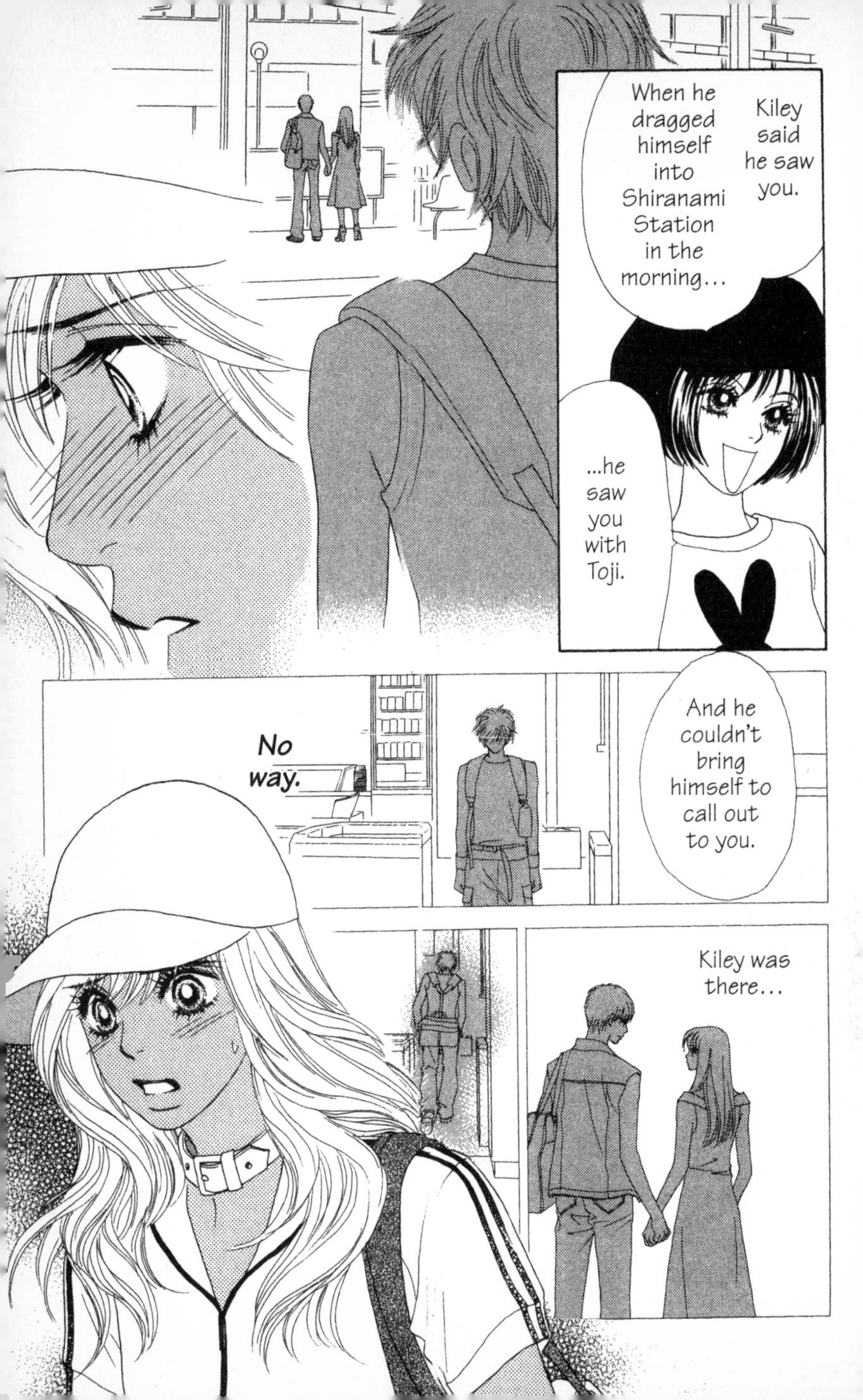
Kiley said he saw you.
When he dragged himself into Shiranami Station in the morning...
...he saw you with Toji.
And he couldn't bring himself to call out to you.
No way.
Kiley was there...

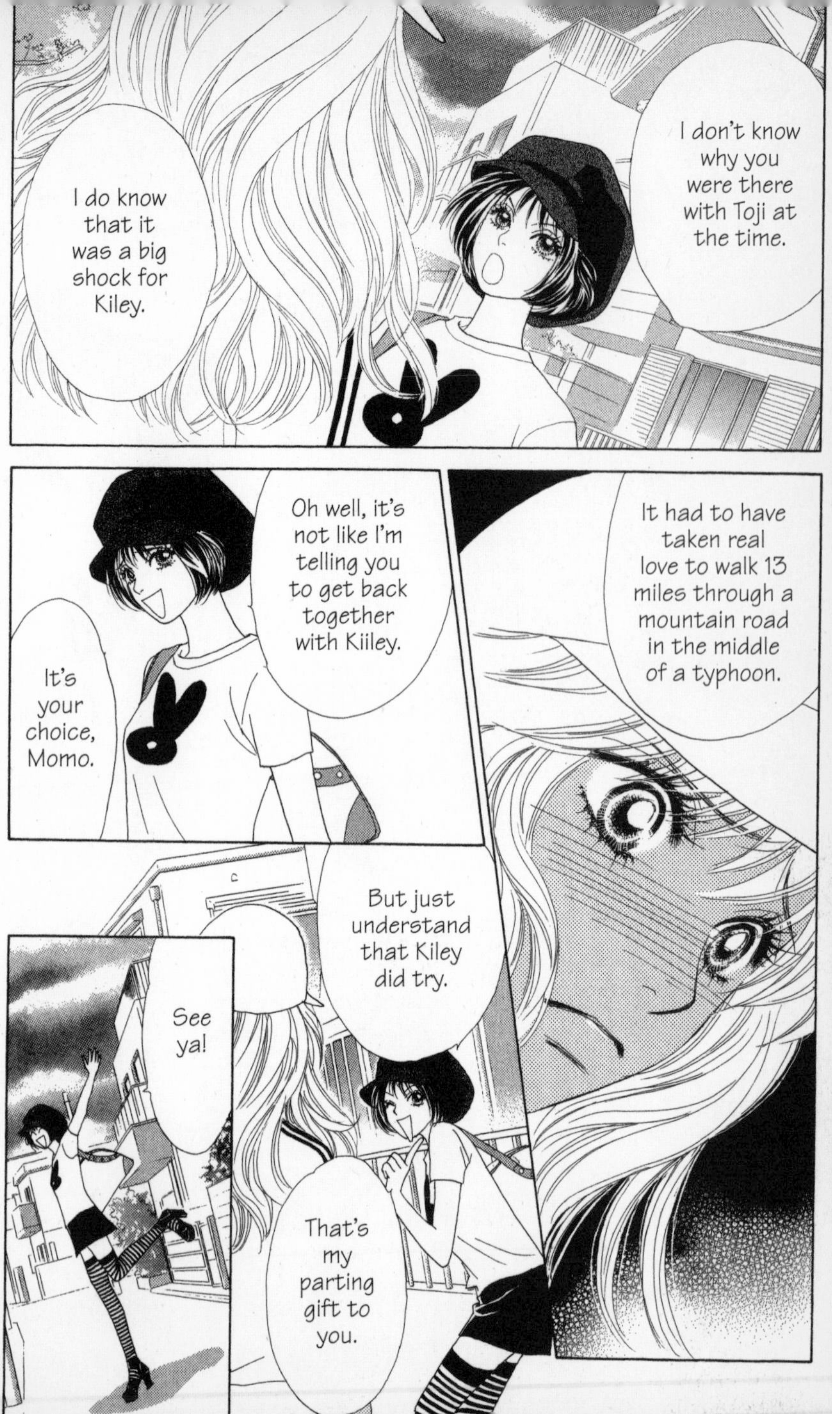
I don't know why you were there with Toji at the time.
I do know that it was a big shock for Kiley.
It had to have taken real love to walk 13 miles through a mountain road in the middle of a typhoon.
Oh well, it's not like I'm telling you to get back together with Kiiley.
It's your choice, Momo.
But just understand that Kiley did try.
That's my parting gift to you.
See ya!

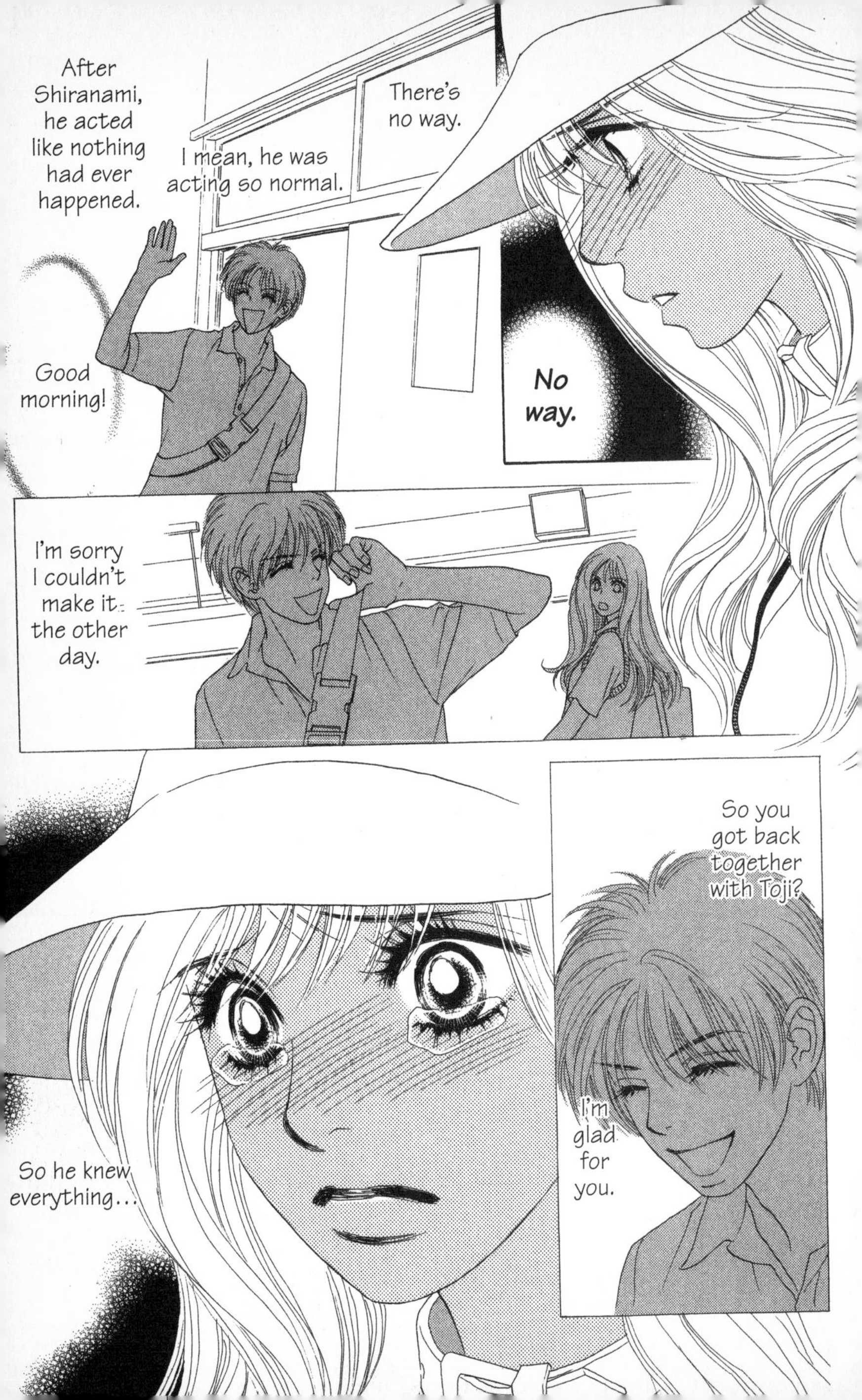
After Shiranami, he acted like nothing had ever happened.
I mean, he was acting so normal.
There's no way.
No way.
Good morning!
I'm sorry I couldn't make it the other day.
So you got back together with Toji?
I'm glad for you.
So he knew everything...

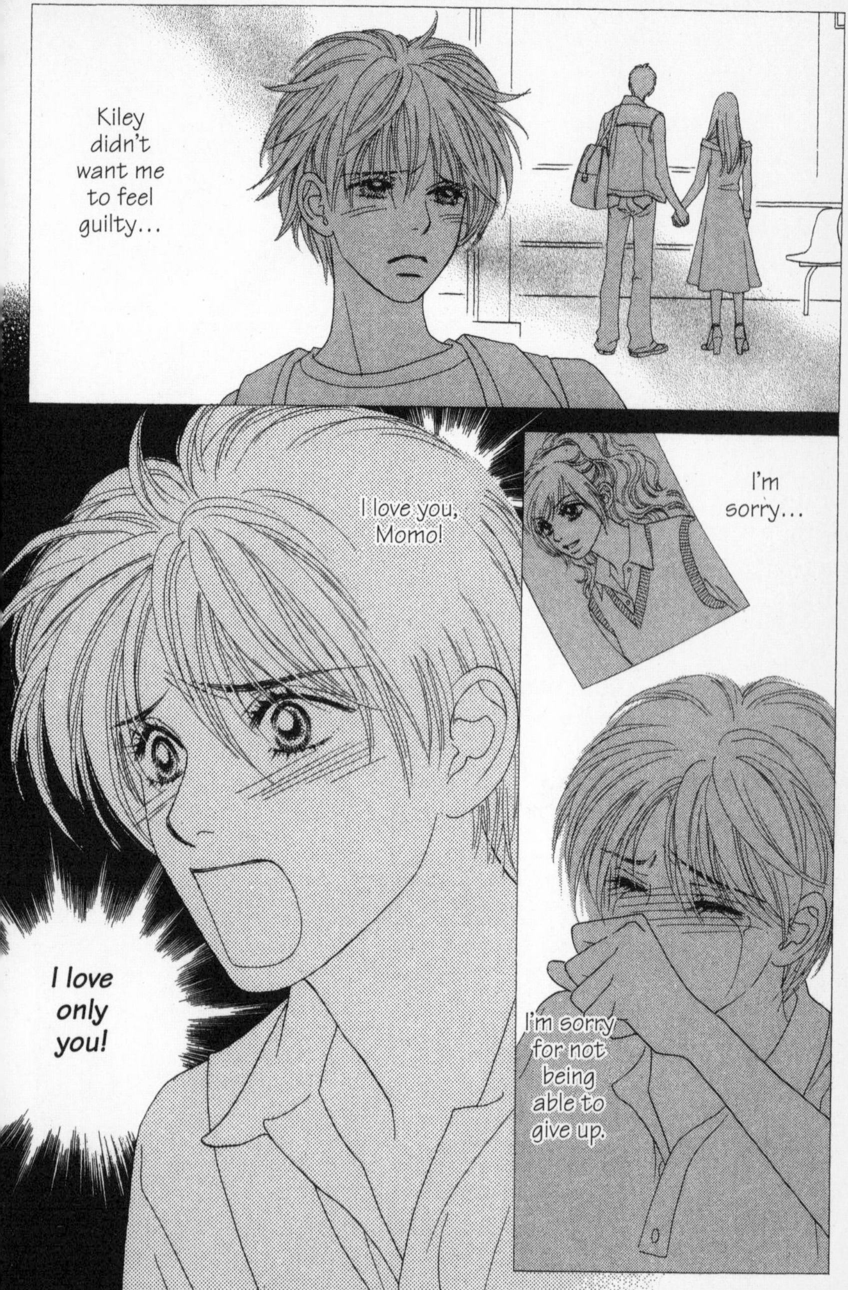
Kiley didn't want me to feel guilty...
I'm sorry...
I'm sorry for not being able to give up.
I love you, Momo!
I love only you!

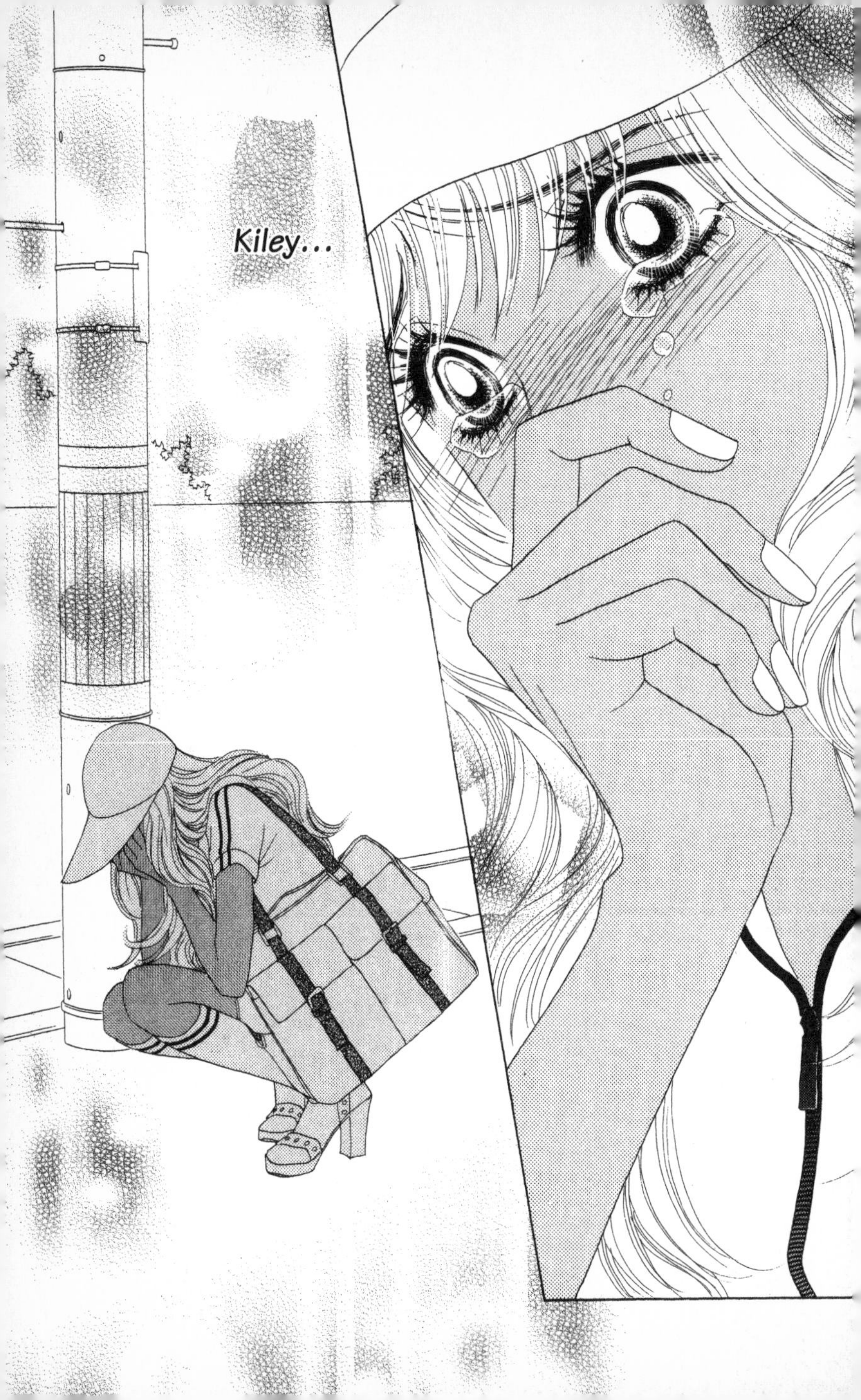
Kiley…

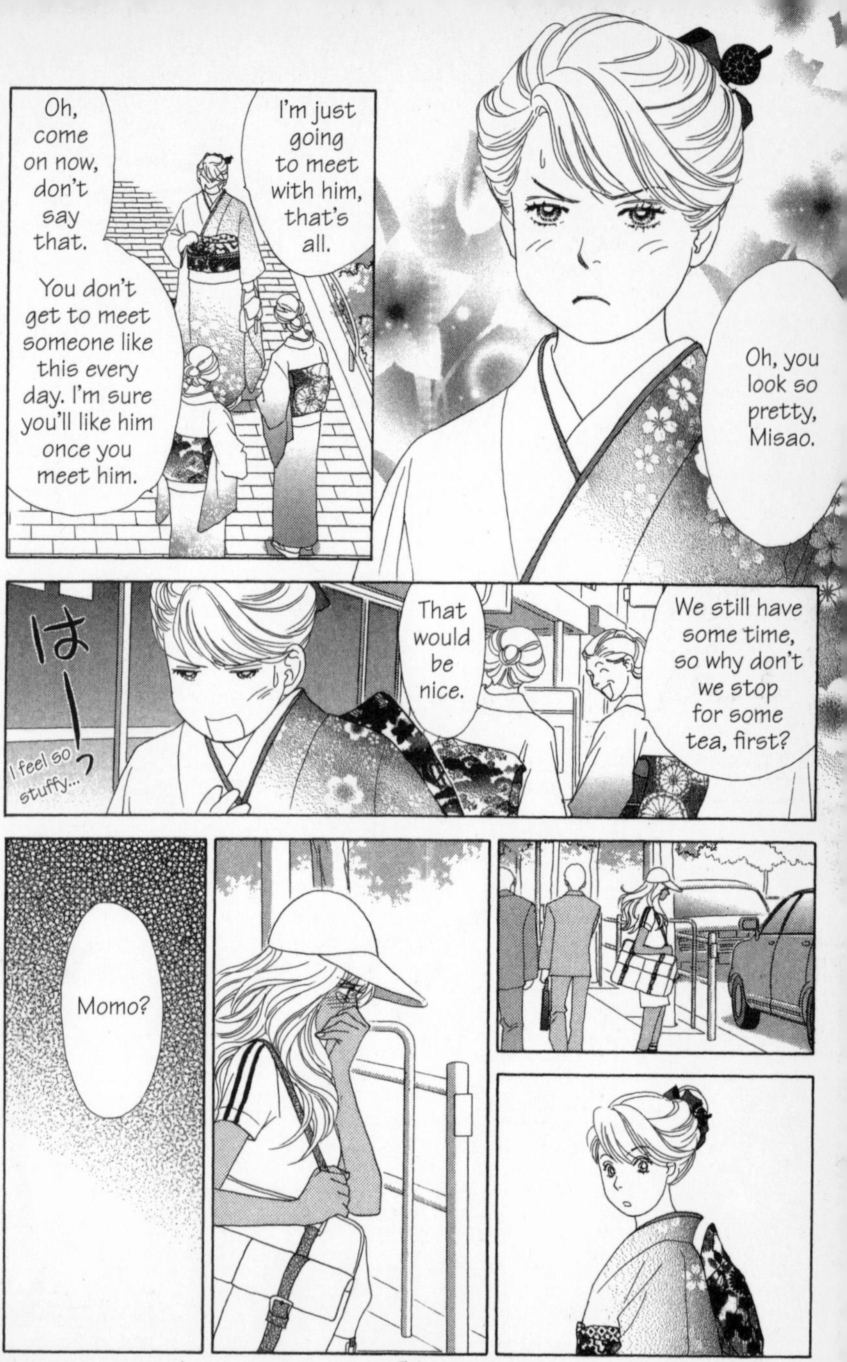
Oh, you look so pretty, Misao.
I'm just going to meet with him, that's all.
Oh, come on now, don't say that.
You don't get to meet someone like this every day. I'm sure you'll like him once you meet him.
We still have some time, so why don't we stop for some tea, first?
That would be nice.
はーっ
I feel so stuffy...
Momo?

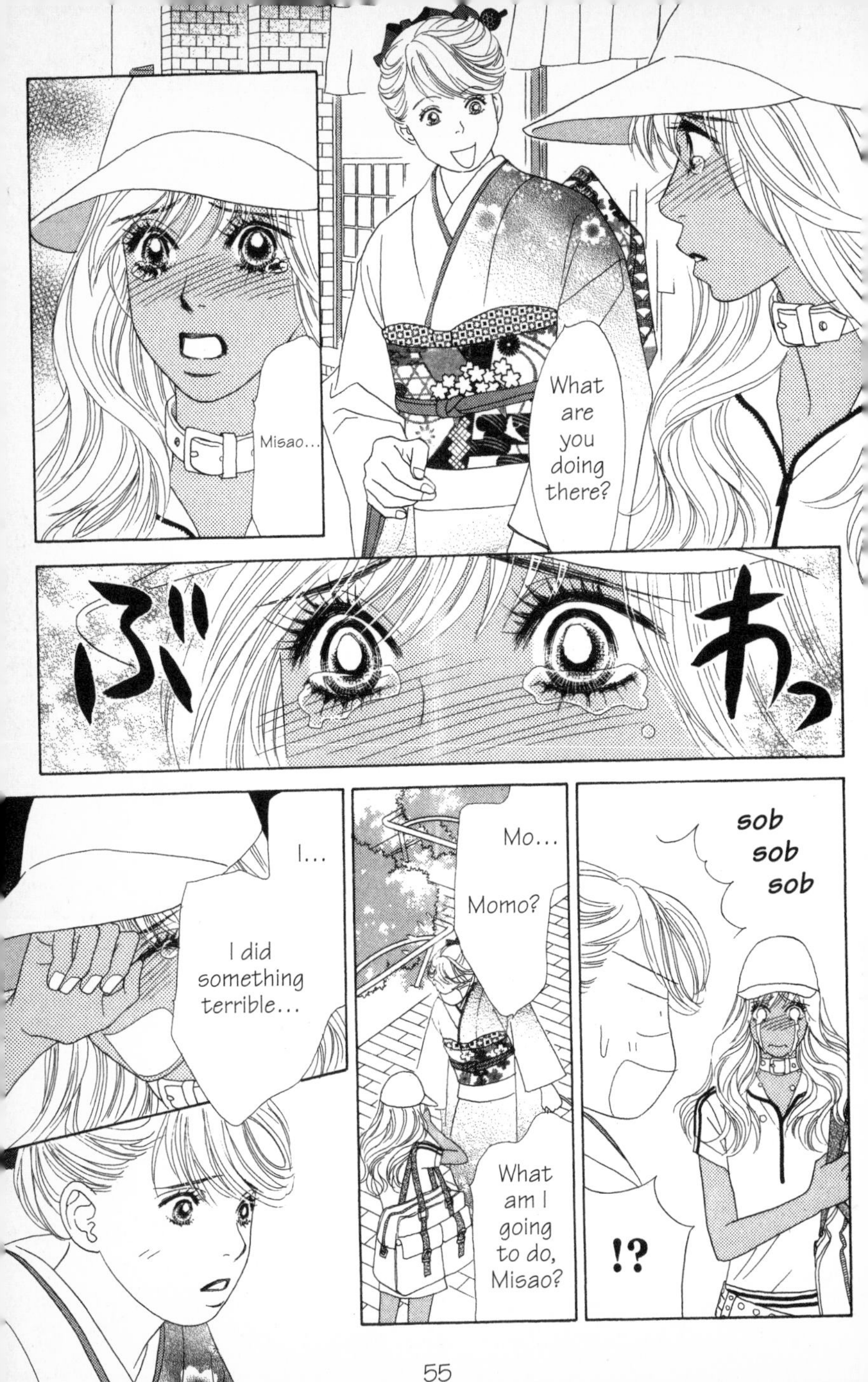
What are you doing there?
Misao...
ぶわっ
sob sob sob
!?
Mo...
Momo?
What am I going to do, Misao?
I...
I did something terrible...

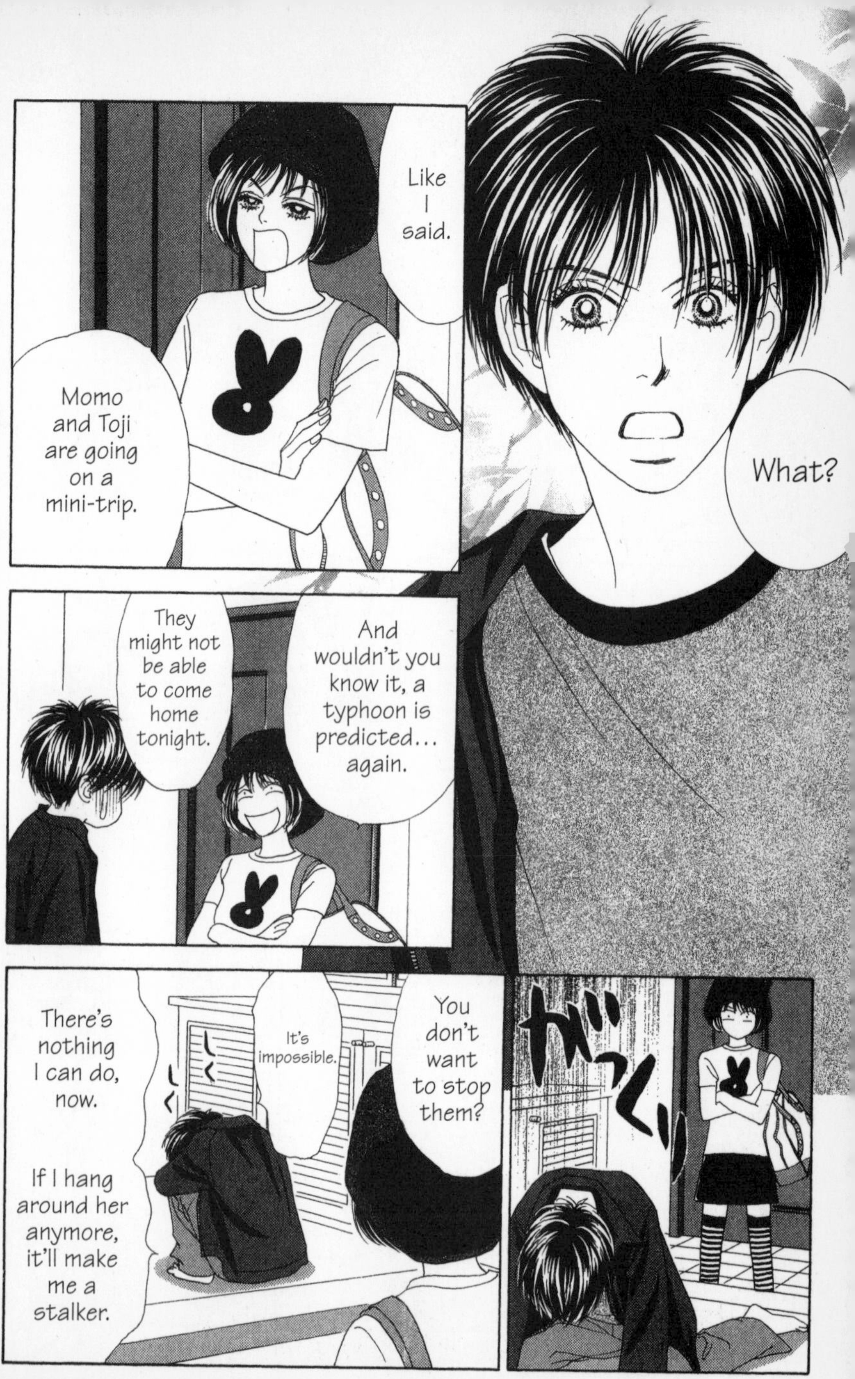
What?
Like I said.
Momo and Toji are going on a mini-trip.
And wouldn't you know it, a typhoon is predicted… again.
They might not be able to come home tonight.
がっくり
You don't want to stop them?
It's impossible.
しくしく
There's nothing I can do, now.
If I hang around her anymore, it'll make me a stalker.

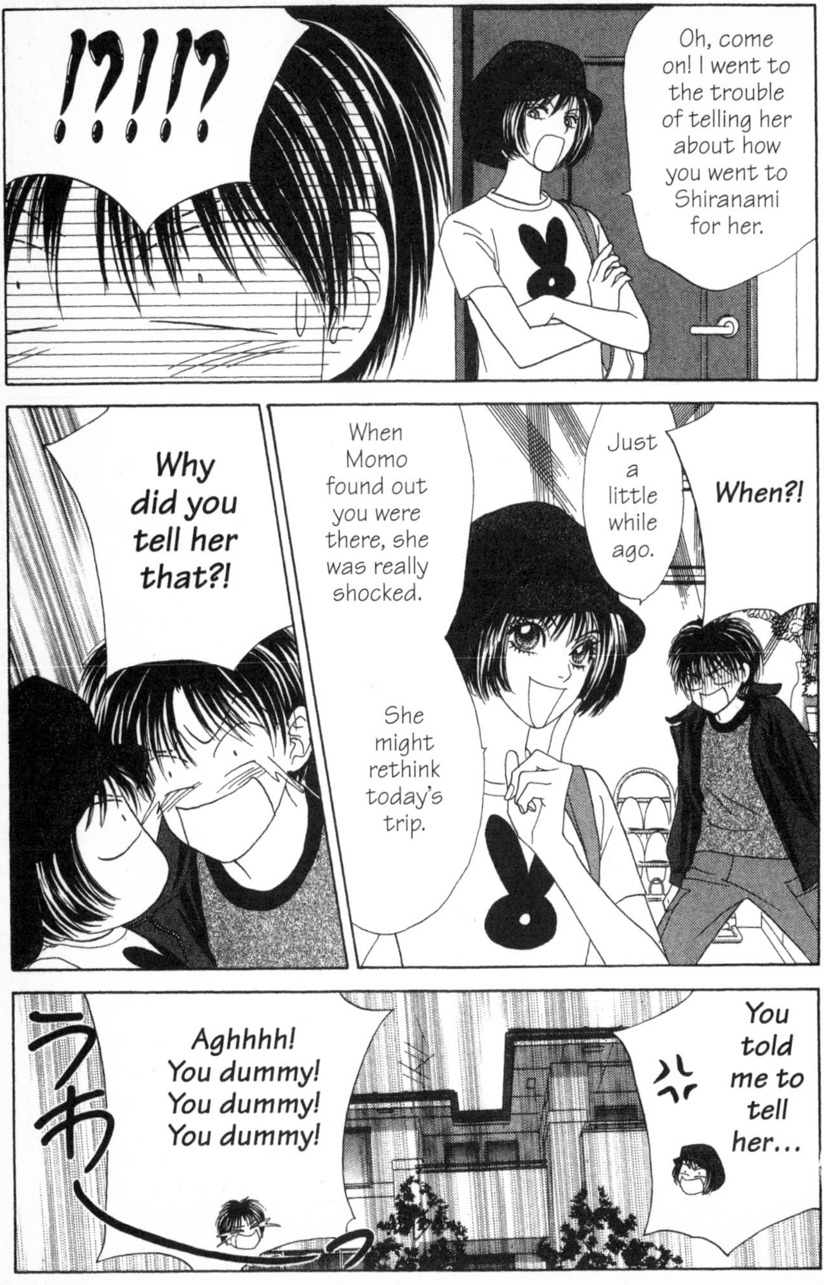
Oh, come on! I went to the trouble of telling her about how you went to Shiranami for her.
!?!?
When?!
Just a little while ago.
When Momo found out you were there, she was really shocked.
She might rethink today's trip.
Why did you tell her that?!
You told me to tell her...
Aghhhh! You dummy! You dummy! You dummy!
うわーっ

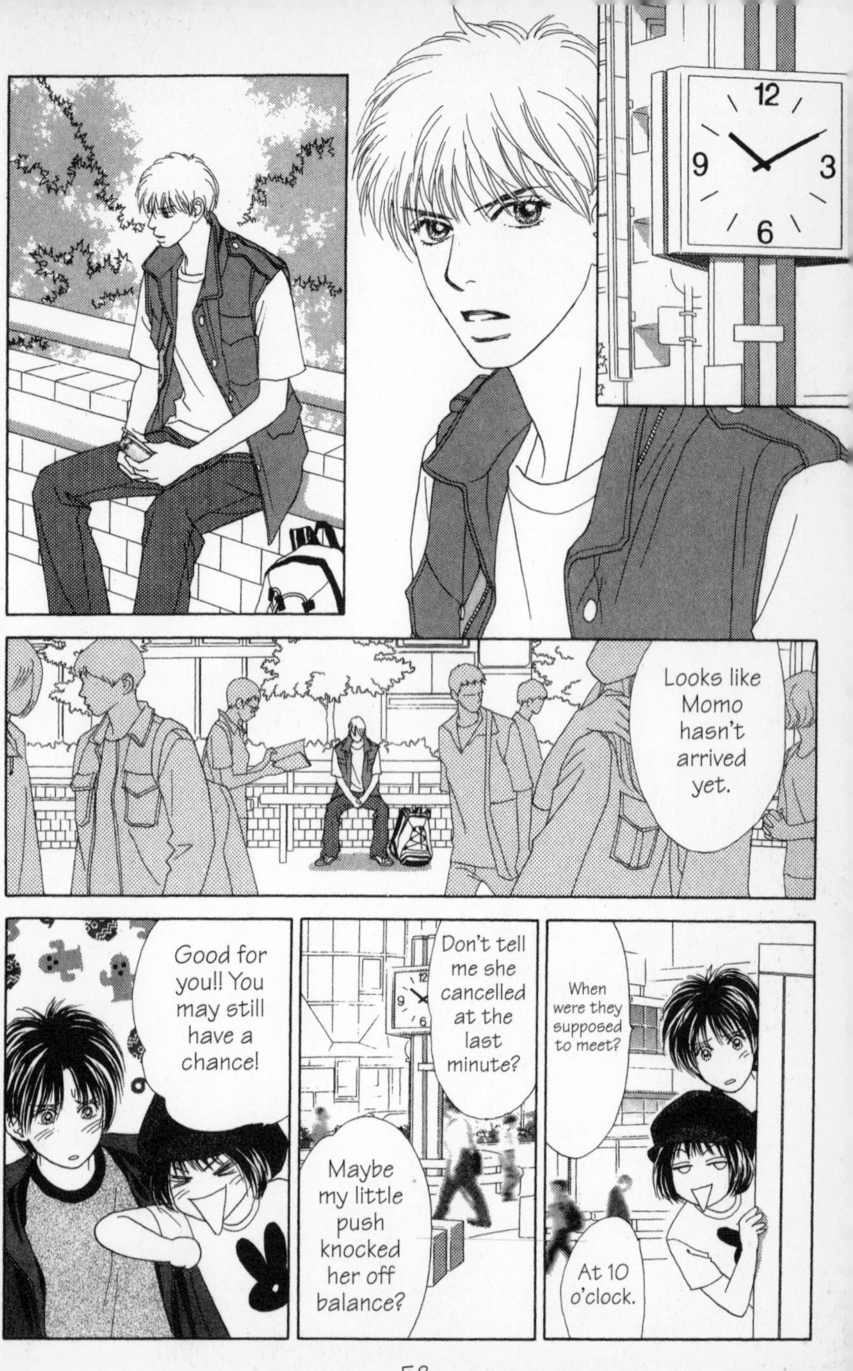
Looks like Momo hasn't arrived yet.
When were they supposed to meet?
At 10 o'clock.
Don't tell me she cancelled at the last minute?
Maybe my little push knocked her off balance?
Good for you!! You may still have a chance!

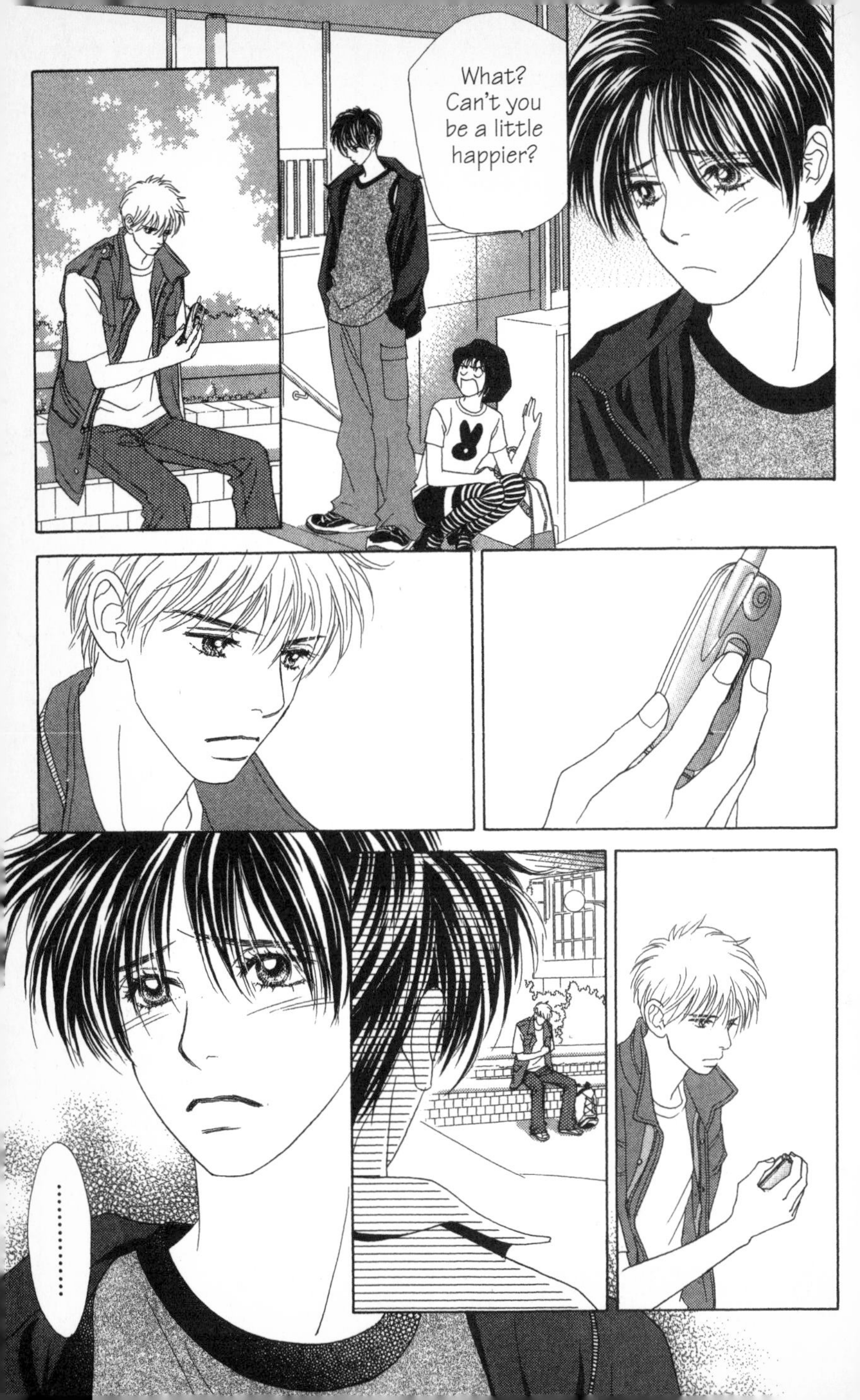
What? Can't you be a little happier?
....

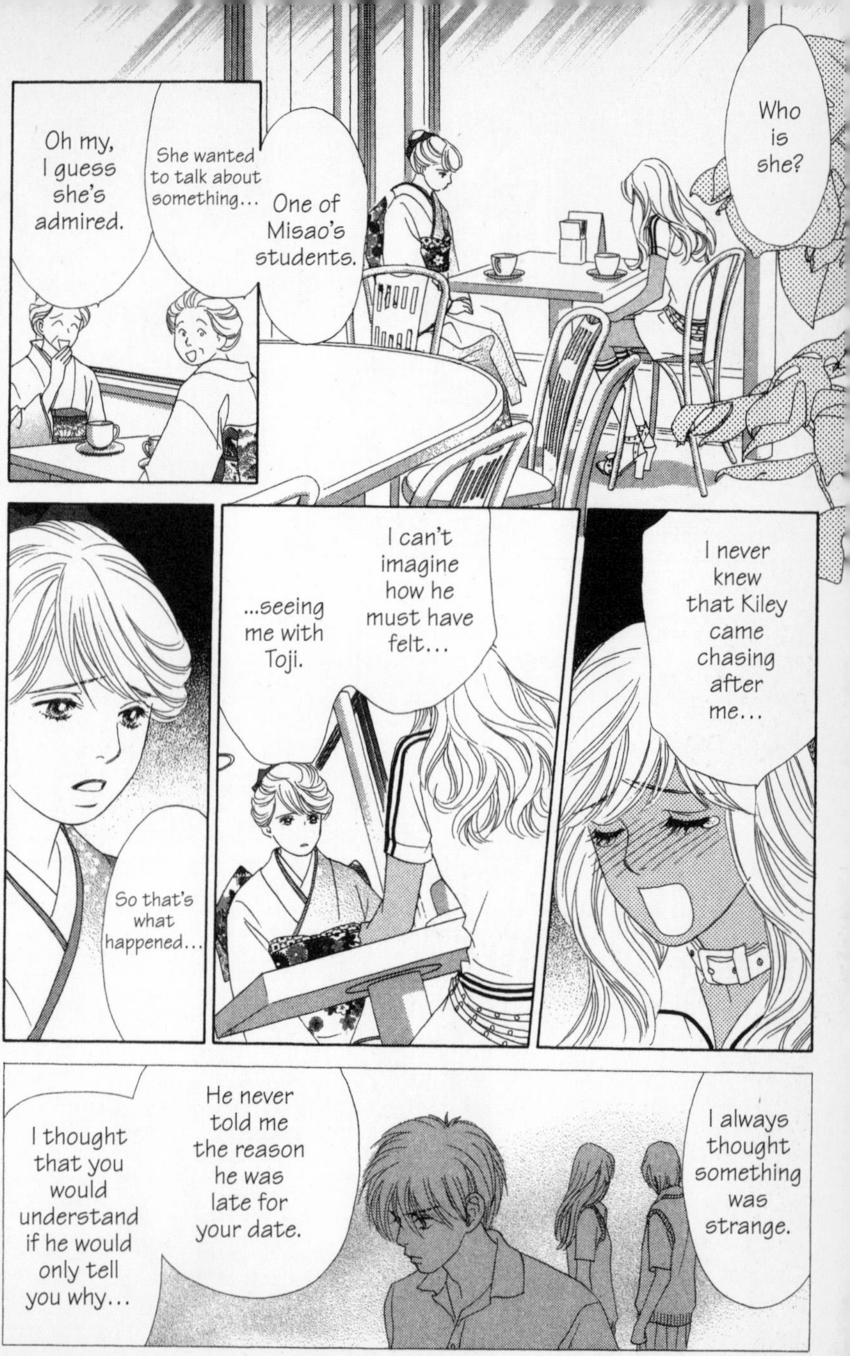
Who is she?
One of Misao's students.
She wanted to talk about something...
Oh my, I guess she's admired.
I never knew that Kiley came chasing after me...
I can't imagine how he must have felt...
...seeing me with Toji.
So that's what happened...
I always thought something was strange.
He never told me the reason he was late for your date.
I thought that you would understand if he would only tell you why...

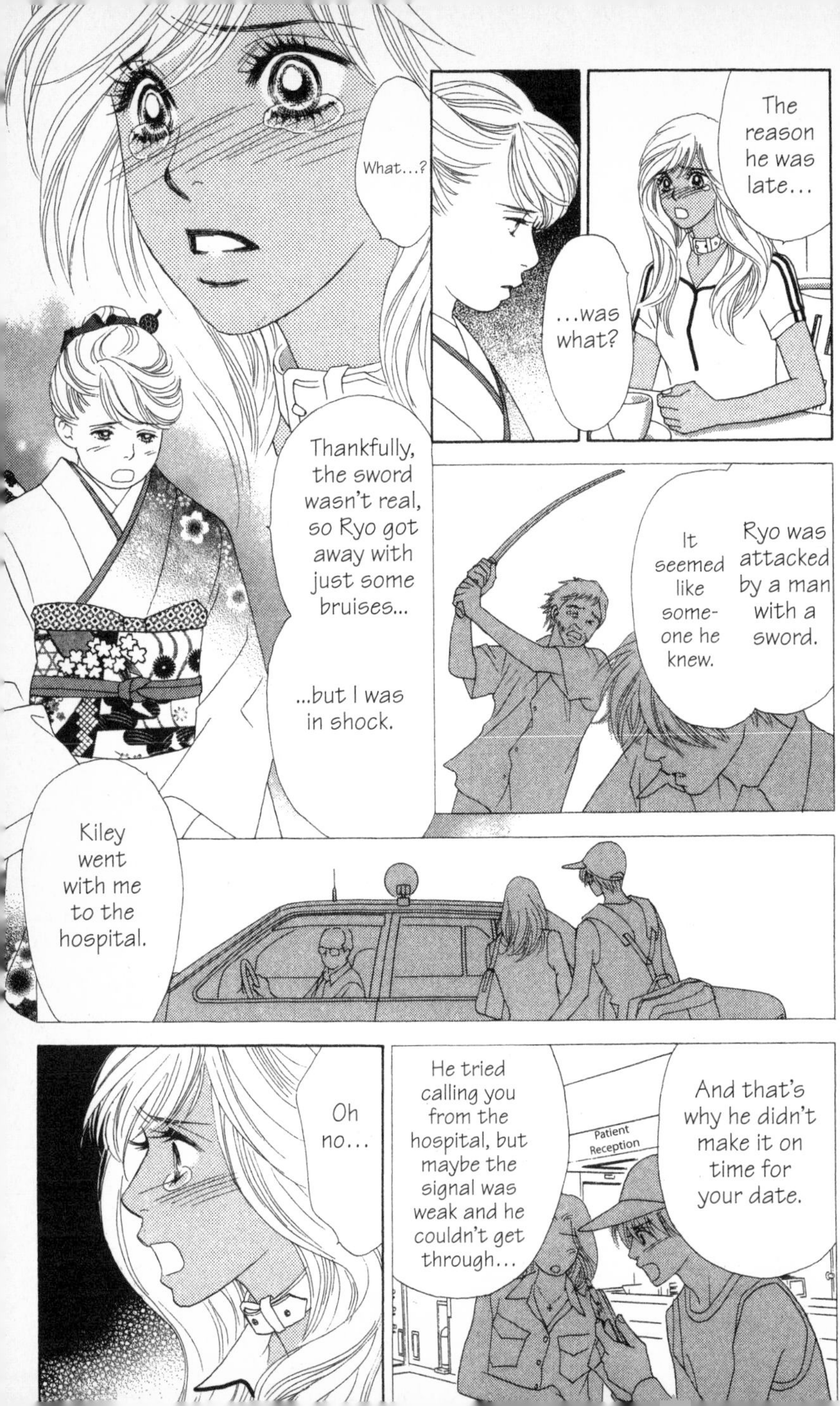

The reason he was late…
…was what?
Ryo was attacked by a man with a sword.
It seemed like someone he knew.
What…?
Thankfully, the sword wasn't real, so Ryo got away with just some bruises...
...but I was in shock.
Kiley went with me to the hospital.
And that's why he didn't make it on time for your date.
He tried calling you from the hospital, but maybe the signal was weak and he couldn't get through…
Patient Reception
Oh no…

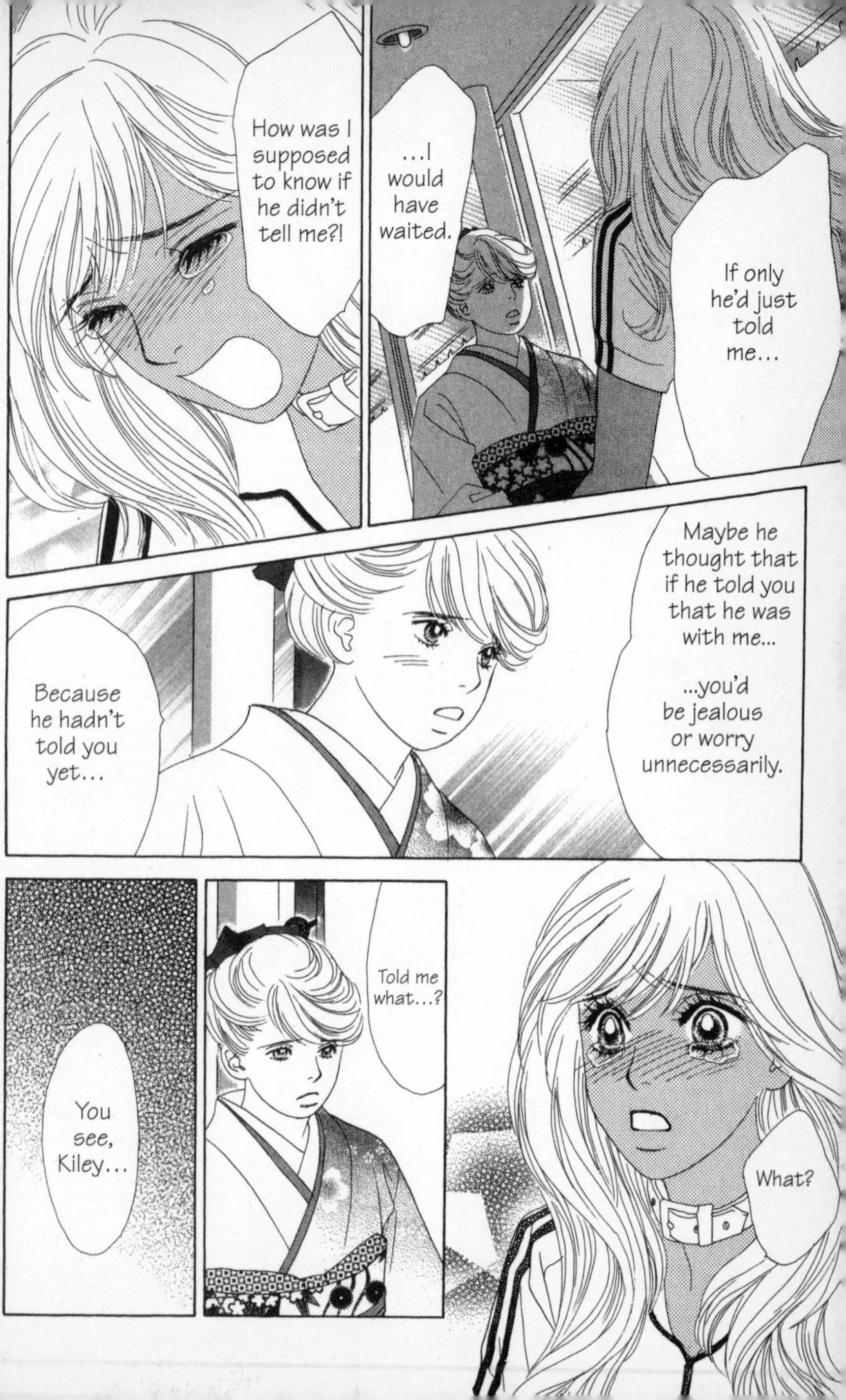
If only he'd just told me…
…I would have waited.
How was I supposed to know if he didn't tell me?!
Maybe he thought that if he told you that he was with me...
...you'd be jealous or worry unnecessarily.
Because he hadn't told you yet…
What?
Told me what…?
You see, Kiley…

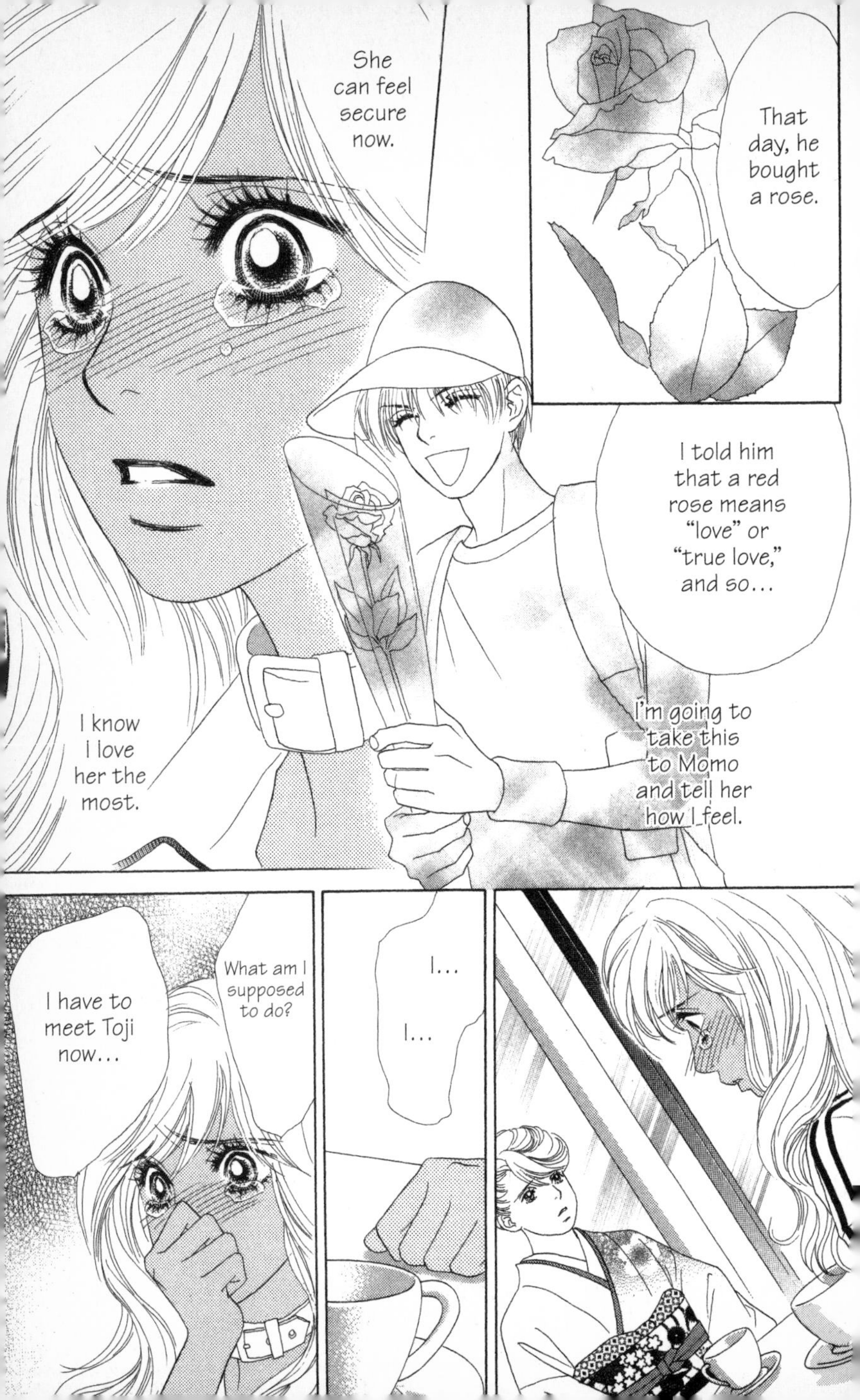
That day, he bought a rose.
I told him that a red rose means "love" or "true love," and so…
I'm going to take this to Momo and tell her how I feel.
She can feel secure now.
I know I love her the most.
I…
I…
What am I supposed to do?
I have to meet Toji now…

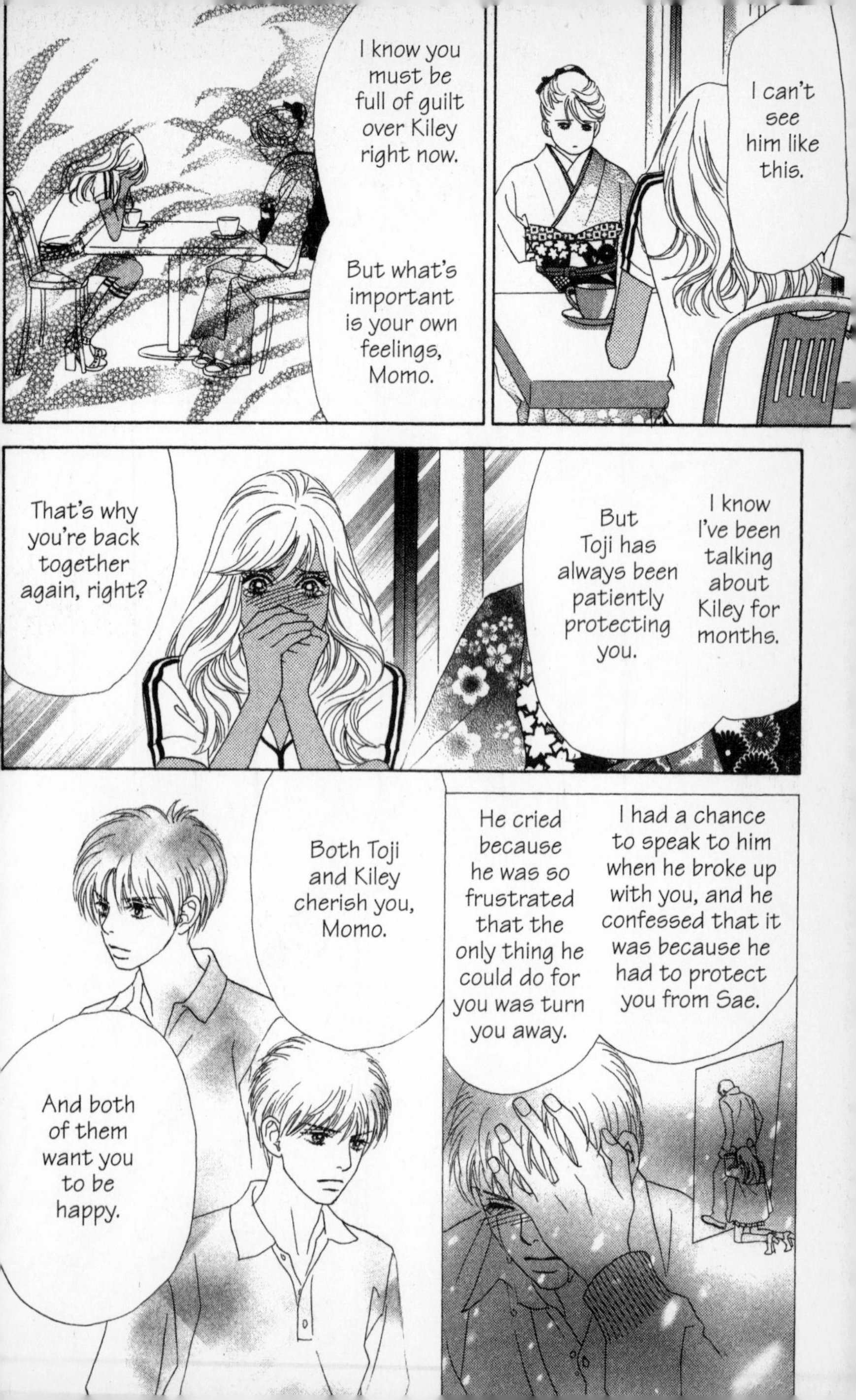
I can't see him like this.
I know you must be full of guilt over Kiley right now.
But what's important is your own feelings, Momo.
I know I've been talking about Kiley for months.
But Toji has always been patiently protecting you.
That's why you're back together again, right?
I had a chance to speak to him when he broke up with you, and he confessed that it was because he had to protect you from Sae.
He cried because he was so frustrated that the only thing he could do for you was turn you away.
Both Toji and Kiley cherish you, Momo.
And both of them want you to be happy.

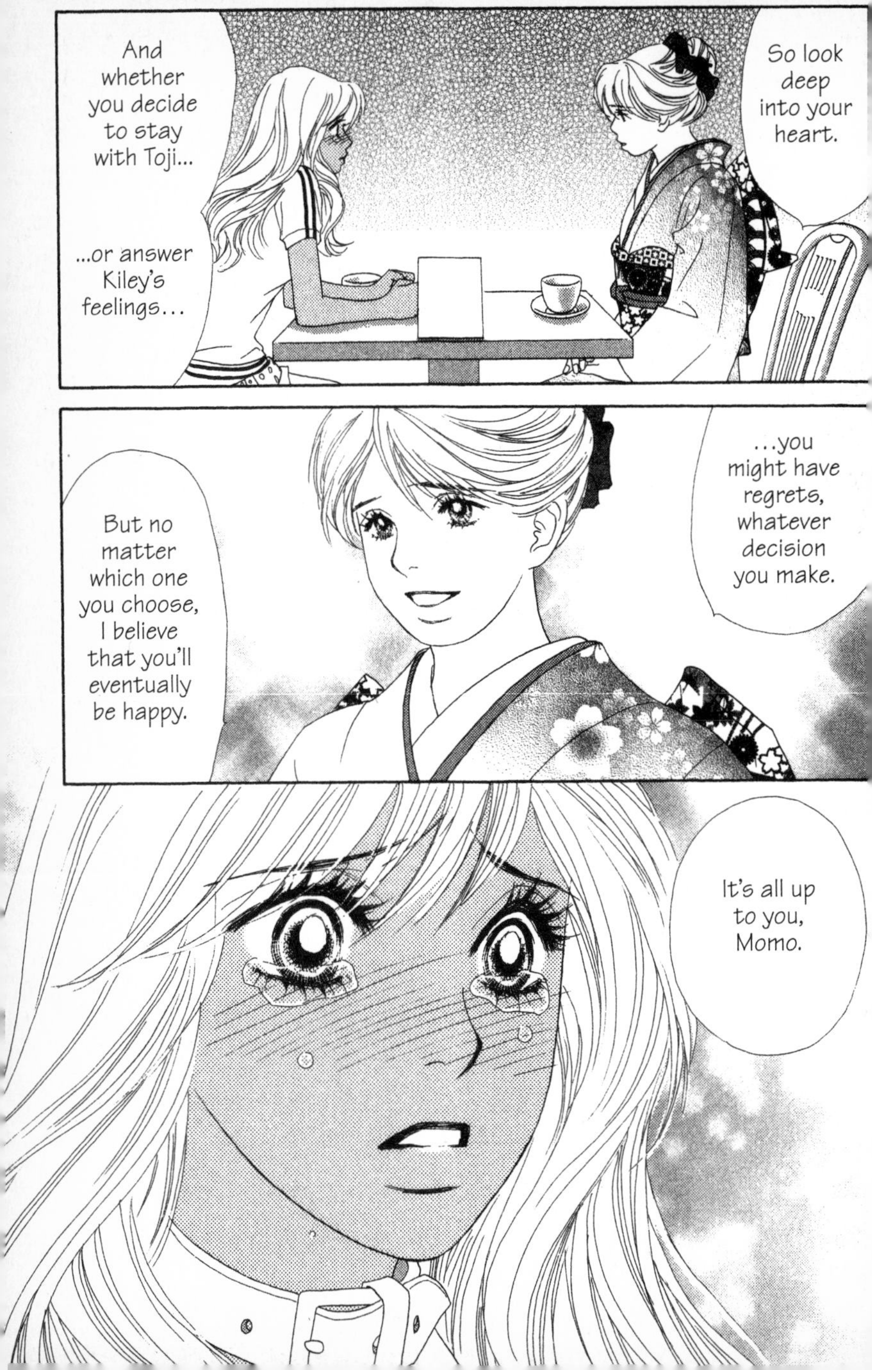

So look deep into your heart.
And whether you decide to stay with Toji...
...or answer Kiley's feelings...
...you might have regrets, whatever decision you make.
But no matter which one you choose, I believe that you'll eventually be happy.
It's all up to you, Momo.

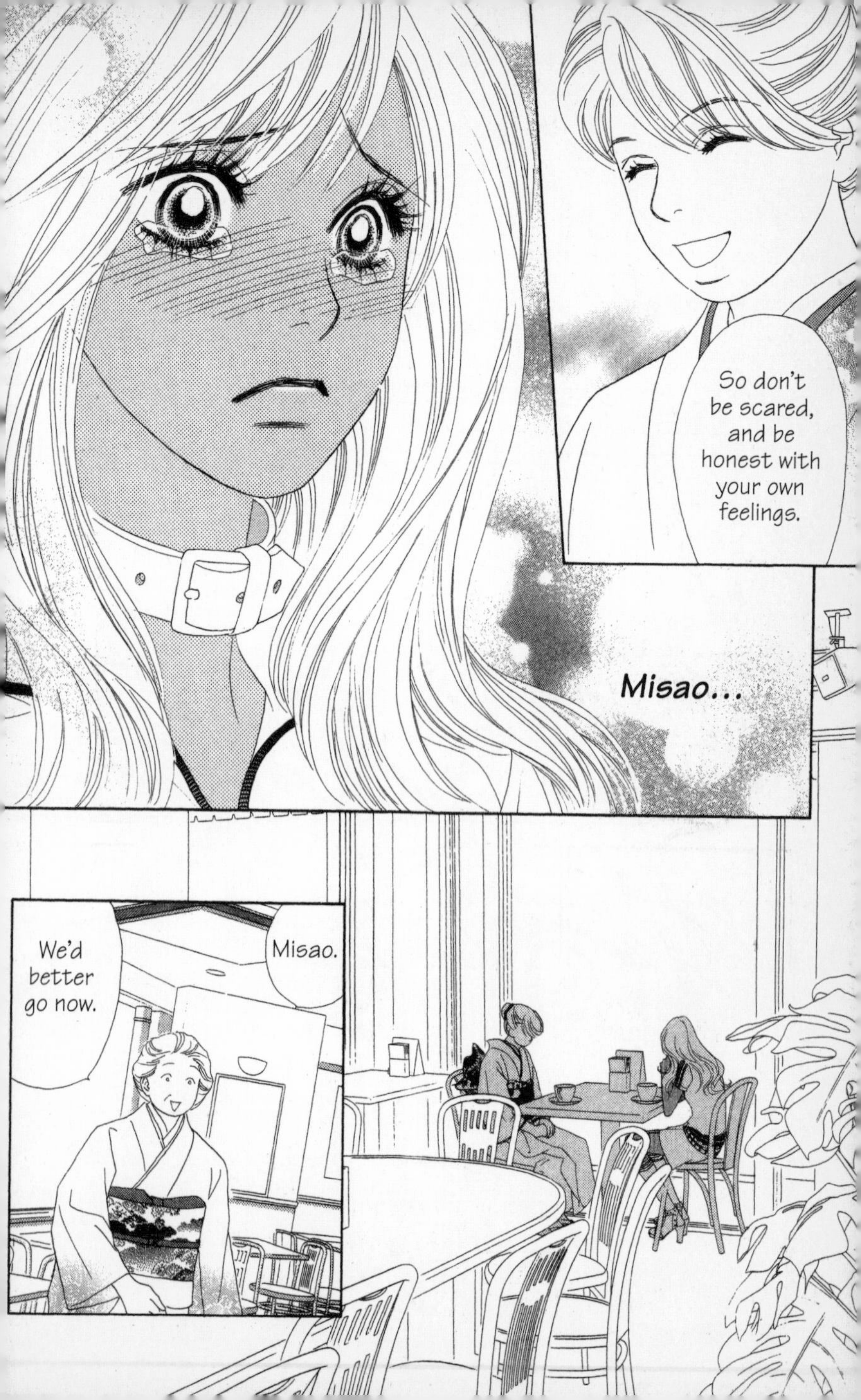
So don't be scared, and be honest with your own feelings.
Misao...
Misao.
We'd better go now.

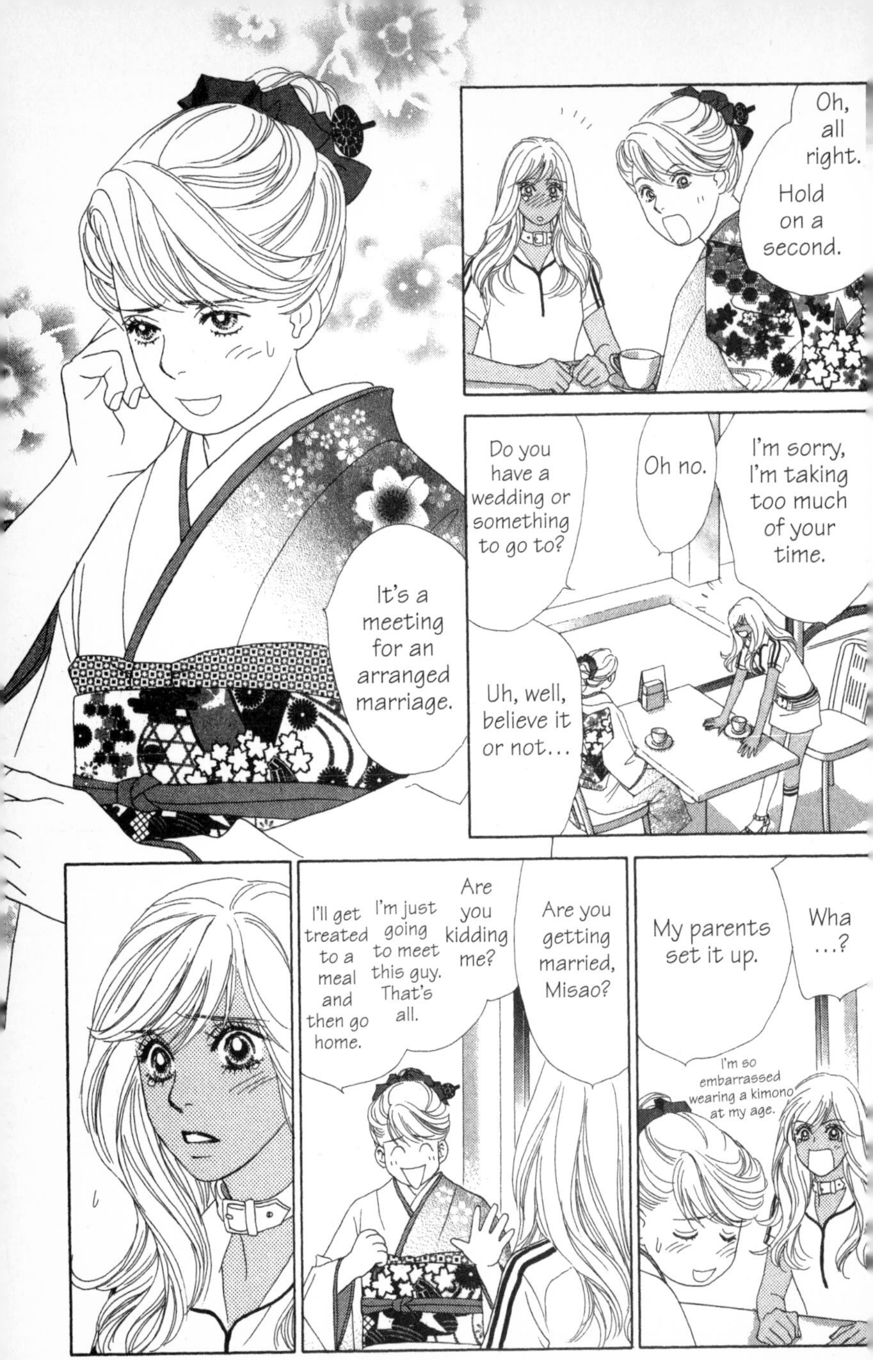
Oh, all right.
Hold on a second.
I'm sorry, I'm taking too much of your time.
Oh no.
Do you have a wedding or something to go to?
Uh, well, believe it or not…
It's a meeting for an arranged marriage.
Wha …?
My parents set it up.
I'm so embarrassed wearing a kimono at my age.
Are you getting married, Misao?
Are you kidding me?
I'm just going to meet this guy. That's all.
I'll get treated to a meal and then go home.

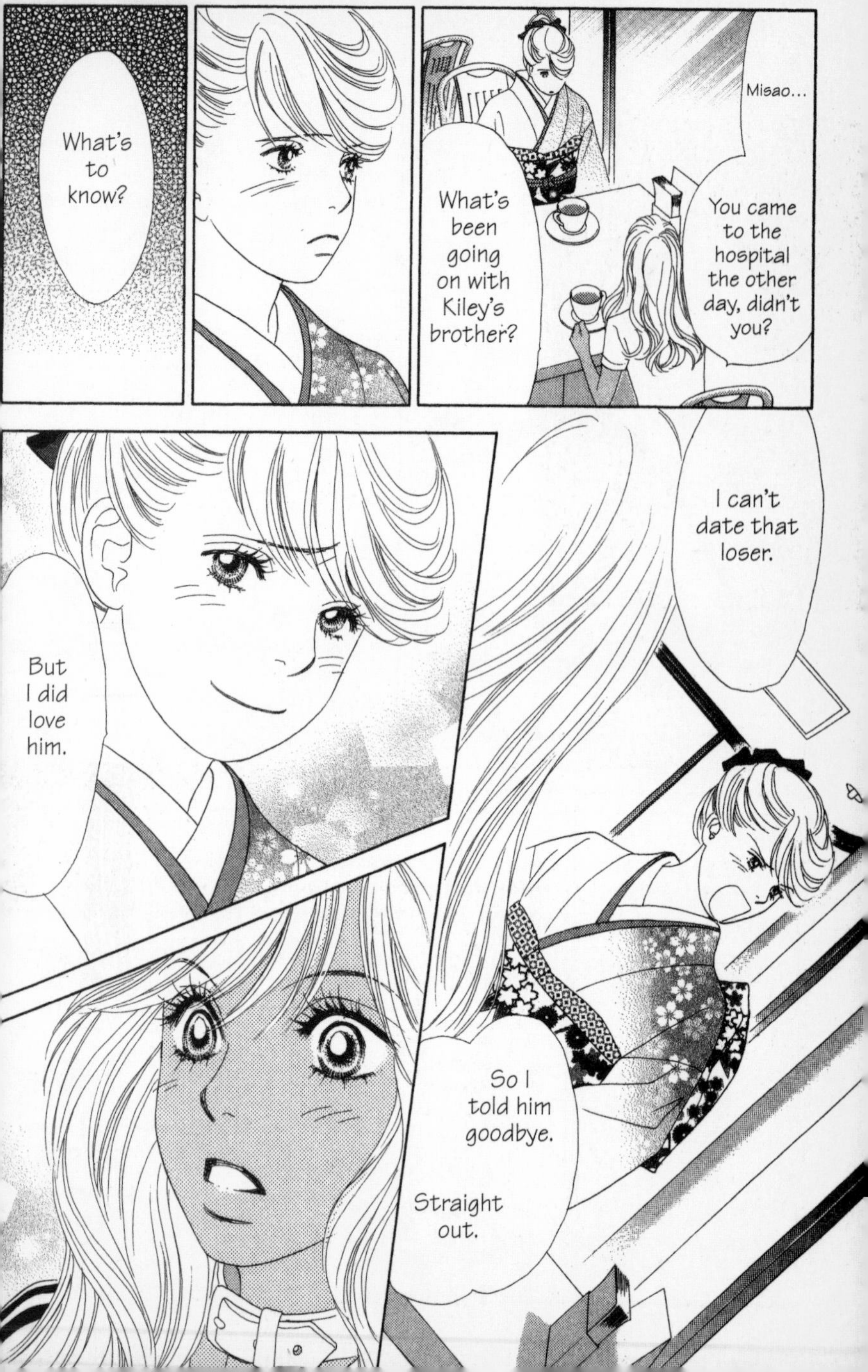
Misao…
You came to the hospital the other day, didn't you?
What's been going on with Kiley's brother?
What's to know?
I can't date that loser.
But I did love him.
So I told him goodbye.
Straight out.

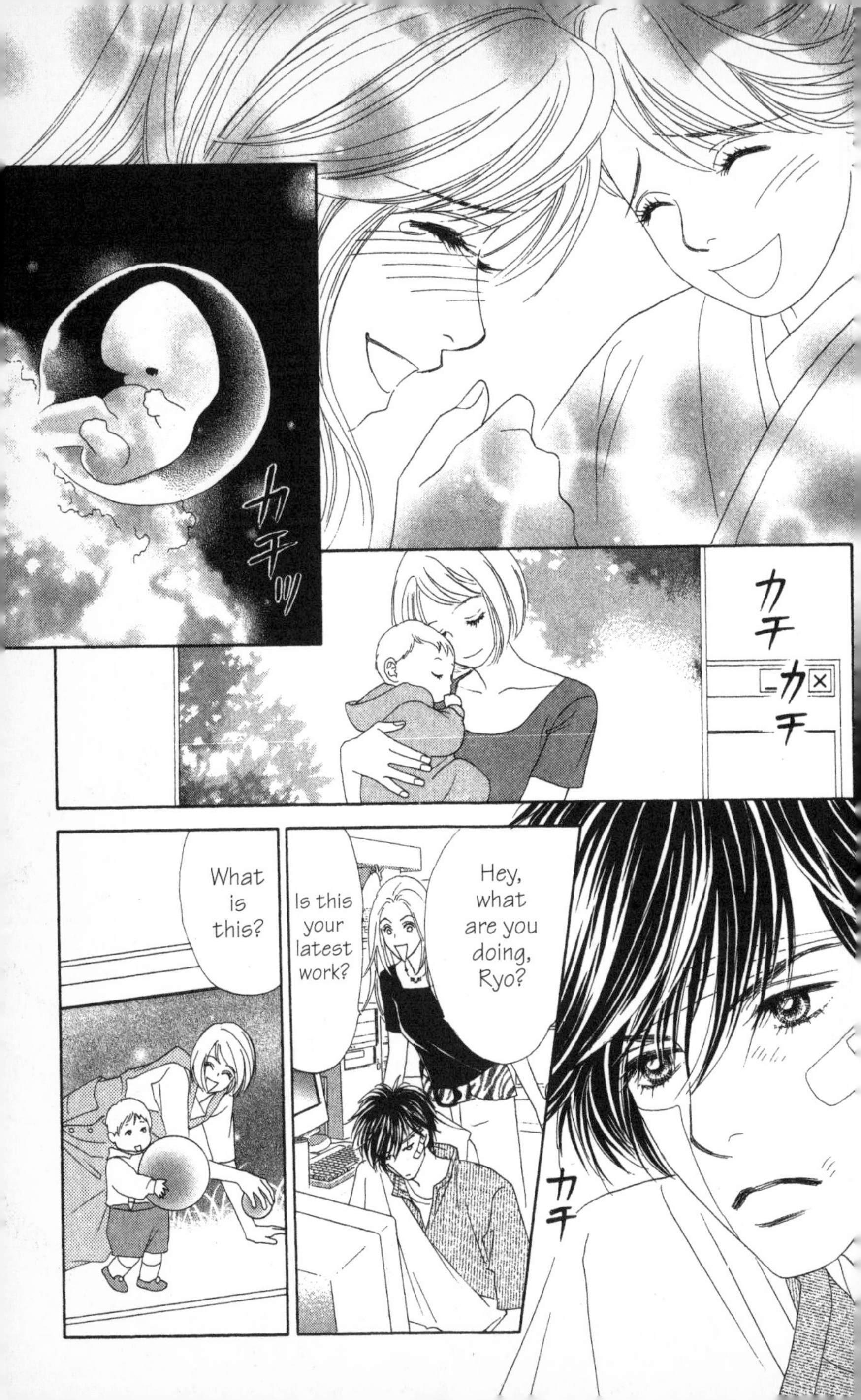

カチッ
カチ
カチ
カチ
カチ
Hey, what are you doing, Ryo?
Is this your latest work?
What is this?

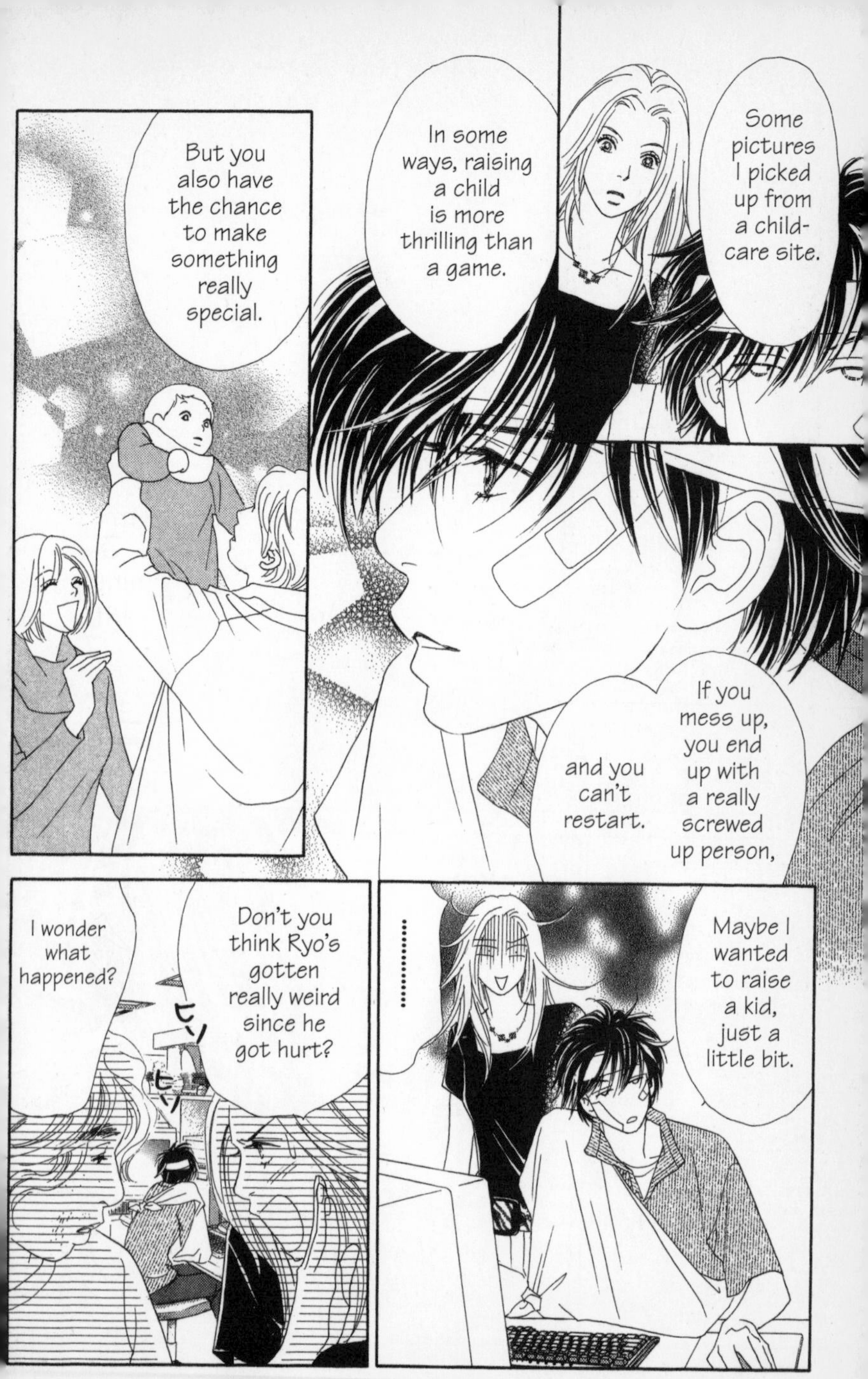
Some pictures I picked up from a child-care site.
In some ways, raising a child is more thrilling than a game.
If you mess up, you end up with a really screwed up person,
and you can't restart.
But you also have the chance to make something really special.
Maybe I wanted to raise a kid, just a little bit.
……
Don't you think Ryo's gotten really weird since he got hurt?
I wonder what happened?
ヒソ ヒソ

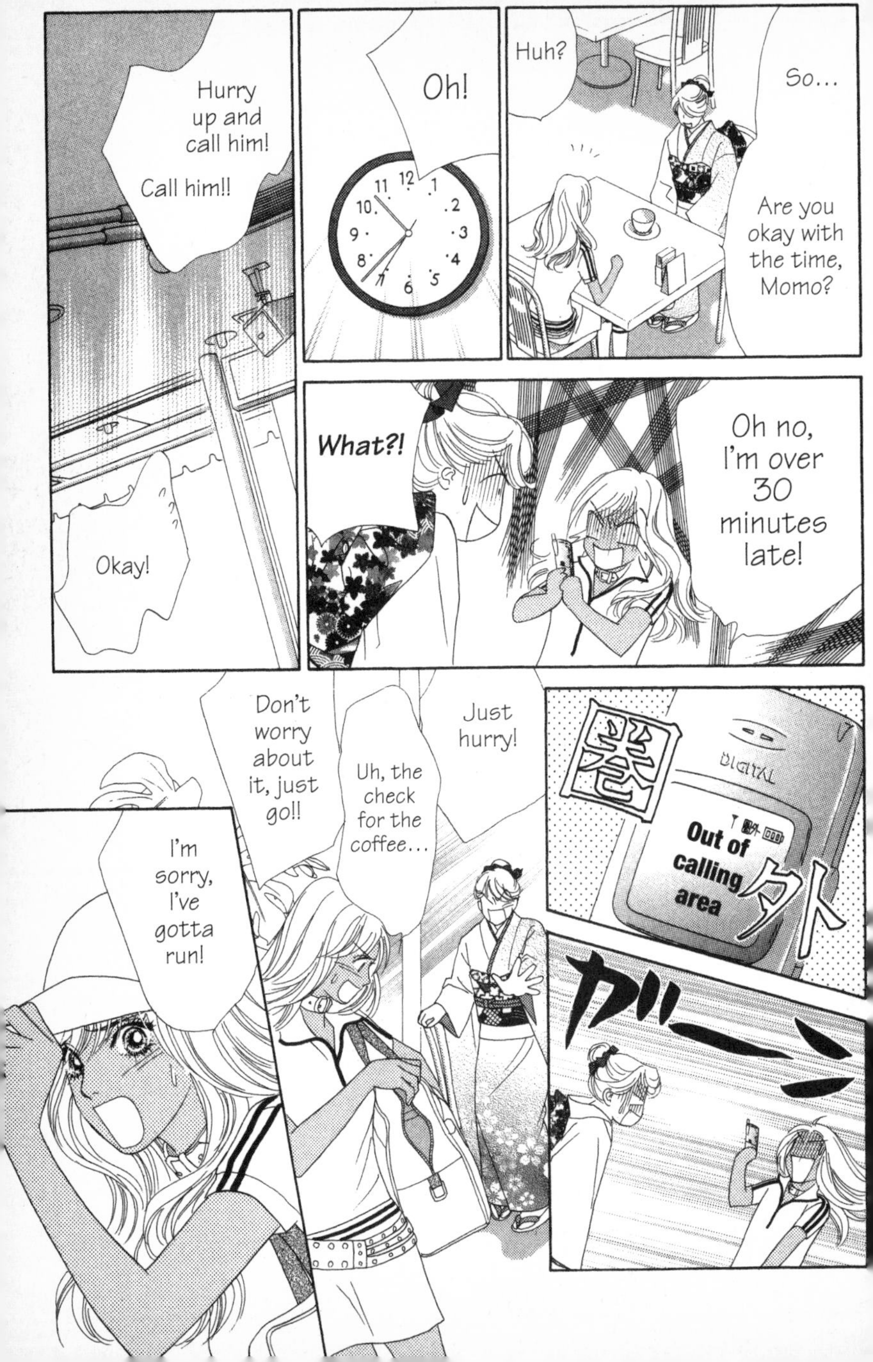
So...
Are you okay with the time, Momo?
Huh?
Oh!
Oh no, I'm over 30 minutes late!
What?!
Hurry up and call him!
Call him!!
Okay!
圏
Out of calling area
タト
ガーン
Just hurry!
Uh, the check for the coffee...
Don't worry about it, just go!!
I'm sorry, I've gotta run!

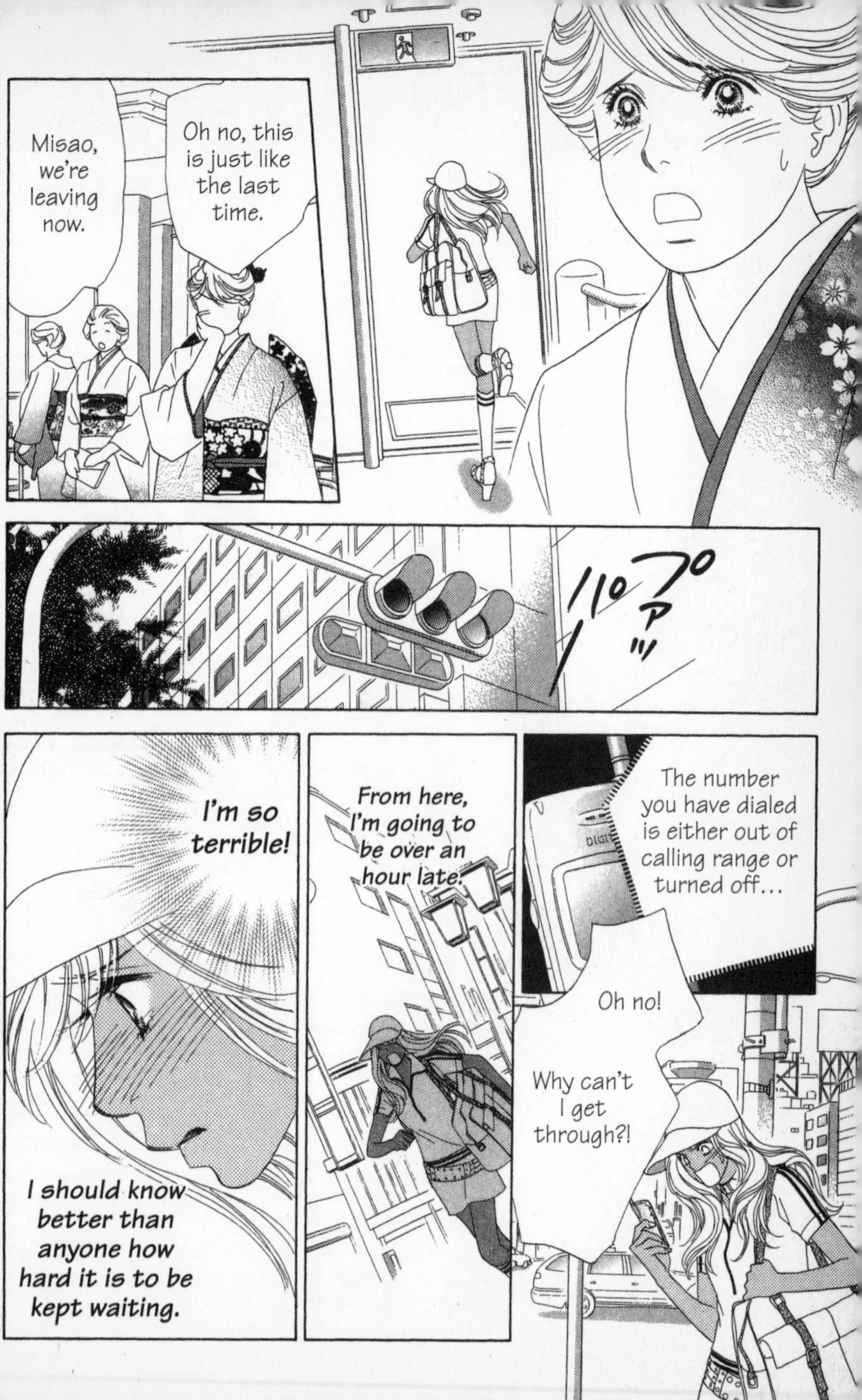
Oh no, this is just like the last time.
Misao, we're leaving now.
パァッ
The number you have dialed is either out of calling range or turned off...
Oh no!
Why can't I get through?!
From here, I'm going to be over an hour late.
I'm so terrible!
I should know better than anyone how hard it is to be kept waiting.

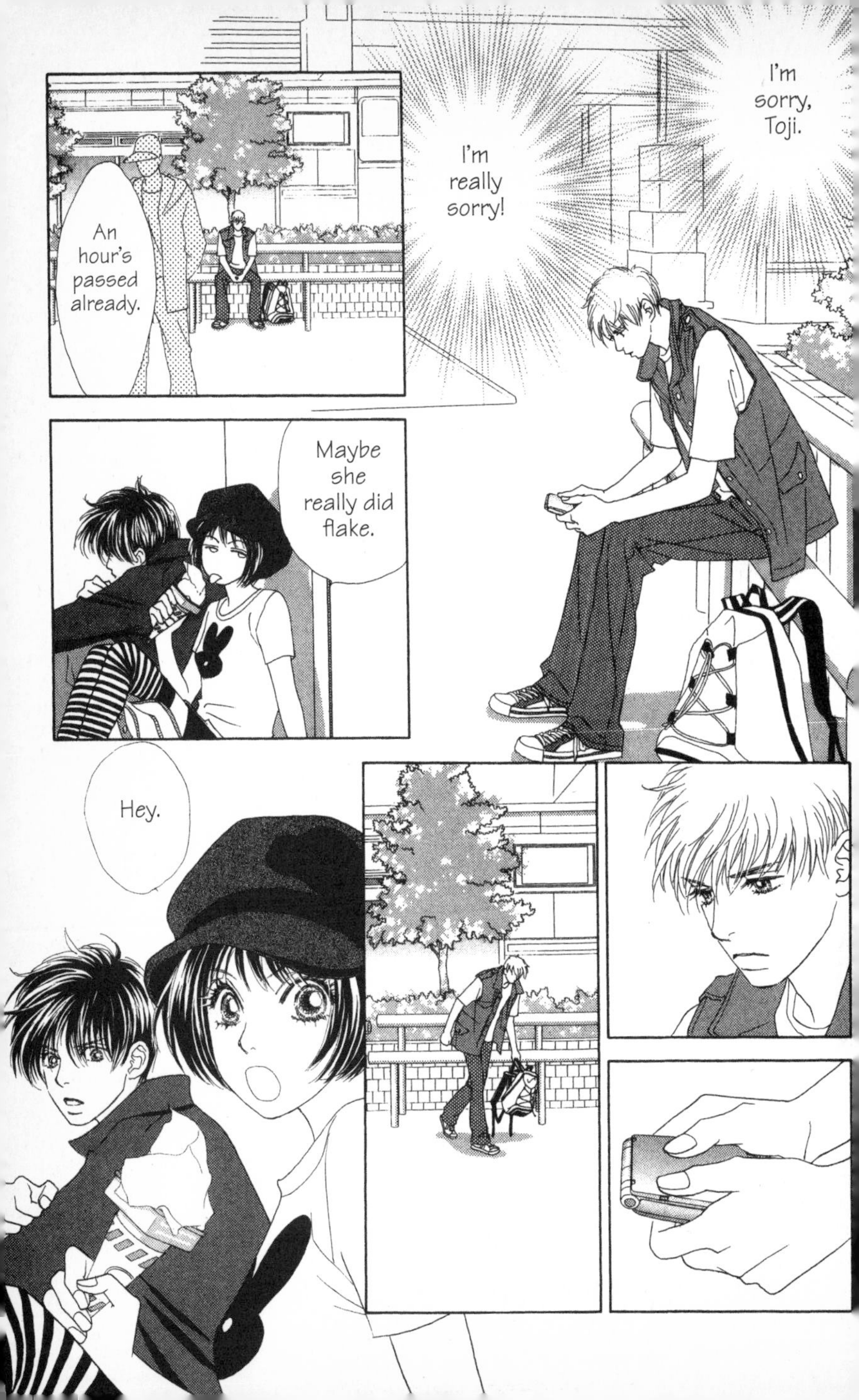
I'm sorry, Toji.
I'm really sorry!
An hour's passed already.
Maybe she really did flake.
Hey.

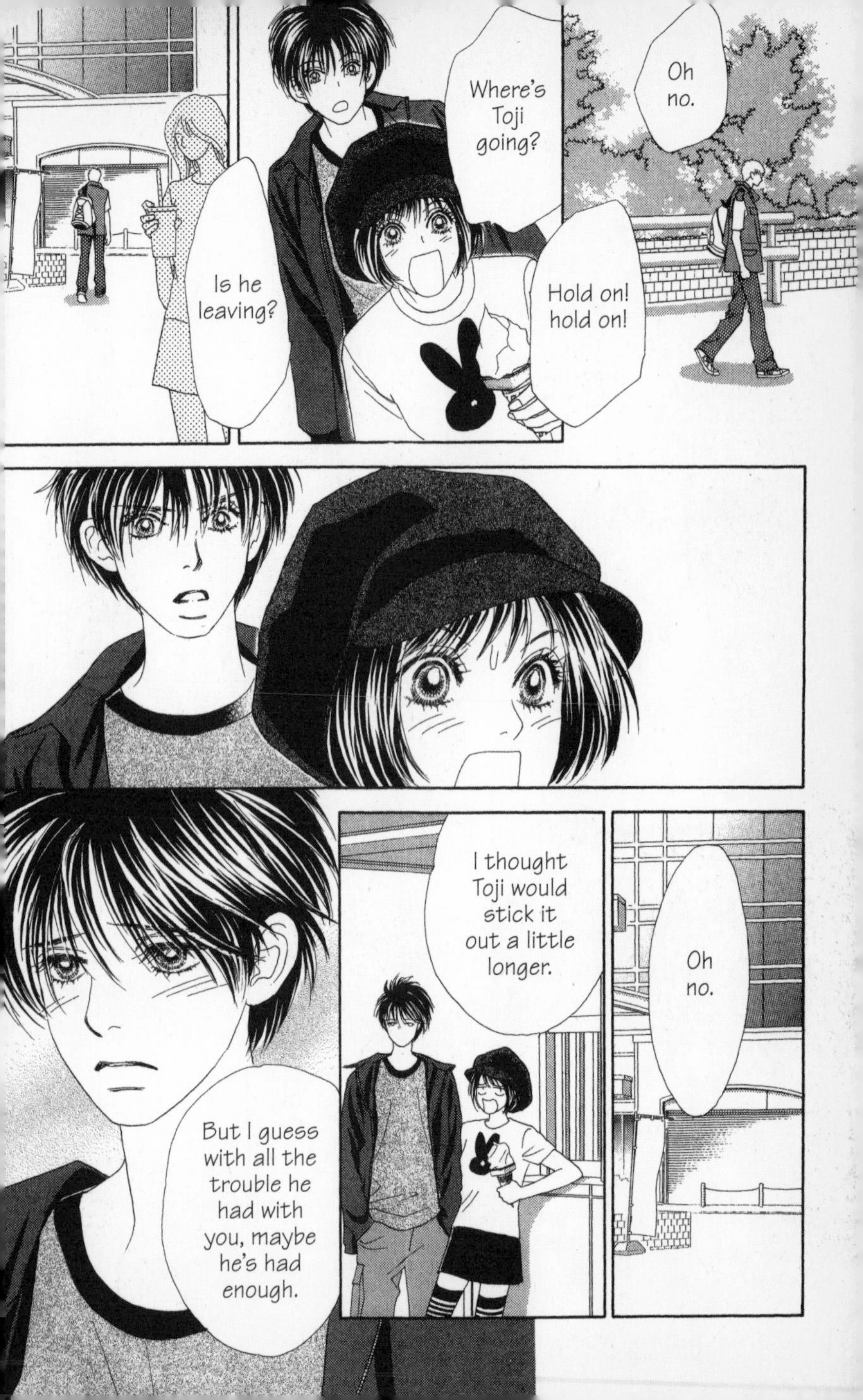
Oh no.
Where's Toji going?
Hold on! hold on!
Is he leaving?
Oh no.
I thought Toji would stick it out a little longer.
But I guess with all the trouble he had with you, maybe he's had enough.

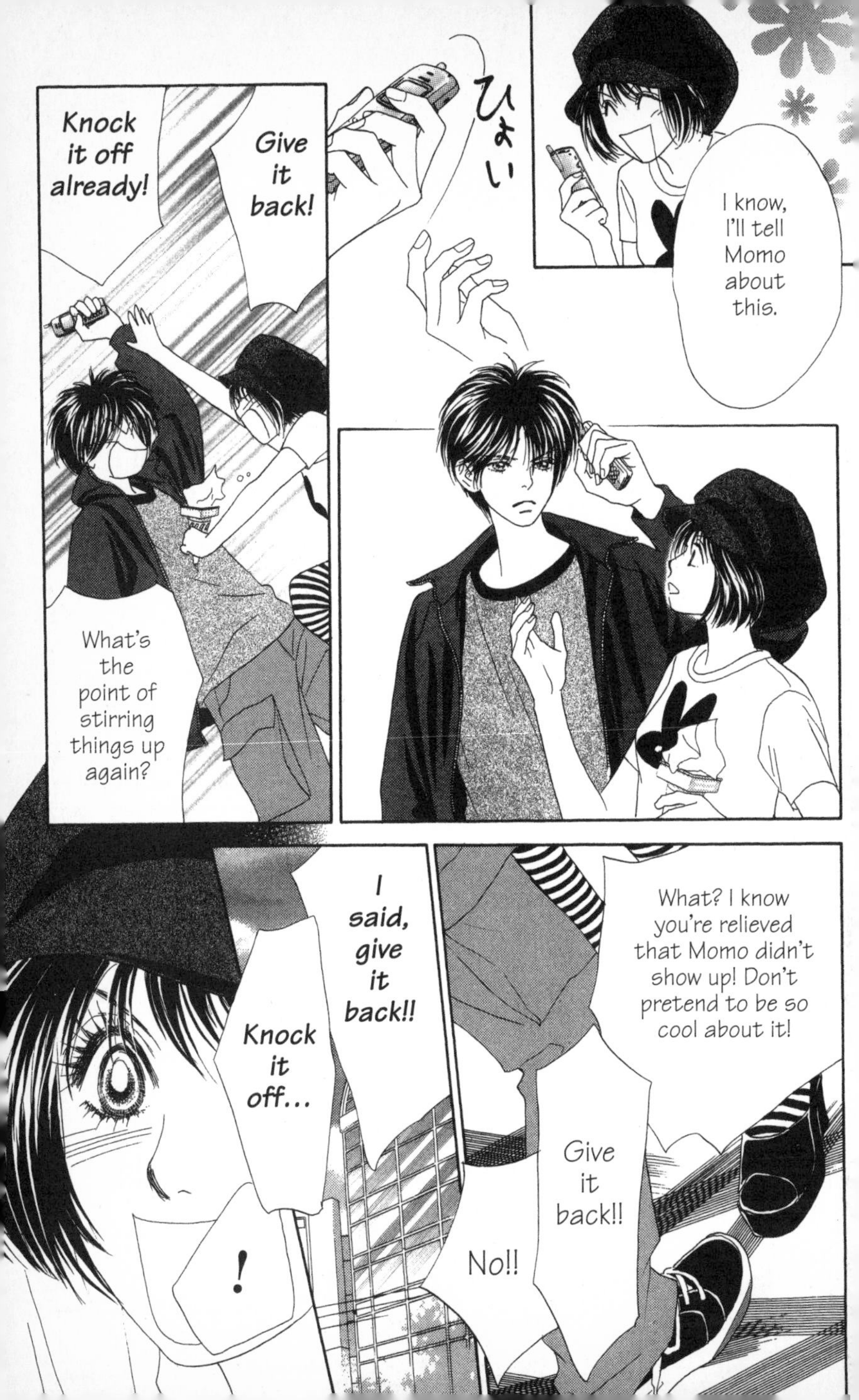
I know, I'll tell Momo about this.
ひょい
Give it back!
Knock it off already!
What's the point of stirring things up again?
What? I know you're relieved that Momo didn't show up! Don't pretend to be so cool about it!
Give it back!!
No!!
I said, give it back!!
Knock it off...
!

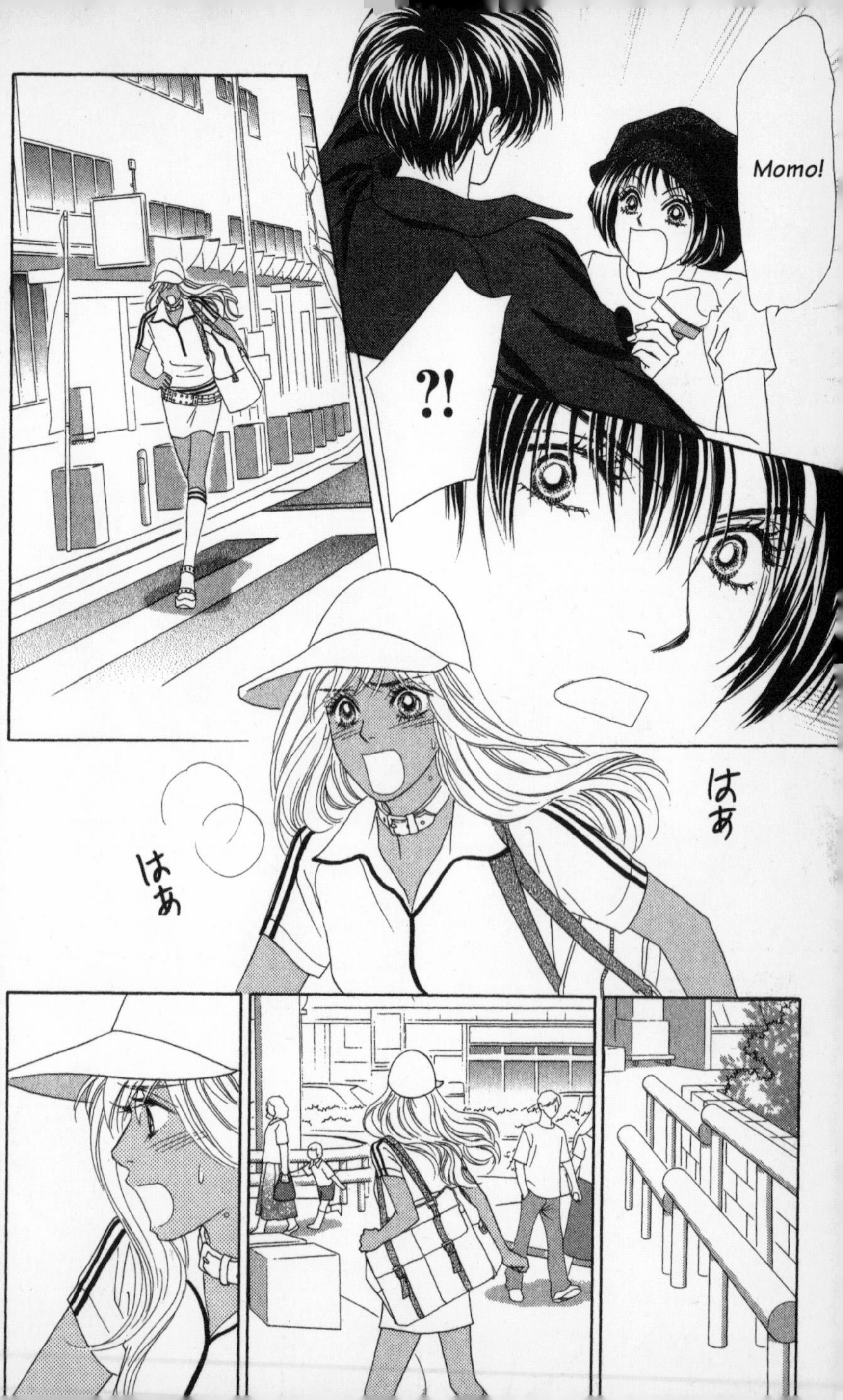
Momo!
?!
はあ
はあ

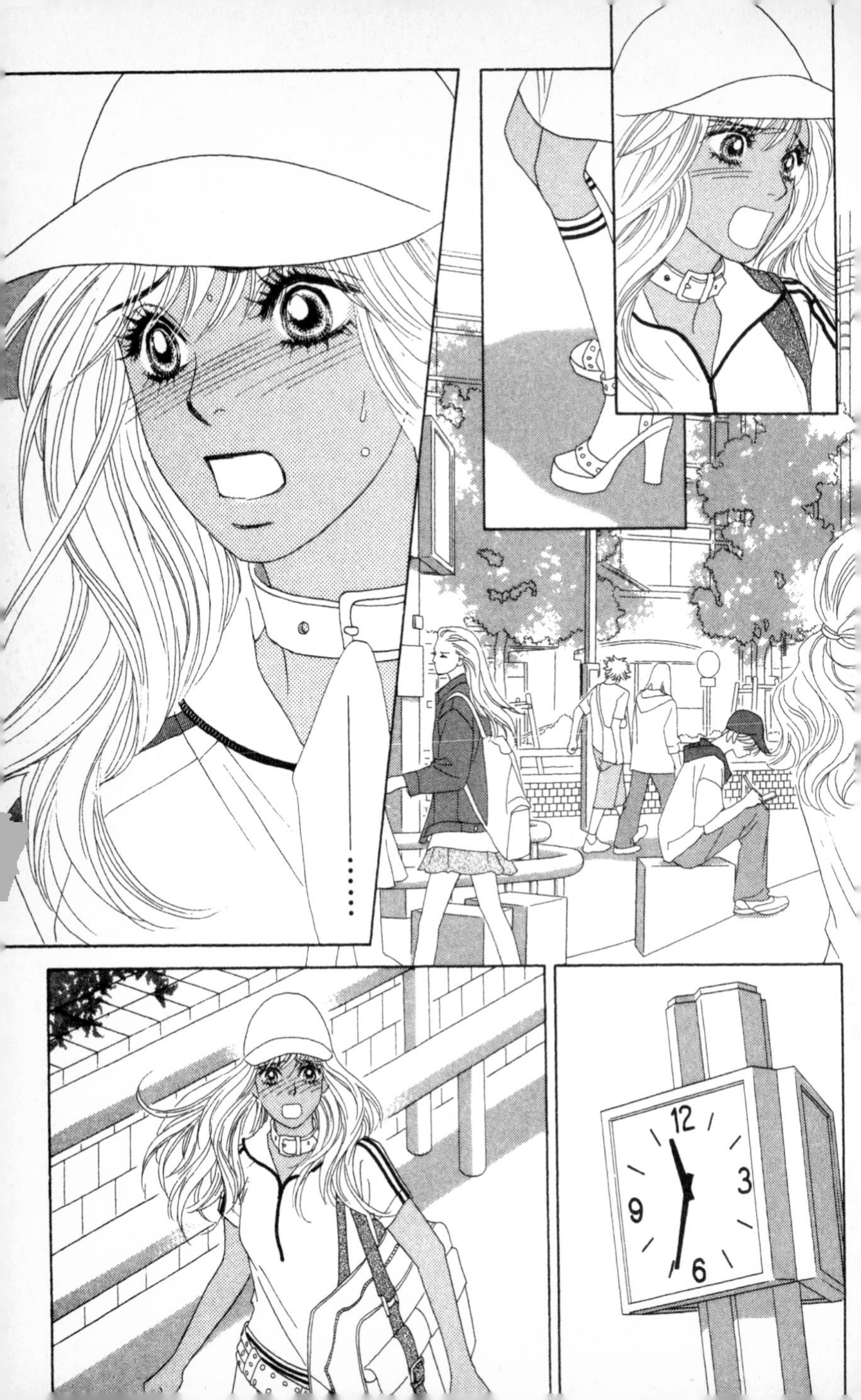

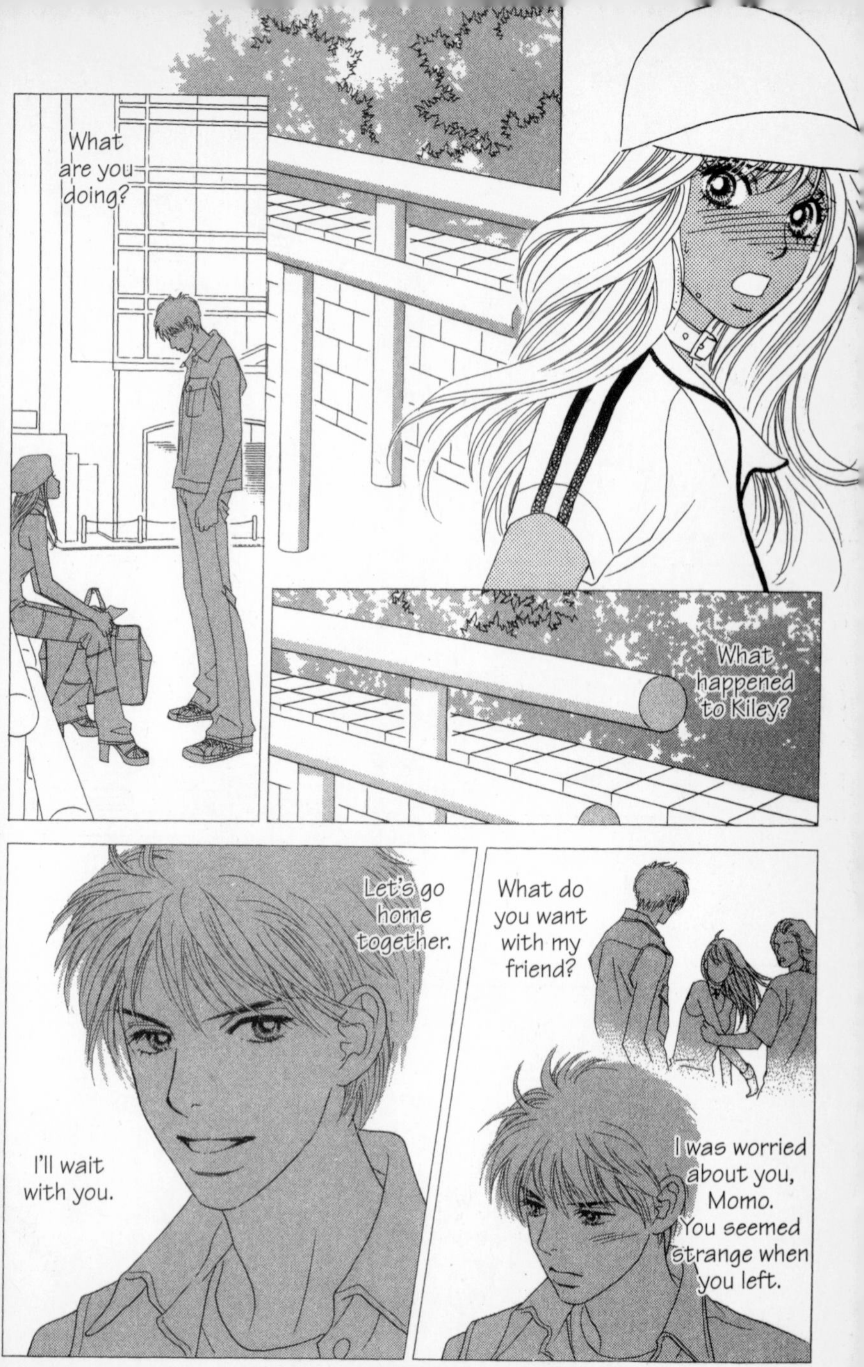
What happened to Kiley?
What are you doing?
What do you want with my friend?
I was worried about you, Momo. You seemed strange when you left.
Let's go home together.
I'll wait with you.

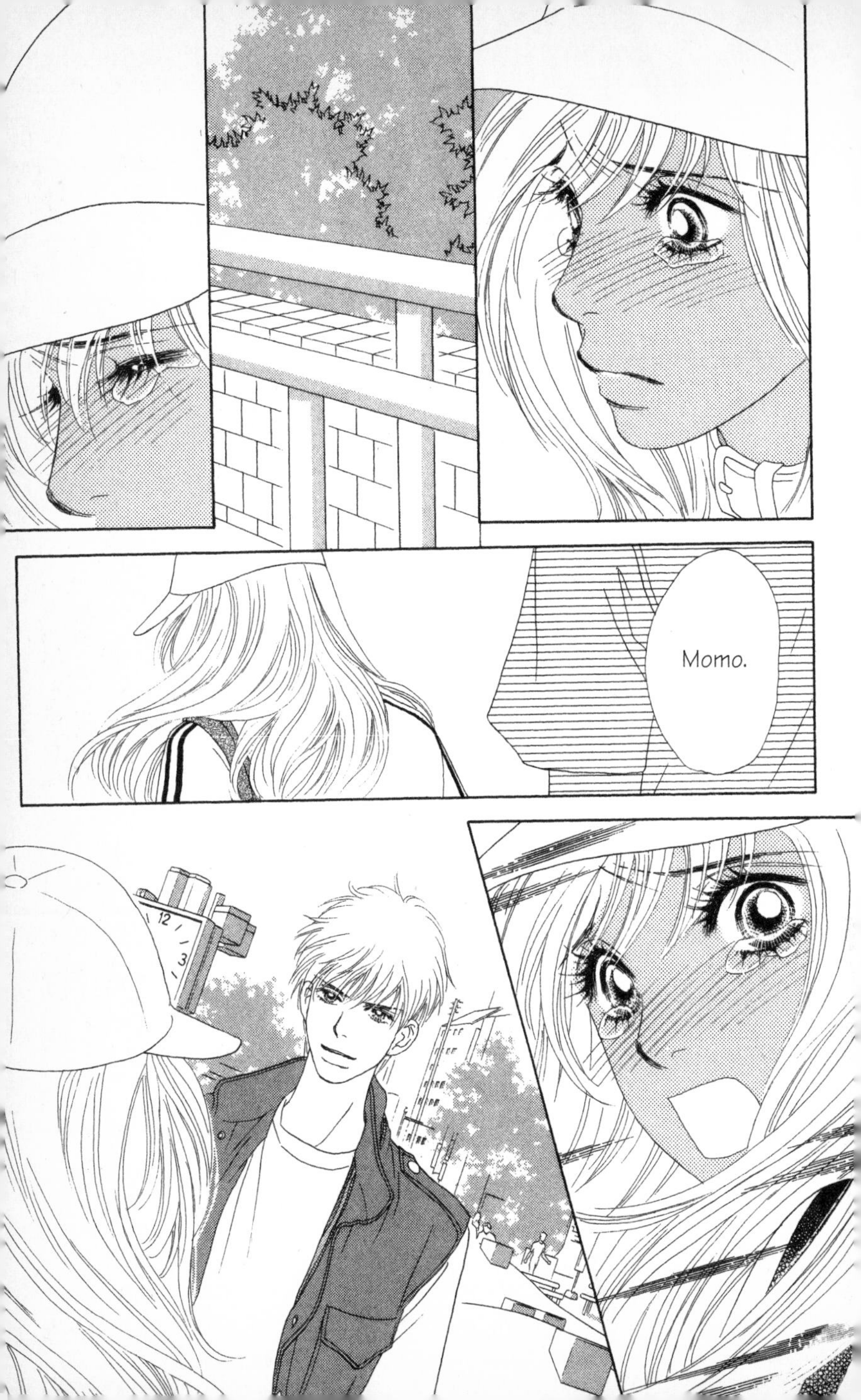
Momo.

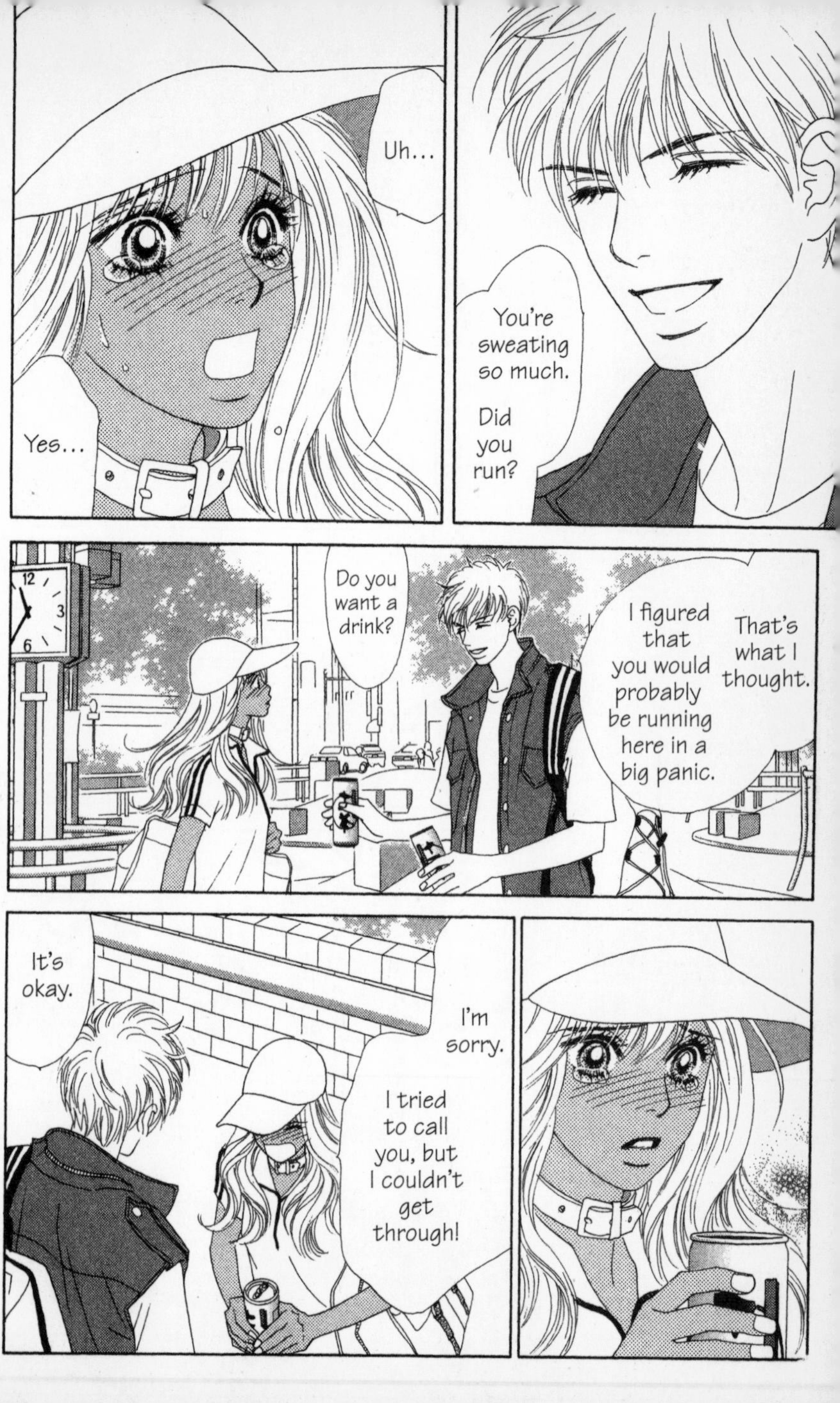
You're sweating so much.
Did you run?
Uh...
Yes...
That's what I thought.
I figured that you would probably be running here in a big panic.
Do you want a drink?
I'm sorry.
I tried to call you, but I couldn't get through!
It's okay.

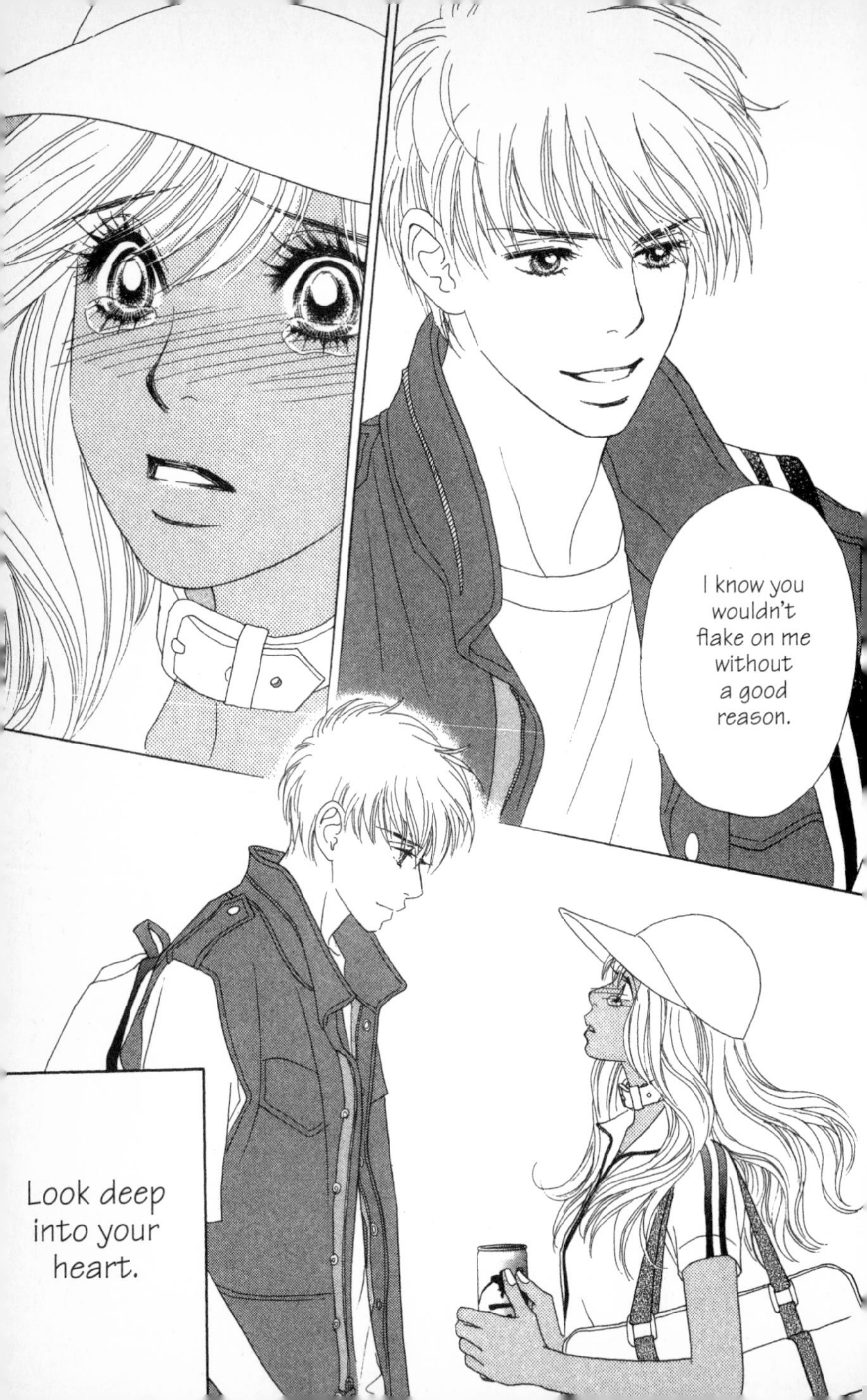
I know you wouldn't flake on me without a good reason.
Look deep into your heart.

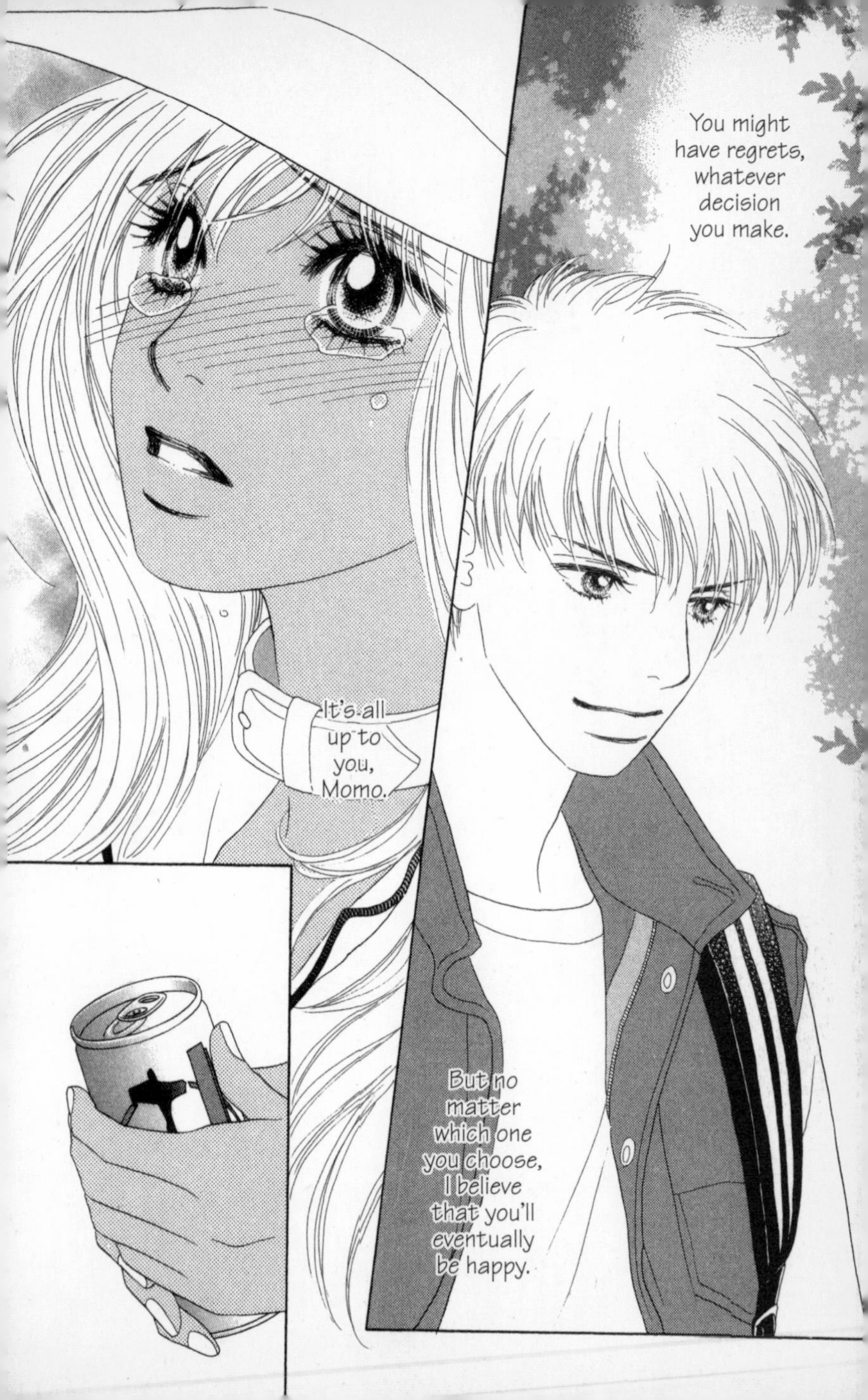
You might have regrets, whatever decision you make.
But no matter which one you choose, I believe that you'll eventually be happy.
It's all up to you, Momo.

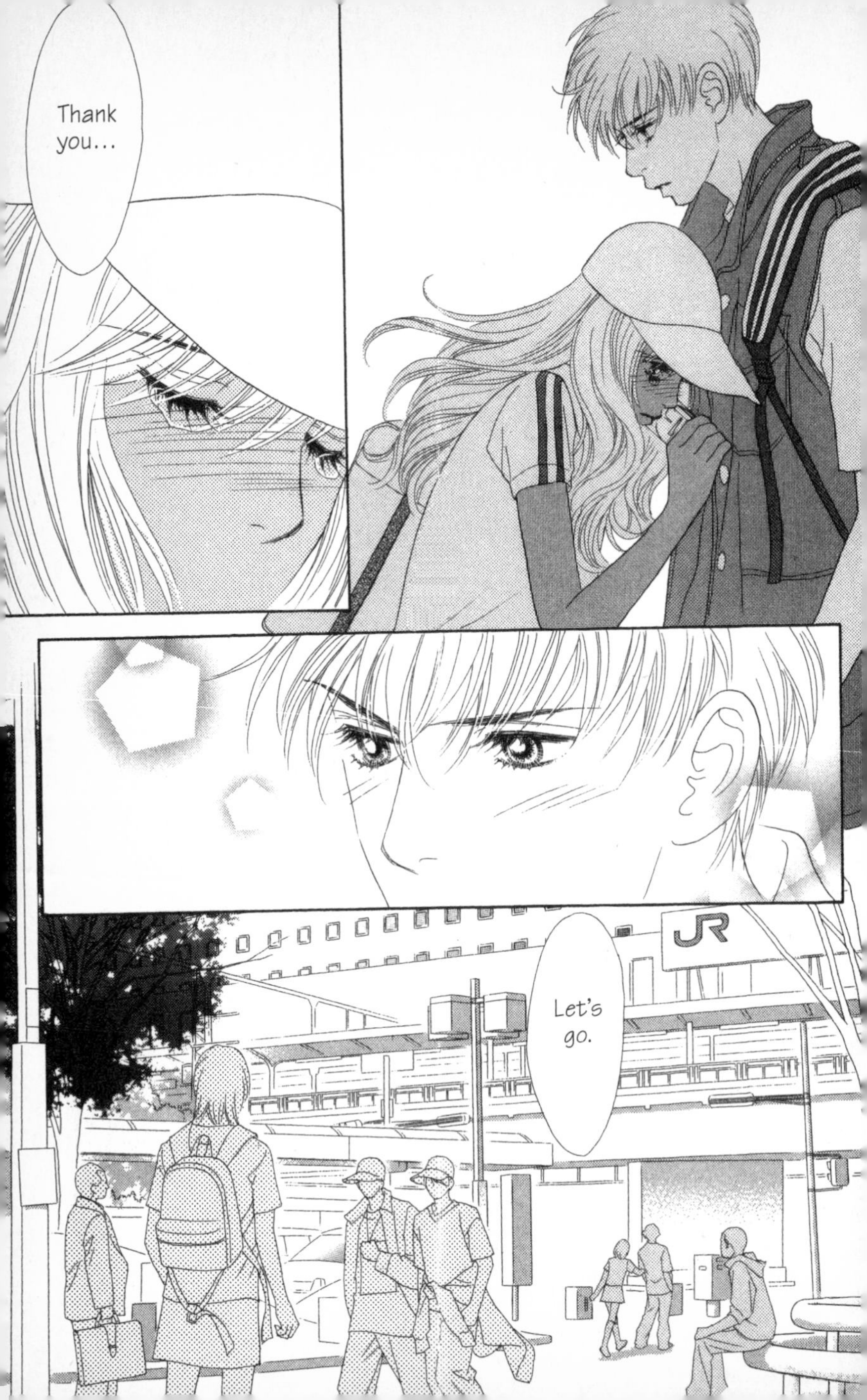
Thank you...
Let's go.

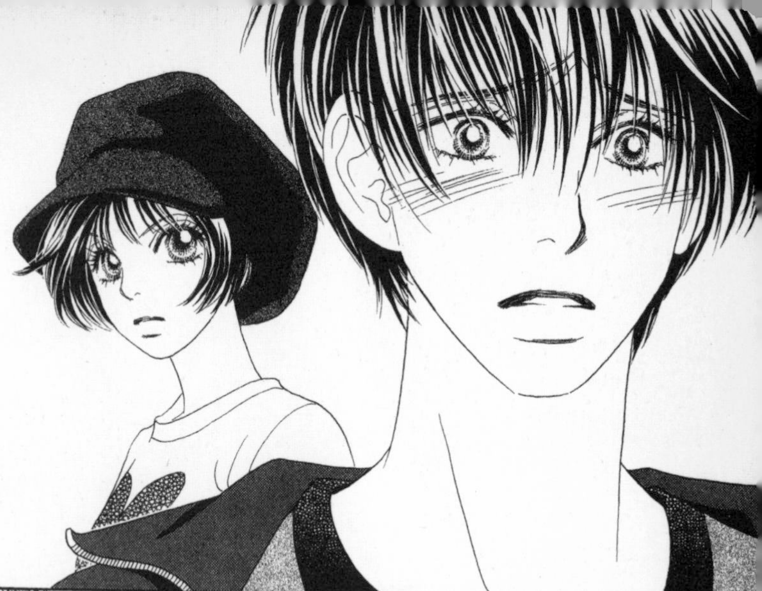

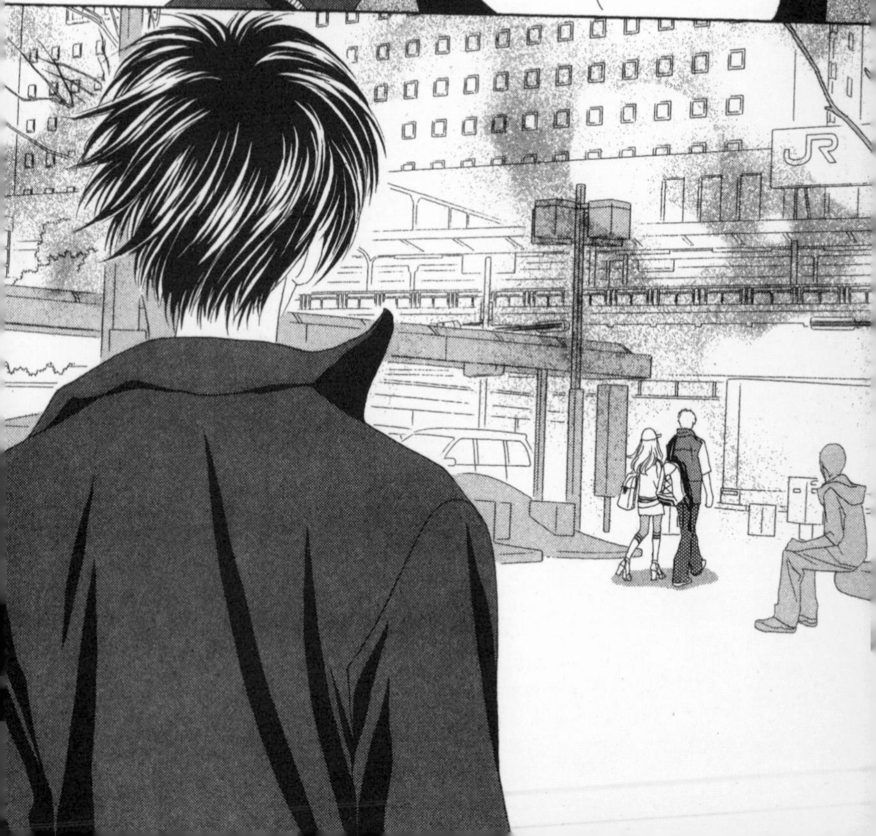
JR

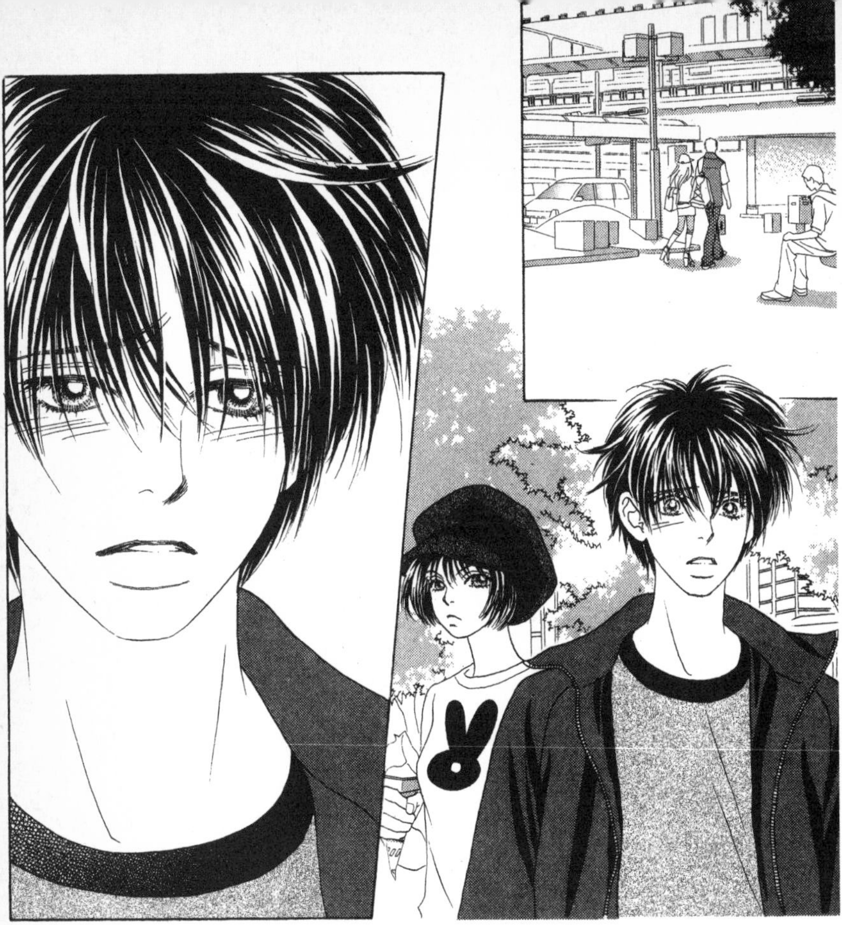

PEACH CLUB

So I began my interview with popstar Sonin. She started out by asking me, "Can I tell you how long I've been a fan?" *That* was a big surprise. Not only did she read the archival books, but she bought *Bessatsu Friend* every month, and even had all of the illustration collections and the *Peach Girl Fan Book*!! Sonin told me, "*Peach Girl* was a big part of my youth." (Tears of joy.) She said that she read *Peach Girl* very deeply, and even named her cat Momo... When she told me that she was a reader, I just assumed that she maybe had a few of the books, but didn't really read them anymore... So thank you, Sonin!! I never knew you were such a fan... I was worried that I might run out of things to talk about during our interview, but I had no need to worry. She talked so passionately that my editors were very impressed. I was so happy to have had the chance to talk to her! -Miwa

(To be continued.)

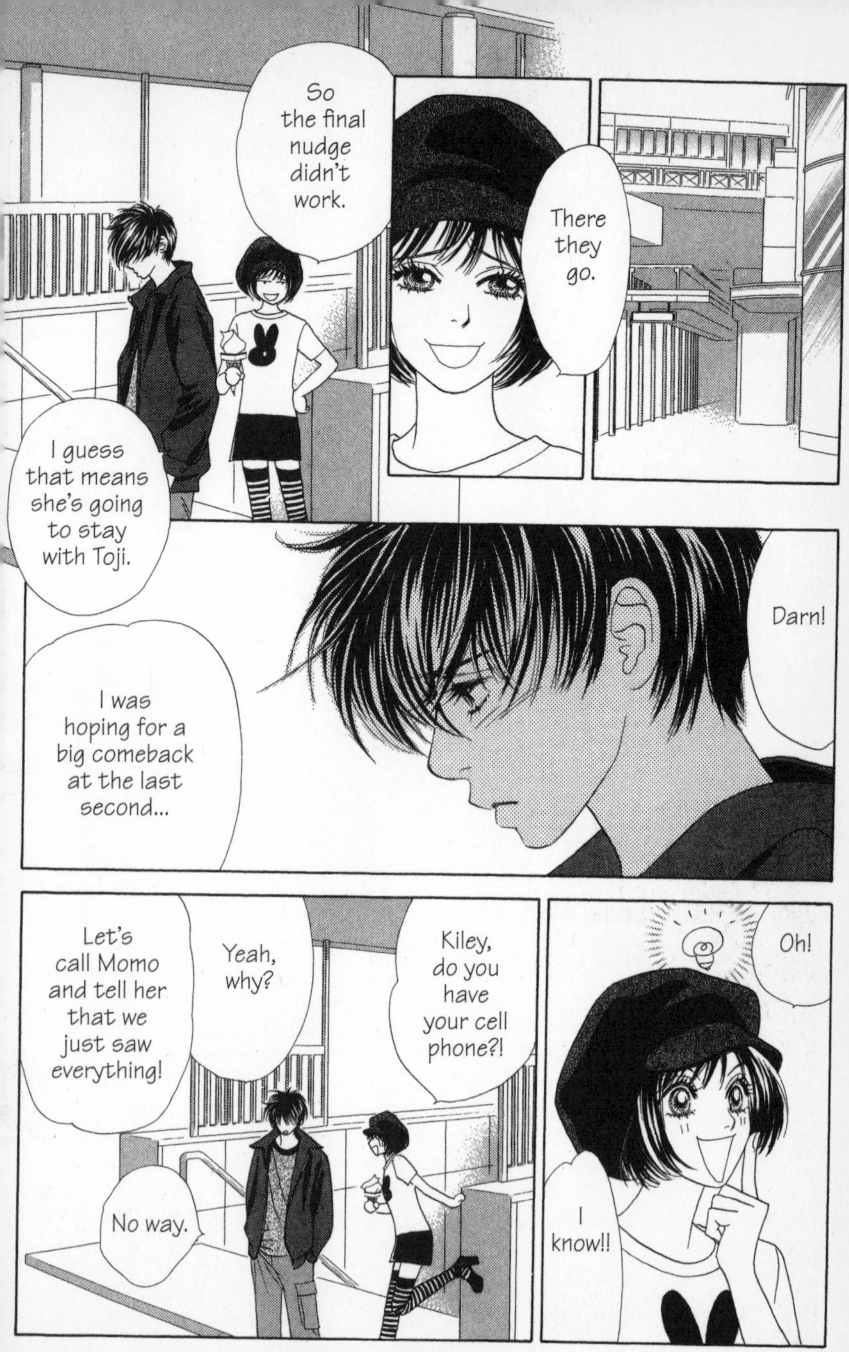
There they go.
So the final nudge didn't work.
I guess that means she's going to stay with Toji.
Darn!
I was hoping for a big comeback at the last second...
Oh!
I know!!
Kiley, do you have your cell phone?!
Yeah, why?
Let's call Momo and tell her that we just saw everything!
No way.

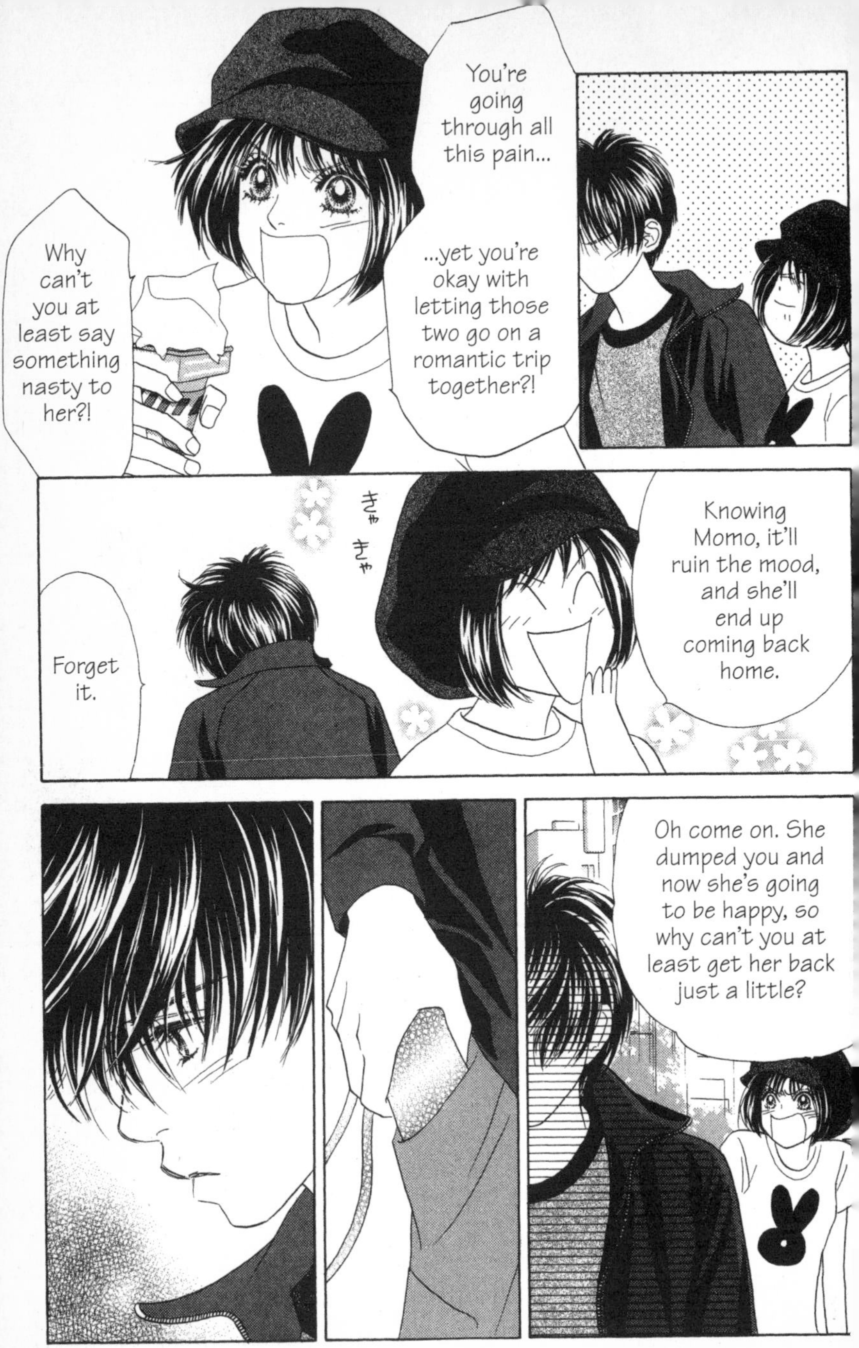
You're going through all this pain...
...yet you're okay with letting those two go on a romantic trip together?!
Why can't you at least say something nasty to her?!
Knowing Momo, it'll ruin the mood, and she'll end up coming back home.
きゃ きゃ
Forget it.
Oh come on. She dumped you and now she's going to be happy, so why can't you at least get her back just a little?

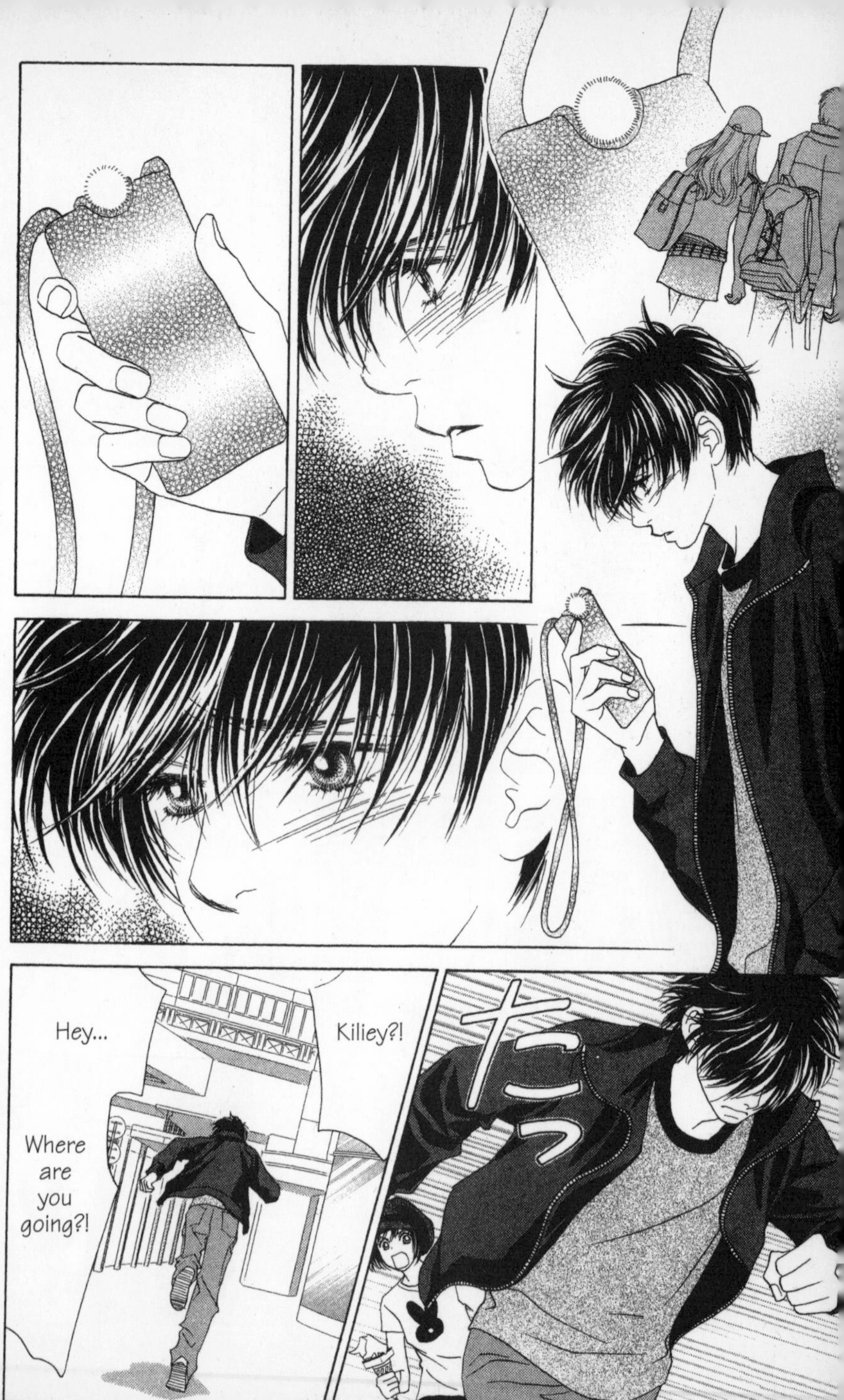
Kiliey?!
Hey...
Where are you going?!

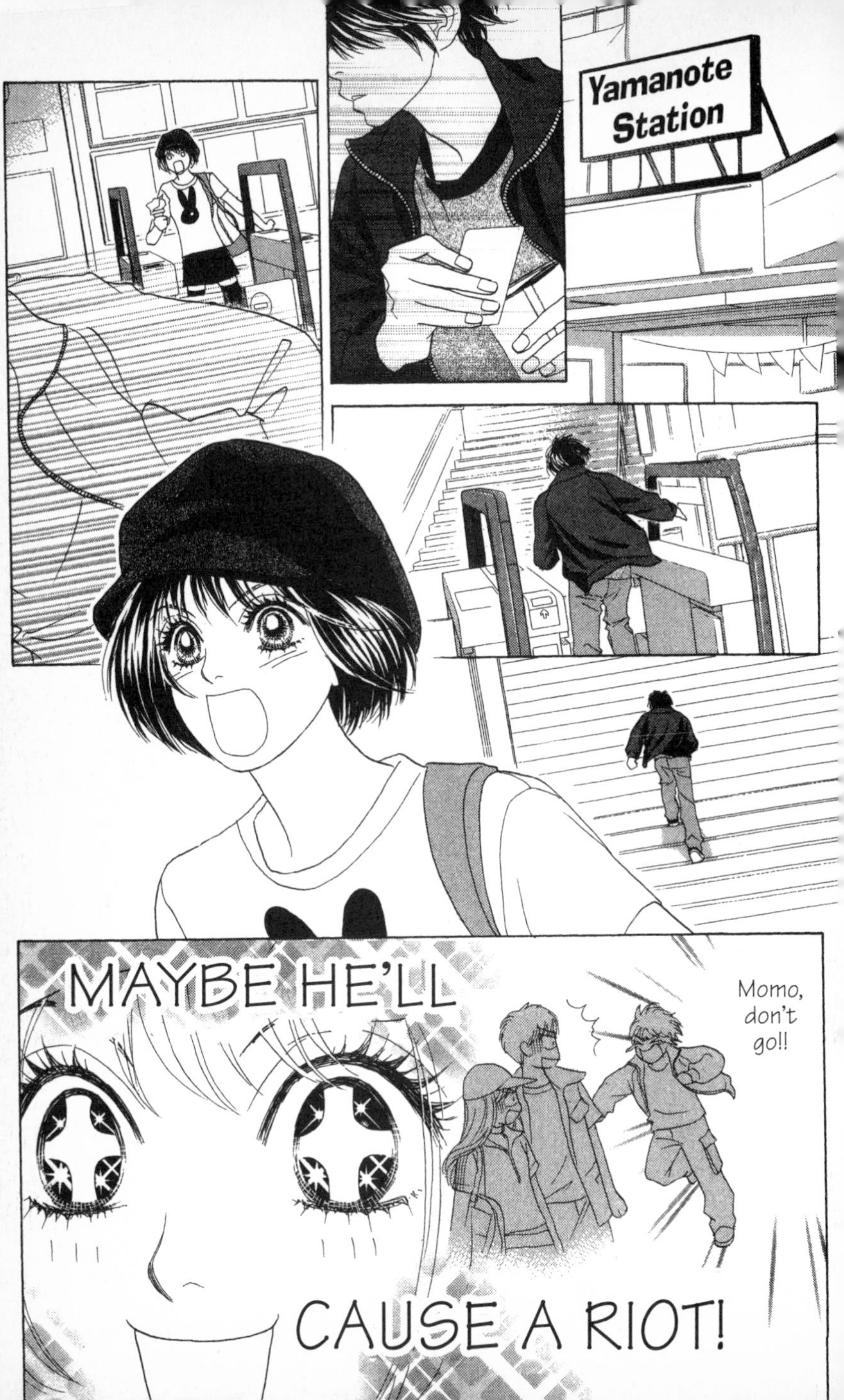
Yamanote Station
MAYBE HE'LL
Momo, don't go!!
CAUSE A RIOT!

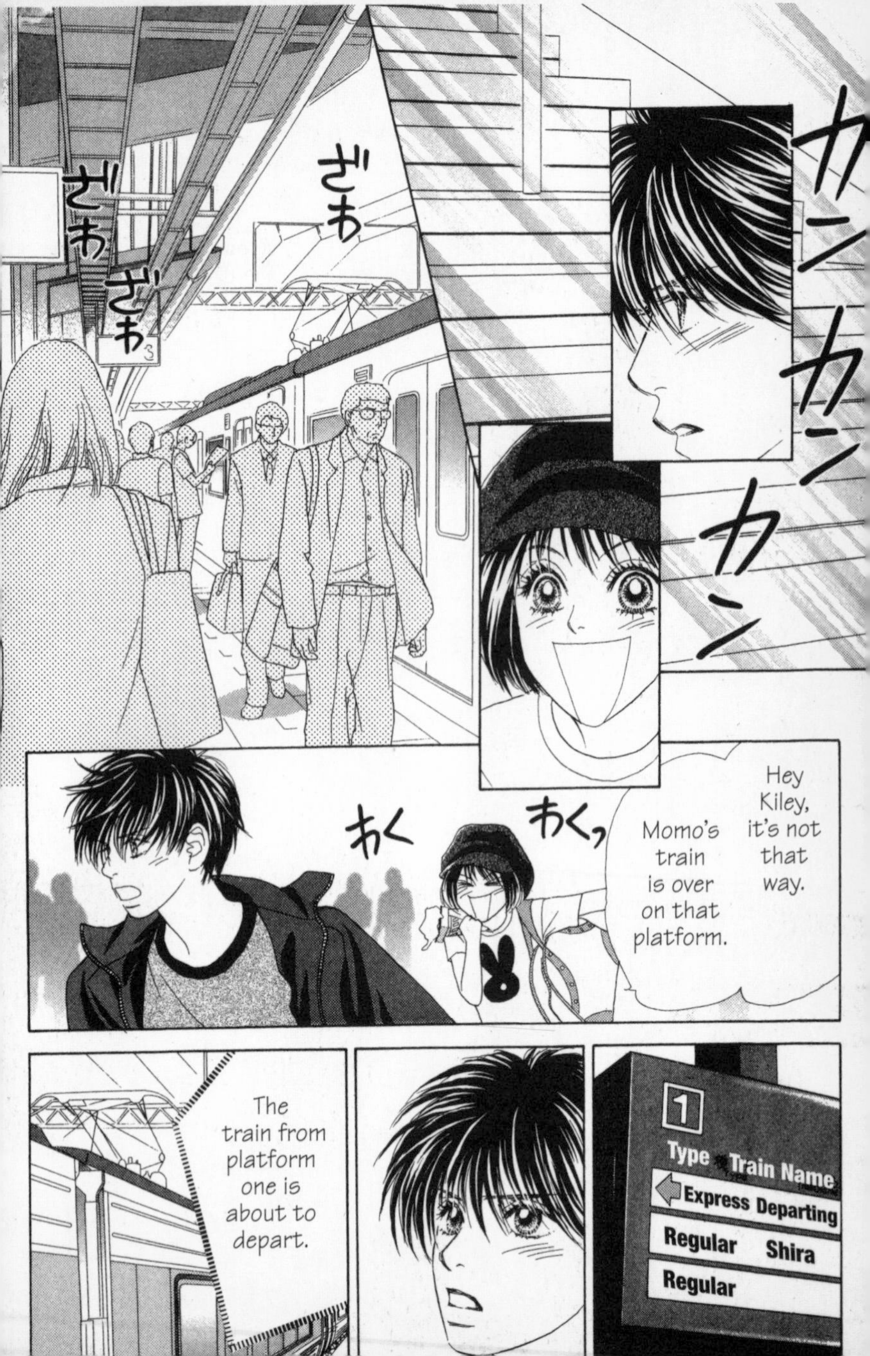

カンカンカン
ざわ
ざわ
ざわ
Hey Kiley, it's not that way.
Momo's train is over on that platform.
わくっ
わく
1
Type
Train Name
Express Departing
Regular Shira
Regular
The train from platform one is about to depart.

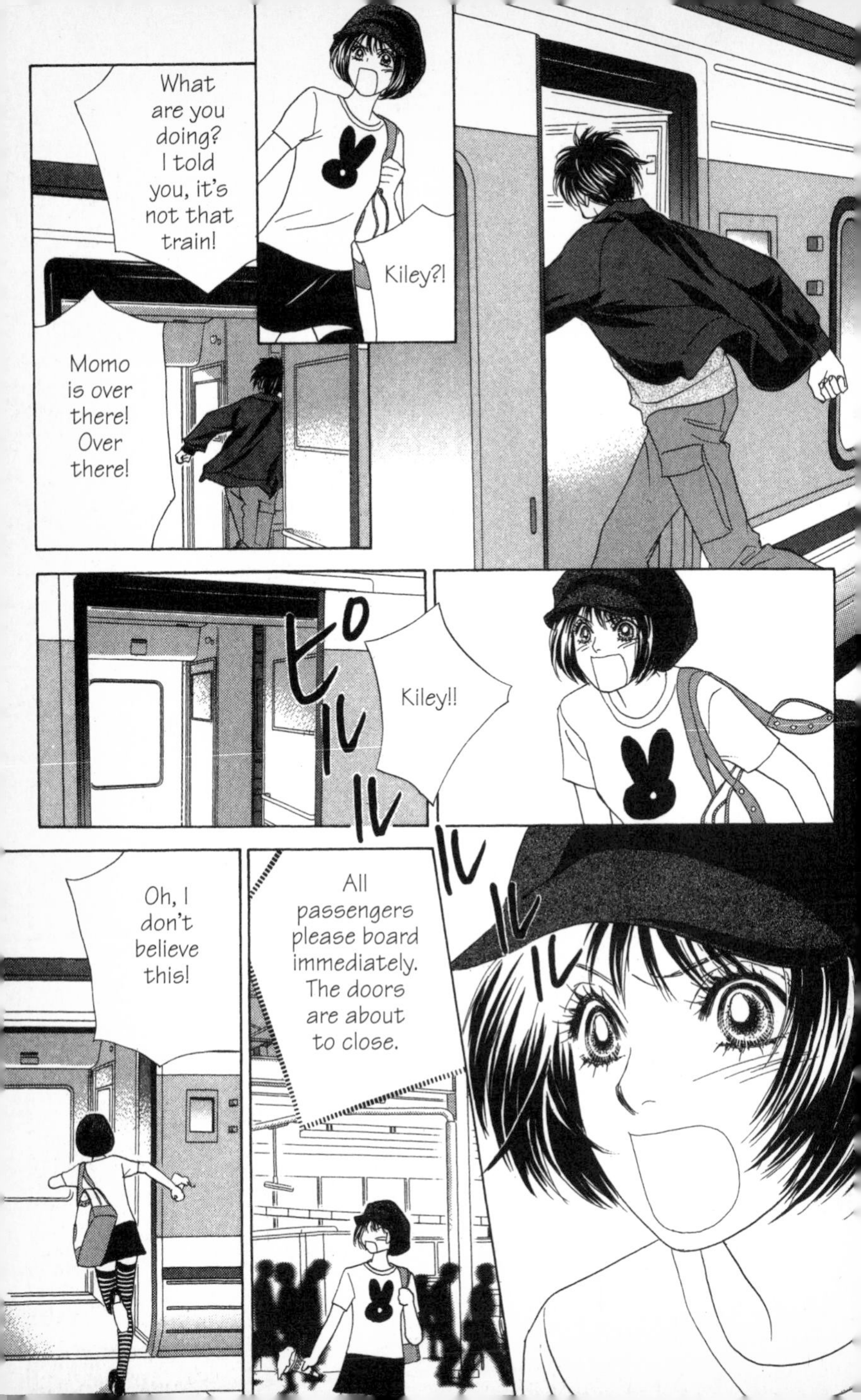
Kiley?!
What are you doing? I told you, it's not that train!
Momo is over there! Over there!
Kiley!!
ピルルルルル
All passengers please board immediately. The doors are about to close.
Oh, I don't believe this!

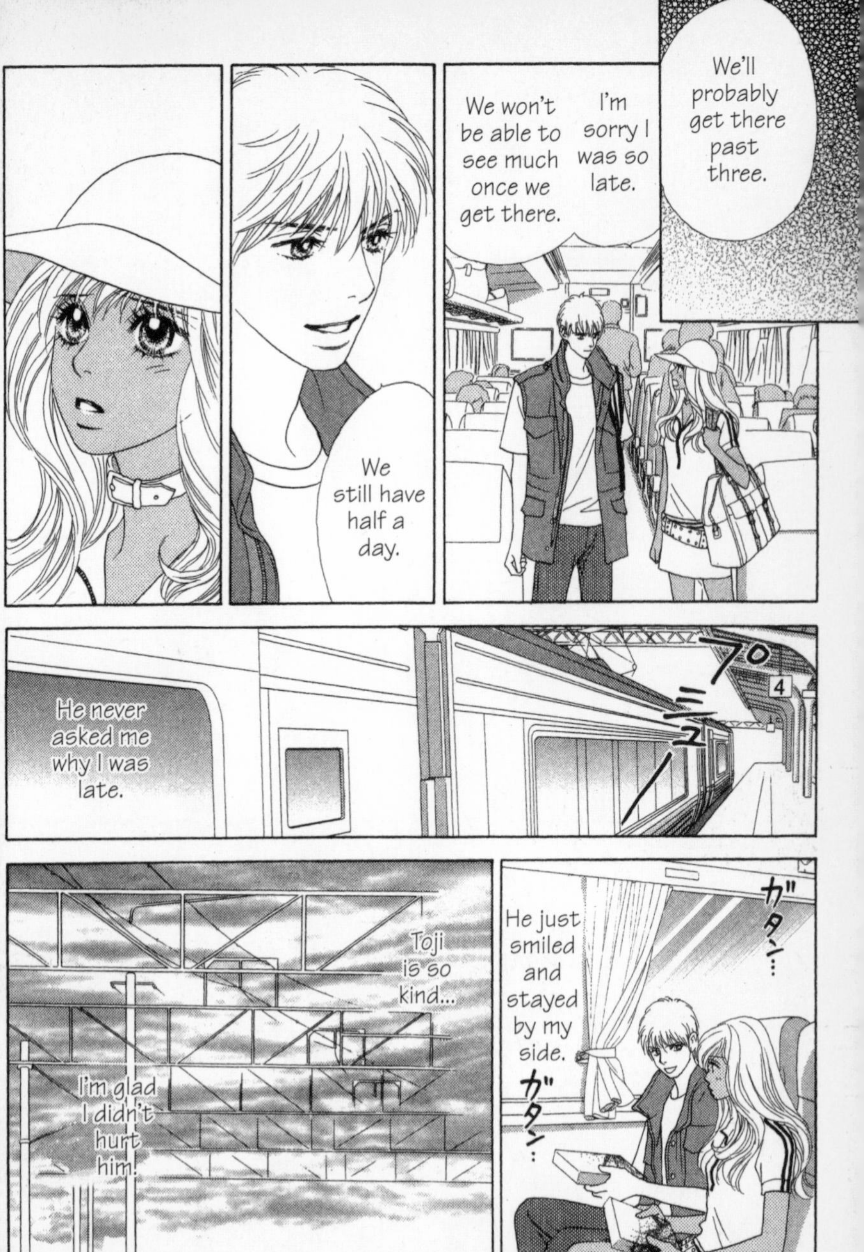
We'll probably get there past three.
I'm sorry I was so late.
We won't be able to see much once we get there.
We still have half a day.
プシュー
He never asked me why I was late.
ガタン…
He just smiled and stayed by my side.
ガタン…
Toji is so kind...
I'm glad I didn't hurt him.

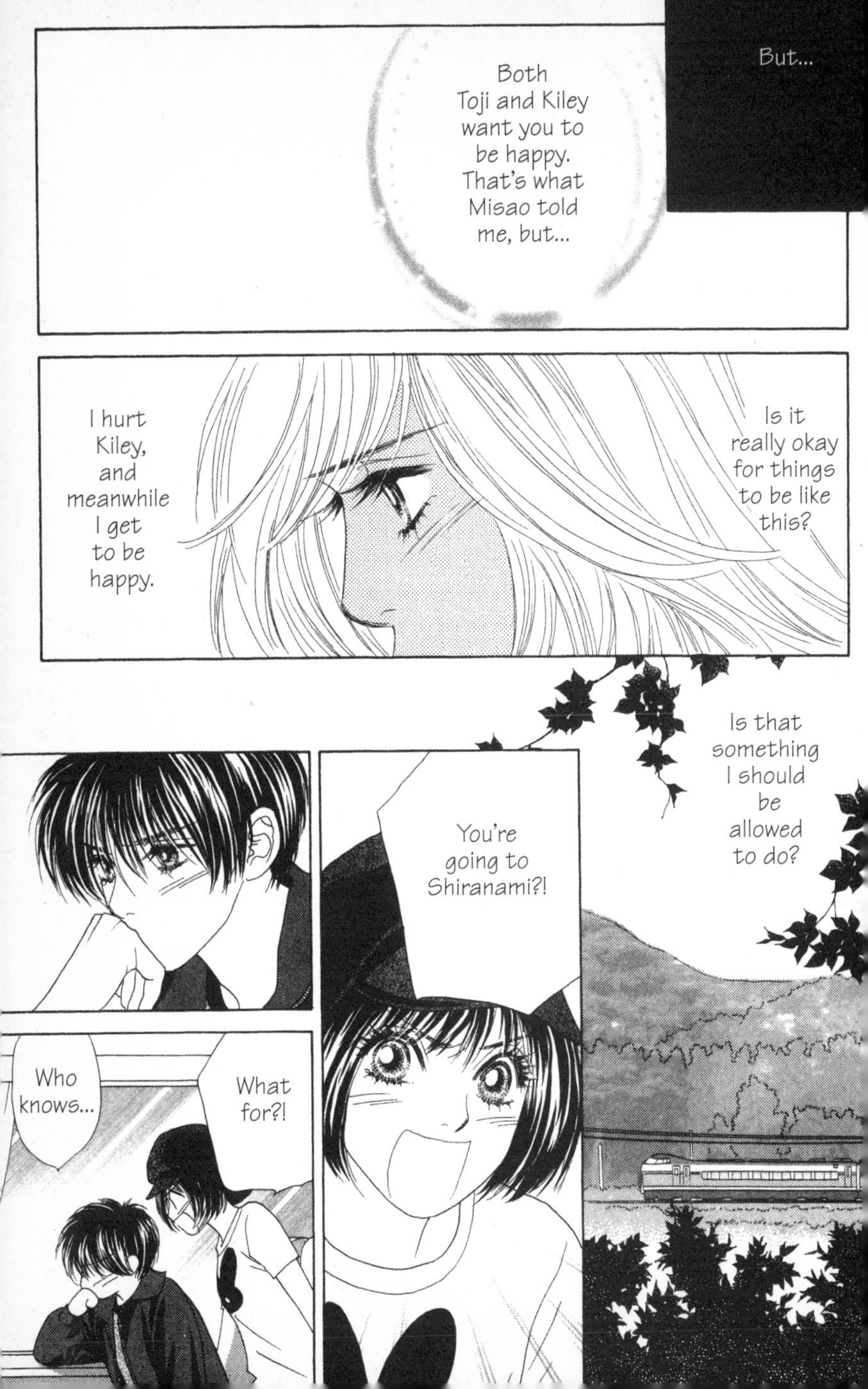
But...
Both Toji and Kiley want you to be happy. That's what Misao told me, but...
Is it really okay for things to be like this?
I hurt Kiley, and meanwhile I get to be happy.
Is that something I should be allowed to do?
You're going to Shiranami?!
What for?!
Who knows...

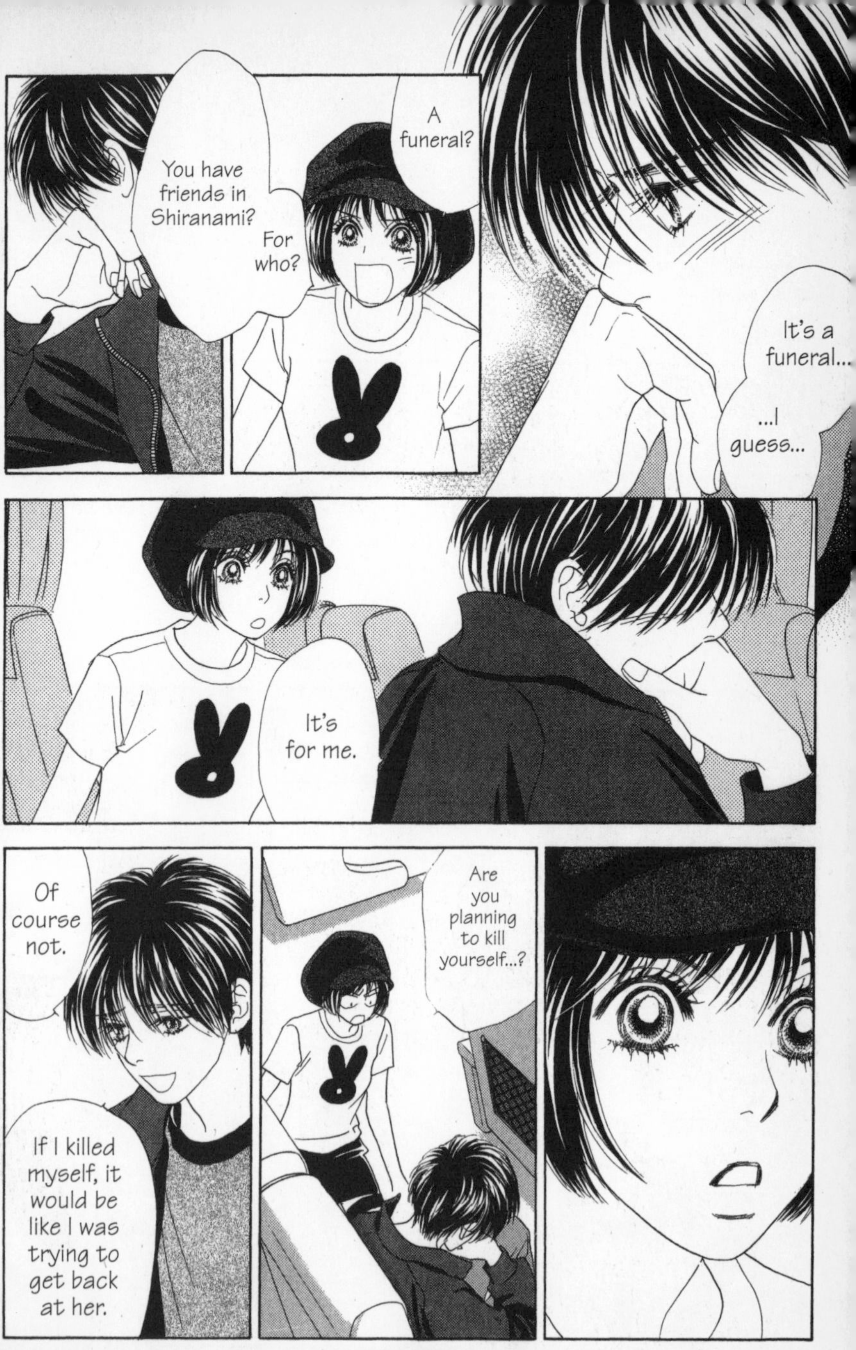
It's a funeral...
...I guess...
A funeral?
For who?
You have friends in Shiranami?
It's for me.
Are you planning to kill yourself...?
Of course not.
If I killed myself, it would be like I was trying to get back at her.

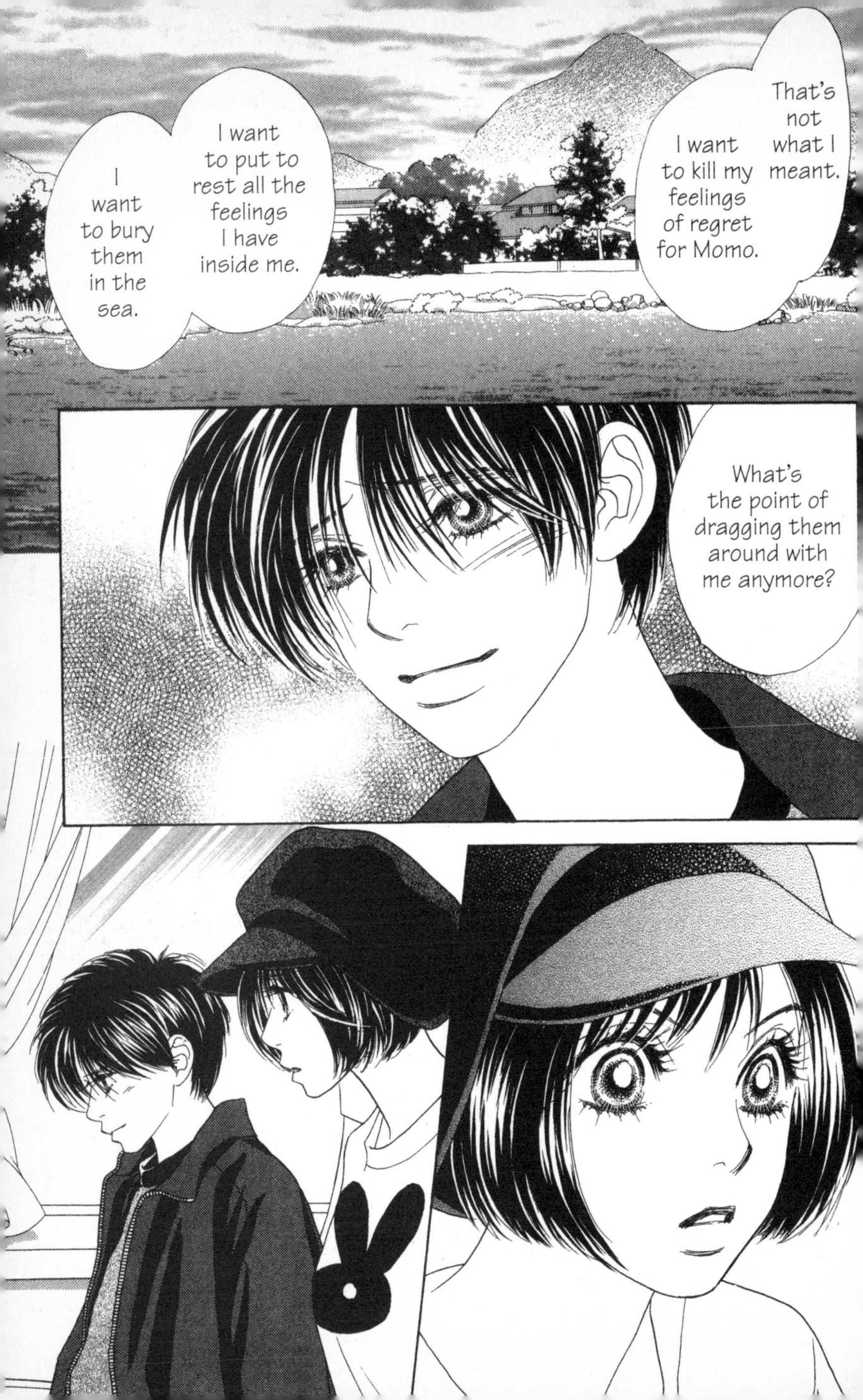
That's not what I meant.
I want to kill my feelings of regret for Momo.
I want to put to rest all the feelings I have inside me.
I want to bury them in the sea.
What's the point of dragging them around with me anymore?

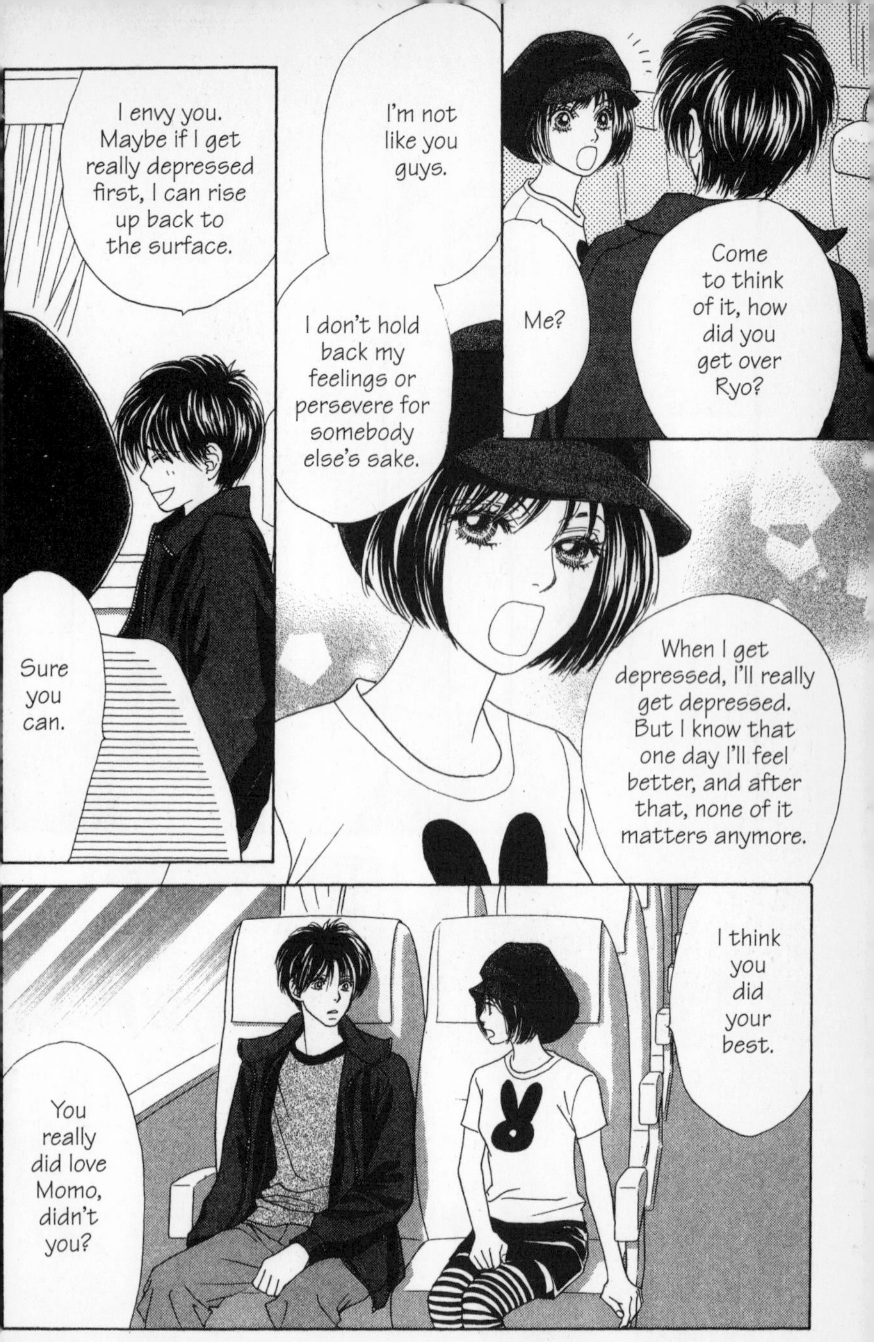
Come to think of it, how did you get over Ryo?
Me?
I'm not like you guys.
I don't hold back my feelings or persevere for somebody else's sake.
When I get depressed, I'll really get depressed. But I know that one day I'll feel better, and after that, none of it matters anymore.
I envy you. Maybe if I get really depressed first, I can rise up back to the surface.
Sure you can.
I think you did your best.
You really did love Momo, didn't you?

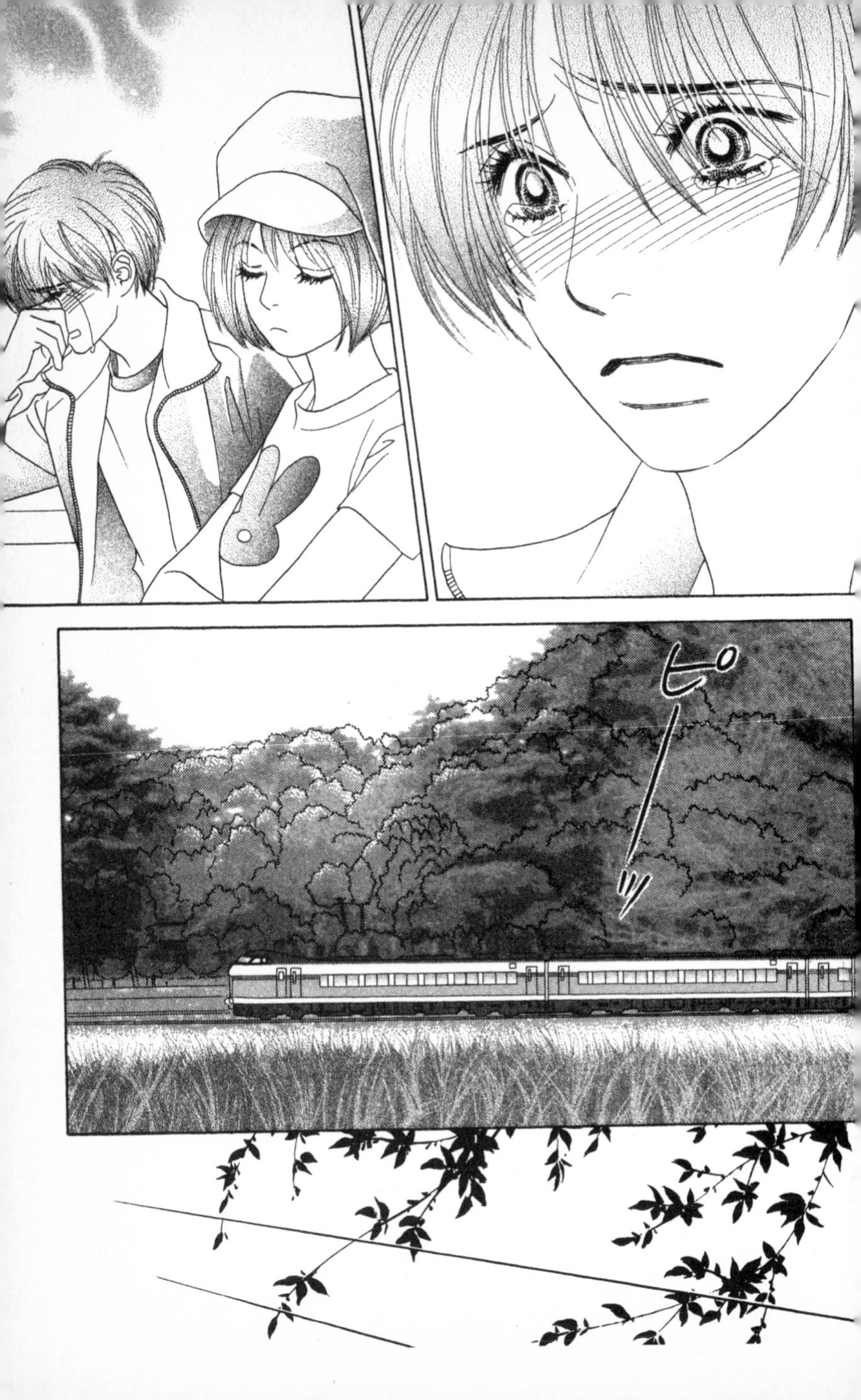
ピーッ

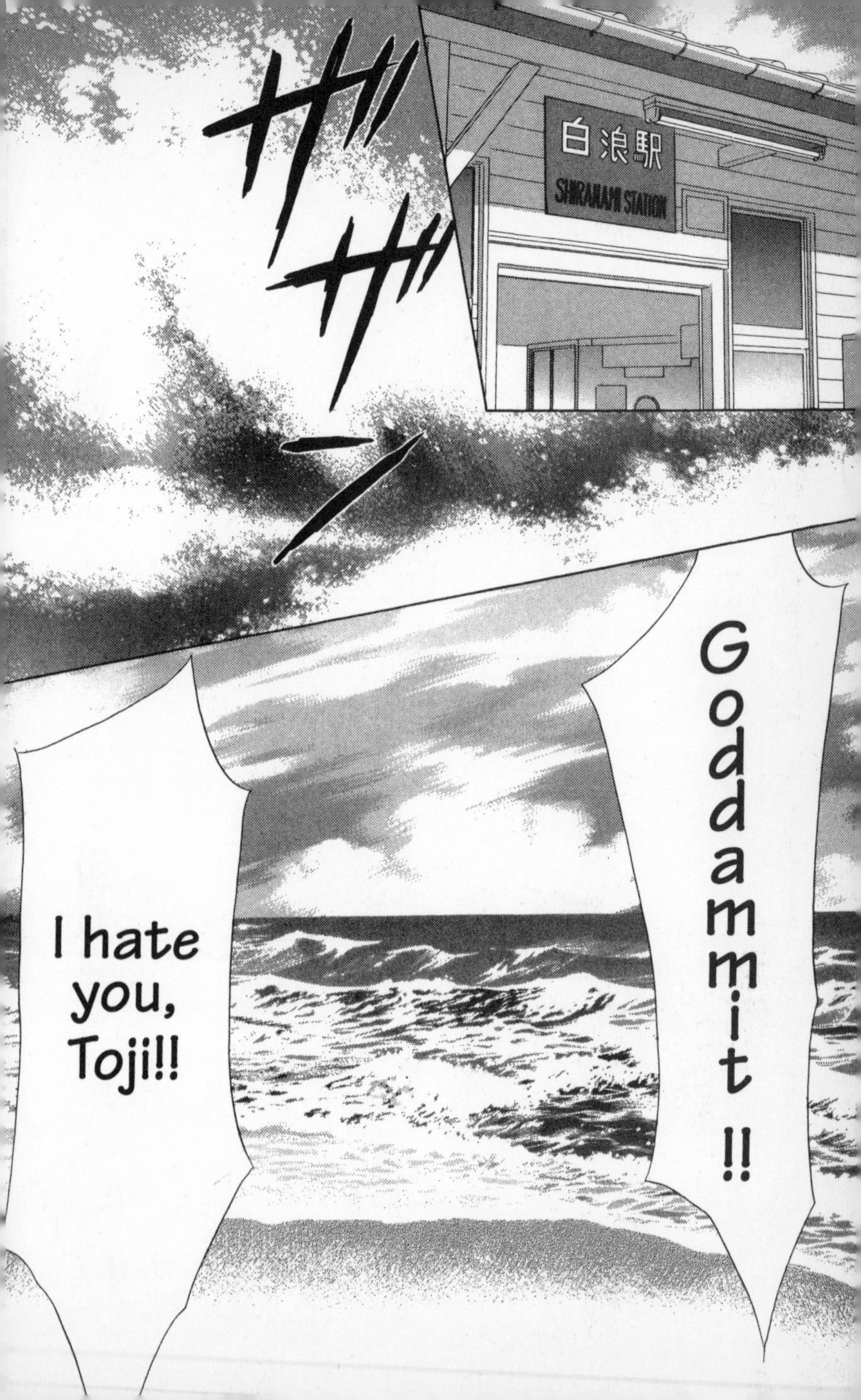

白浪駅
SHIRANAMI STATION
ザザーン
Goddammit!!
I hate you, Toji!!

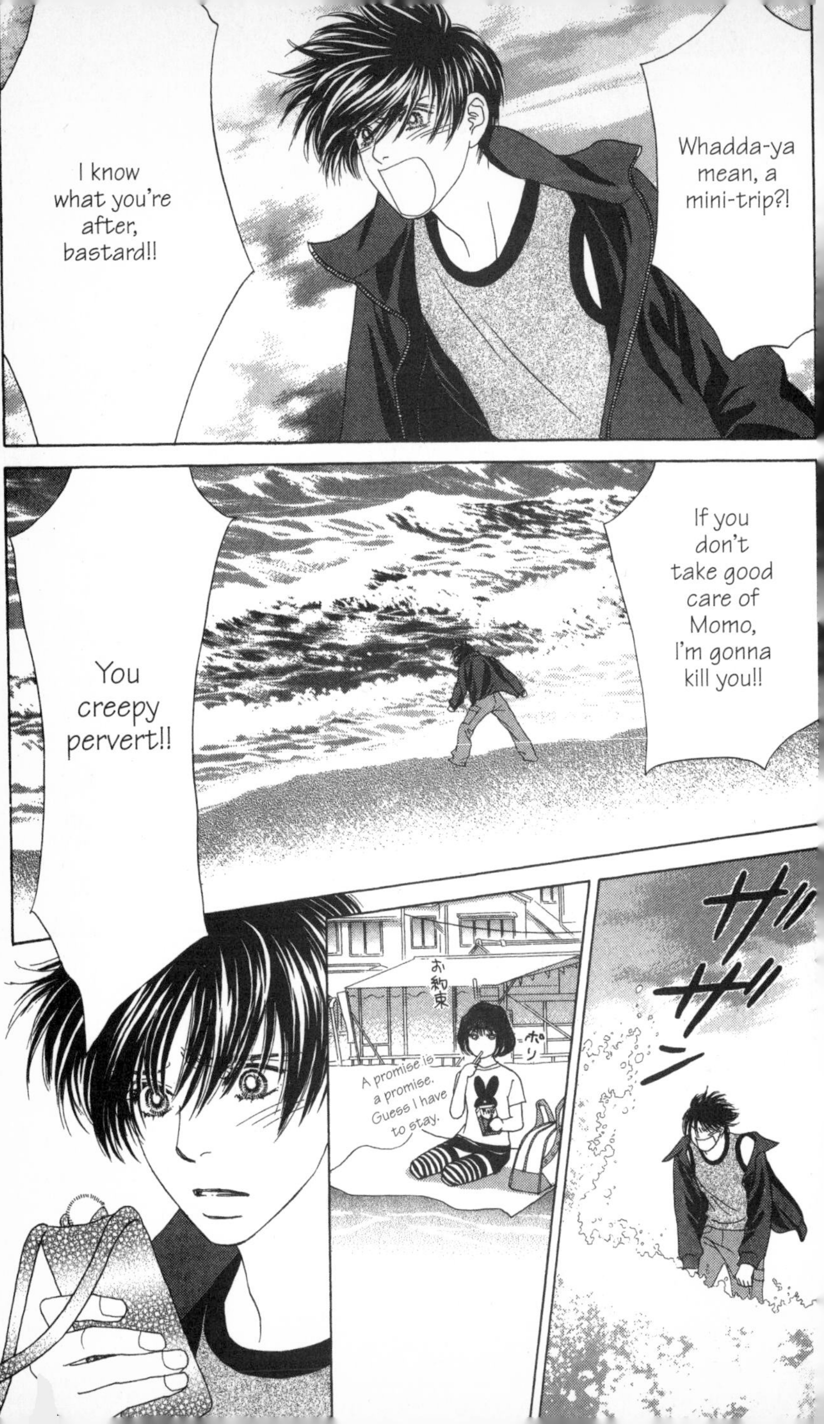
Whadda-ya mean, a mini-trip?!
I know what you're after, bastard!!
If you don't take good care of Momo, I'm gonna kill you!!
You creepy pervert!!
ザザン
お約束
ポリ
A promise is a promise. Guess I have to stay.

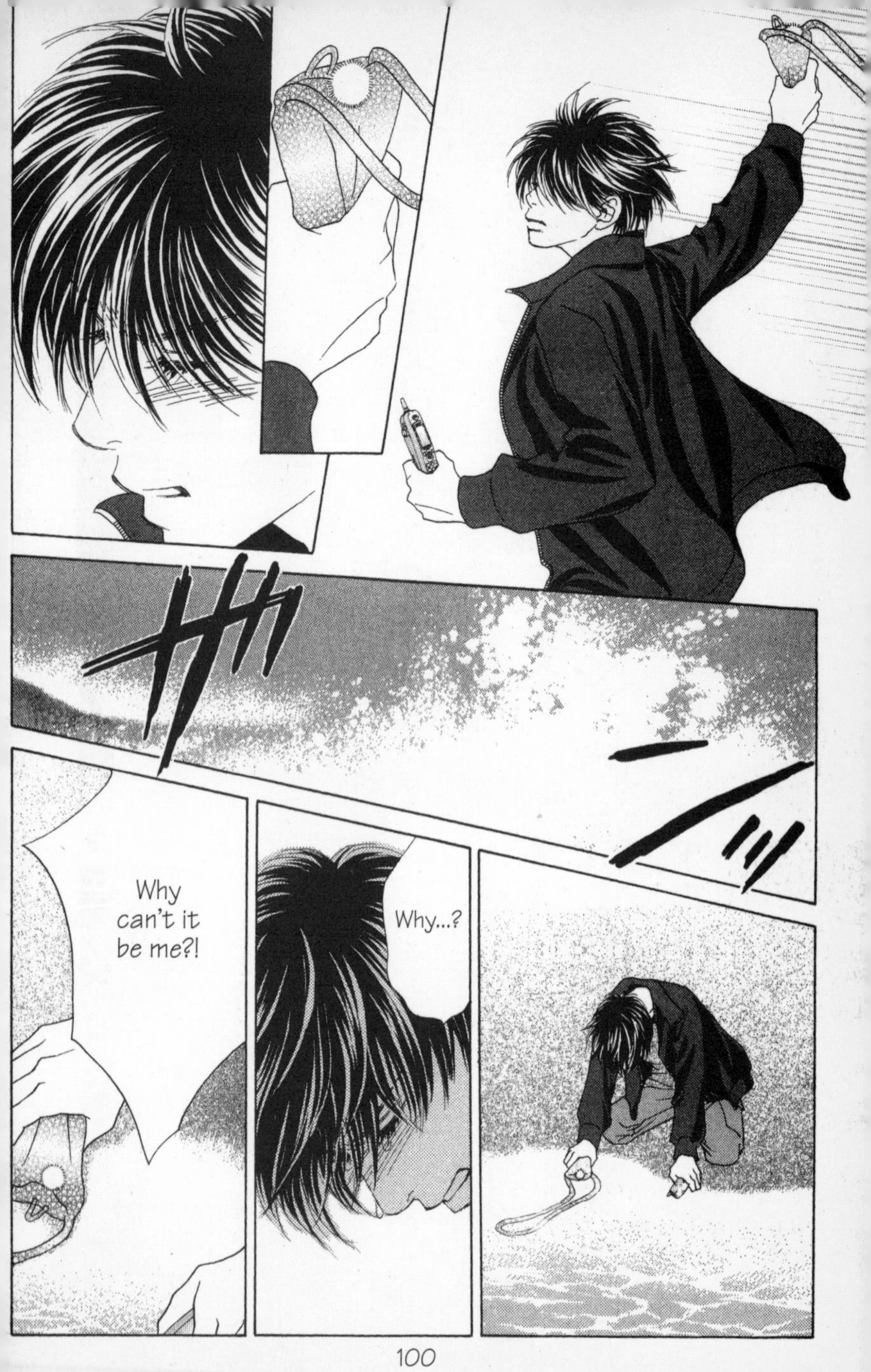
Why...?
Why can't it be me?!

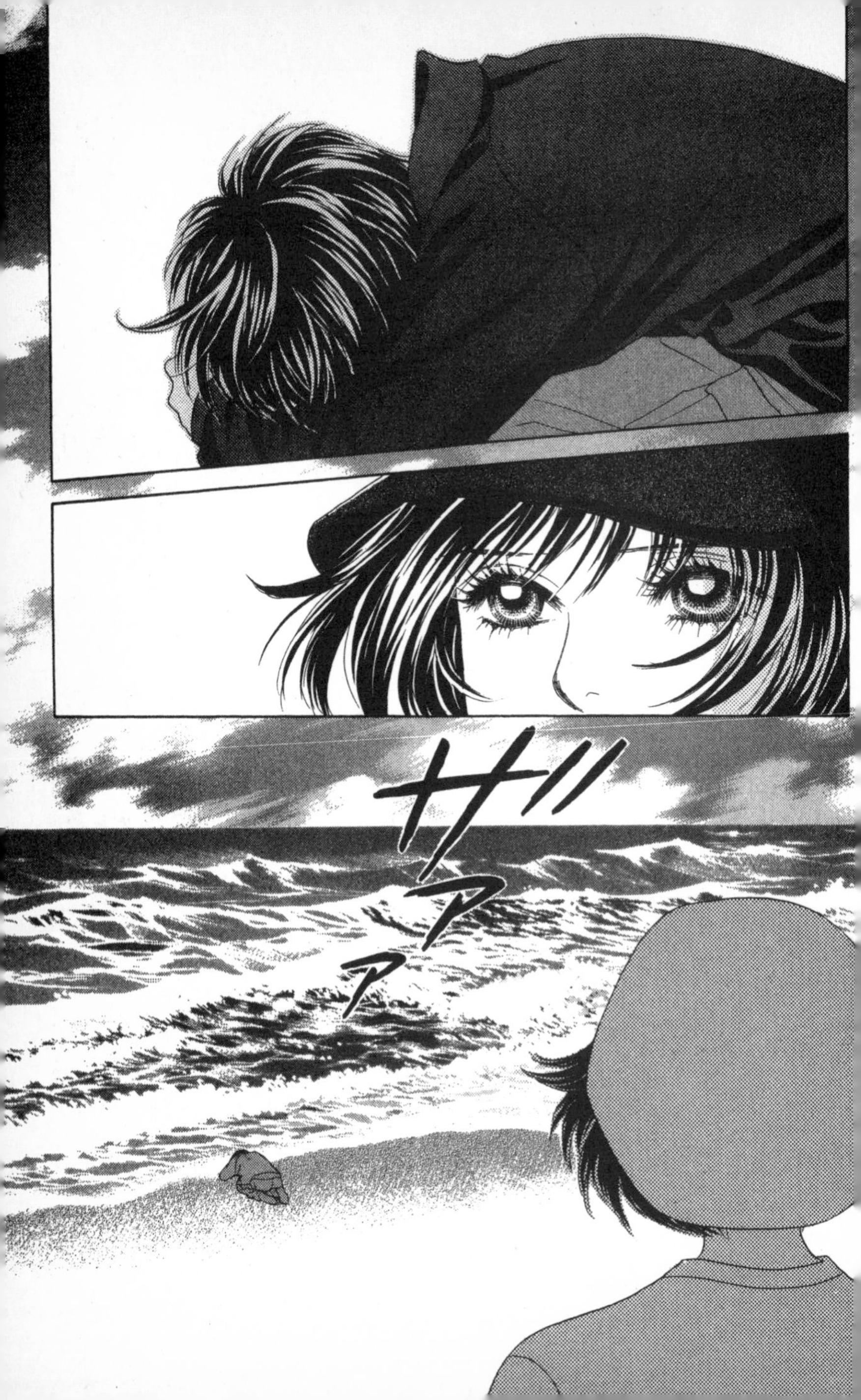
ザァーァ

LOVE KNOTS

LUCKY FORTUNE

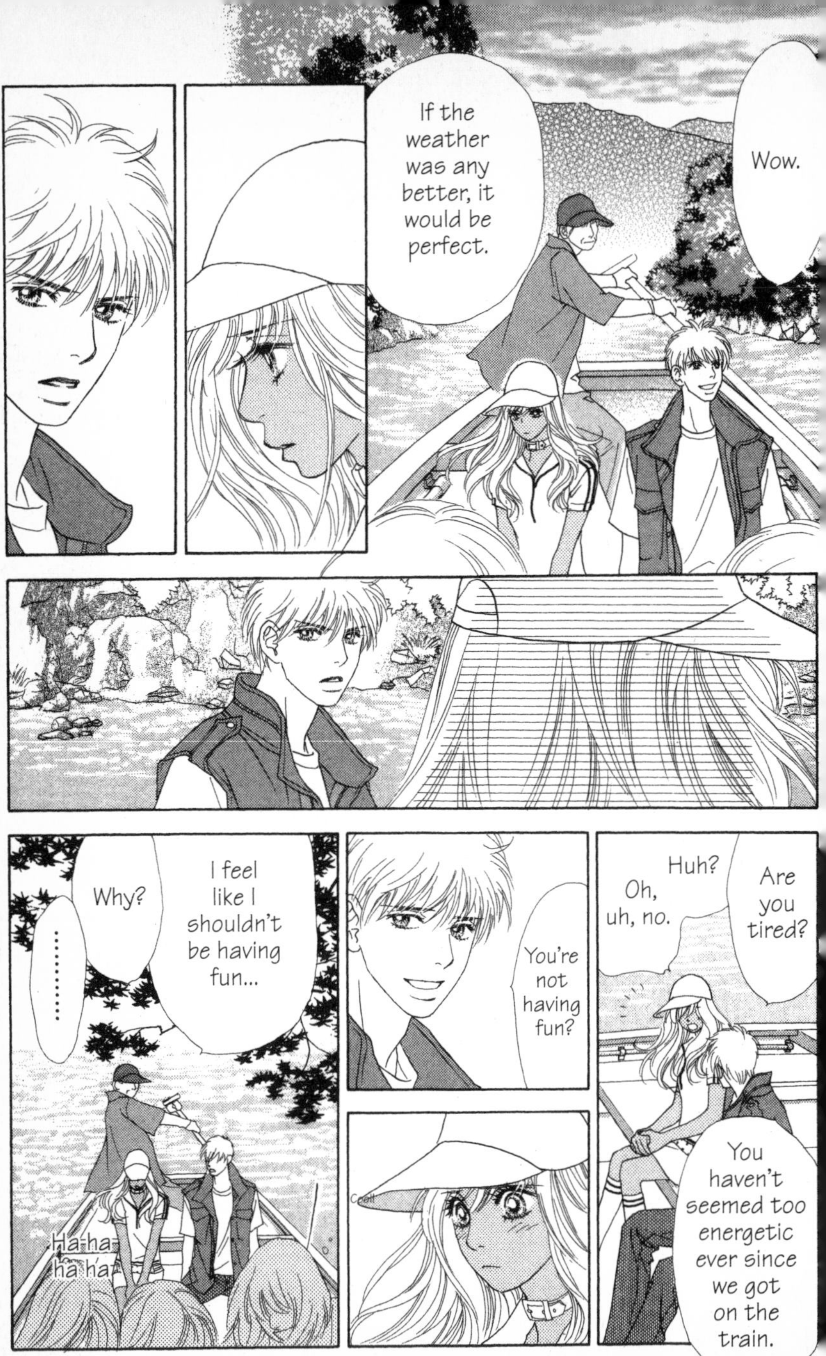
Wow.
If the weather was any better, it would be perfect.
Are you tired?
Huh?
Oh, uh, no.
You haven't seemed too energetic ever since we got on the train.
You're not having fun?
I feel like I shouldn't be having fun...
Why?
....
Ha-ha-ha-ha

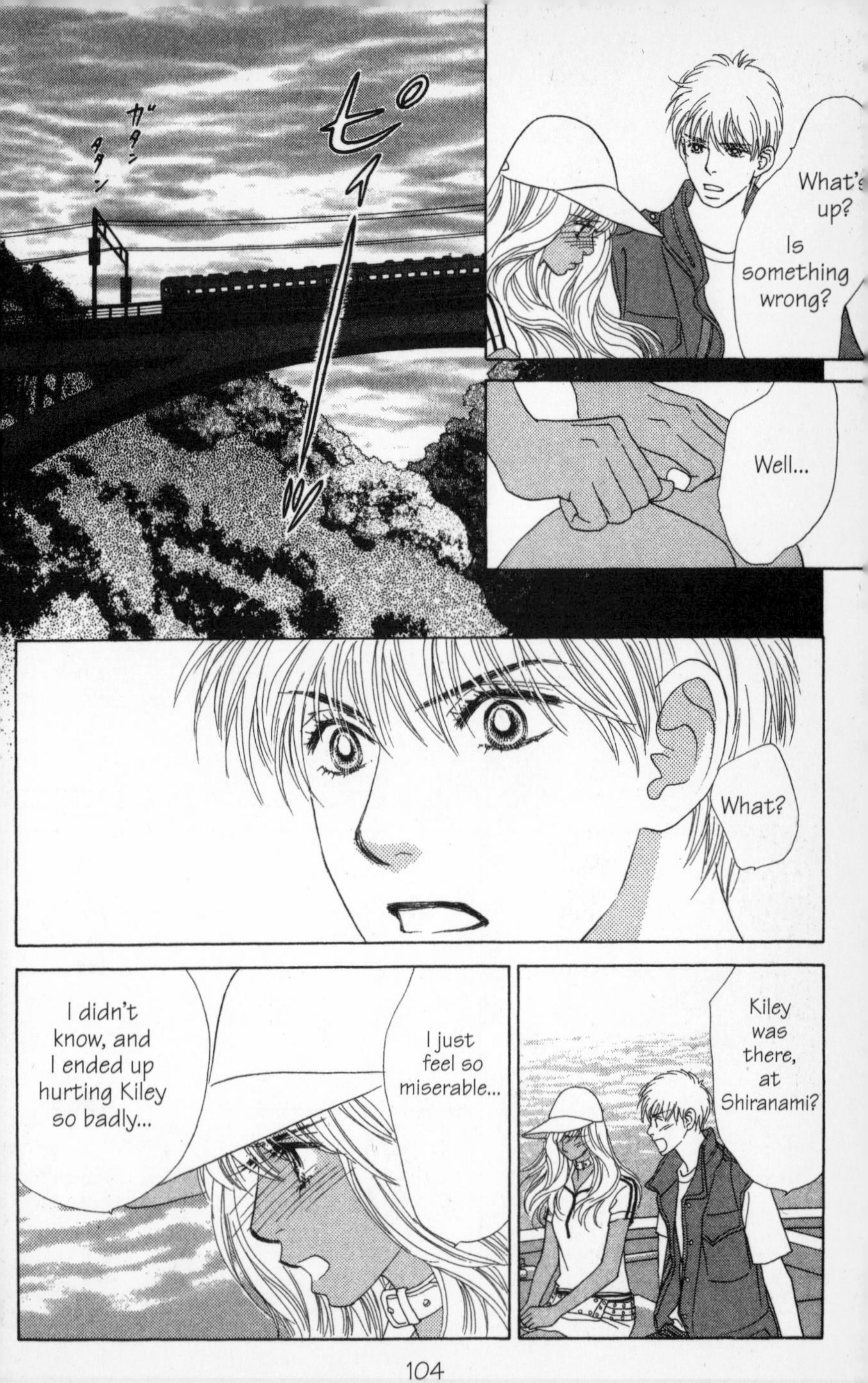
What's up?
Is something wrong?
Well...
ガタン
タタン
ピィー
What?
Kiley was there, at Shiranami?
I just feel so miserable...
I didn't know, and I ended up hurting Kiley so badly...

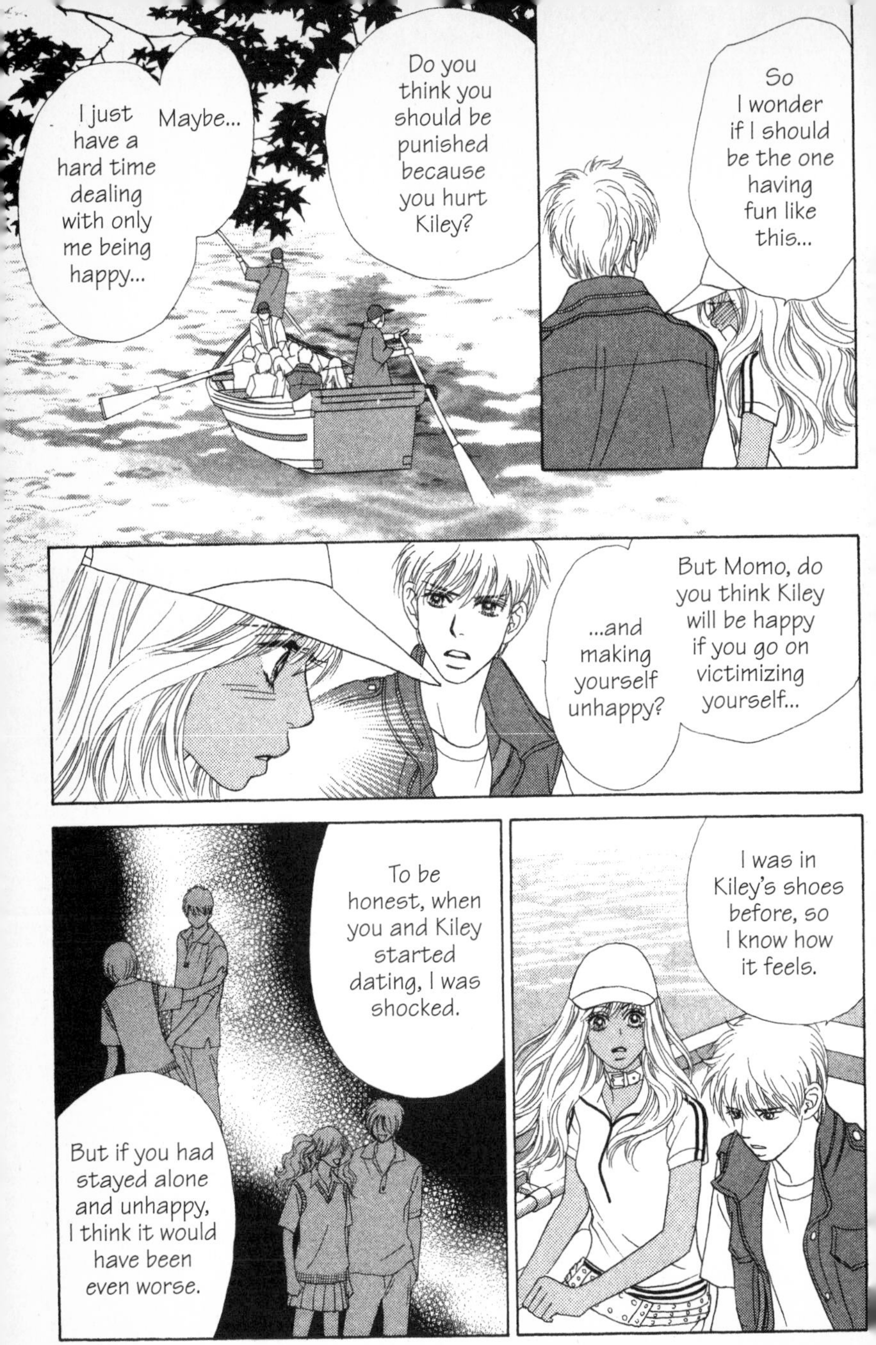
So I wonder if I should be the one having fun like this...
Do you think you should be punished because you hurt Kiley?
Maybe...
I just have a hard time dealing with only me being happy...
But Momo, do you think Kiley will be happy if you go on victimizing yourself...
...and making yourself unhappy?
I was in Kiley's shoes before, so I know how it feels.
To be honest, when you and Kiley started dating, I was shocked.
But if you had stayed alone and unhappy, I think it would have been even worse.

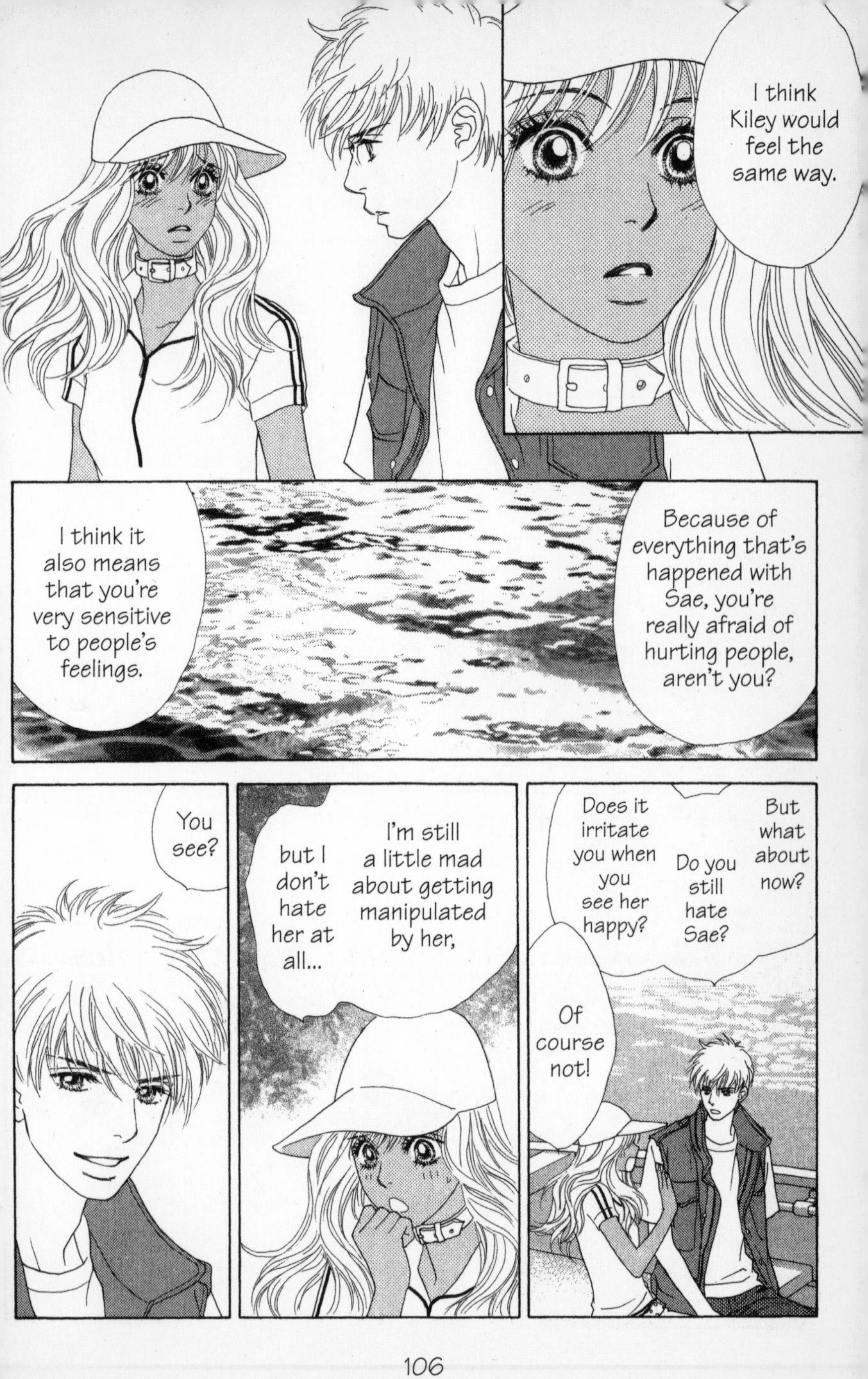
I think Kiley would feel the same way.
Because of everything that's happened with Sae, you're really afraid of hurting people, aren't you?
I think it also means that you're very sensitive to people's feelings.
But what about now?
Do you still hate Sae?
Does it irritate you when you see her happy?
Of course not!
I'm still a little mad about getting manipulated by her,
but I don't hate her at all...
You see?

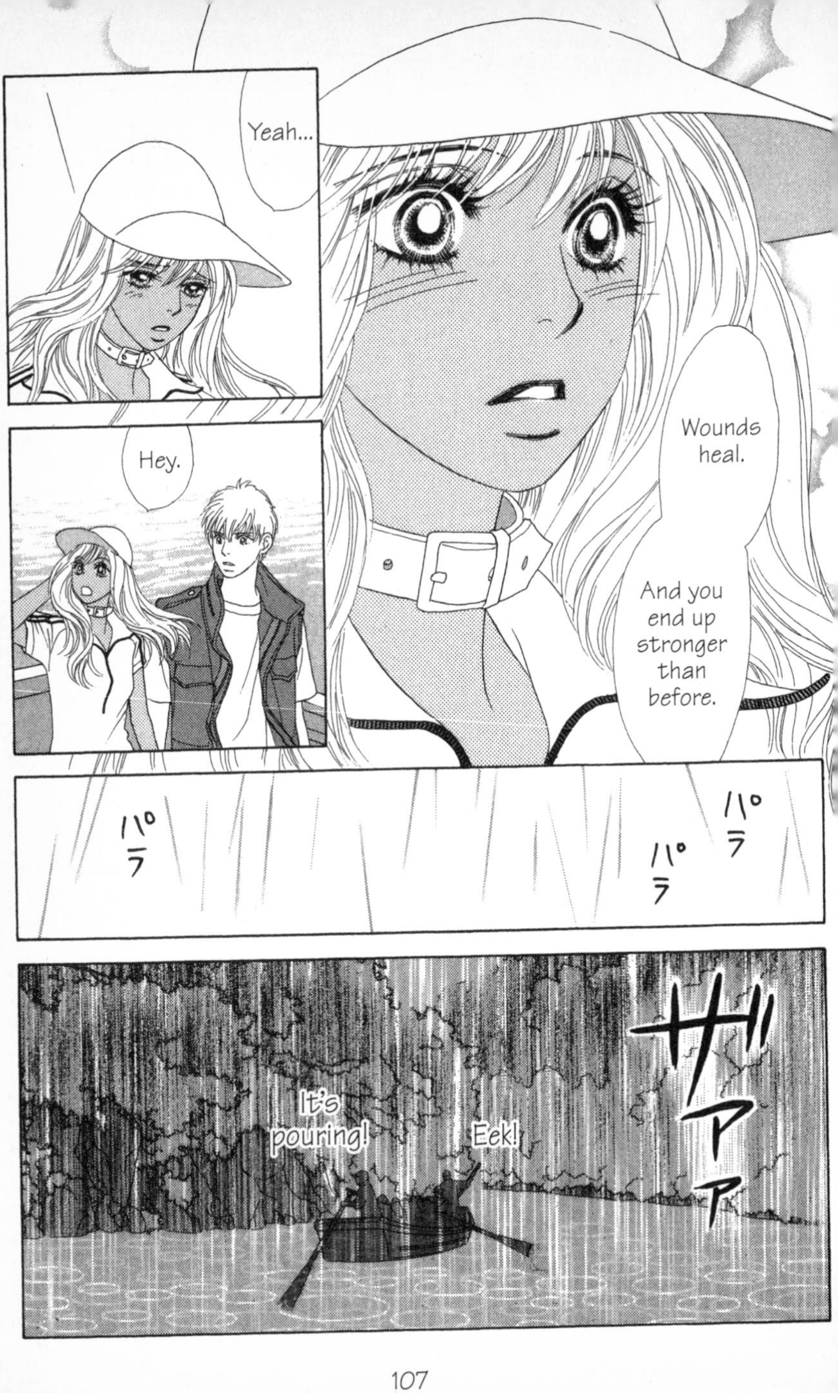
Wounds heal.
And you end up stronger than before.
Yeah...
Hey.
パラ
パラ
パラ
ザァァ
Eek!
It's pouring!

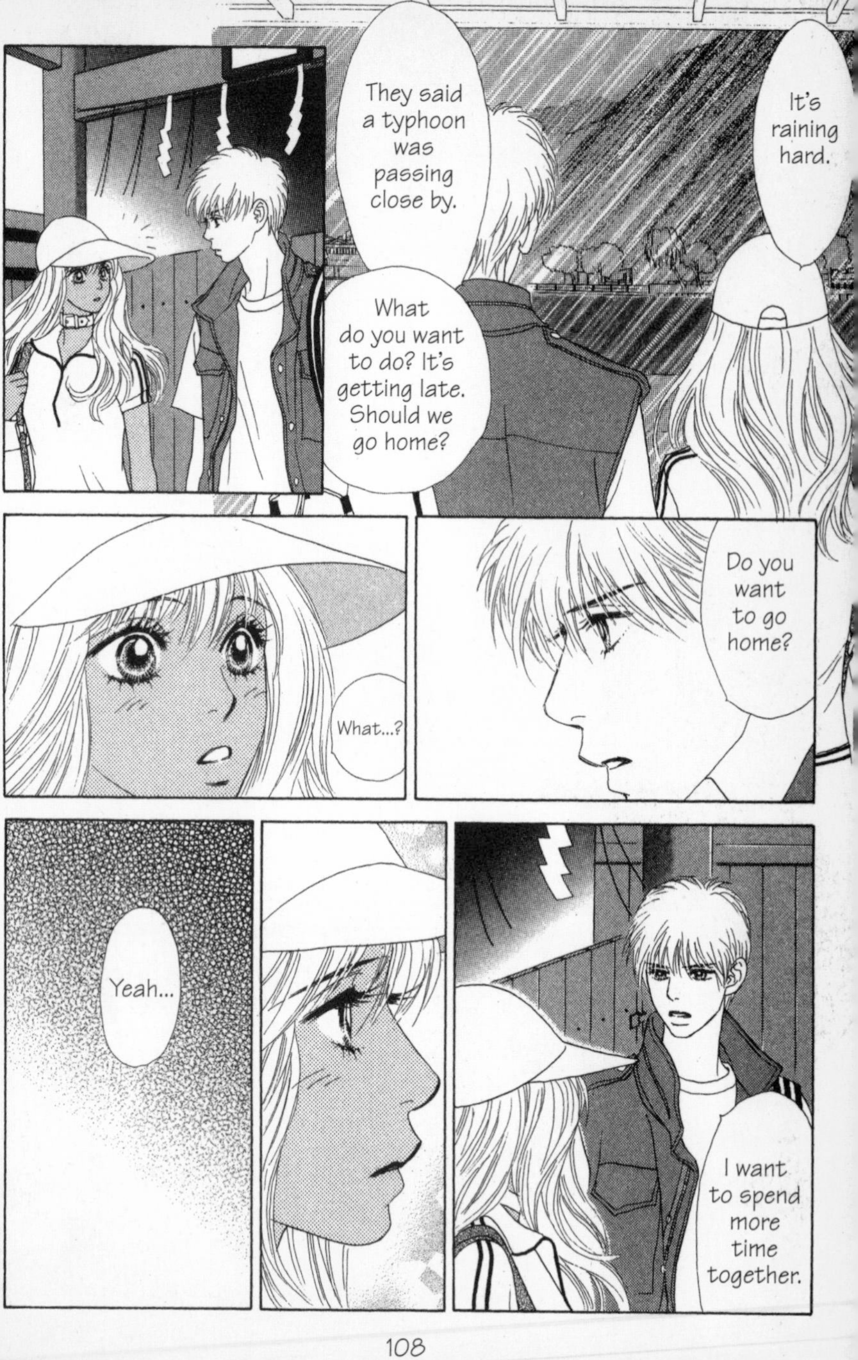
It's raining hard.
They said a typhoon was passing close by.
What do you want to do? It's getting late. Should we go home?
Do you want to go home?
What...?
I want to spend more time together.
Yeah...

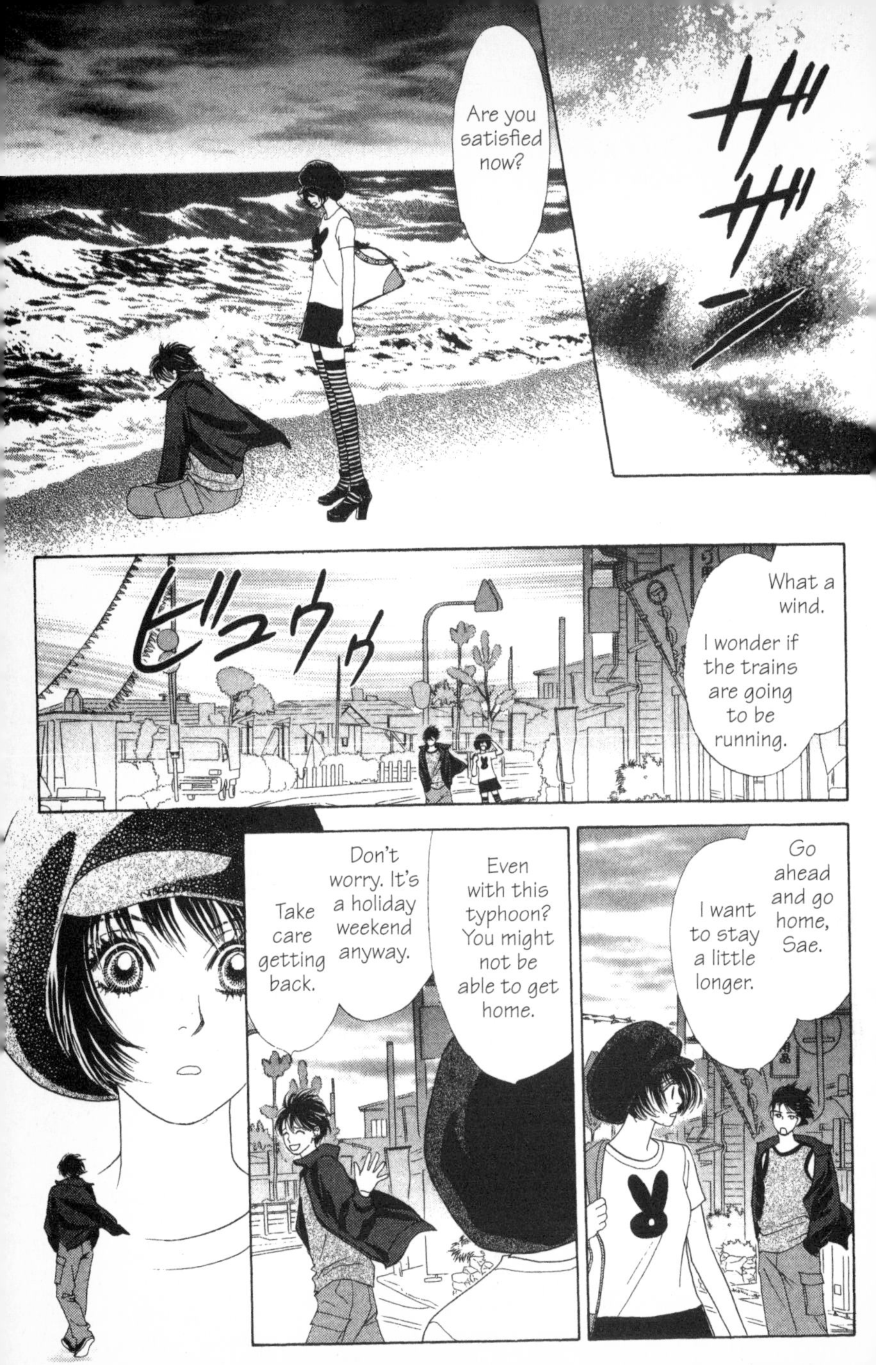
ザザーン
Are you satisfied now?
ビュウゥ
What a wind.
I wonder if the trains are going to be running.
Go ahead and go home, Sae.
I want to stay a little longer.
Even with this typhoon? You might not be able to get home.
Don't worry. It's a holiday weekend anyway.
Take care getting back.

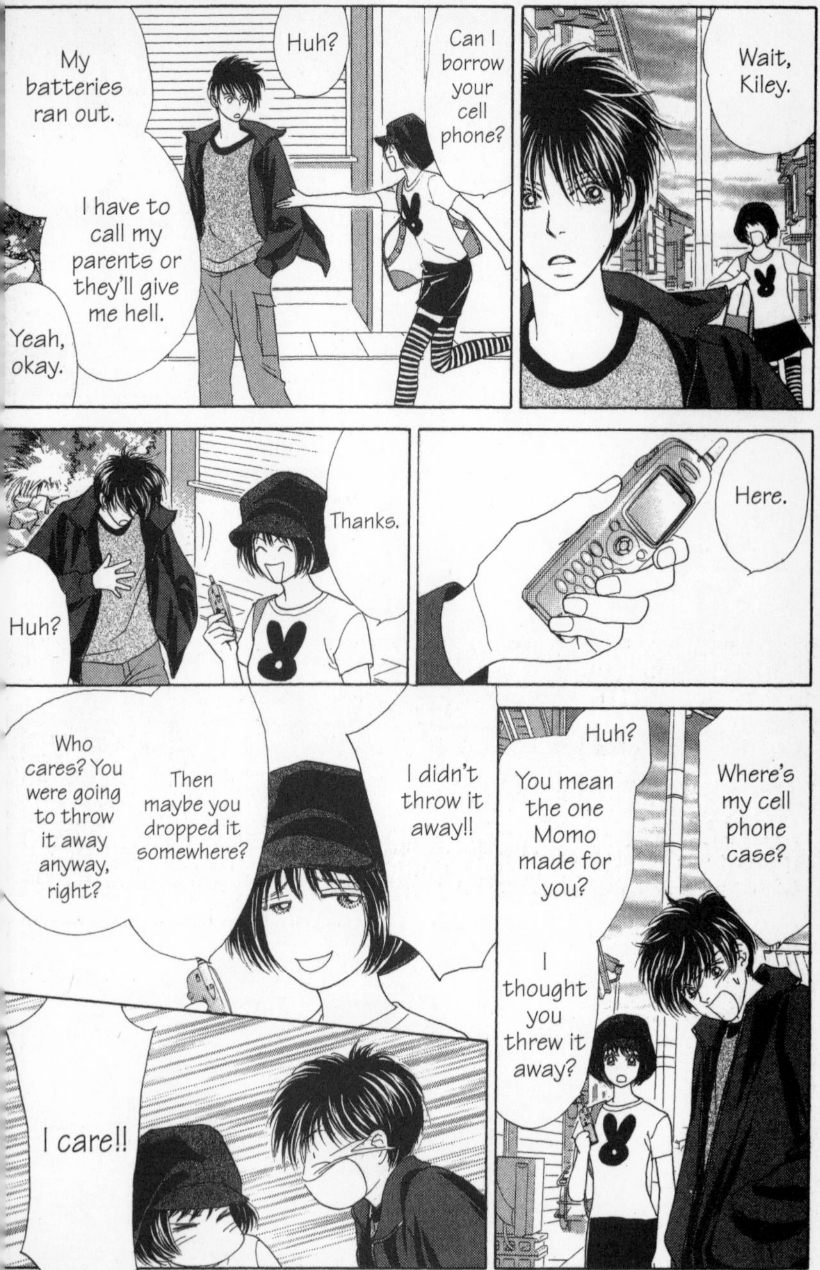
Wait, Kiley.
Can I borrow your cell phone?
Huh?
My batteries ran out.
I have to call my parents or they'll give me hell.
Yeah, okay.
Here.
Thanks.
Huh?
Where's my cell phone case?
Huh?
You mean the one Momo made for you?
I thought you threw it away?
I didn't throw it away!!
Then maybe you dropped it somewhere?
Who cares? You were going to throw it away anyway, right?
I care!!

I'm going to go look for it!!

Looks like you're still hung up on her.

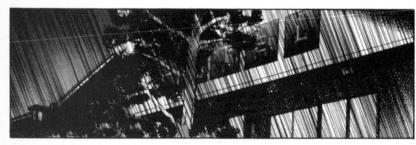

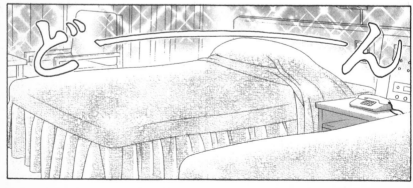

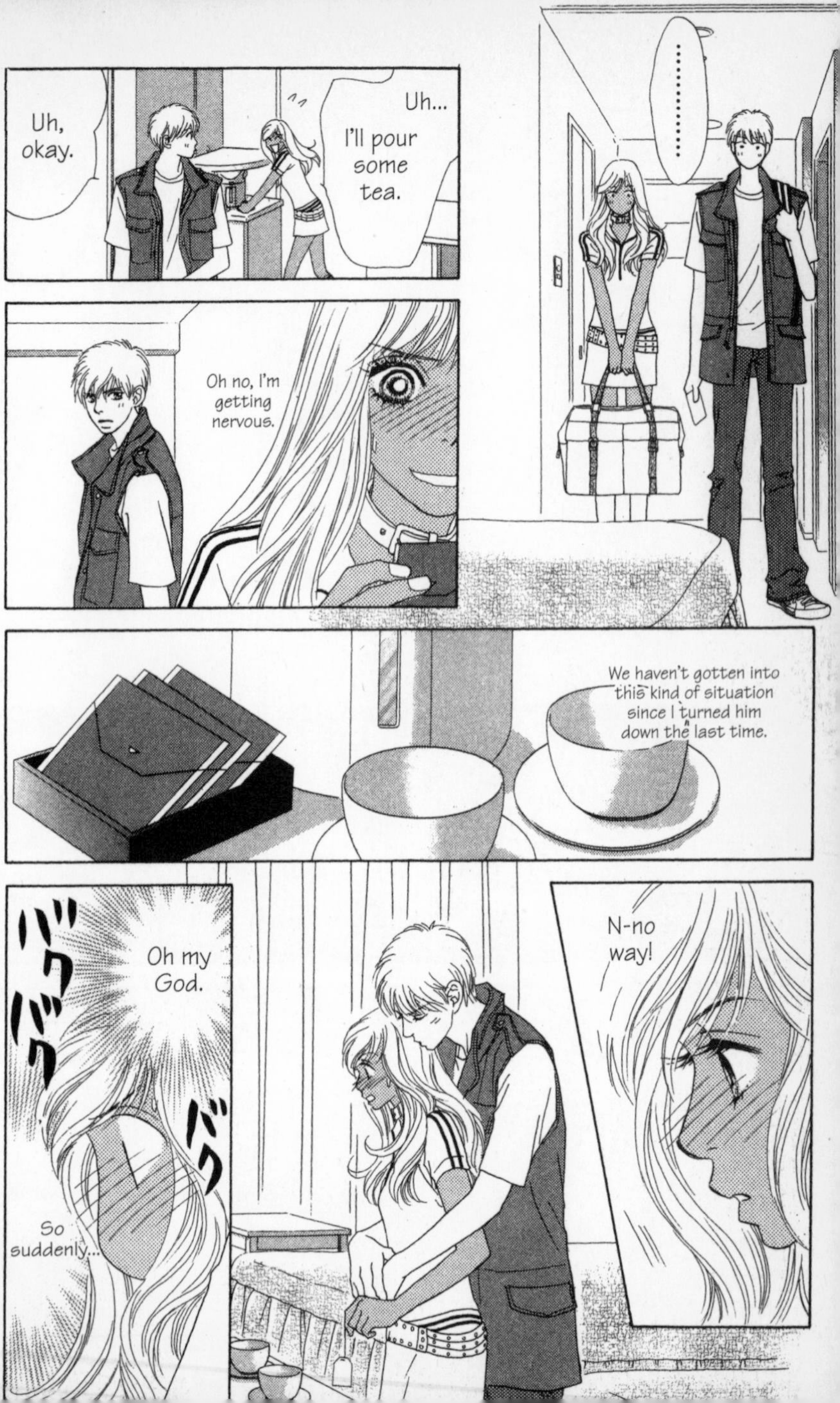
......
Uh...
I'll pour some tea.
Uh, okay.
Oh no, I'm getting nervous.
We haven't gotten into this kind of situation since I turned him down the last time.
N-no way!
Oh my God.
バクバク
So suddenly...

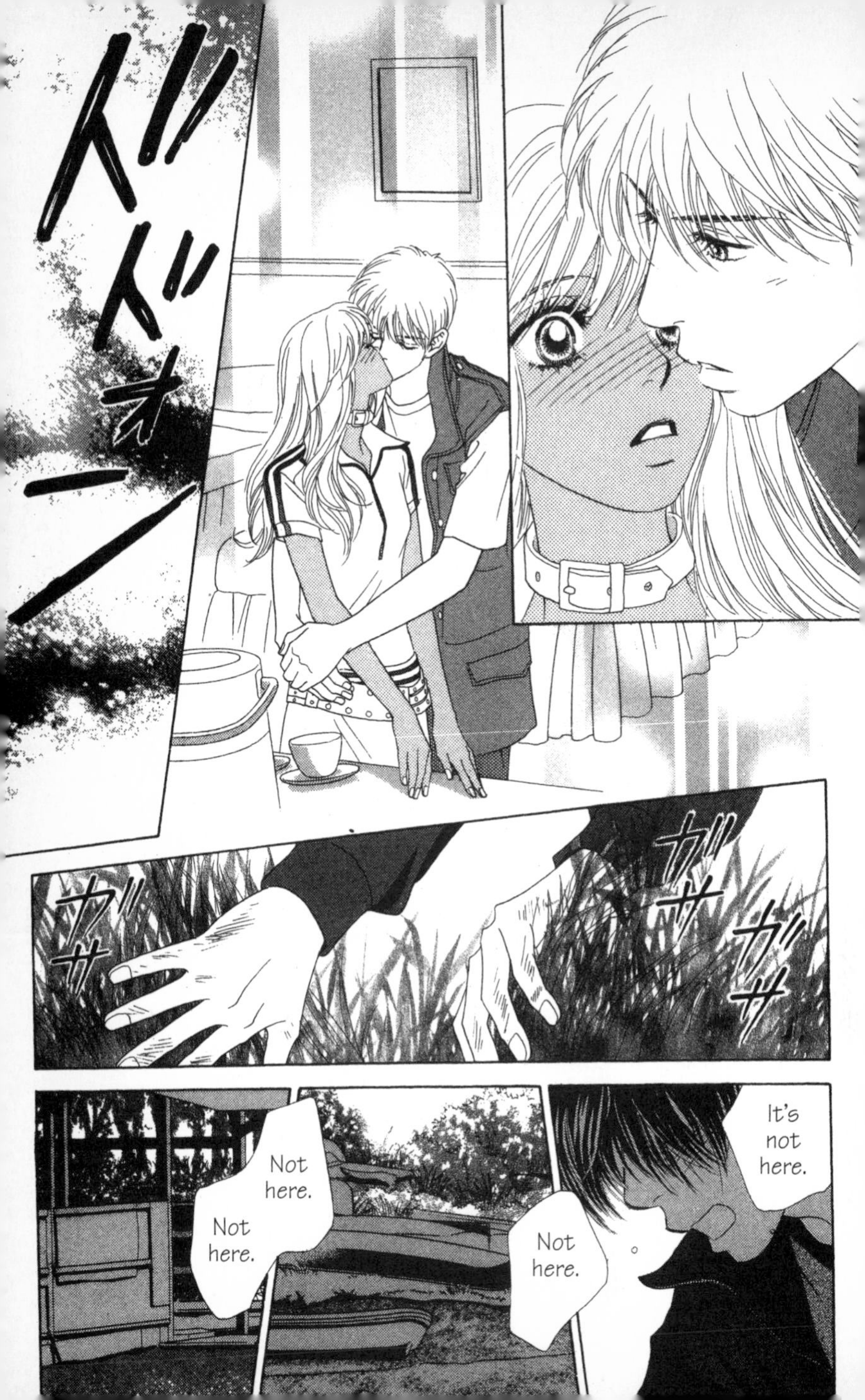

ガサ
ガサ
ガサ
It's not here.
Not here.
Not here.
Not here.

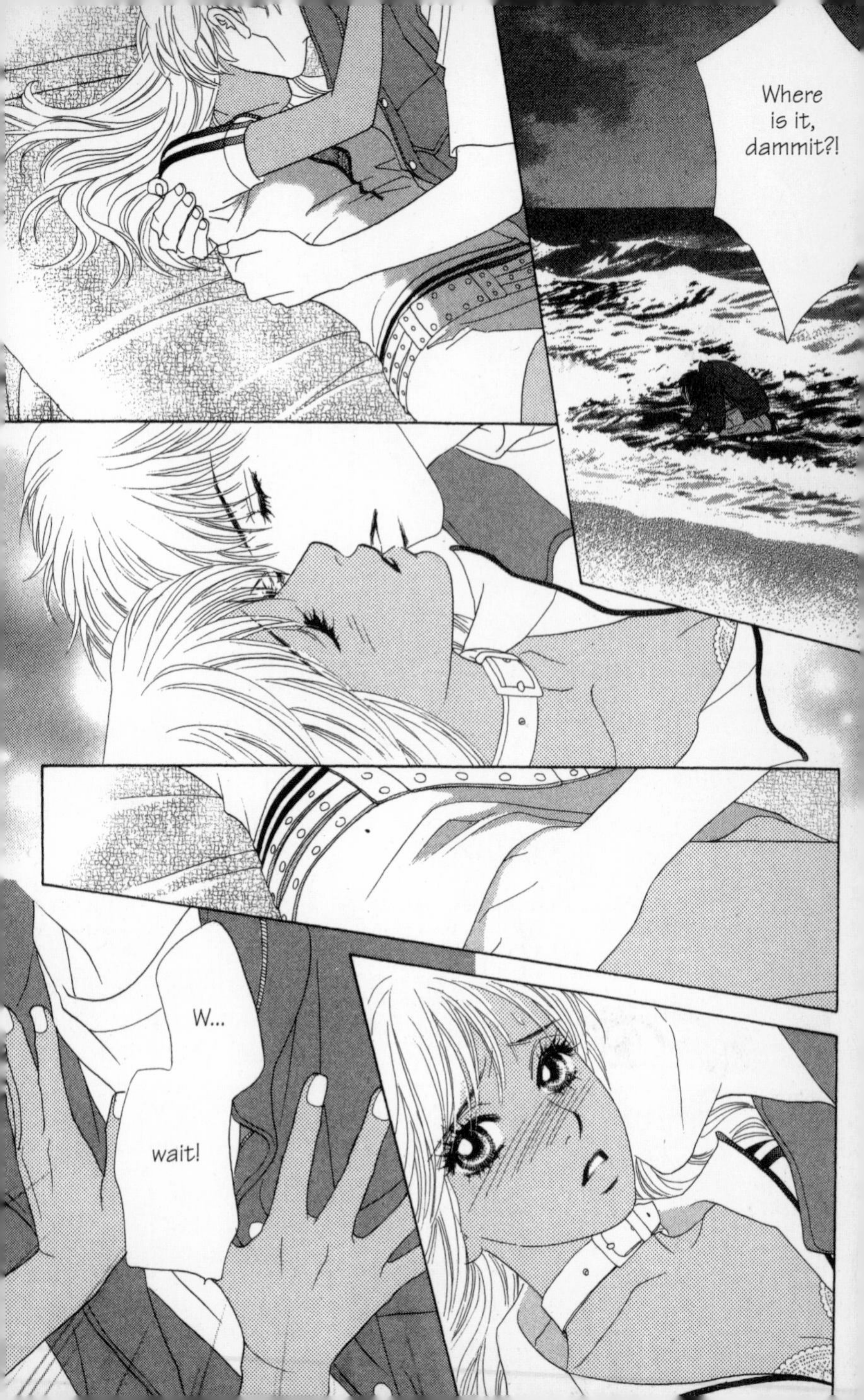
Where is it, dammit?!
W...
wait!

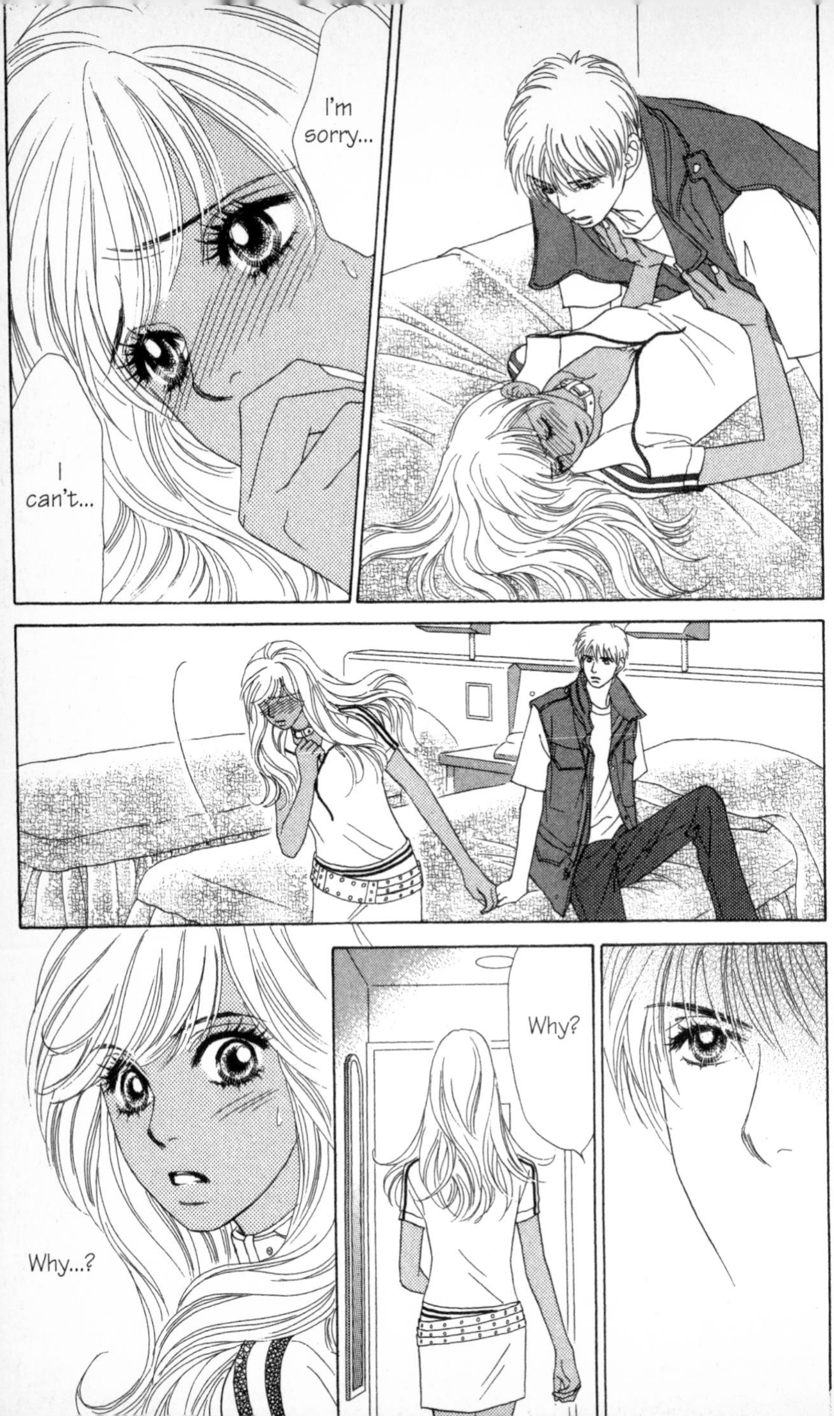
I'm sorry...
I can't...
Why?
Why...?

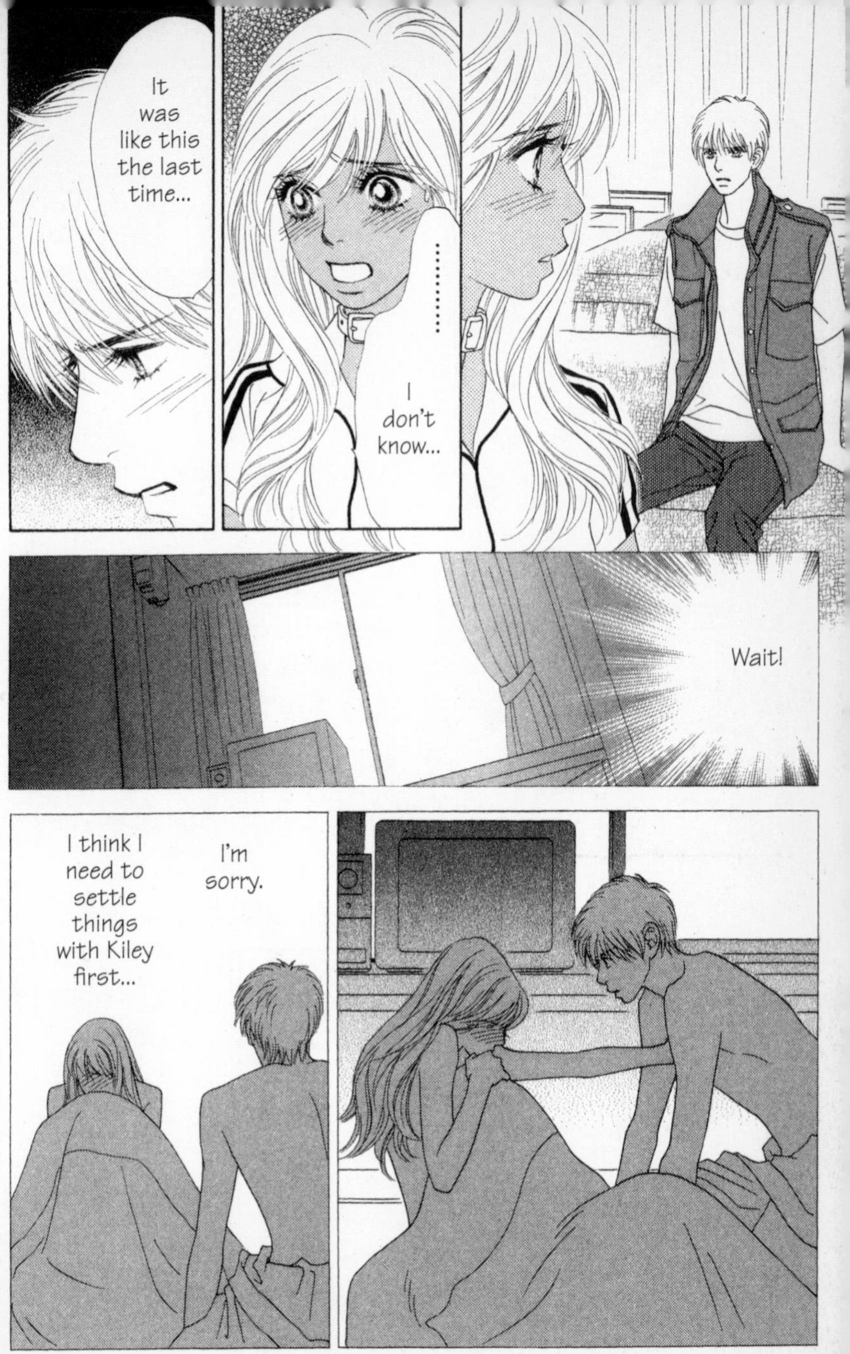
......
I don't know...
It was like this the last time...
Wait!
I'm sorry.
I think I need to settle things with Kiley first...

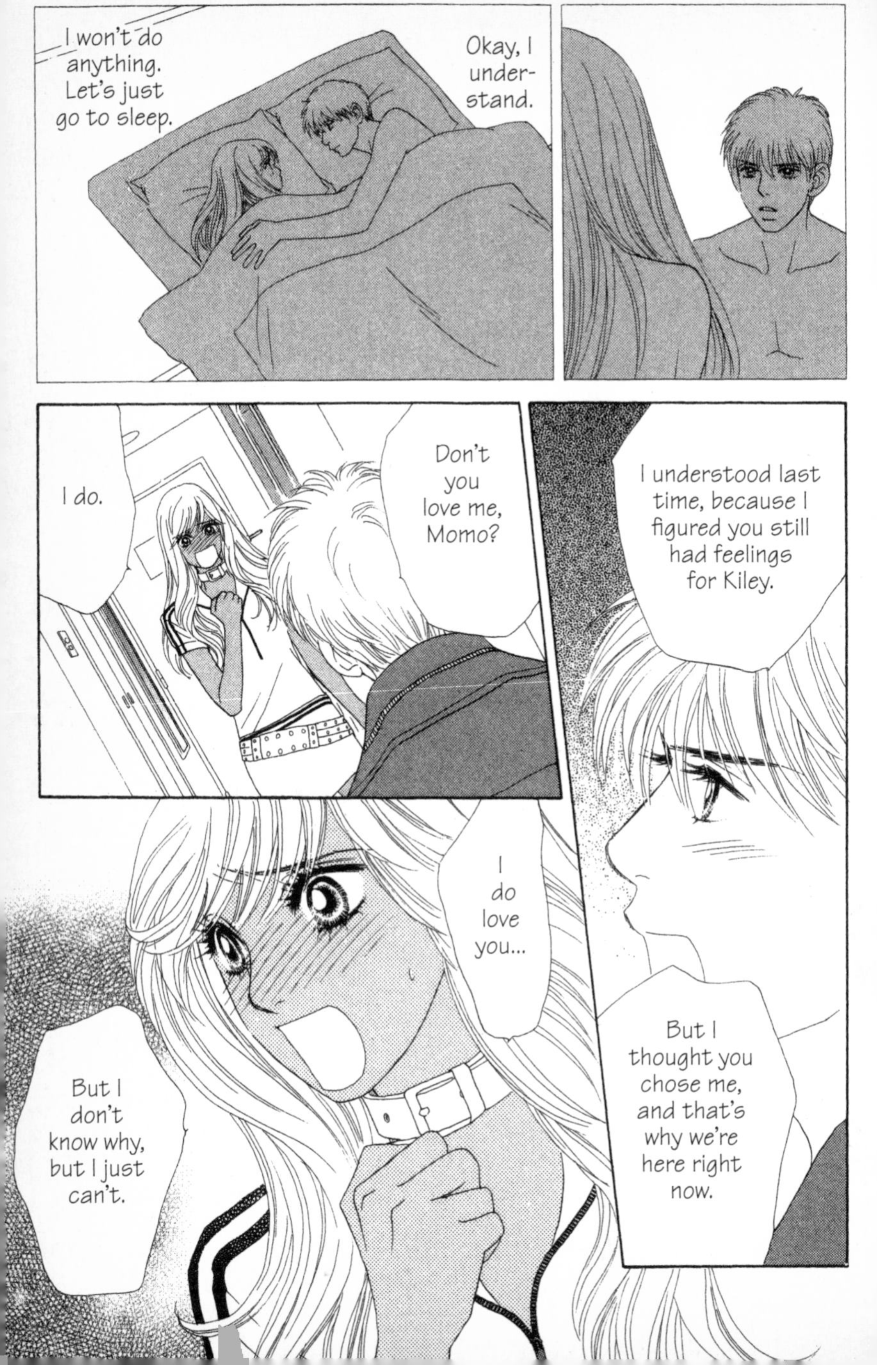
Okay, I understand.
I won't do anything. Let's just go to sleep.
I understood last time, because I figured you still had feelings for Kiley.
But I thought you chose me, and that's why we're here right now.
Don't you love me, Momo?
I do.
I do love you...
But I don't know why, but I just can't.

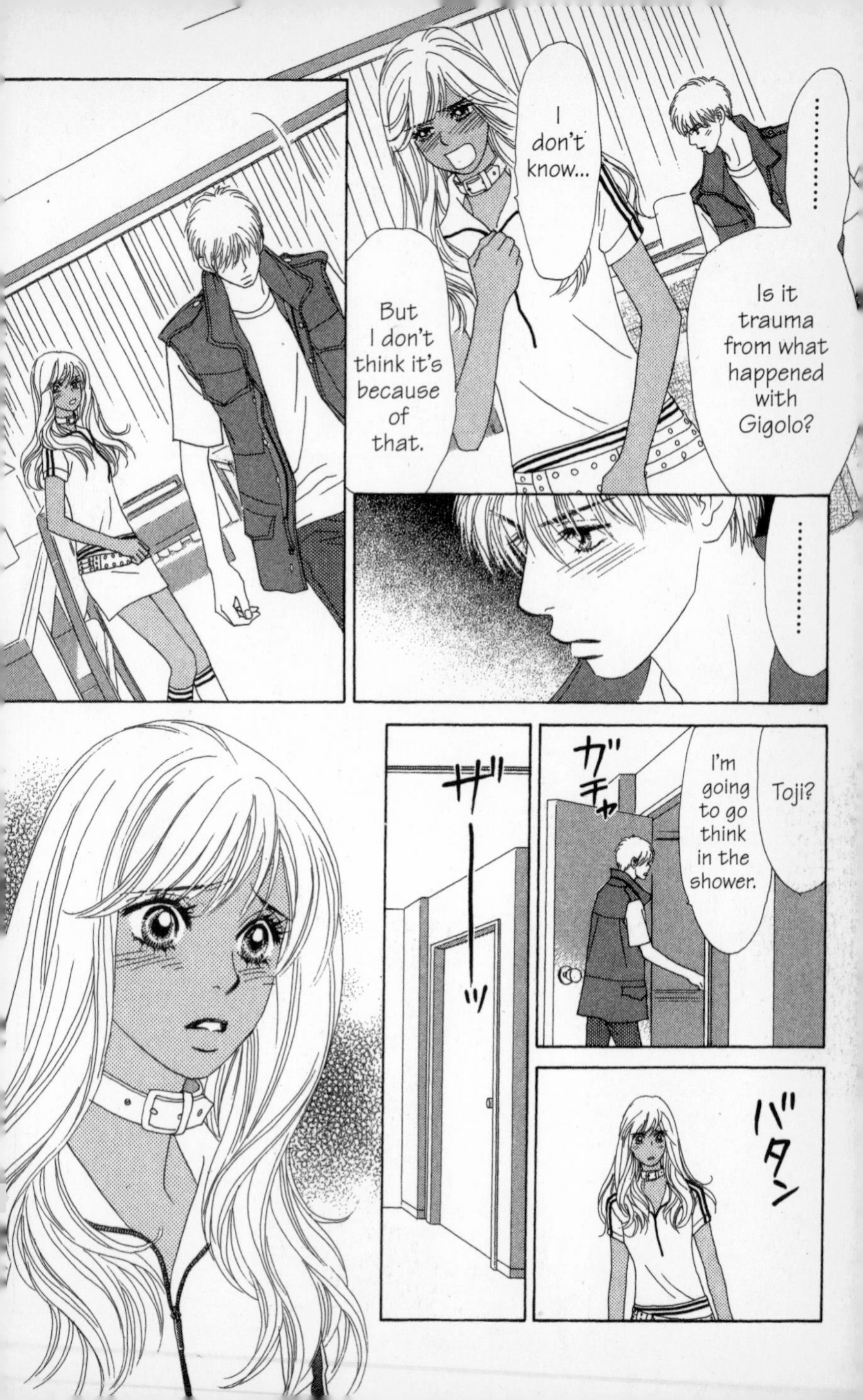

......
Is it trauma from what happened with Gigolo?
I don't know...
But I don't think it's because of that.
......
Toji?
I'm going to go think in the shower.
ガチャ
バタン
ザーーッ

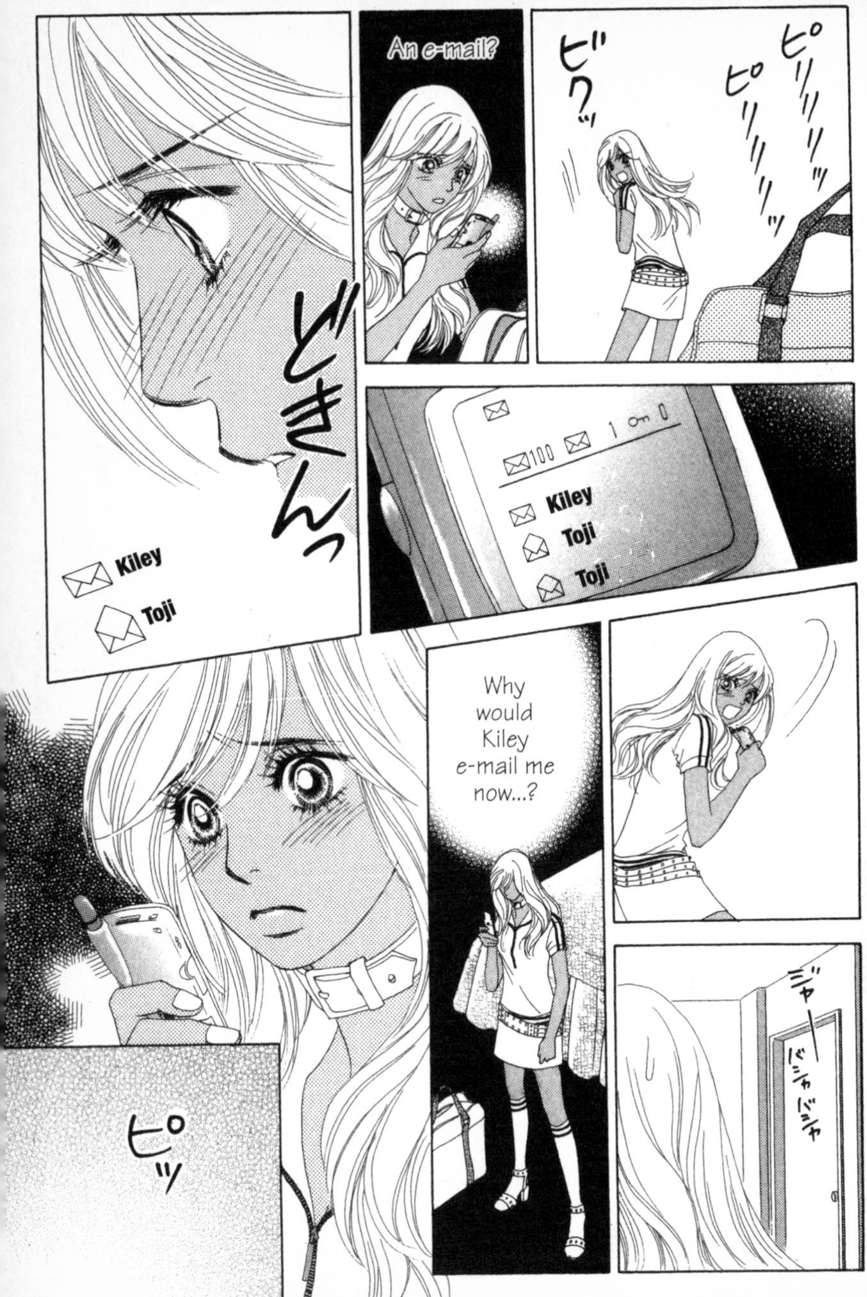
ピリリリリッ
ピリリリリッ
ビクッ
An e-mail?
100
Kiley
Toji
Toji
Kiley
Toji
どきんっ
ジャー
バシャバシャ
Why would Kiley e-mail me now...?
ピッ

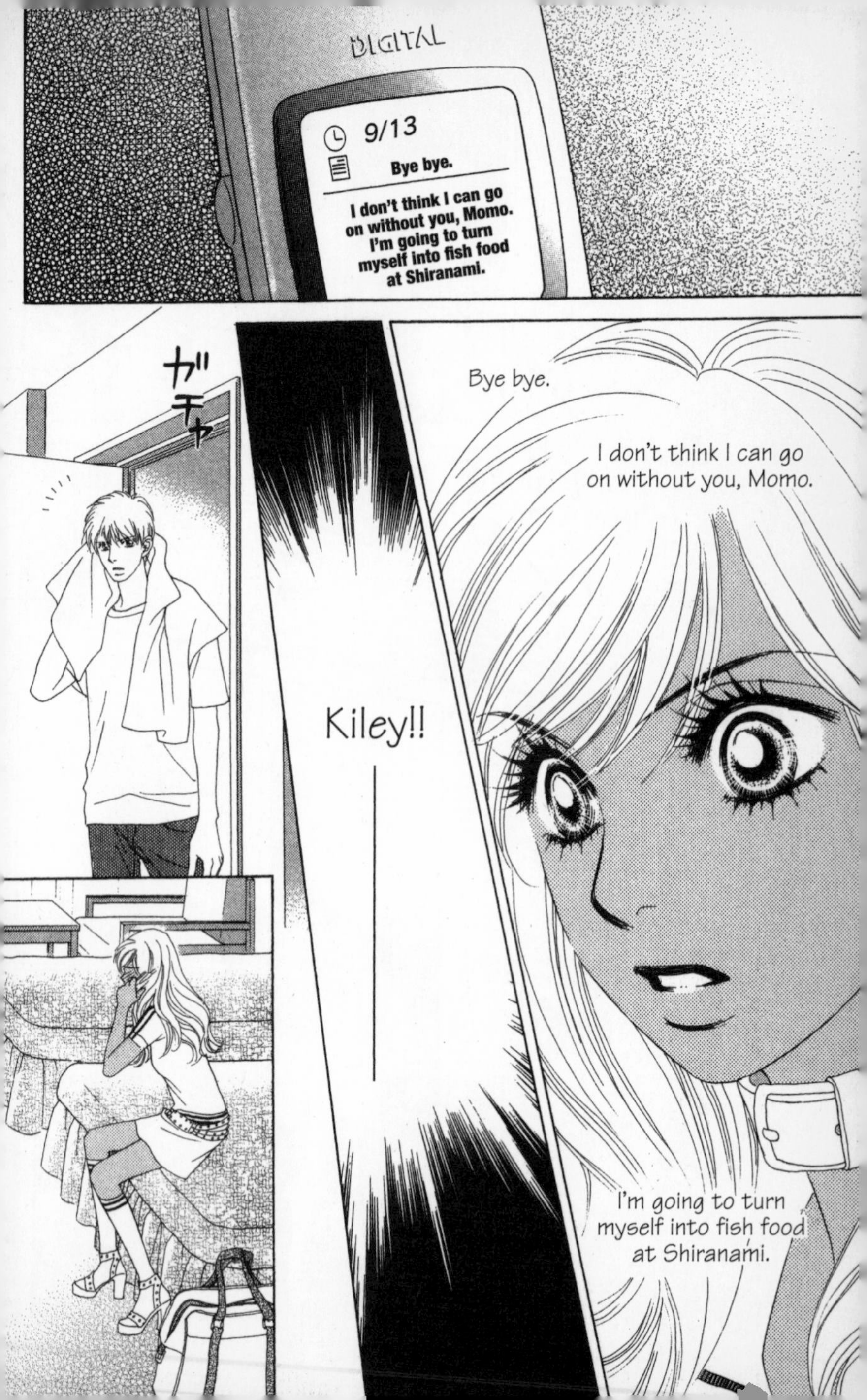
DIGITAL
9/13
Bye bye.
I don't think I can go on without you, Momo. I'm going to turn myself into fish food at Shiranami.
Bye bye.
I don't think I can go on without you, Momo.
I'm going to turn myself into fish food at Shiranami.
Kiley!!
ガチャ

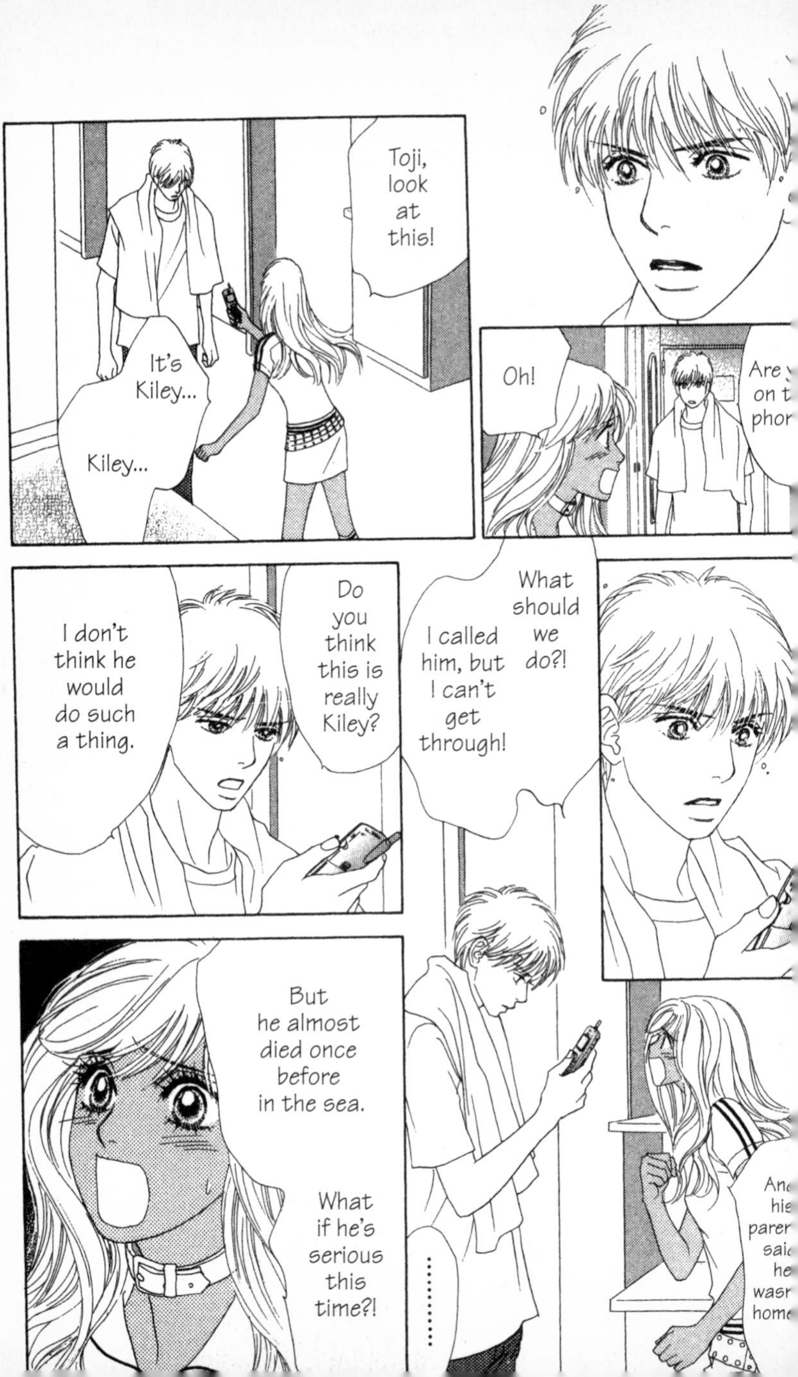

Oh!
Toji, look at this!
It's Kiley...
Kiley...
What should we do?!
I called him, but I can't get through!
Do you think this is really Kiley?
I don't think he would do such a thing.
......
But he almost died once before in the sea.
What if he's serious this time?!

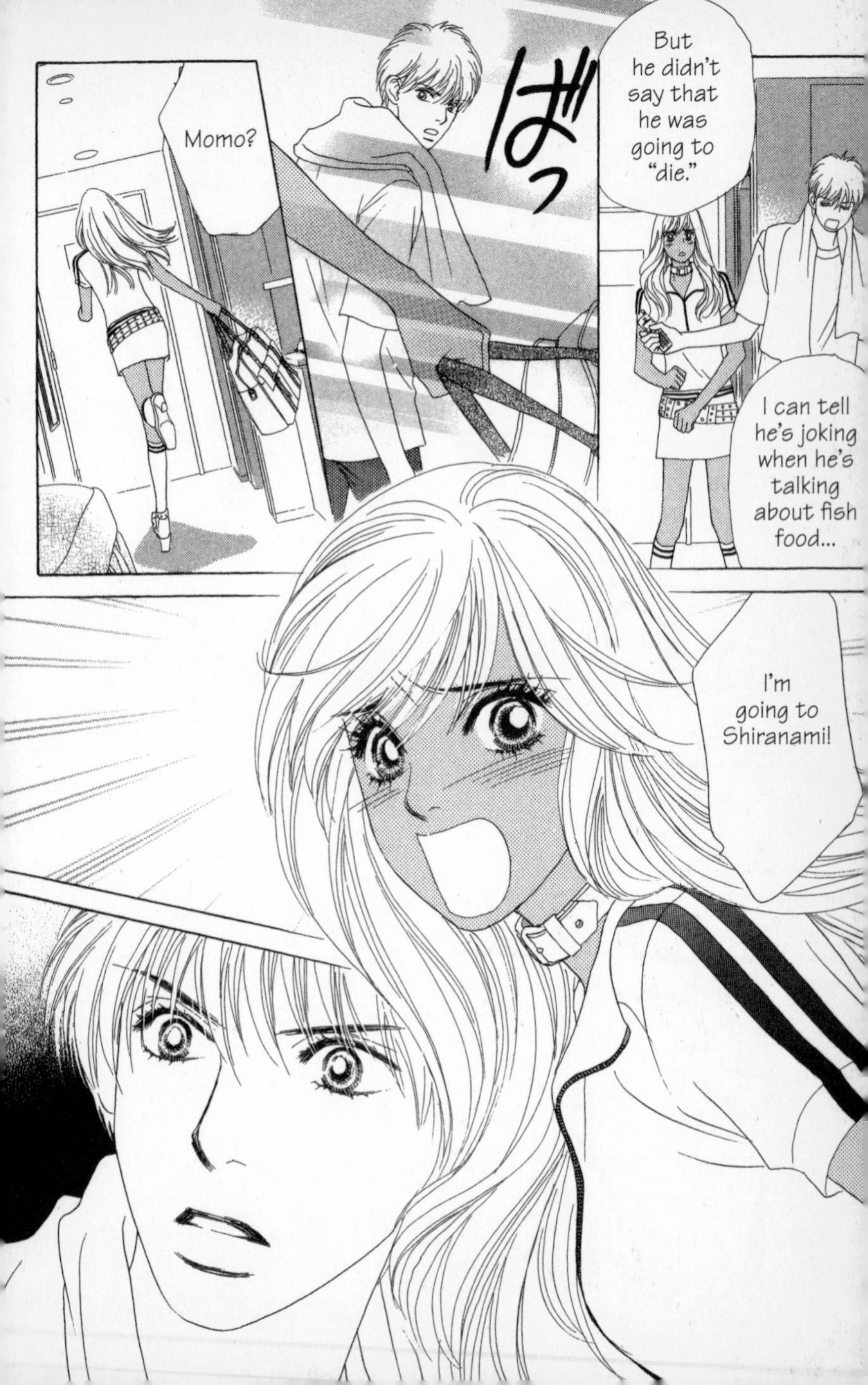
But he didn't say that he was going to "die."
I can tell he's joking when he's talking about fish food...
Momo?
ばっ
I'm going to Shiranami!

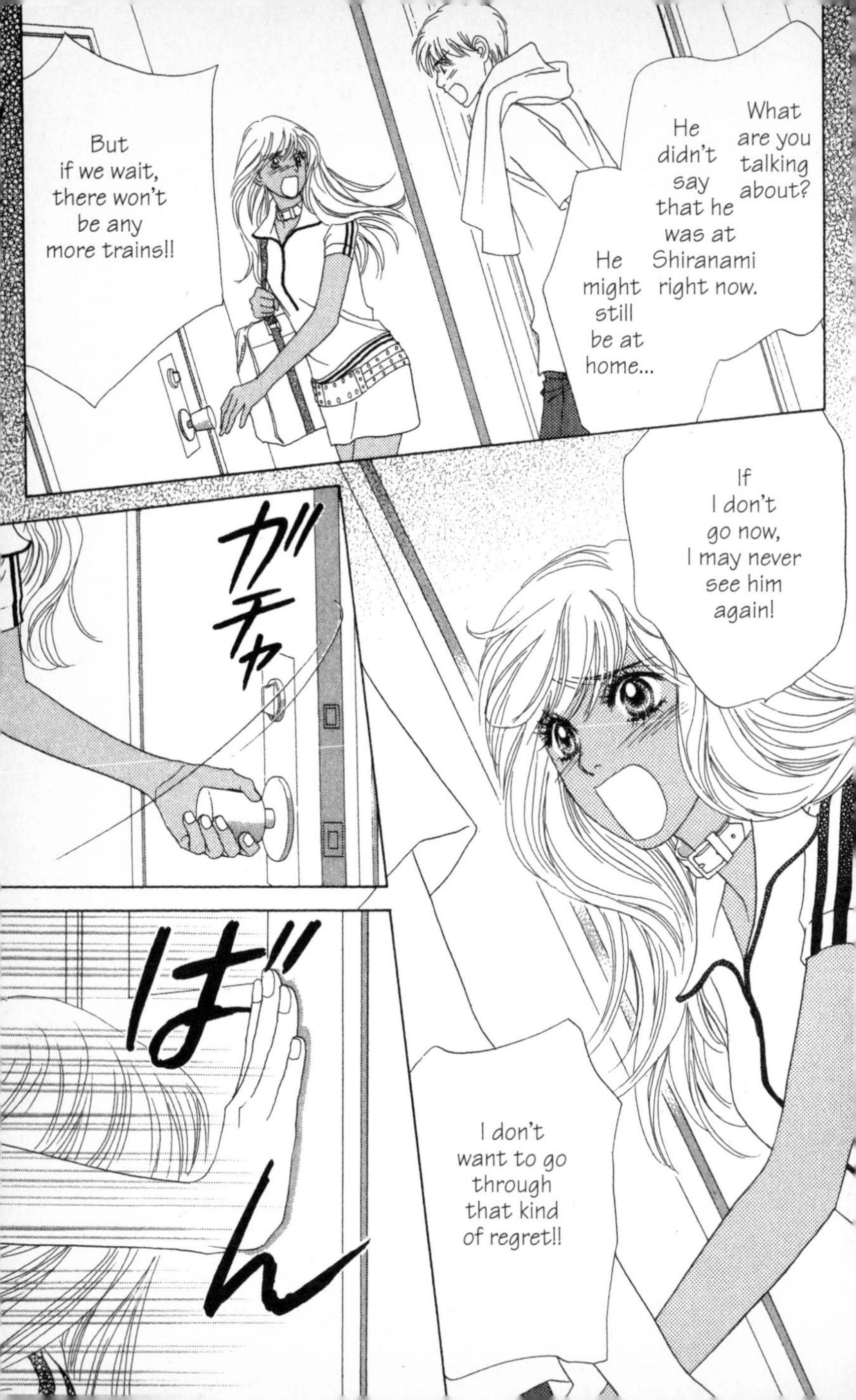
What are you talking about?
He didn't say that he was at Shiranami right now.
He might still be at home...
But if we wait, there won't be any more trains!!
If I don't go now, I may never see him again!
I don't want to go through that kind of regret!!
ガチャ
ばん

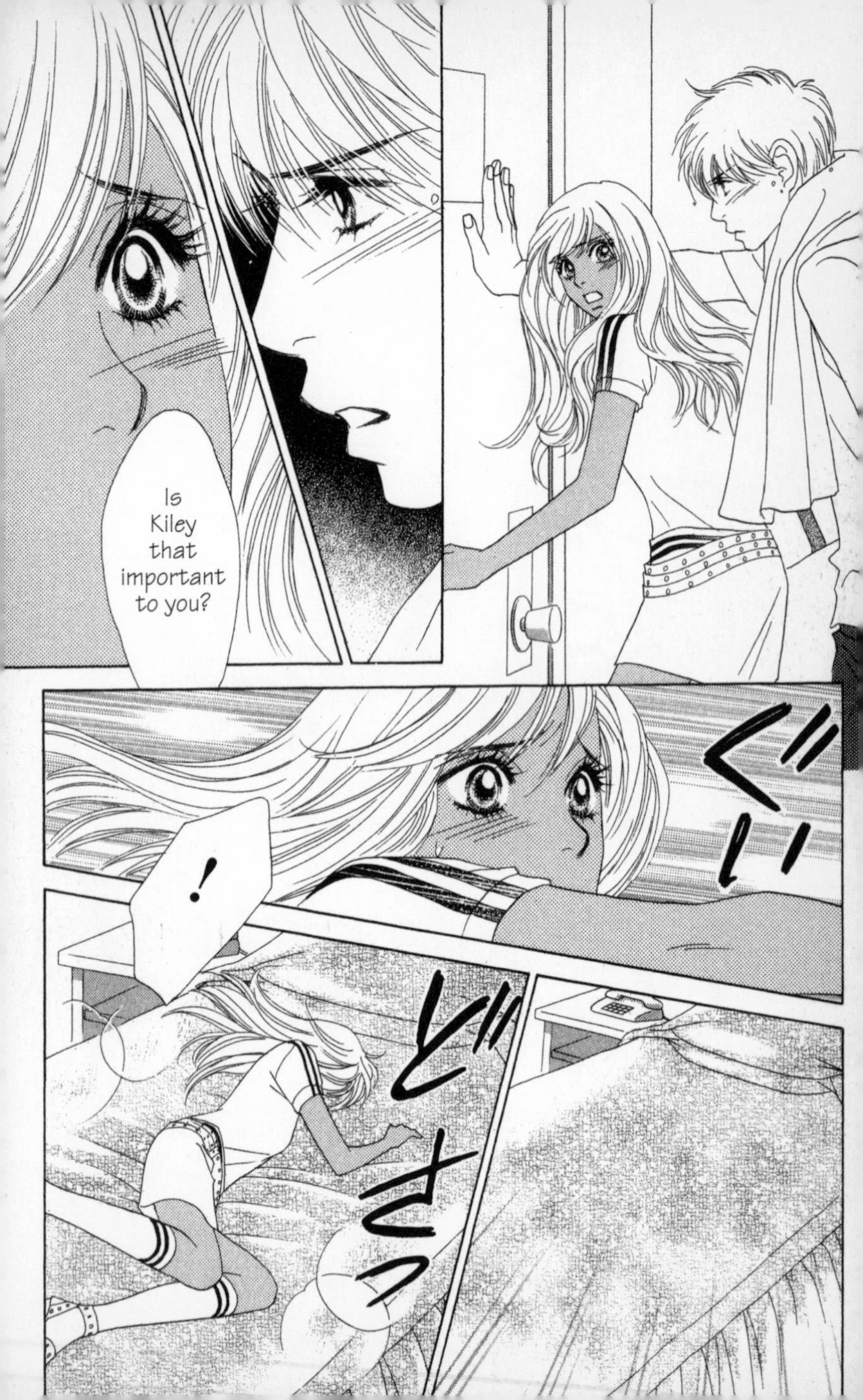
Is Kiley that important to you?
ぐい
!
どさっ

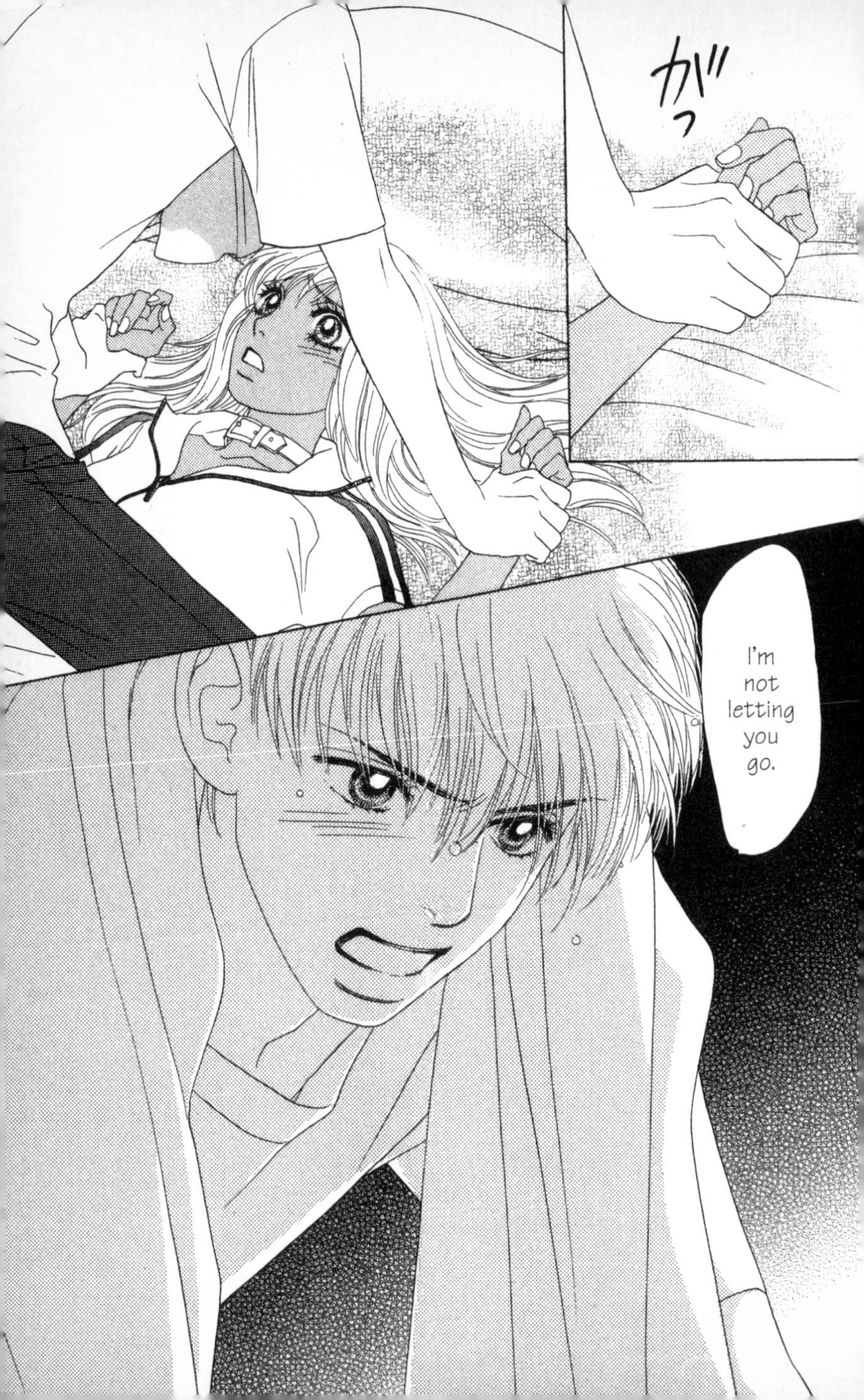
ガッ
I'm not letting you go.

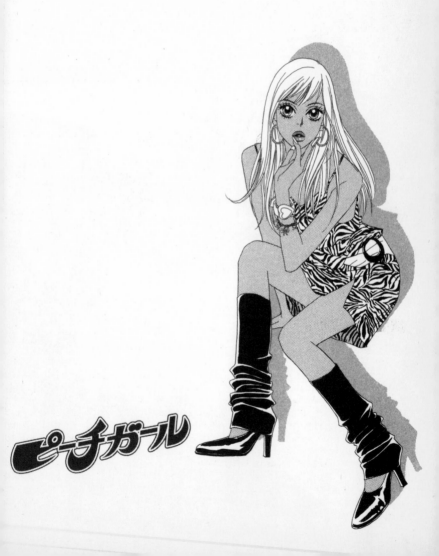

ピーチガール

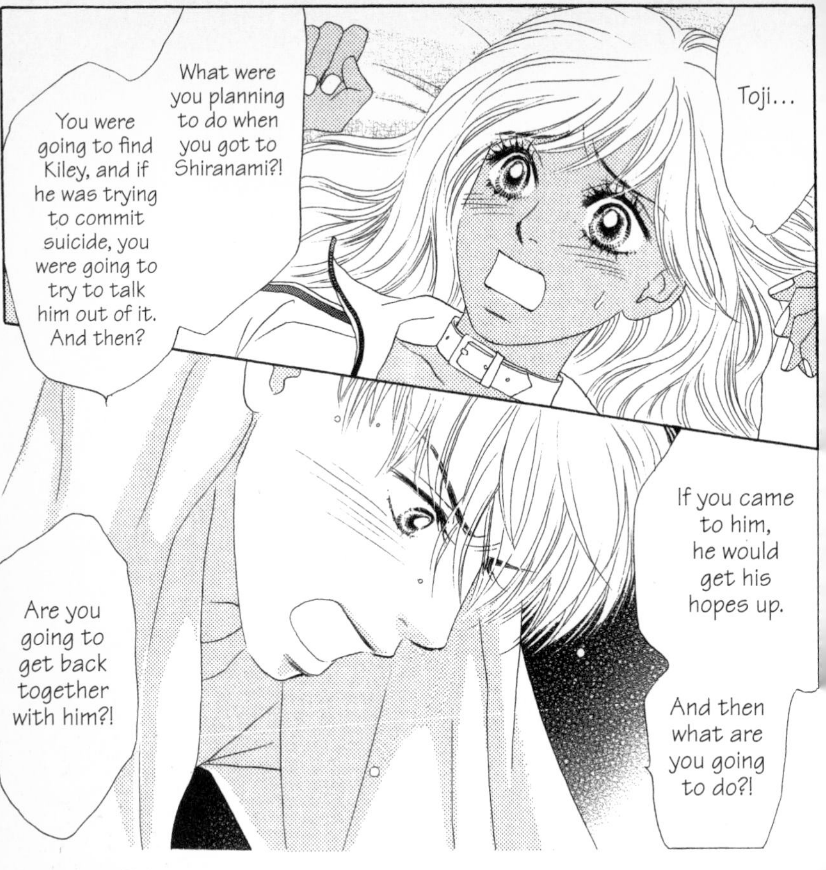
Toji...
What were you planning to do when you got to Shiranami?!
You were going to find Kiley, and if he was trying to commit suicide, you were going to try to talk him out of it. And then?
If you came to him, he would get his hopes up.
And then what are you going to do?!
Are you going to get back together with him?!

PEACH CLUB

I asked popstar Sonin the question, “Have you ever met a girl like Sae?” She answered, “No. Or maybe I have, but I just never realized it.” I thought, “Oh, really?” as we proceeded along. Then Sonin seemed to recall something. “Come to think of it, I did get my shoes thrown into the garbage once.” Hey, that’s totally bullying... But whenever Sonin would find her desk turned over or whatever, she would just assume that it was one of the boys fooling around who had accidentally knocked it over, and she would just set it upright. It seems that she was indifferent to harassment. I would say that basically she doesn’t seem to think that people have bad intentions. She’s such a straight up and kind person who makes me feel better from just being with her. I was really glad to have had the chance to meet her. Thank you, Sonin. That was only two days after I had finished drawing the last episode, but when I think about how many readers are out there who are looking forward to my work like she does, I feel that I have to work harder and stay intense. It was that kind of day. -Miwa

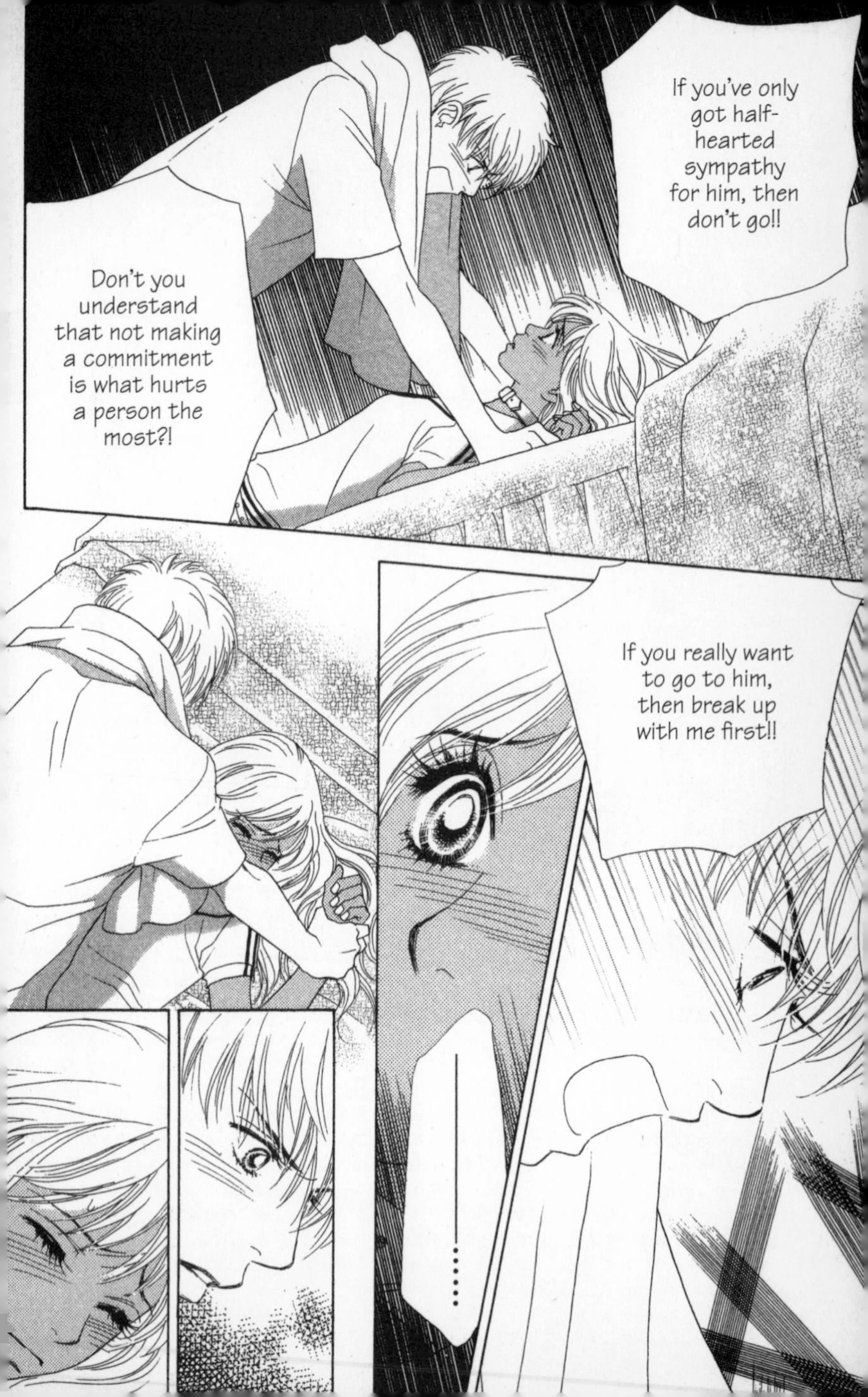
If you've only got half-hearted sympathy for him, then don't go!!
Don't you understand that not making a commitment is what hurts a person the most?!
If you really want to go to him, then break up with me first!!
......

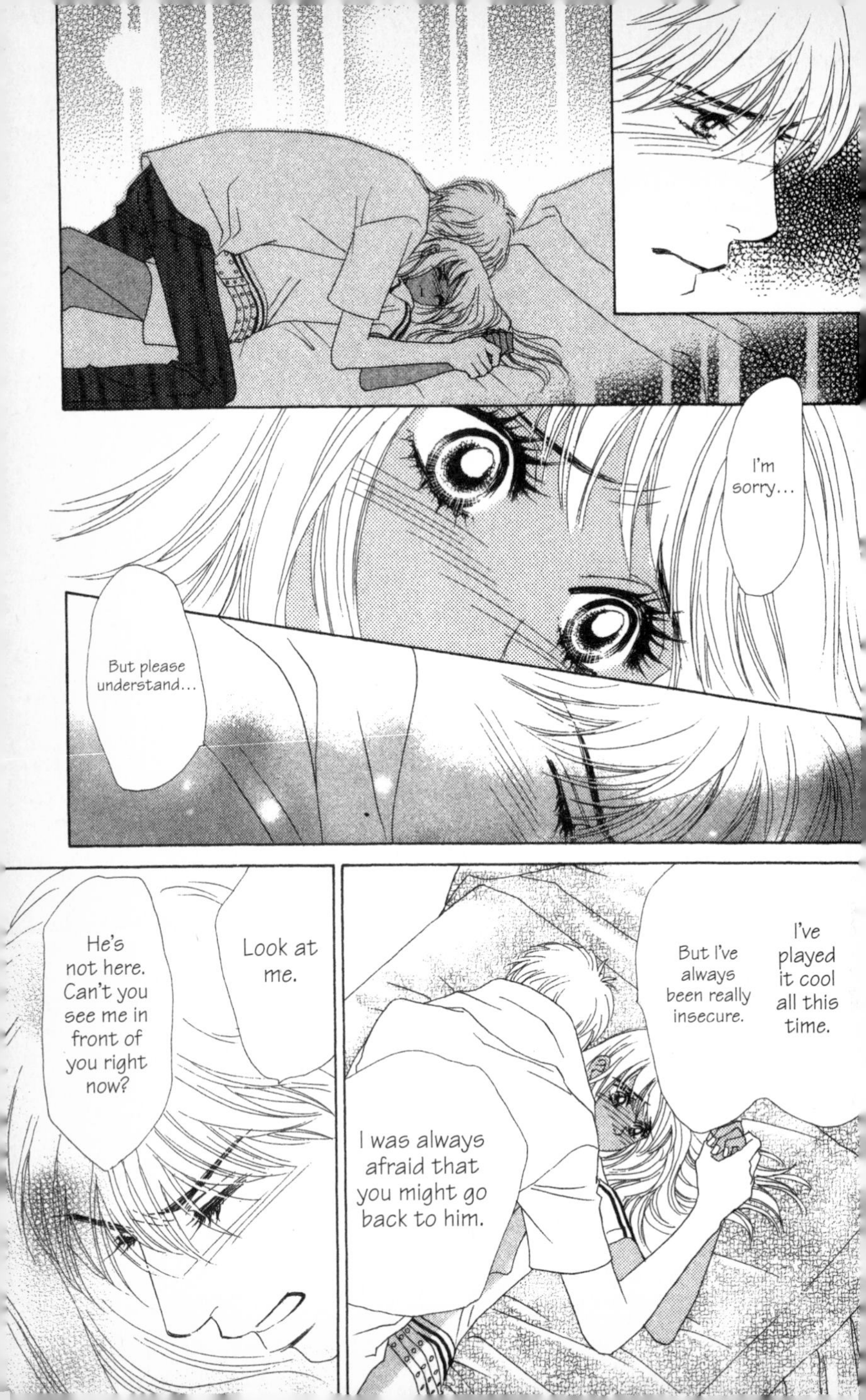
I'm sorry...
But please understand...
I've played it cool all this time.
But I've always been really insecure.
I was always afraid that you might go back to him.
Look at me.
He's not here. Can't you see me in front of you right now?

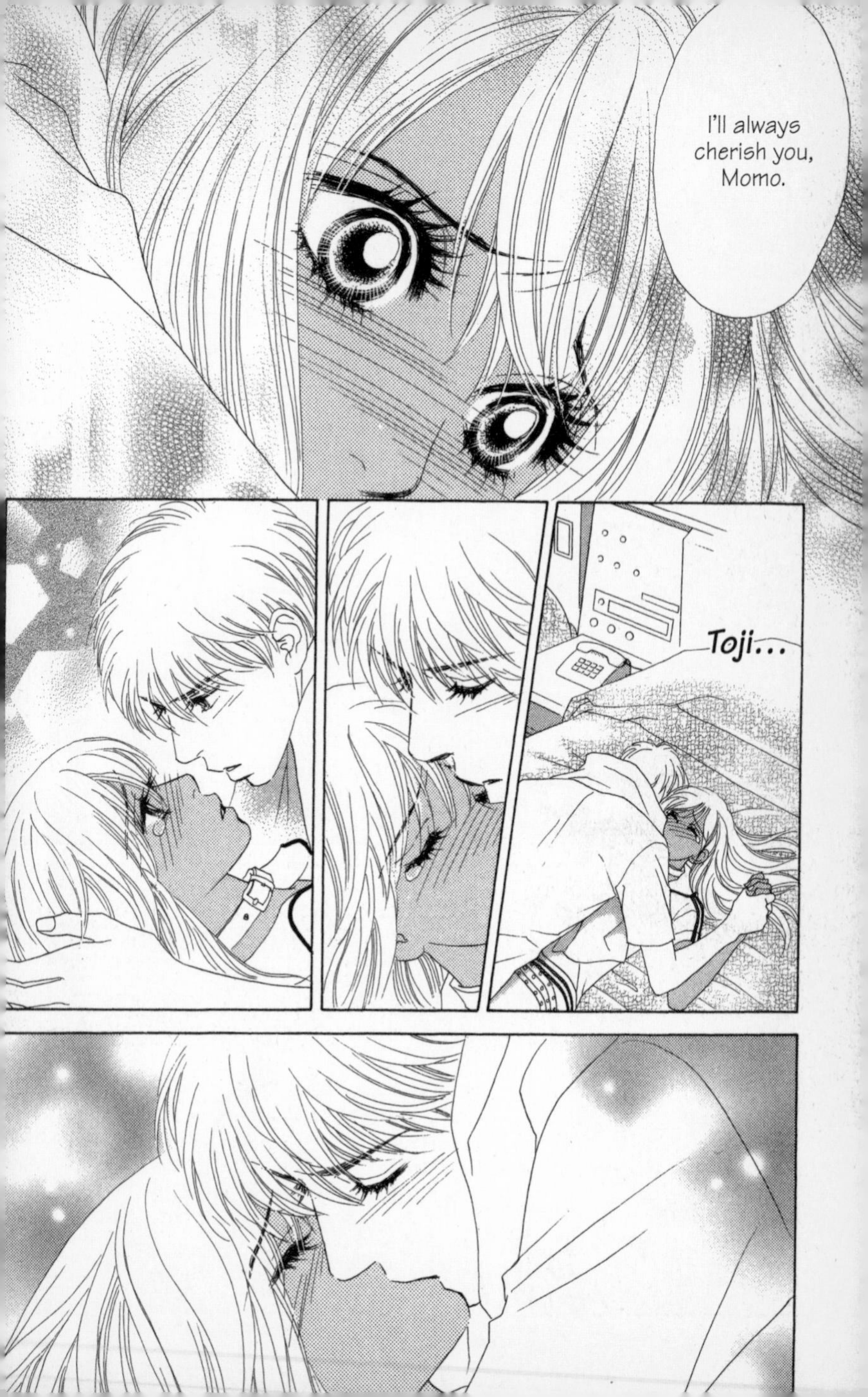
I'll always cherish you, Momo.
Toji...

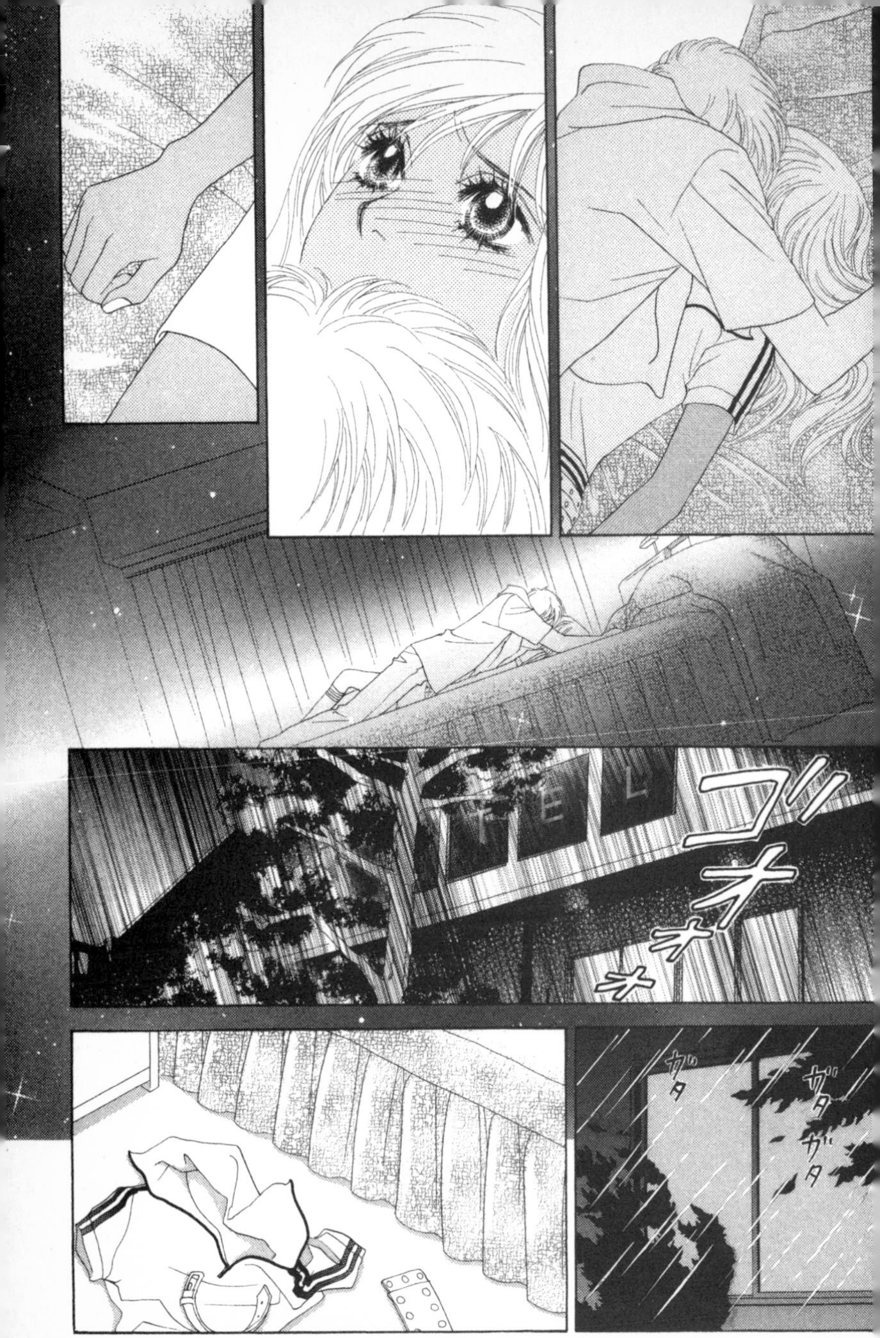
コオオオ
ガタ
ガタ
ガタ

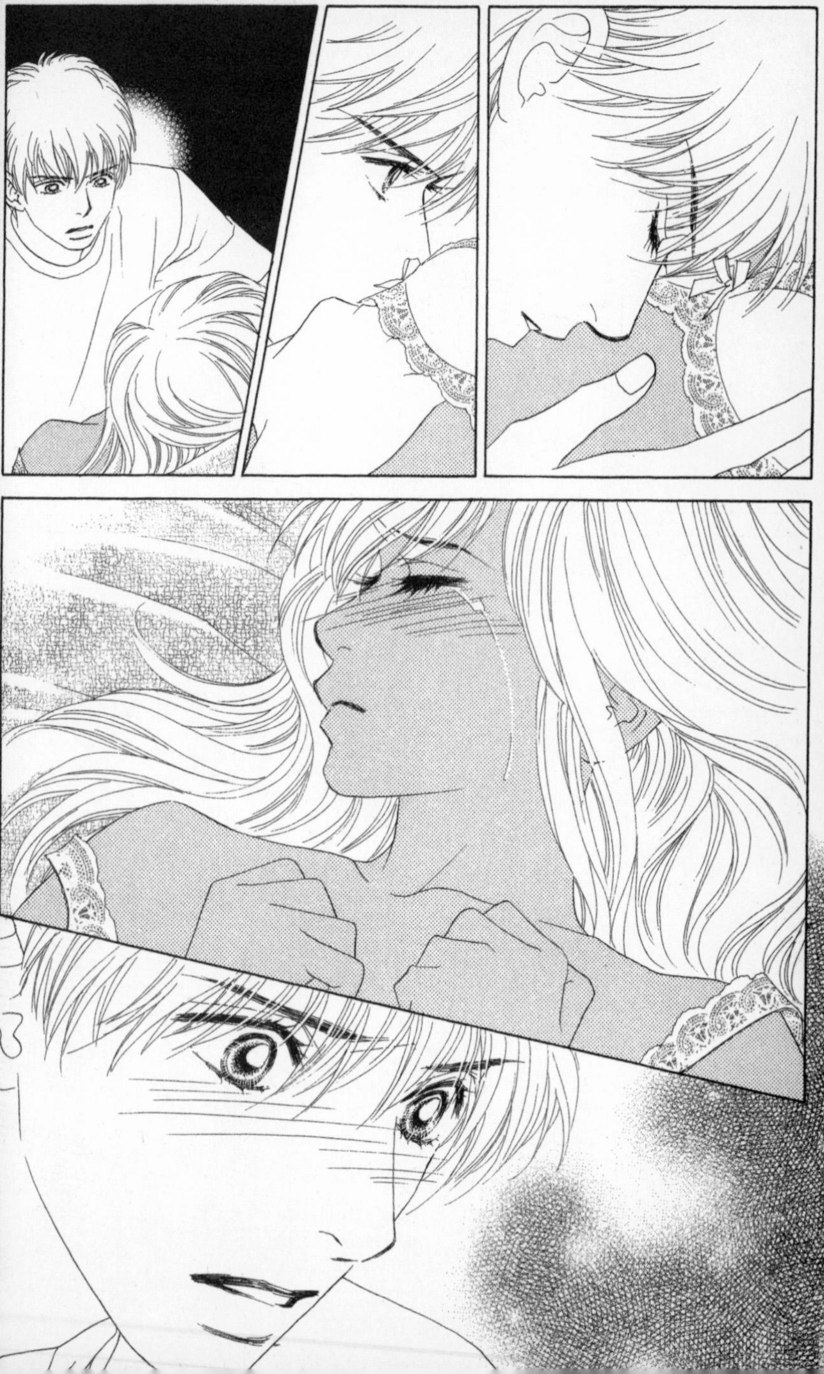

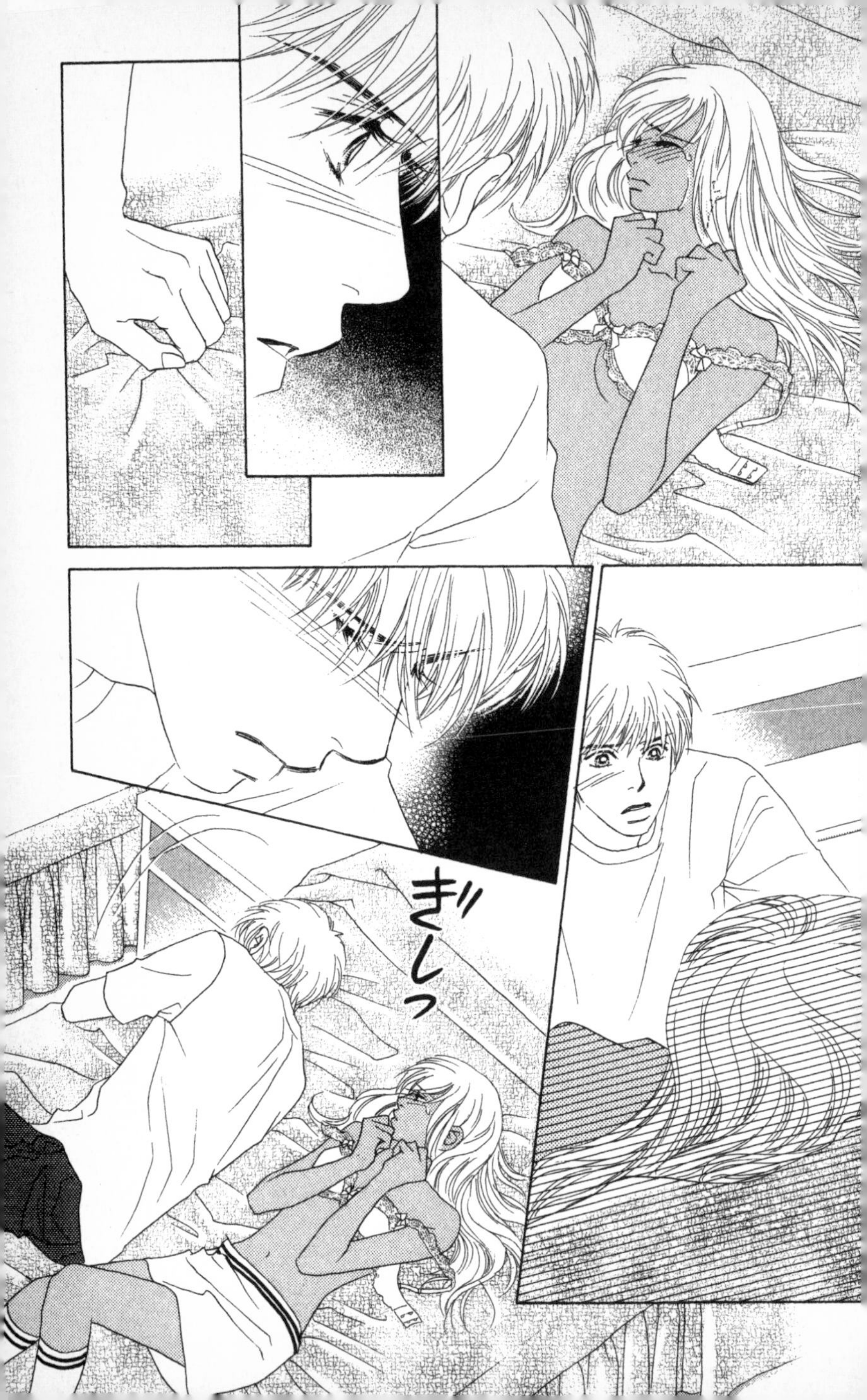
ぎしっ

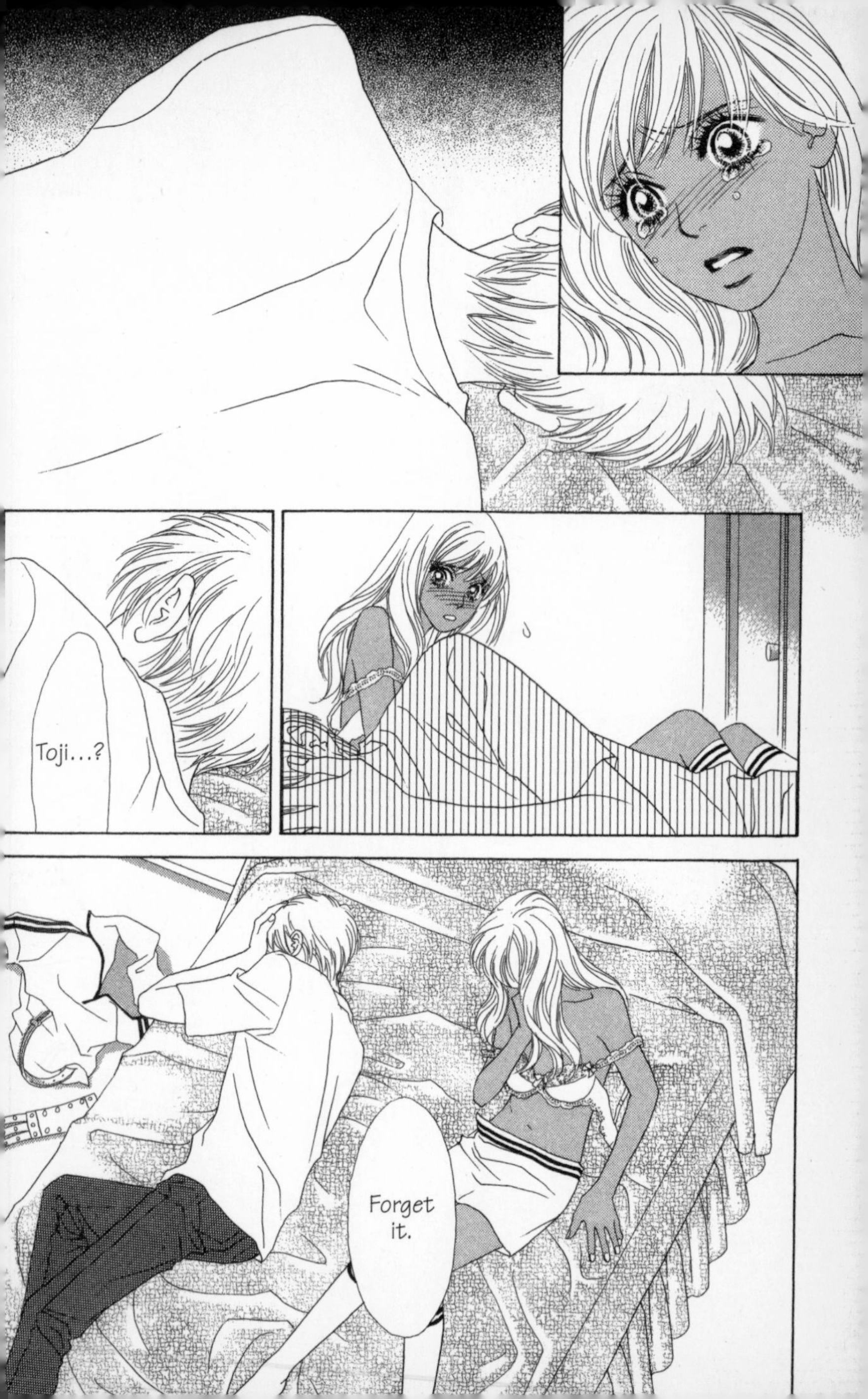
Toji...?
Forget it.

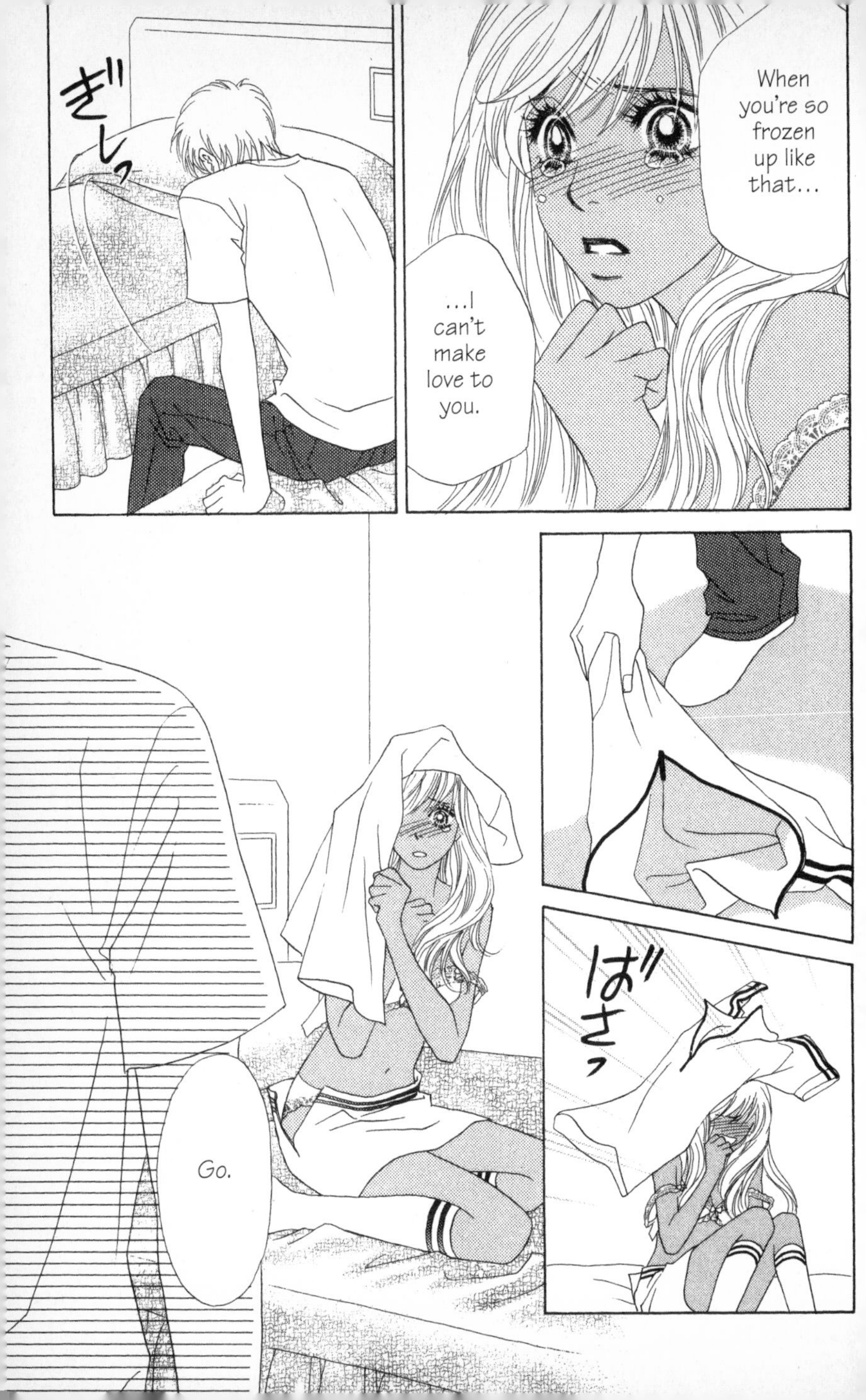
When you're so frozen up like that…
…I can't make love to you.
ぎしっ
ばさっ
Go.

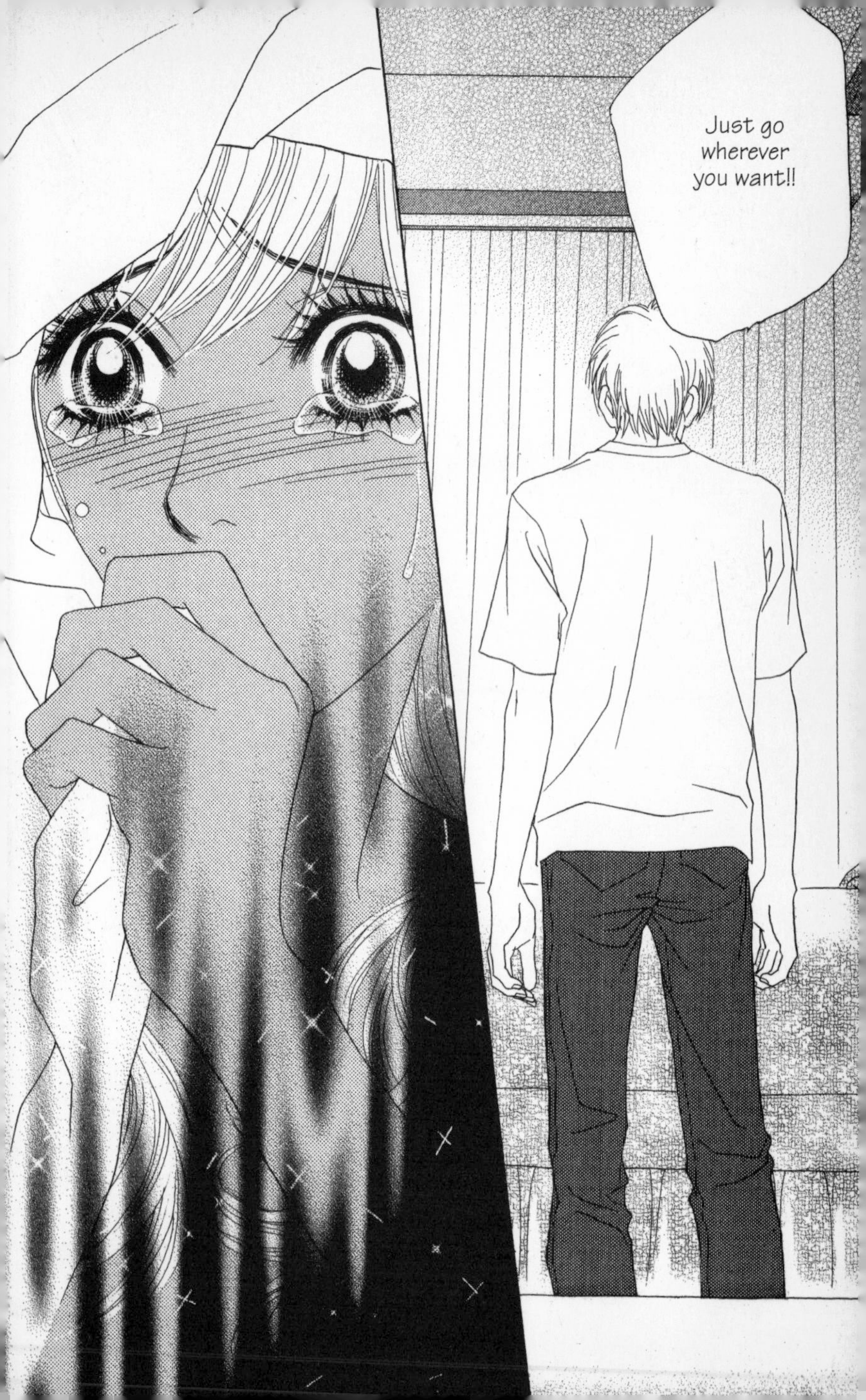
Just go wherever you want!!

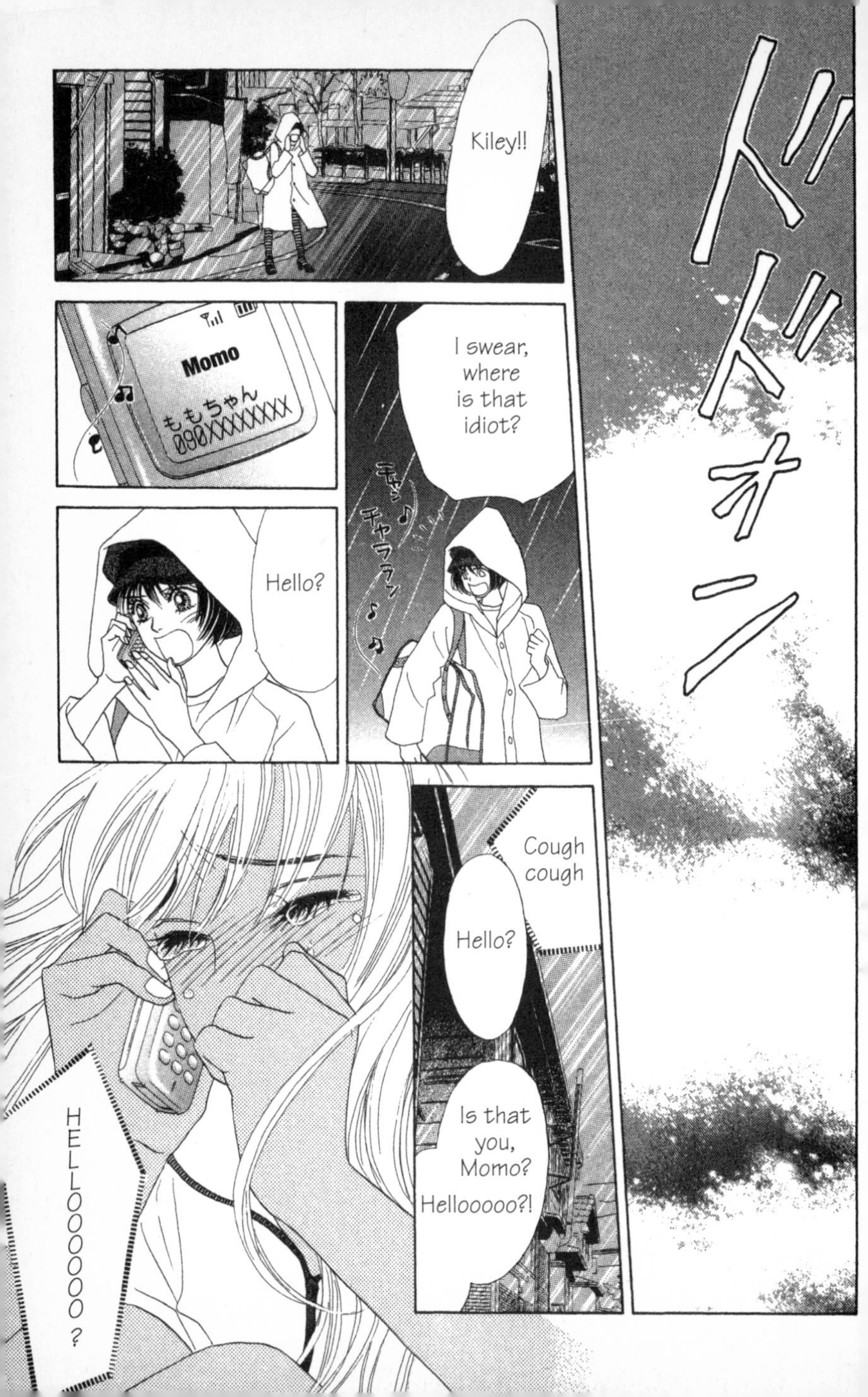
Kiley!!
I swear, where is that idiot?
Momo
ももちゃん
090XXXXXXXX
Hello?
Cough cough
Hello?
Is that you, Momo?
Hellooooo?!
HELLOOOOOOO?

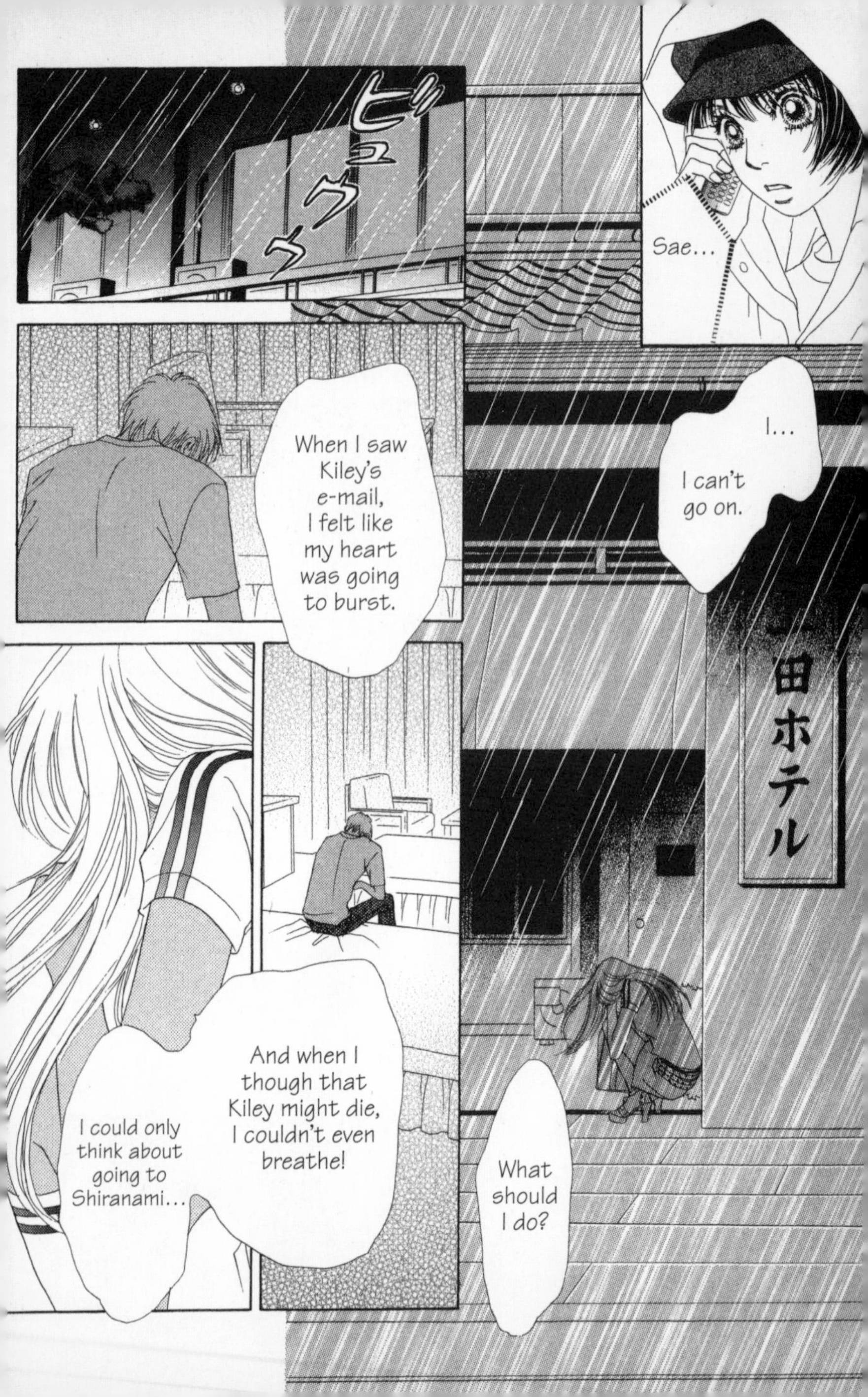
Sae…
I…
I can't go on.
田ホテル
What should I do?
ビュウウ
When I saw Kiley's e-mail, I felt like my heart was going to burst.
And when I though that Kiley might die, I couldn't even breathe!
I could only think about going to Shiranami…

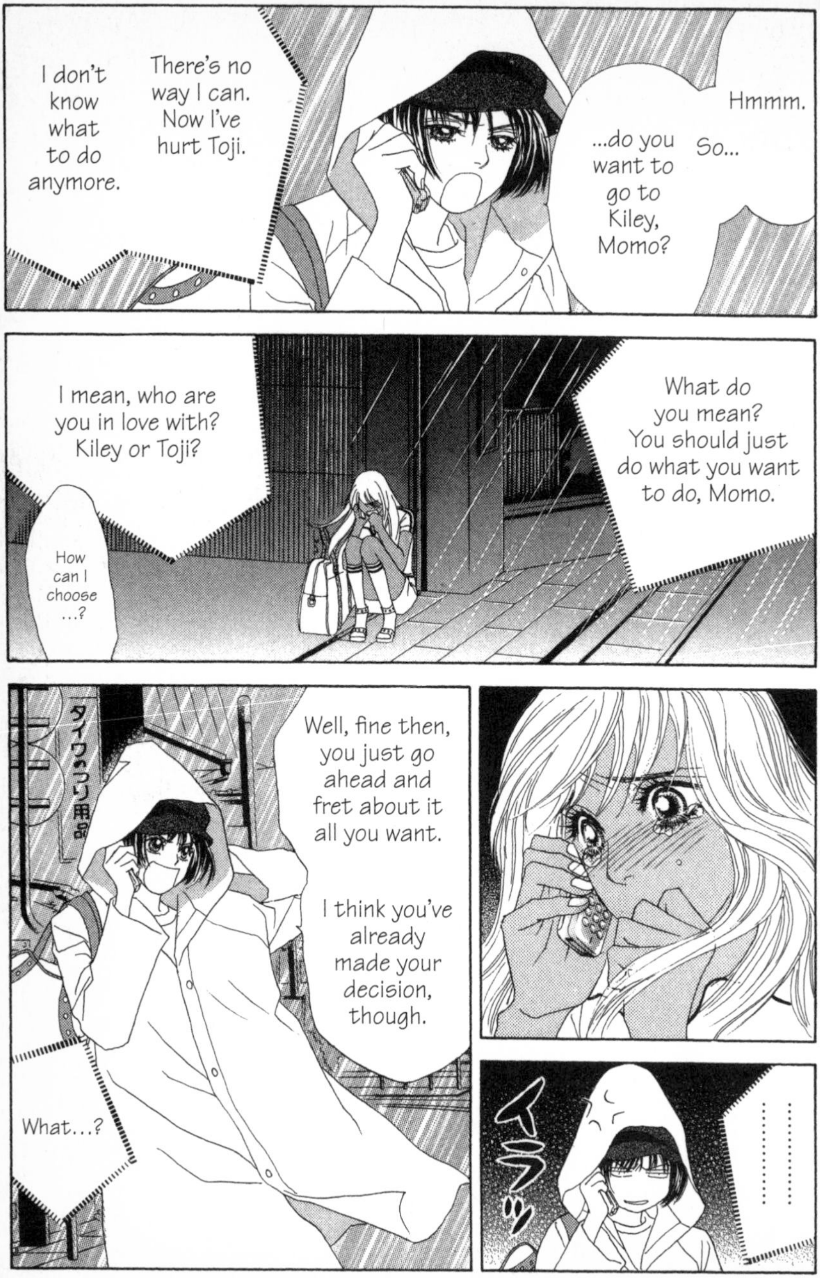
Hmmm.
So...
...do you want to go to Kiley, Momo?
There's no way I can. Now I've hurt Toji.
I don't know what to do anymore.
What do you mean? You should just do what you want to do, Momo.
I mean, who are you in love with? Kiley or Toji?
How can I choose ...?
イラッ
......
Well, fine then, you just go ahead and fret about it all you want.
I think you've already made your decision, though.
タイワのつり用品
What...?

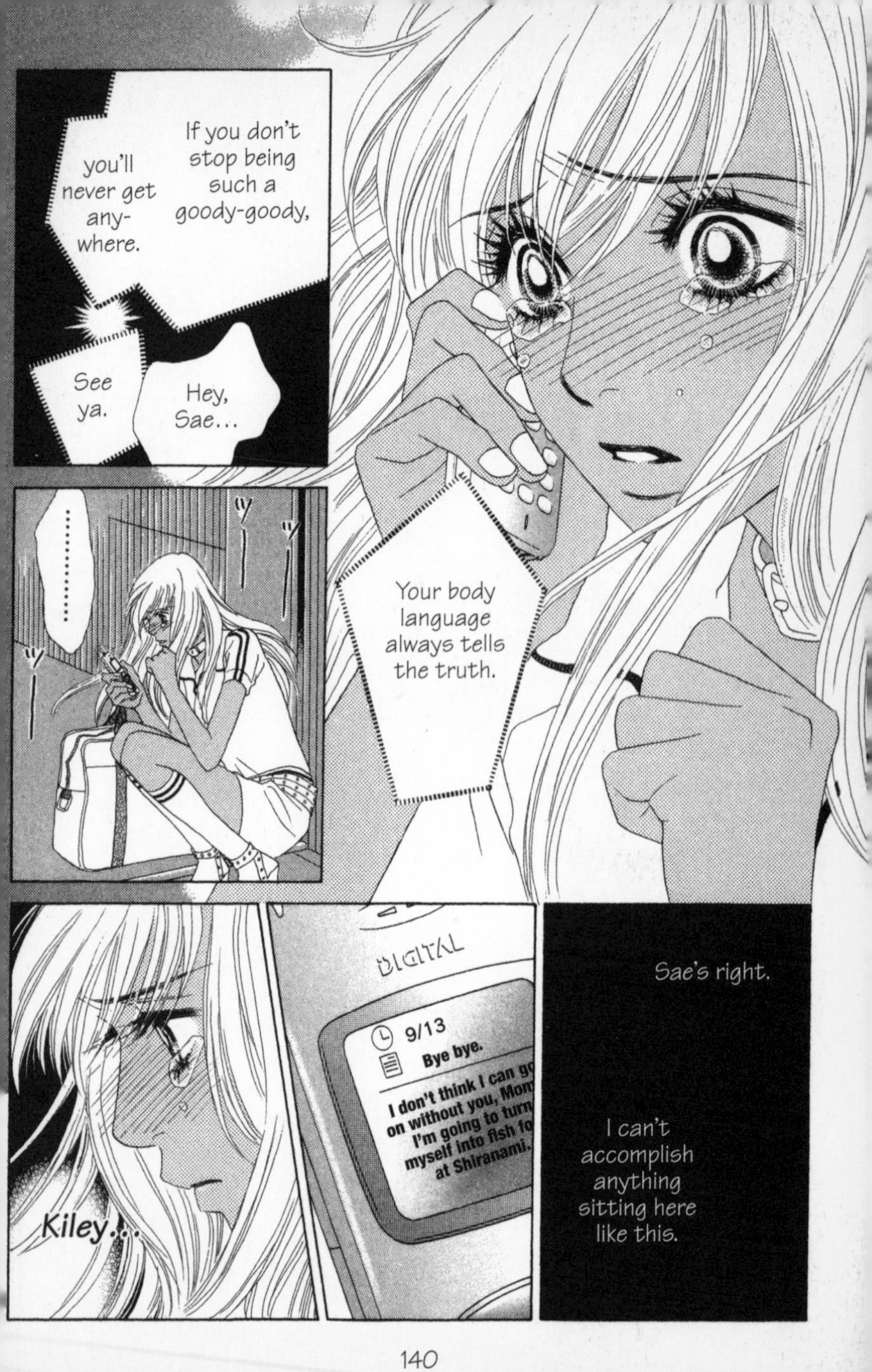
Your body language always tells the truth.
If you don't stop being such a goody-goody,
you'll never get anywhere.
Hey, Sae...
See ya.
......
Sae's right.
I can't accomplish anything sitting here like this.
DIGITAL
9/13
Bye bye.
I don't think I can go on without you, Mom. I'm going to turn myself into fish food at Shiranami.
Kiley...

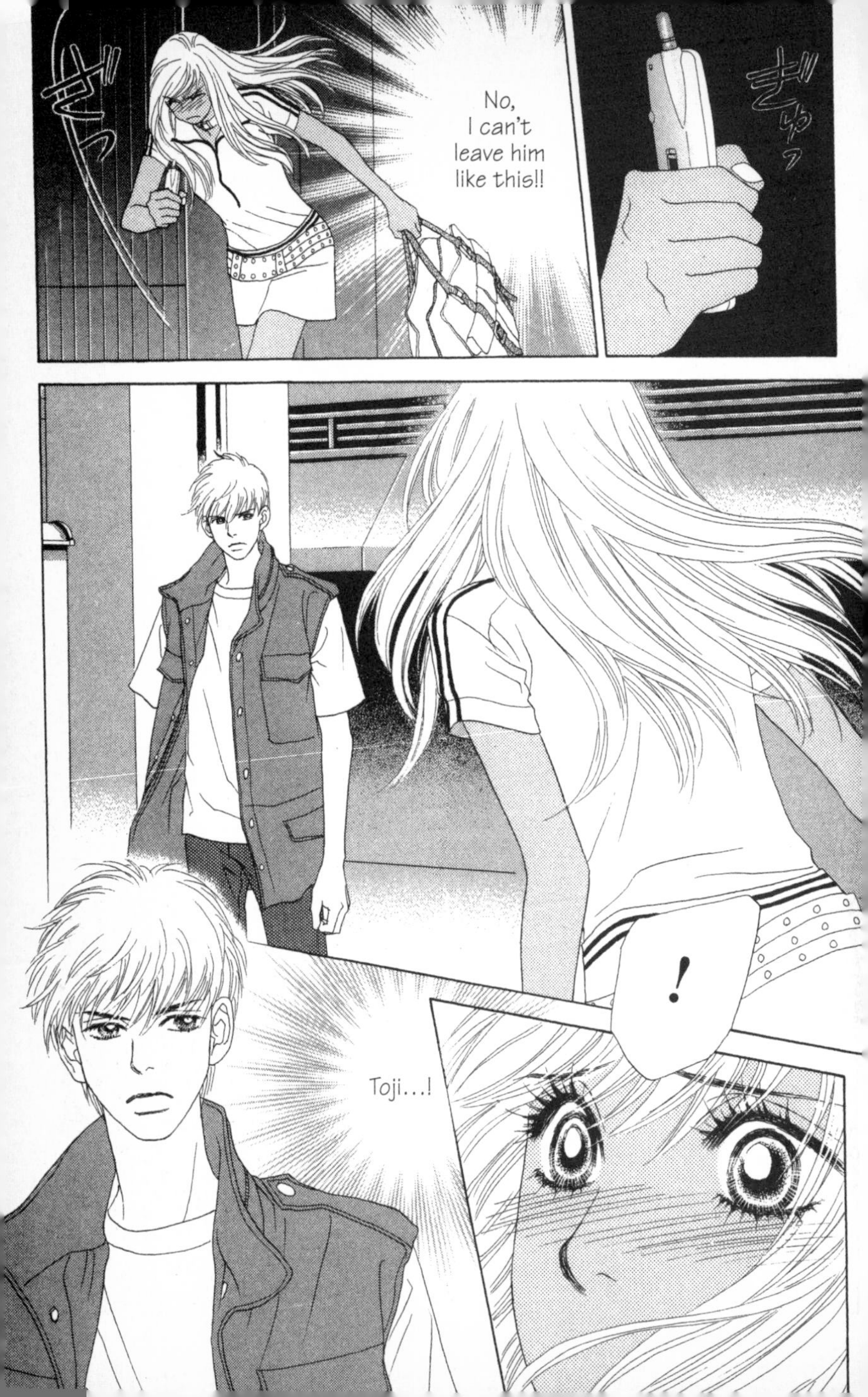
ぎゅっ
ざっ
No, I can't leave him like this!!
!
Toji…!

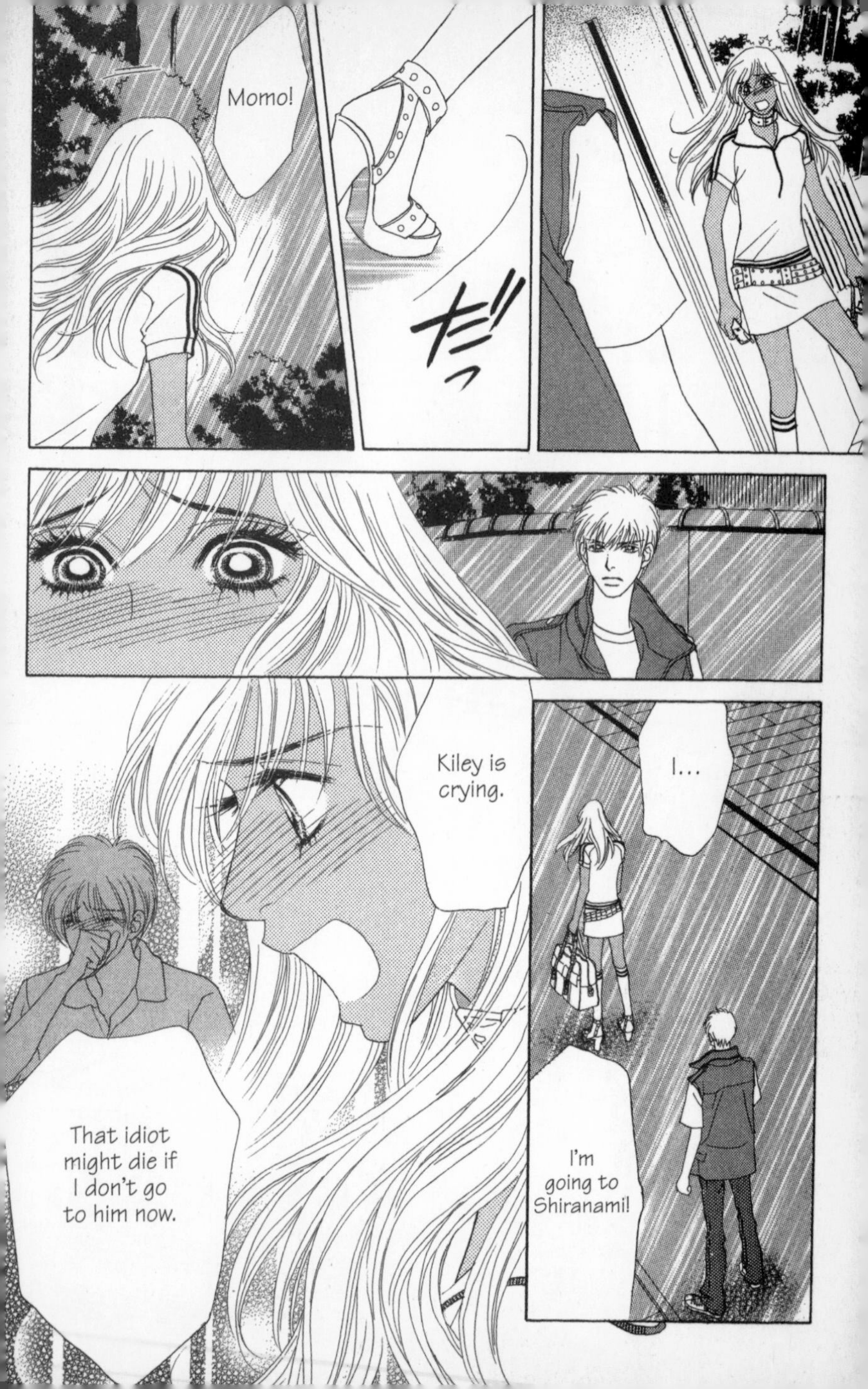

だっ
Momo!
I...
I'm going to Shiranami!
Kiley is crying.
That idiot might die if I don't go to him now.

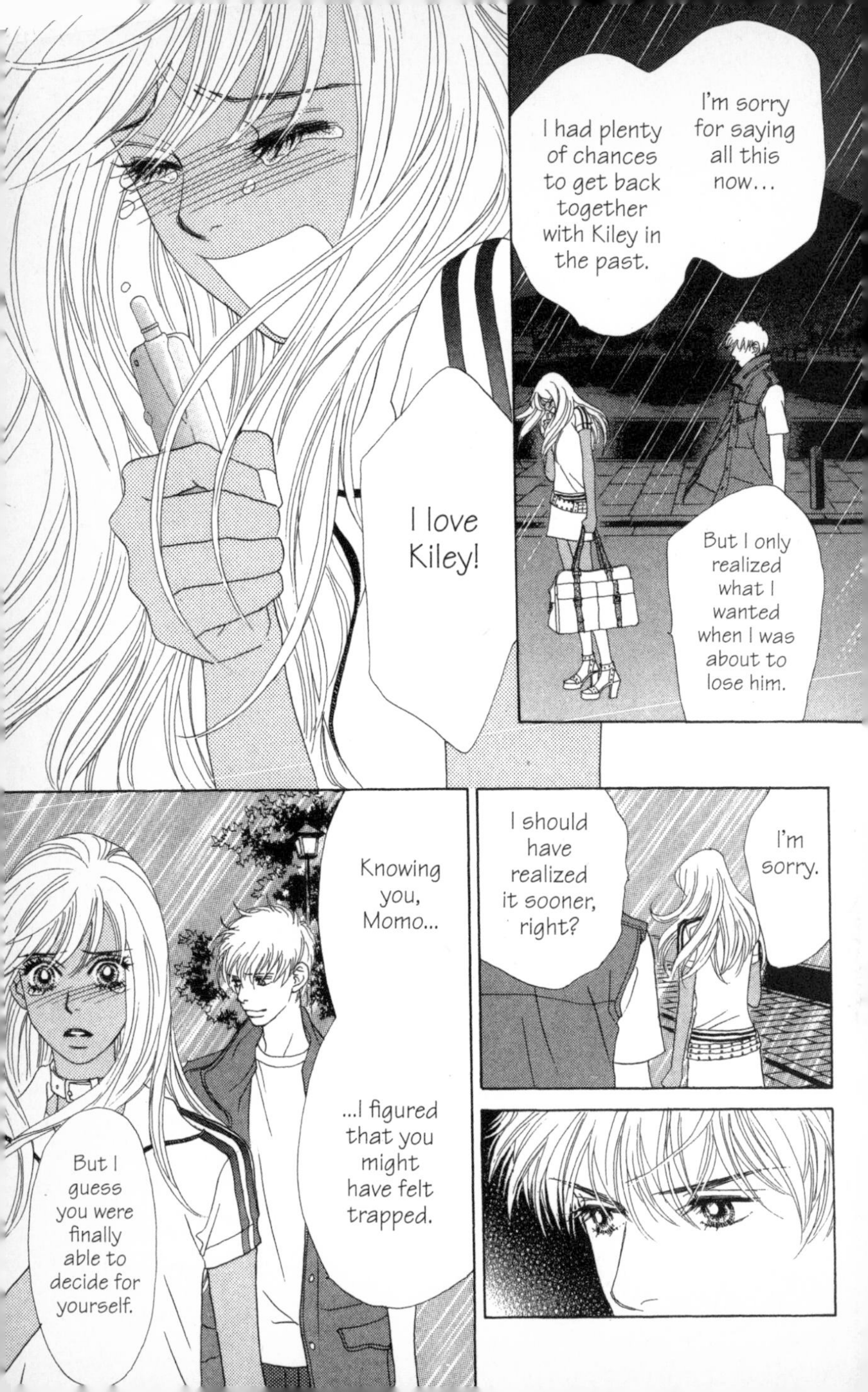
I'm sorry for saying all this now…
I had plenty of chances to get back together with Kiley in the past.
But I only realized what I wanted when I was about to lose him.
I love Kiley!
I'm sorry.
I should have realized it sooner, right?
Knowing you, Momo...
...I figured that you might have felt trapped.
But I guess you were finally able to decide for yourself.

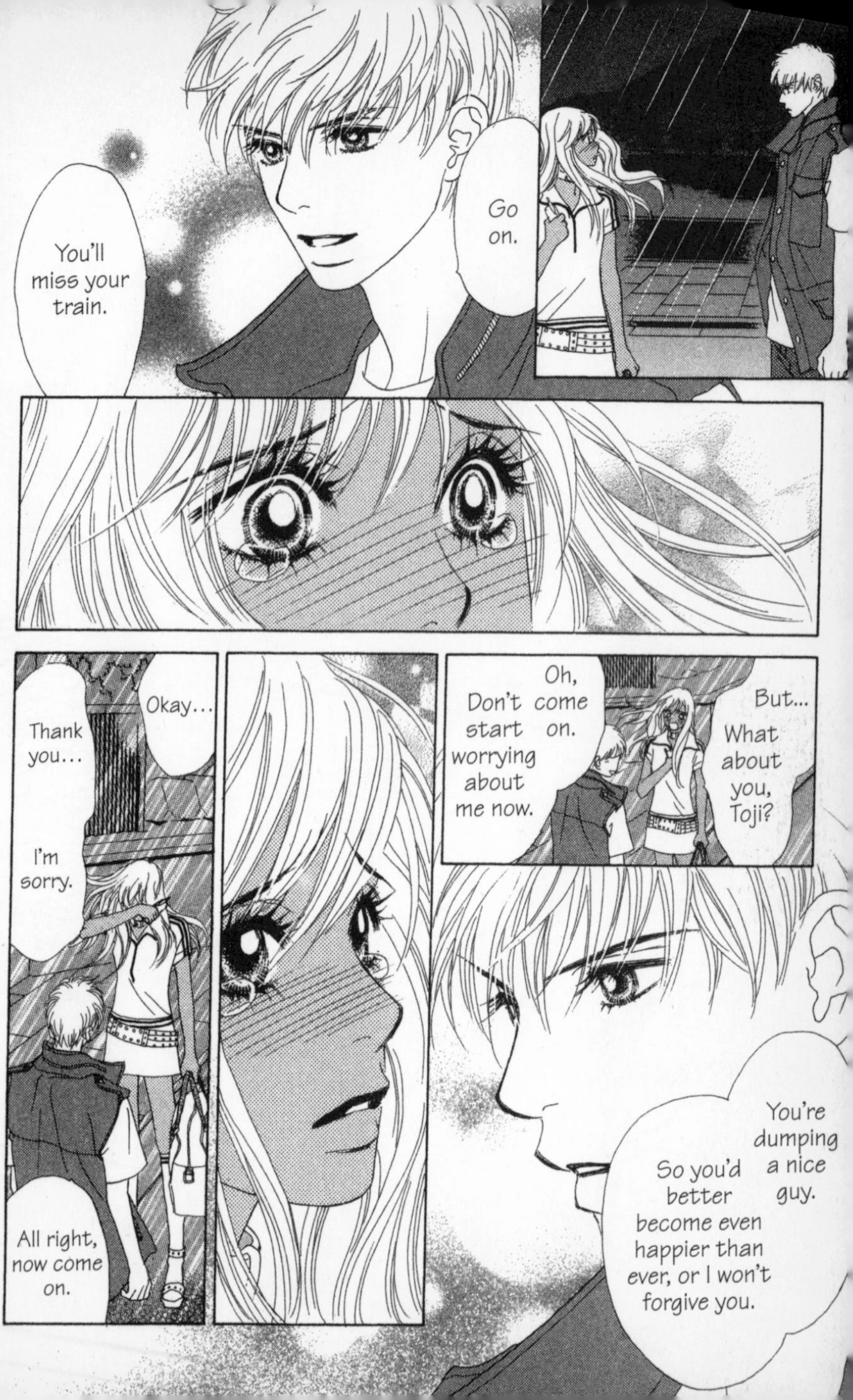
Go on.
You'll miss your train.
But... What about you, Toji?
Oh, come on.
Don't start worrying about me now.
You're dumping a nice guy.
So you'd better become even happier than ever, or I won't forgive you.
Okay...
Thank you...
I'm sorry.
All right, now come on.

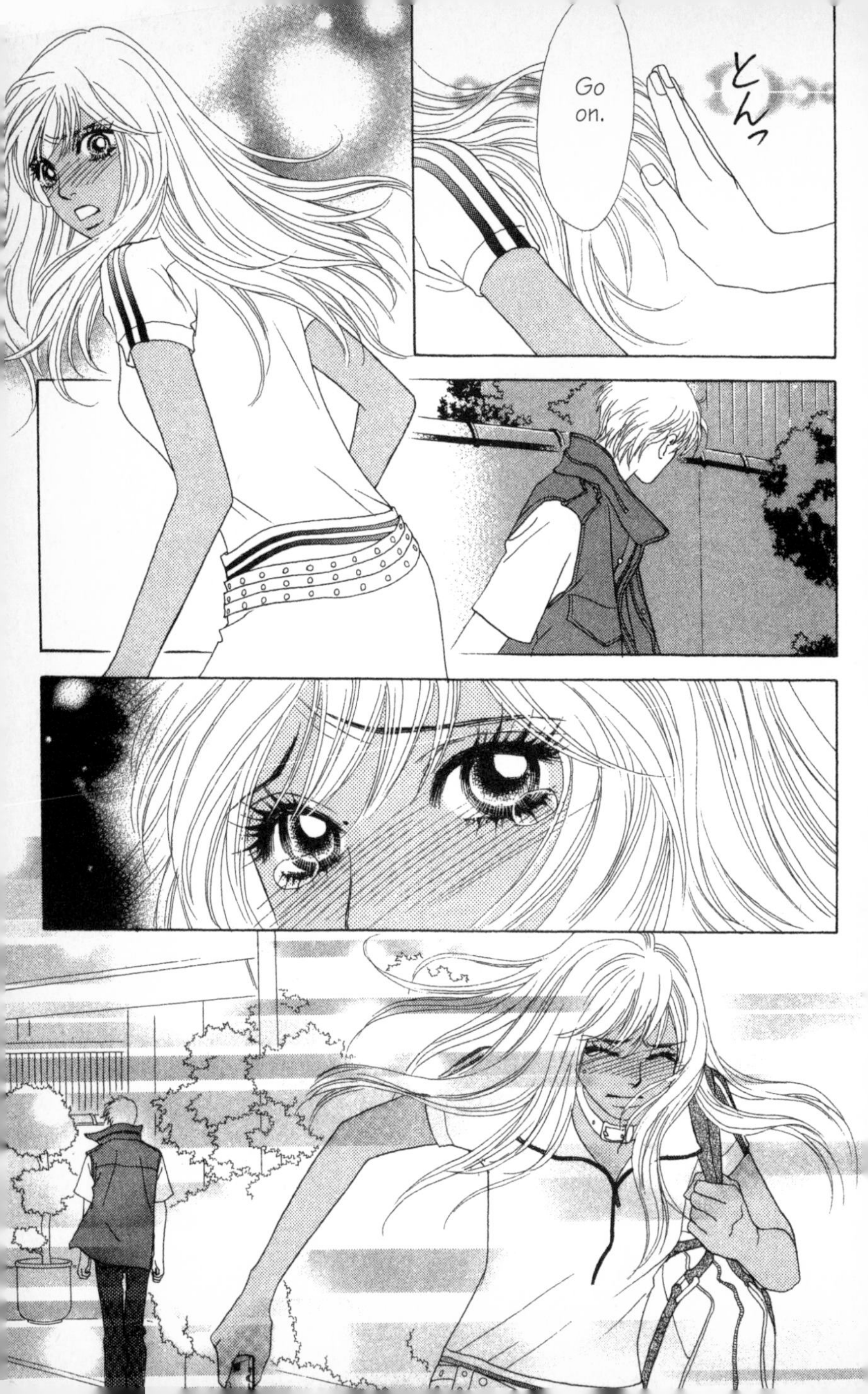
とんっ
Go on.

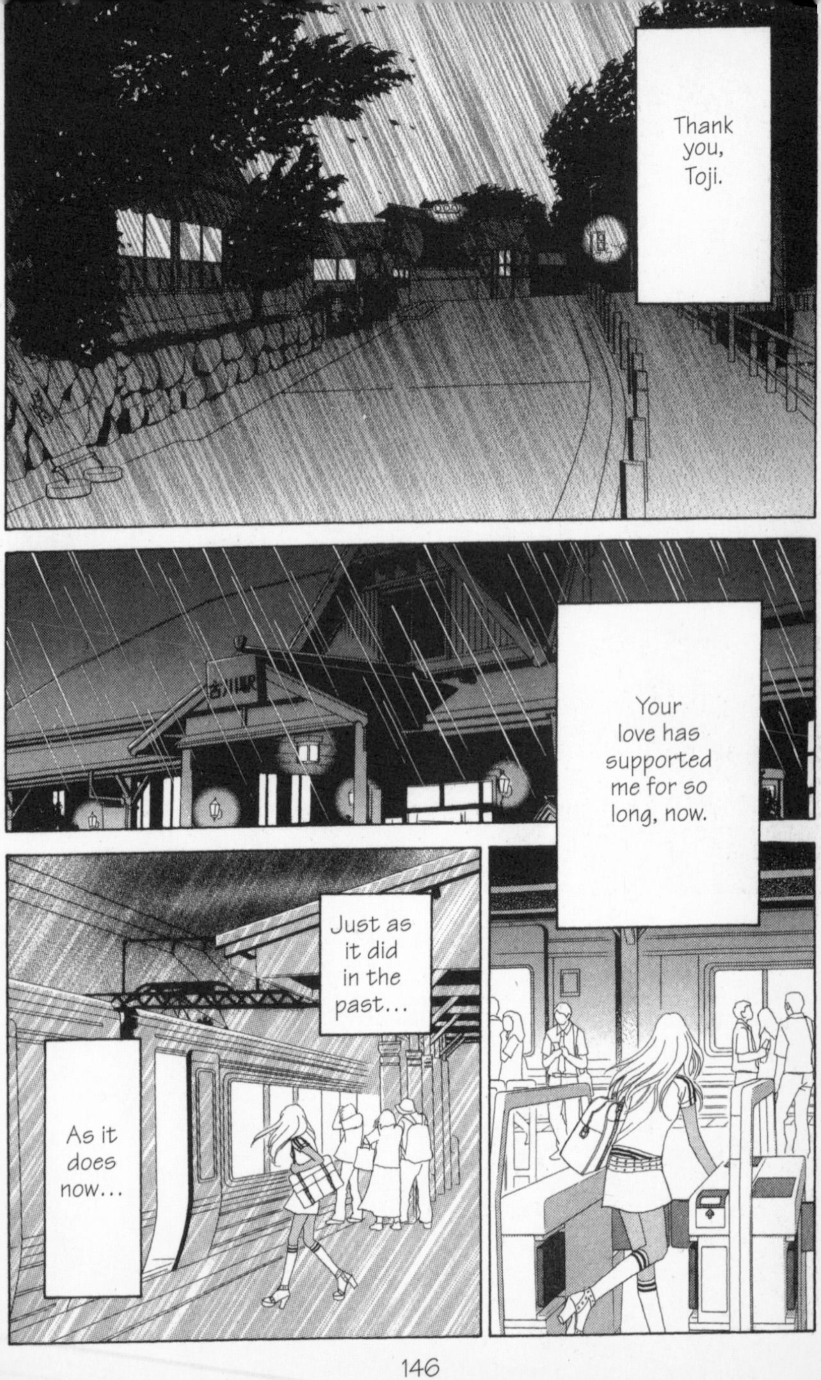
Thank you, Toji.
Your love has supported me for so long, now.
Just as it did in the past...
As it does now...

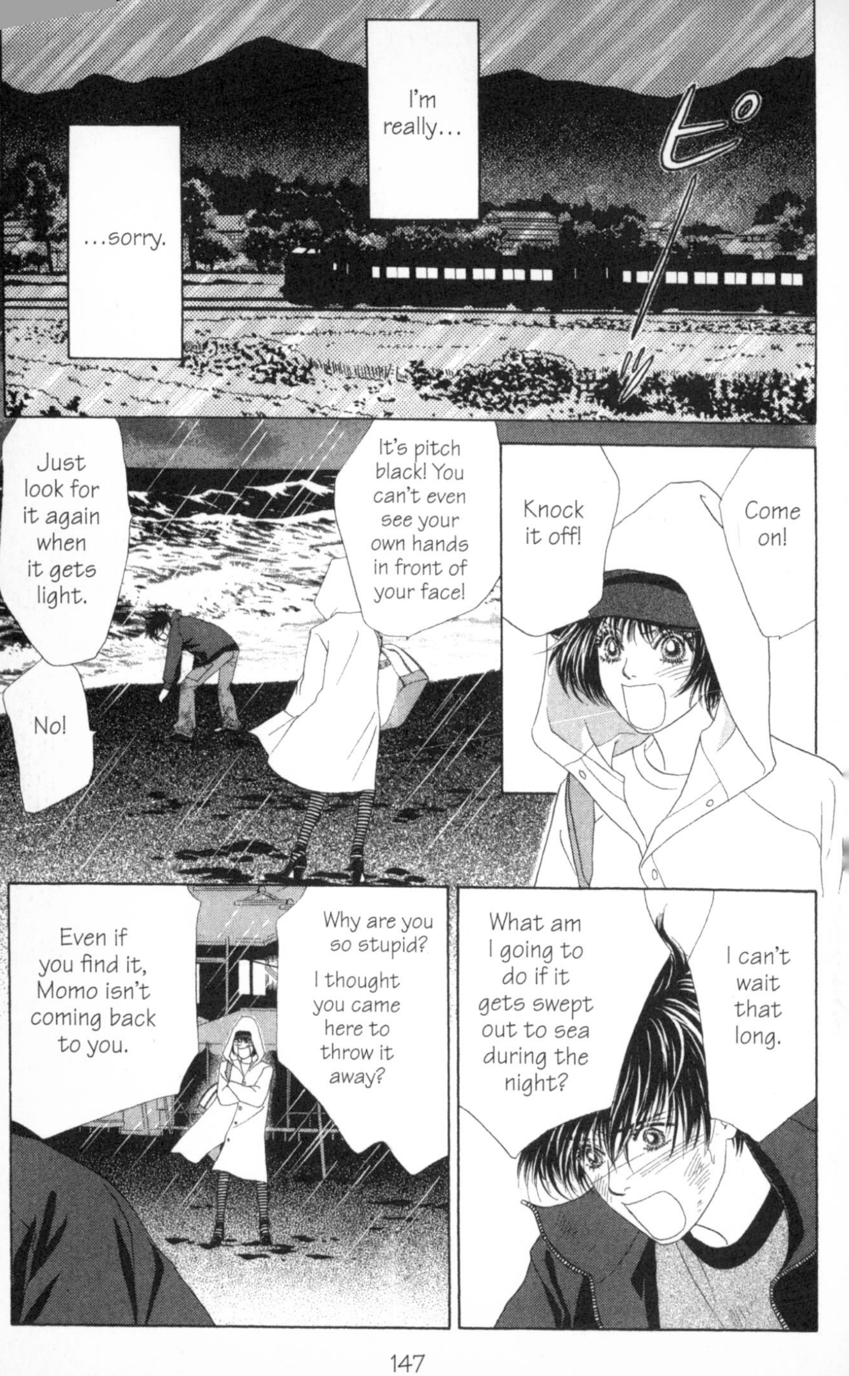
I'm really...
...sorry.
Come on!
Knock it off!
It's pitch black! You can't even see your own hands in front of your face!
Just look for it again when it gets light.
No!
I can't wait that long.
What am I going to do if it gets swept out to sea during the night?
Why are you so stupid?
I thought you came here to throw it away?
Even if you find it, Momo isn't coming back to you.

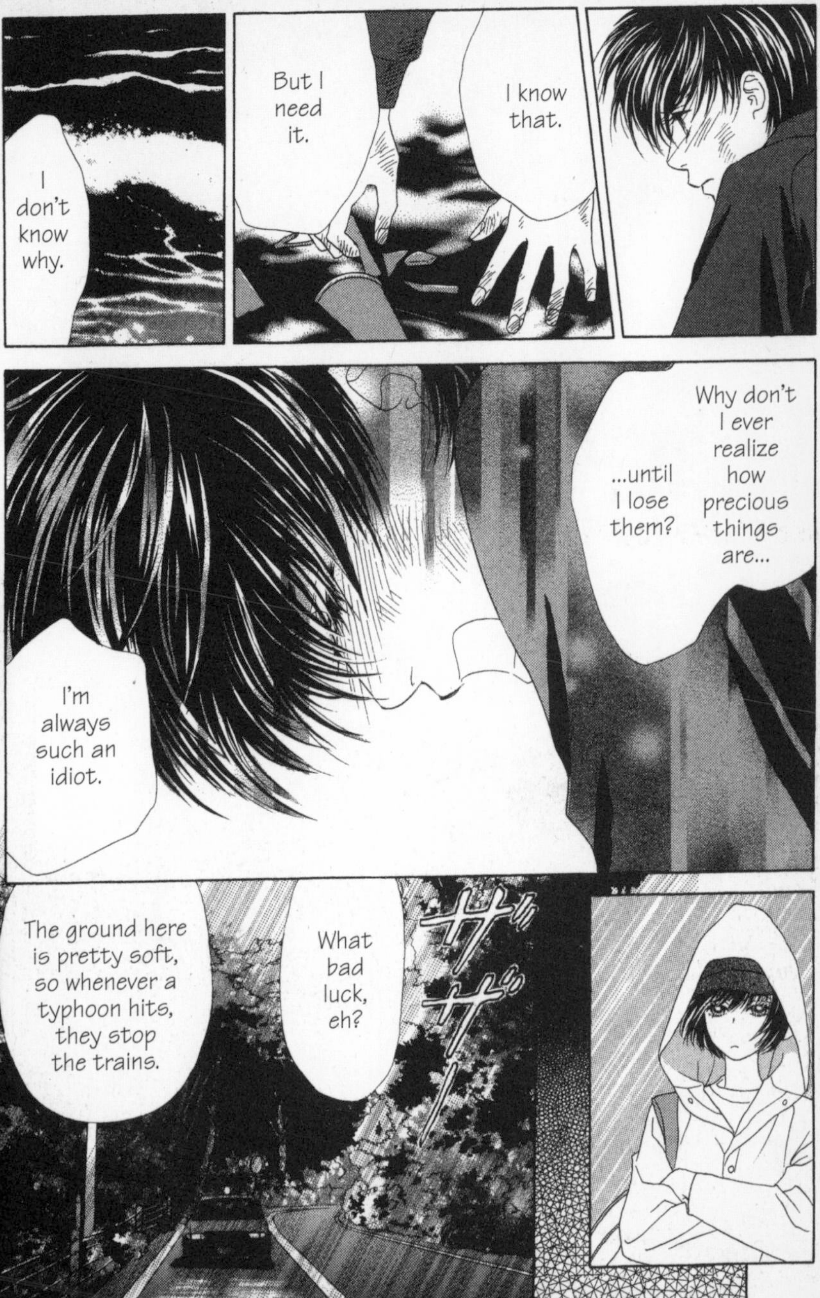
I know that.
But I need it.
I don't know why.
Why don't I ever realize how precious things are...
...until I lose them?
I'm always such an idiot.
ザザー
What bad luck, eh?
The ground here is pretty soft, so whenever a typhoon hits, they stop the trains.

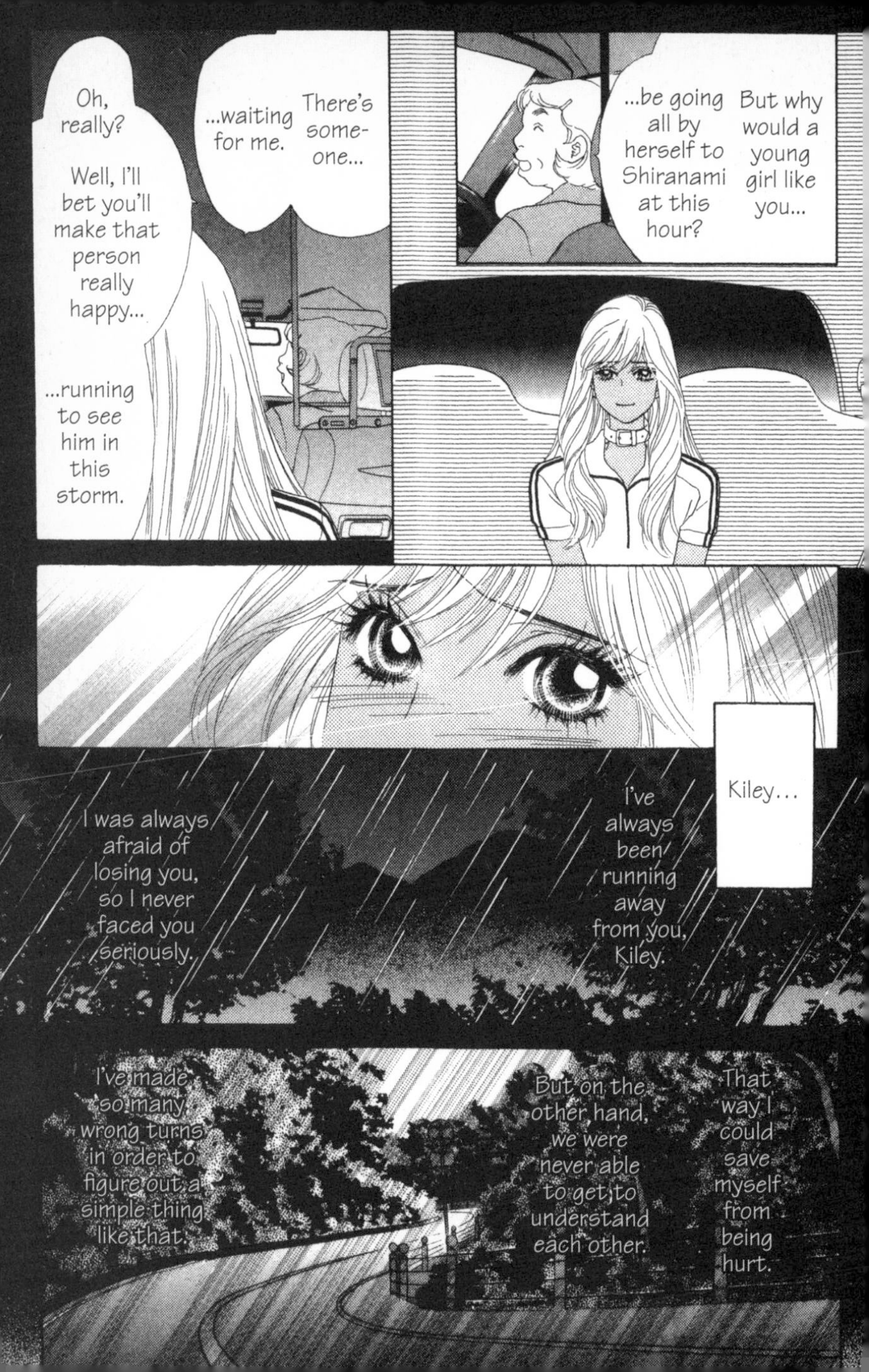
But why would a young girl like you...
...be going all by herself to Shiranami at this hour?
There's some-one...
...waiting for me.
Oh, really?
Well, I'll bet you'll make that person really happy...
...running to see him in this storm.
Kiley...
I've always been running away from you, Kiley.
I was always afraid of losing you, so I never faced you seriously.
That way I could save myself from being hurt.
But on the other hand, we were never able to get to understand each other.
I've made so many wrong turns in order to figure out a simple thing like that.

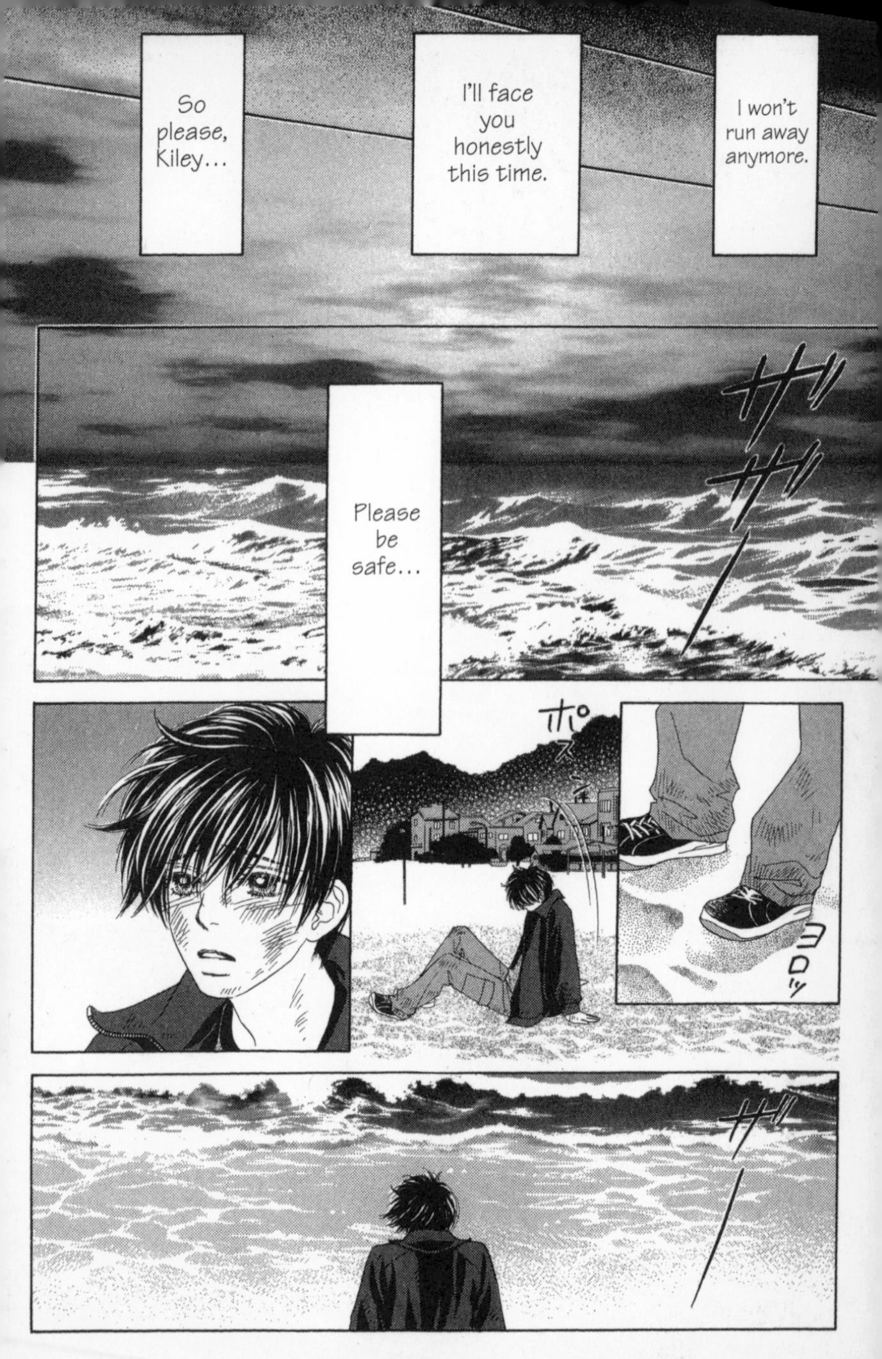
I won't run away anymore.
I'll face you honestly this time.
So please, Kiley...
ザザー
Please be safe...
コロッ
ポスン
ザー

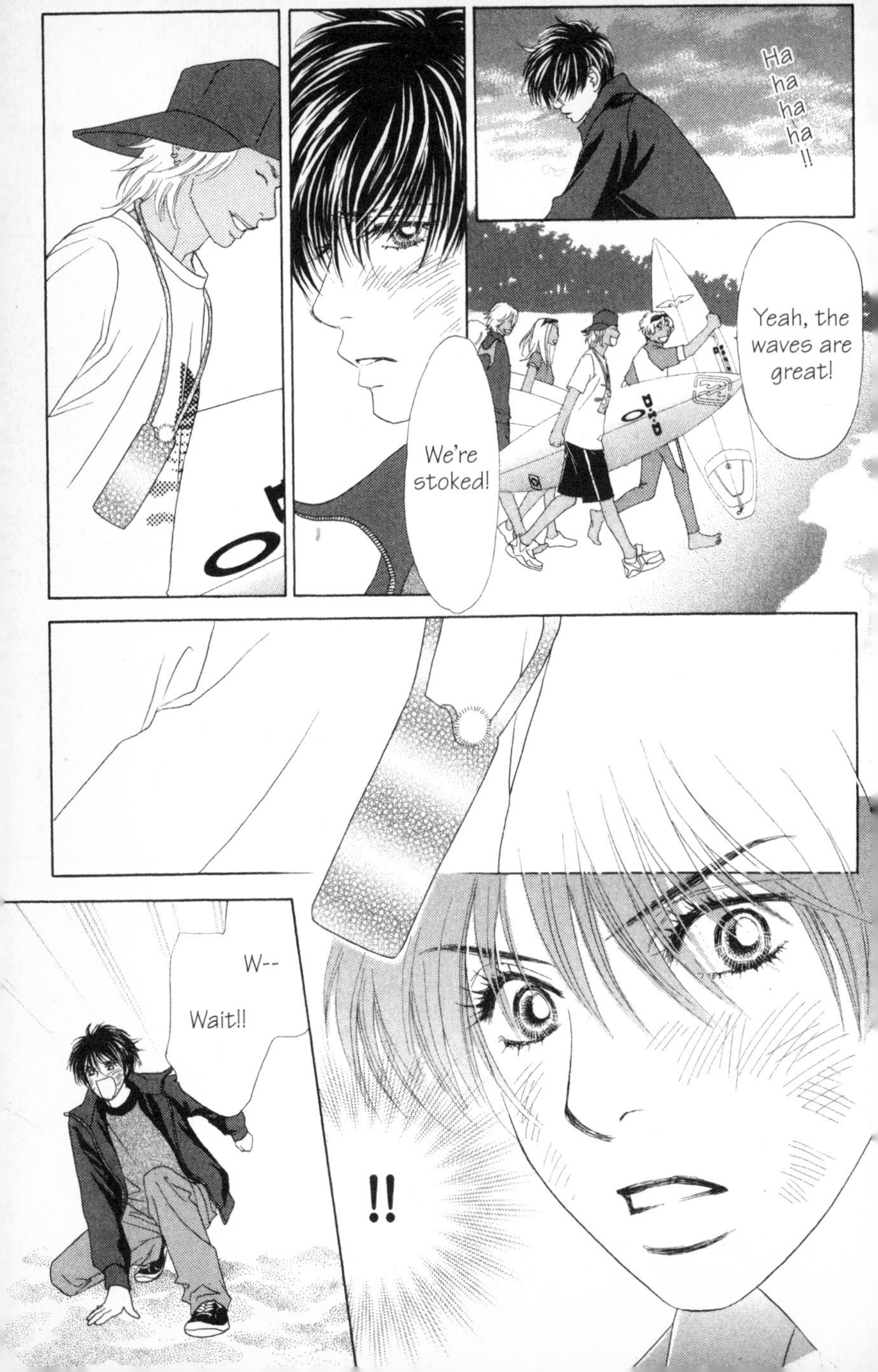
Ha ha ha ha !!
Yeah, the waves are great!
We're stoked!
!!
W--
Wait!!

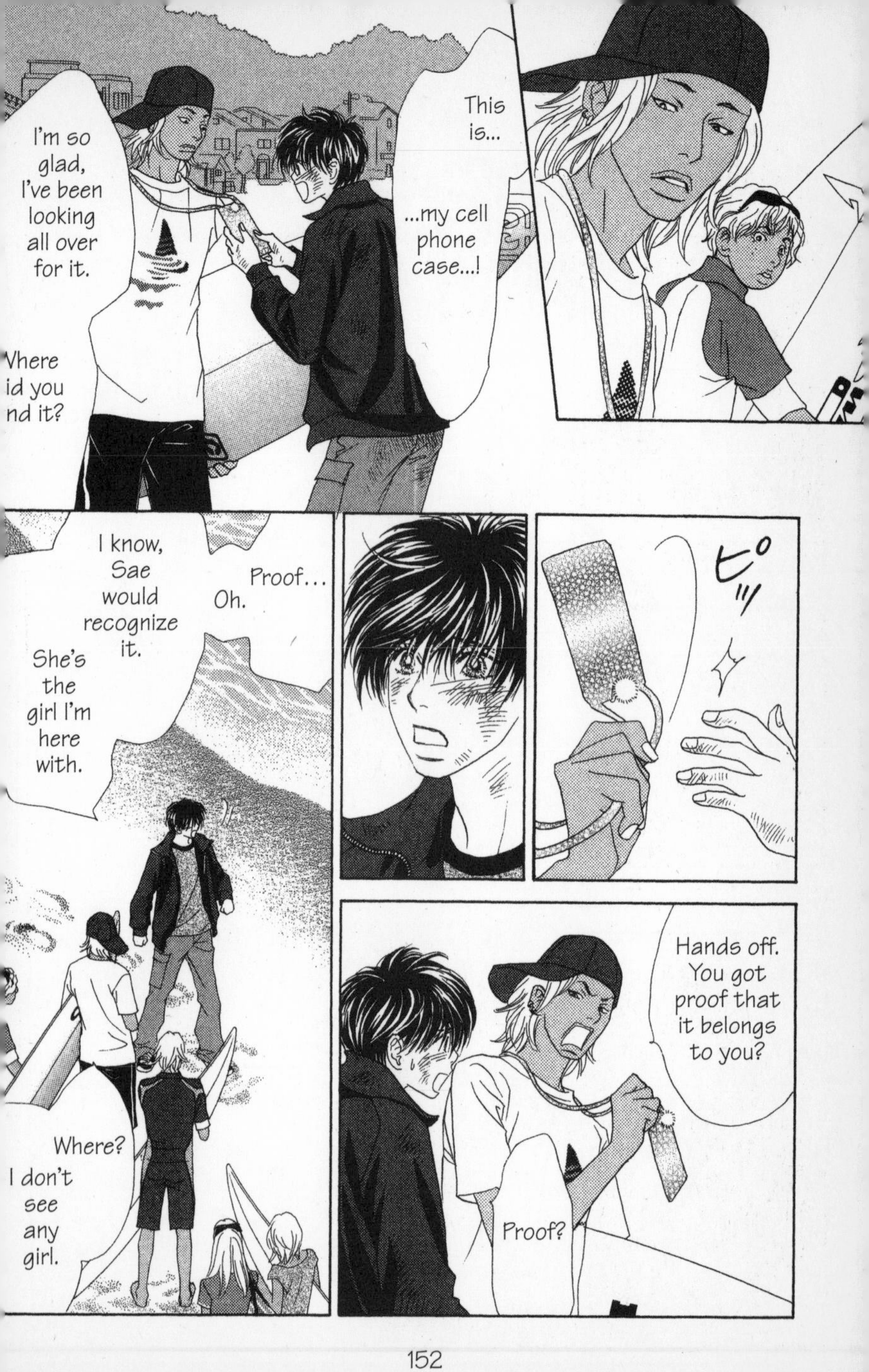
This is...
...my cell phone case...!
I'm so glad, I've been looking all over for it.
Vhere id you nd it?
ピッ
Hands off. You got proof that it belongs to you?
Proof?
Proof...
Oh.
I know, Sae would recognize it.
She's the girl I'm here with.
Where? I don't see any girl.

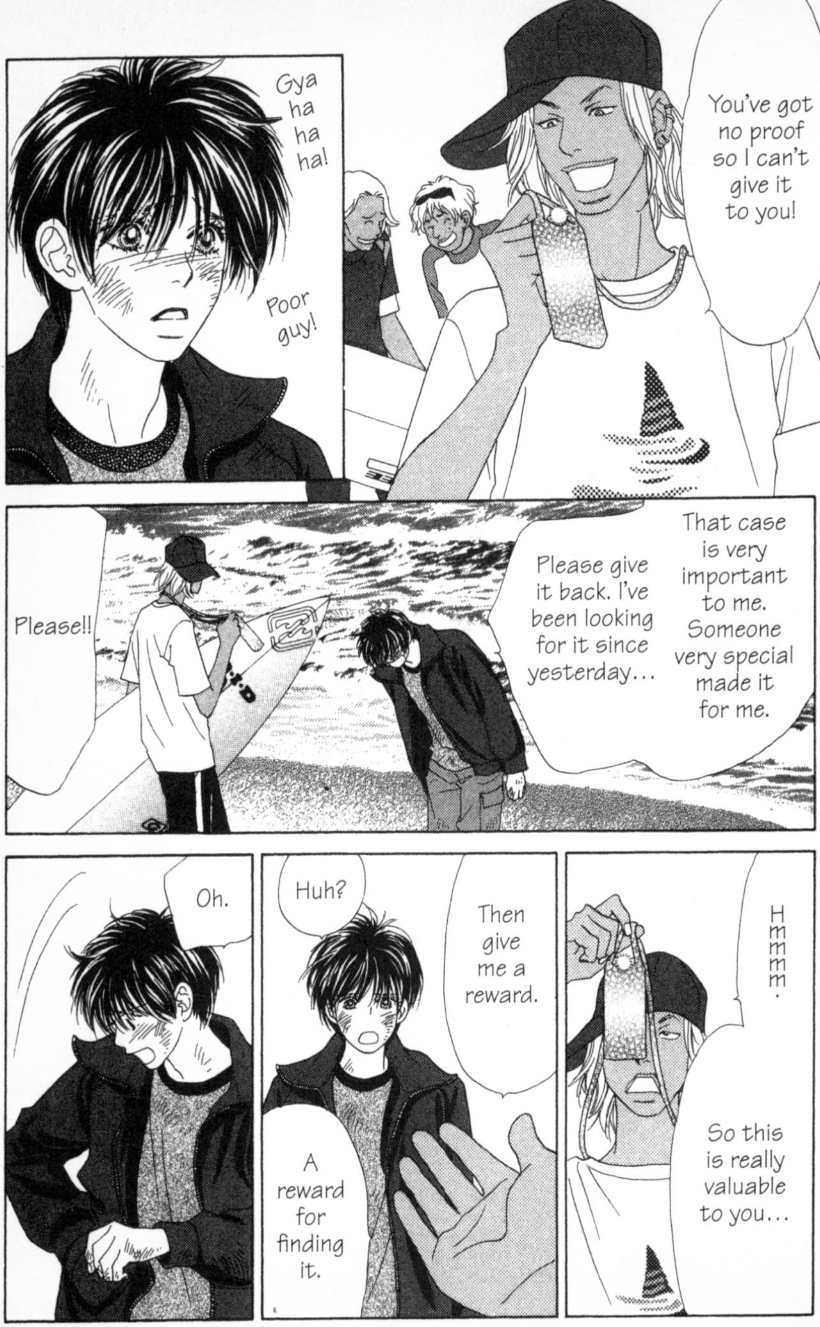
You've got no proof so I can't give it to you!
Gya ha ha ha!
Poor guy!
That case is very important to me. Someone very special made it for me.
Please give it back. I've been looking for it since yesterday…
Please!!
Hmmmm.
So this is really valuable to you…
Then give me a reward.
Huh?
A reward for finding it.
Oh.

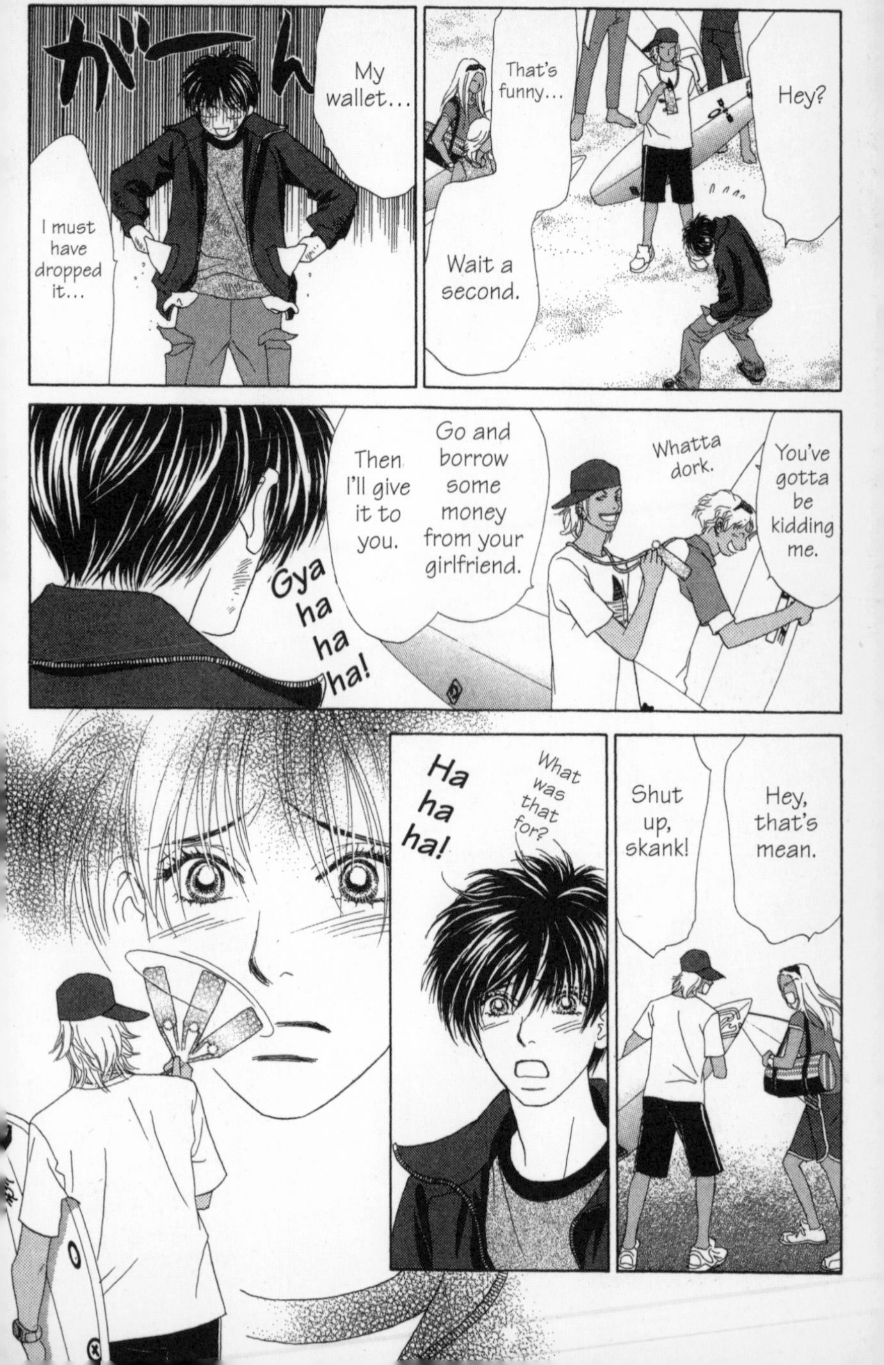
Hey?
That's funny…
Wait a second.
がーん
My wallet…
I must have dropped it…
You've gotta be kidding me.
Whatta dork.
Go and borrow some money from your girlfriend.
Then I'll give it to you.
Gya ha ha ha!
Hey, that's mean.
Shut up, skank!
What was that for?
Ha ha ha!

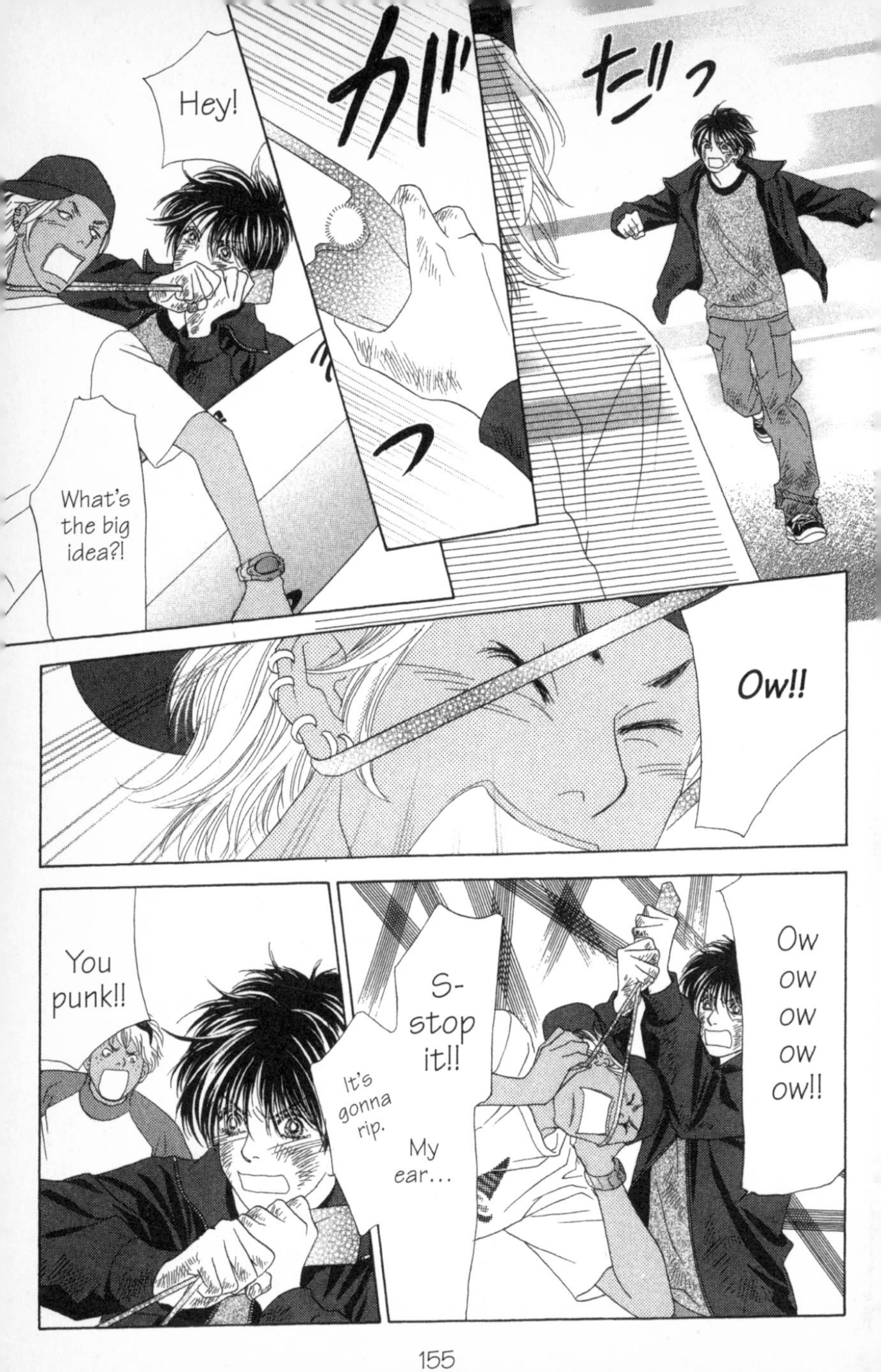
だっ
ガ
っ
Hey!
What's the big idea?!
Ow!!
Ow ow ow ow ow!!
S- stop it!!
It's gonna rip.
My ear...
You punk!!

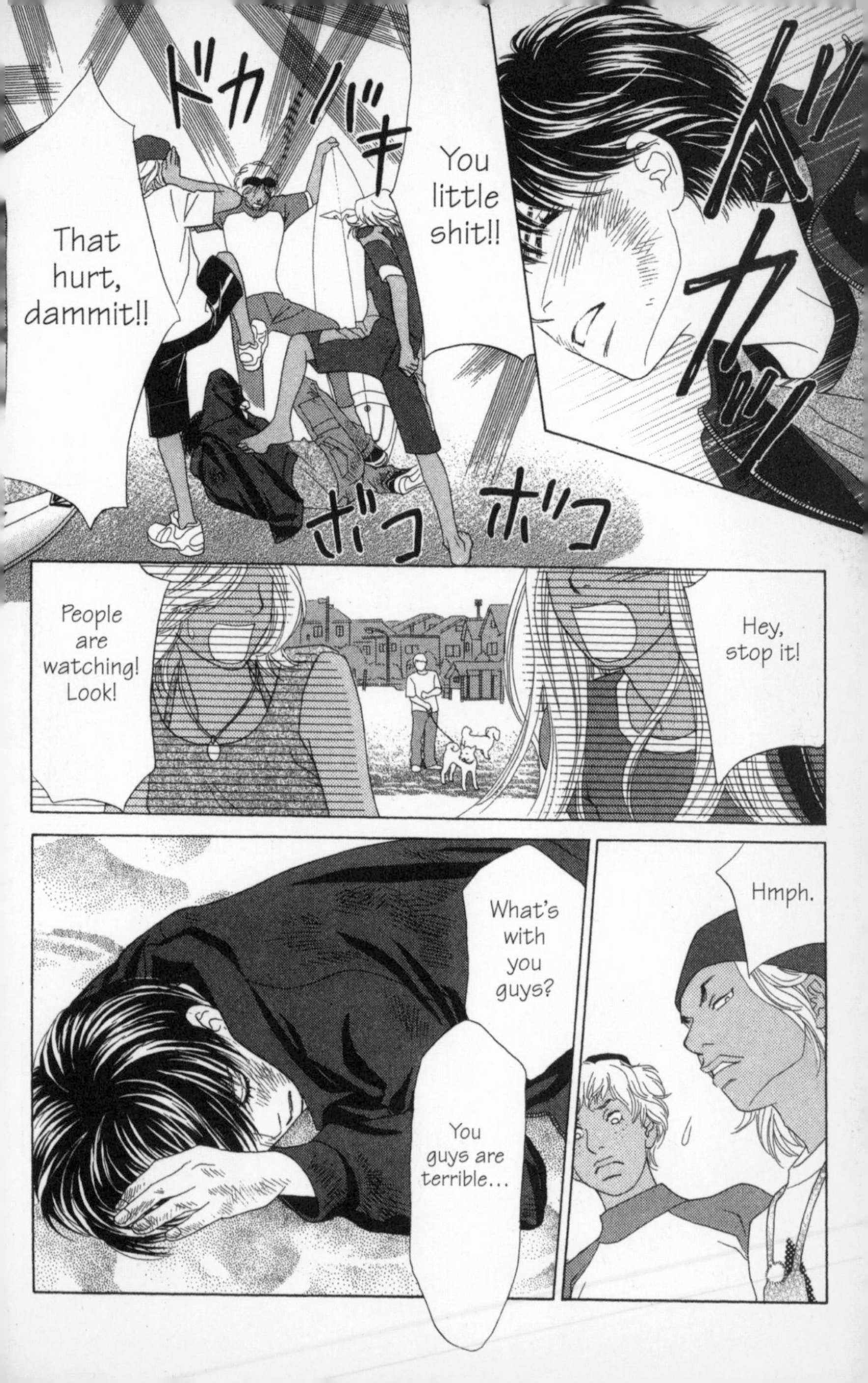
ドカッ
You little shit!!
That hurt, dammit!!
ドカ
バキ
ボコ ボコ
Hey, stop it!
People are watching! Look!
Hmph.
What's with you guys?
You guys are terrible...

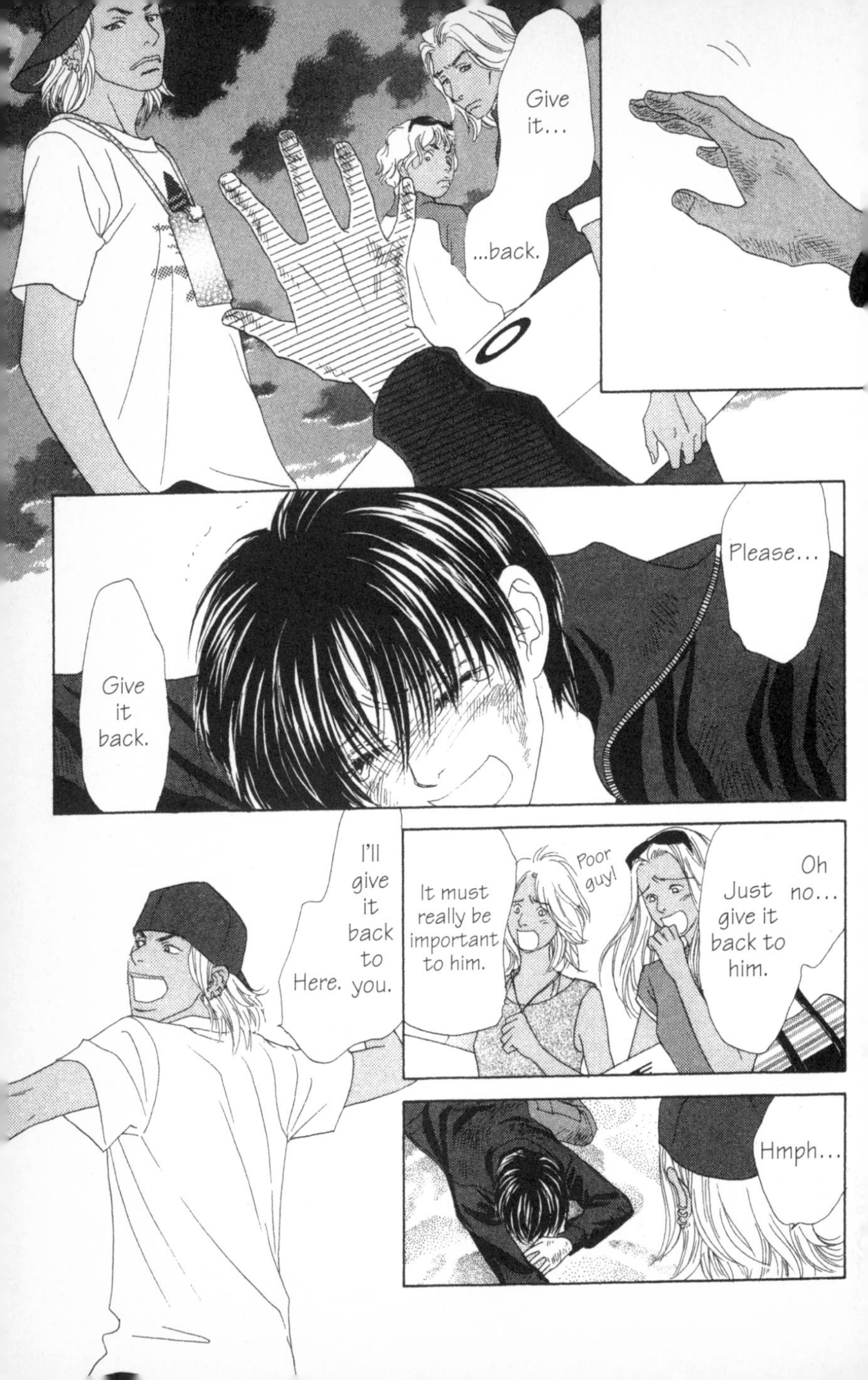
Give it…
...back.
Please…
Give it back.
Oh no… Just give it back to him.
Poor guy!
It must really be important to him.
Hmph…
I'll give it back to you.
Here.

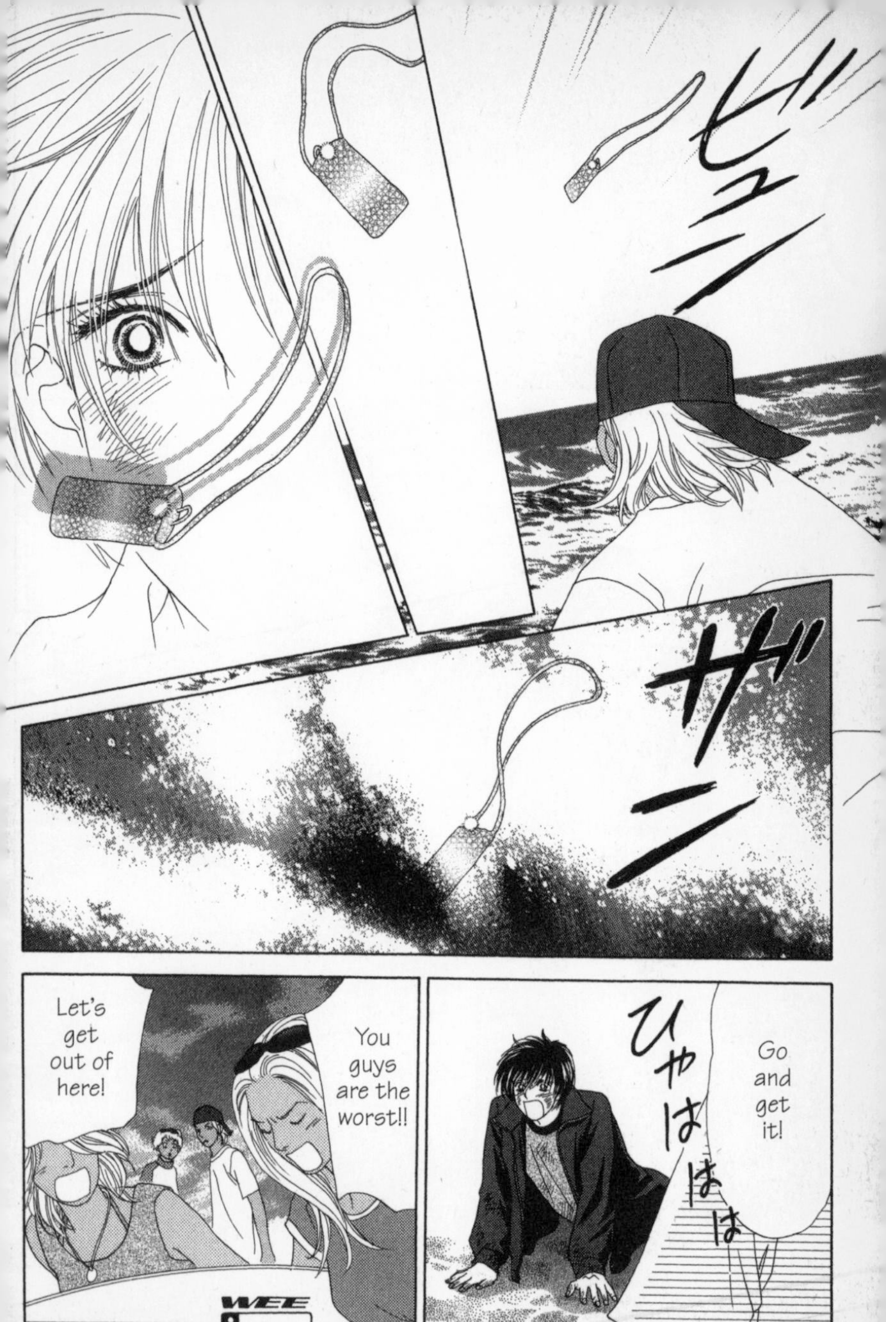

ビュン
ザン
Go and get it!
ひゃははは
You guys are the worst!!
Let's get out of here!
WEE

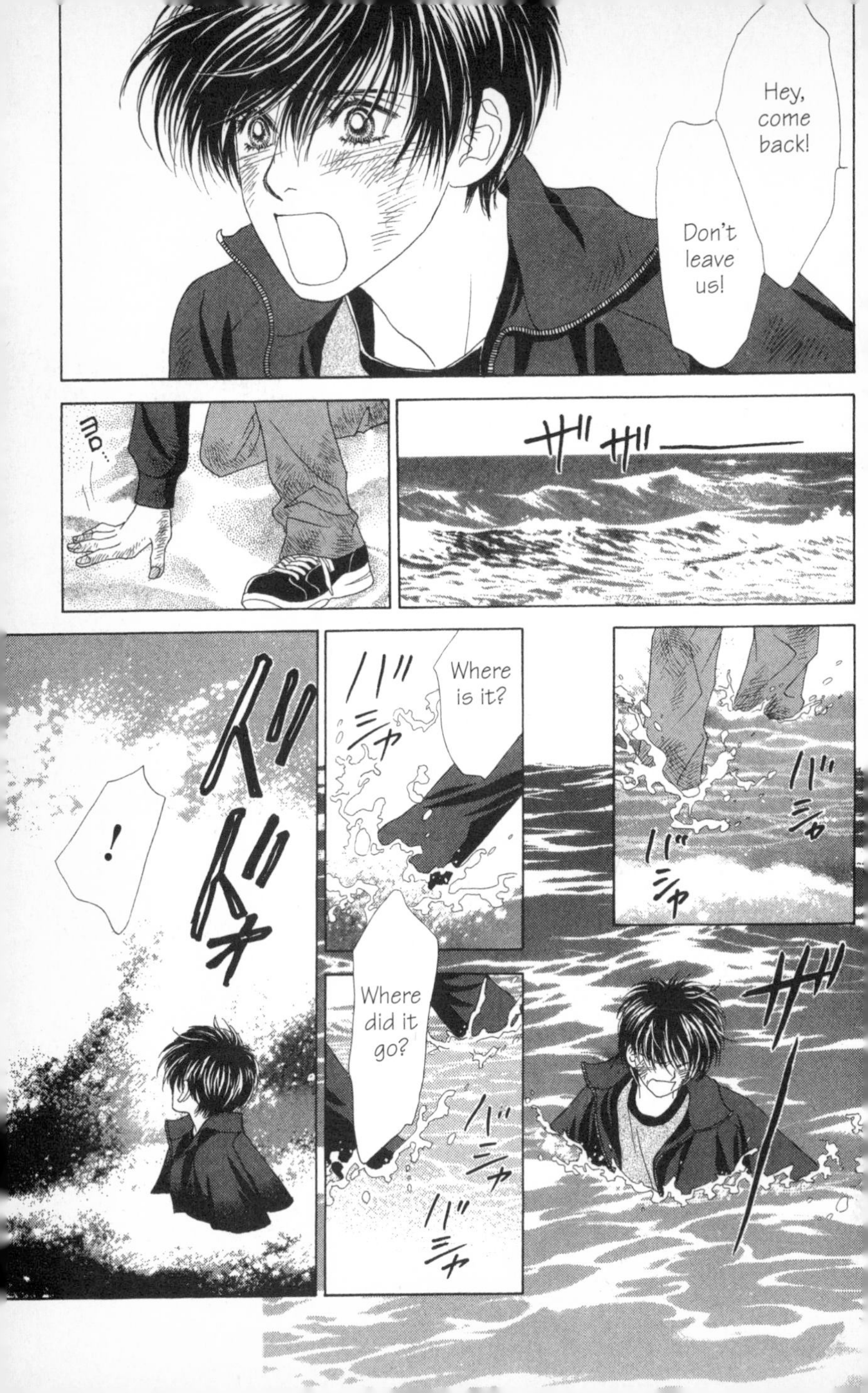
Hey, come back!
Don't leave us!
Where is it?
Where did it go?
!

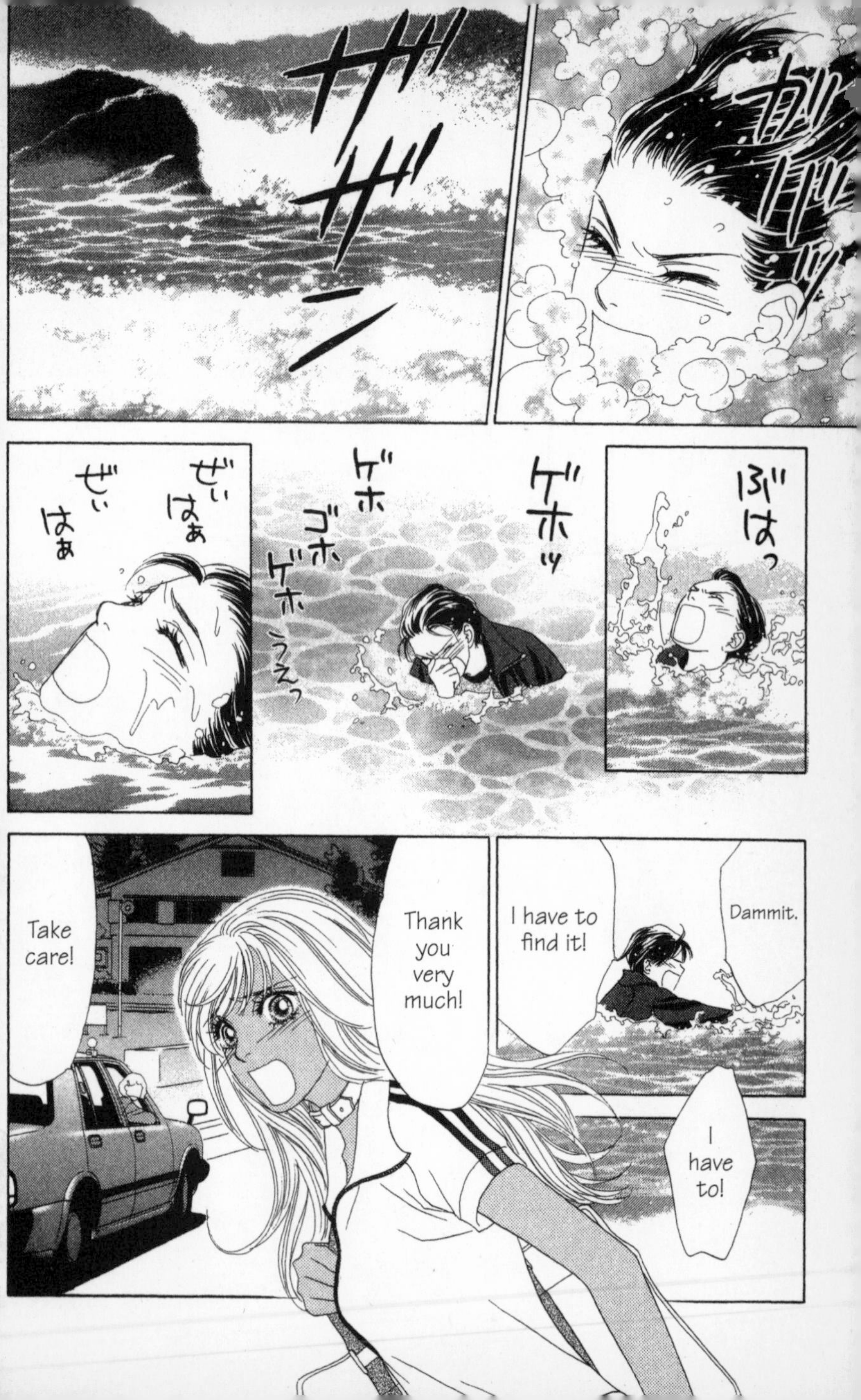
ザザザー
ぶはっ
ゲホッ
ゲホ
ゴホ
ゲホ
うえっ
ぜぃ
はぁ
ぜぃ
はぁ
Dammit.
I have to find it!
I have to!
Thank you very much!
Take care!

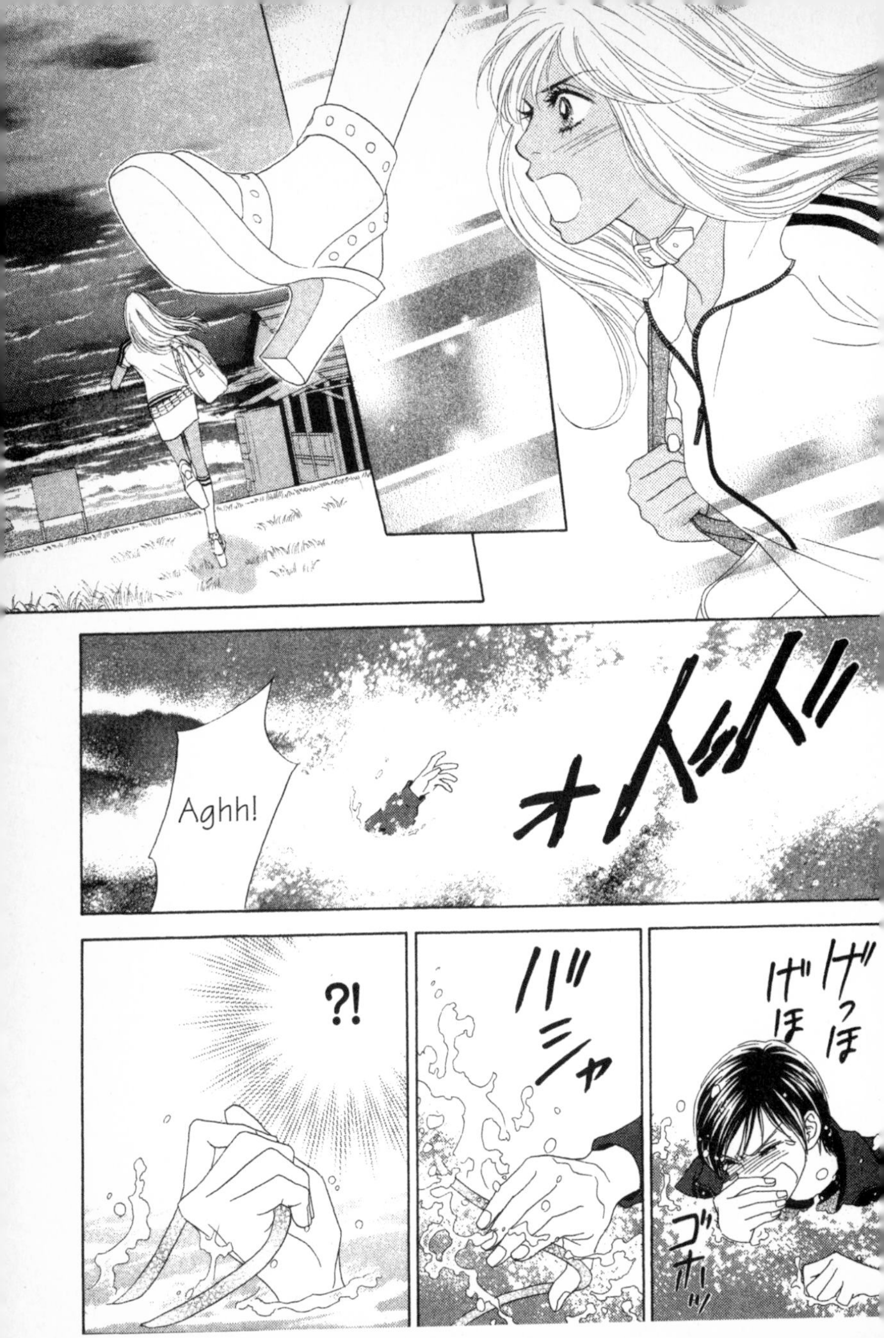
Aghh!
?!
バシャ
げっほ
げほ
ゴホッ

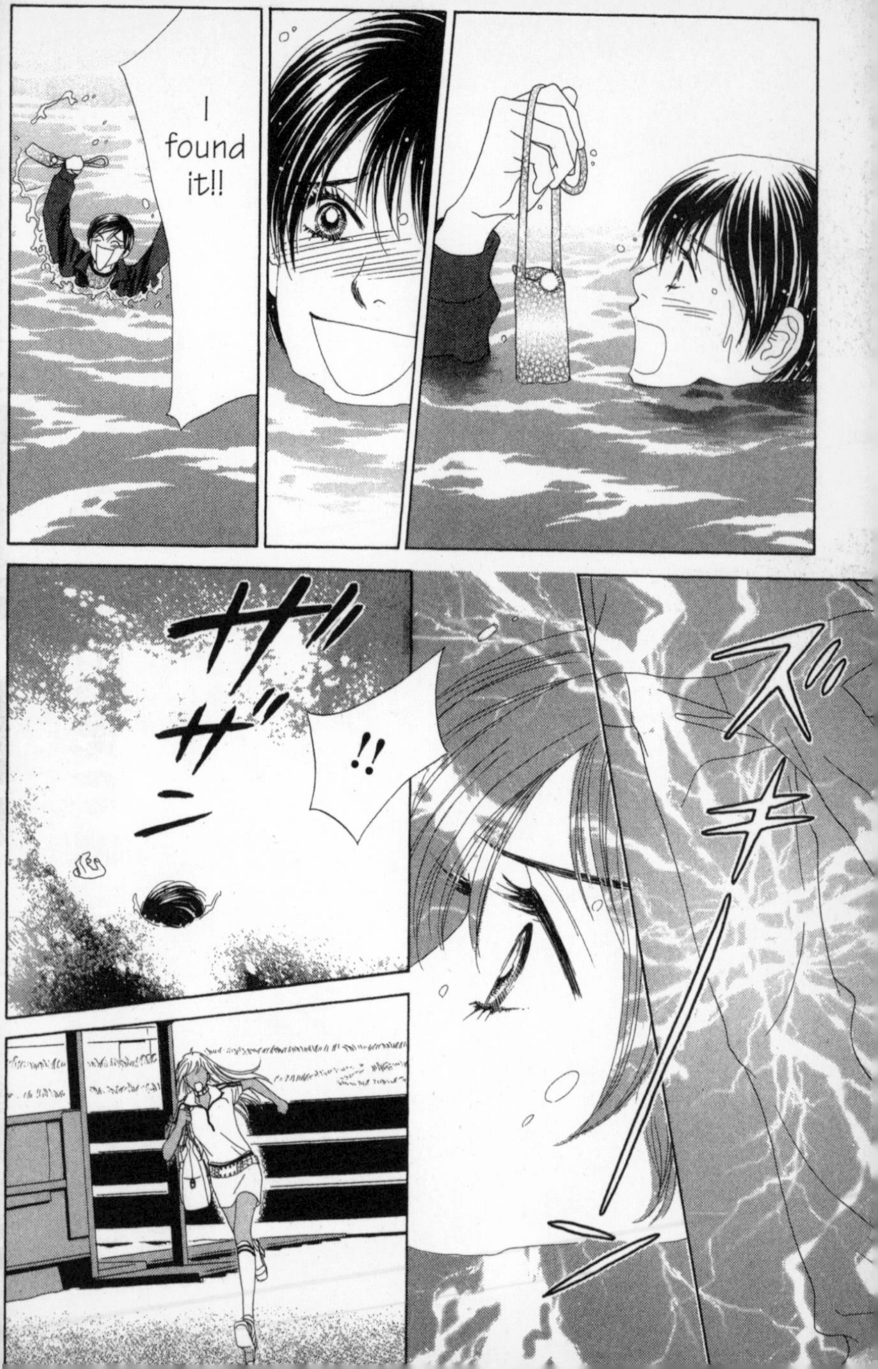

I found it!!
ザザーン
!!
ズキーン

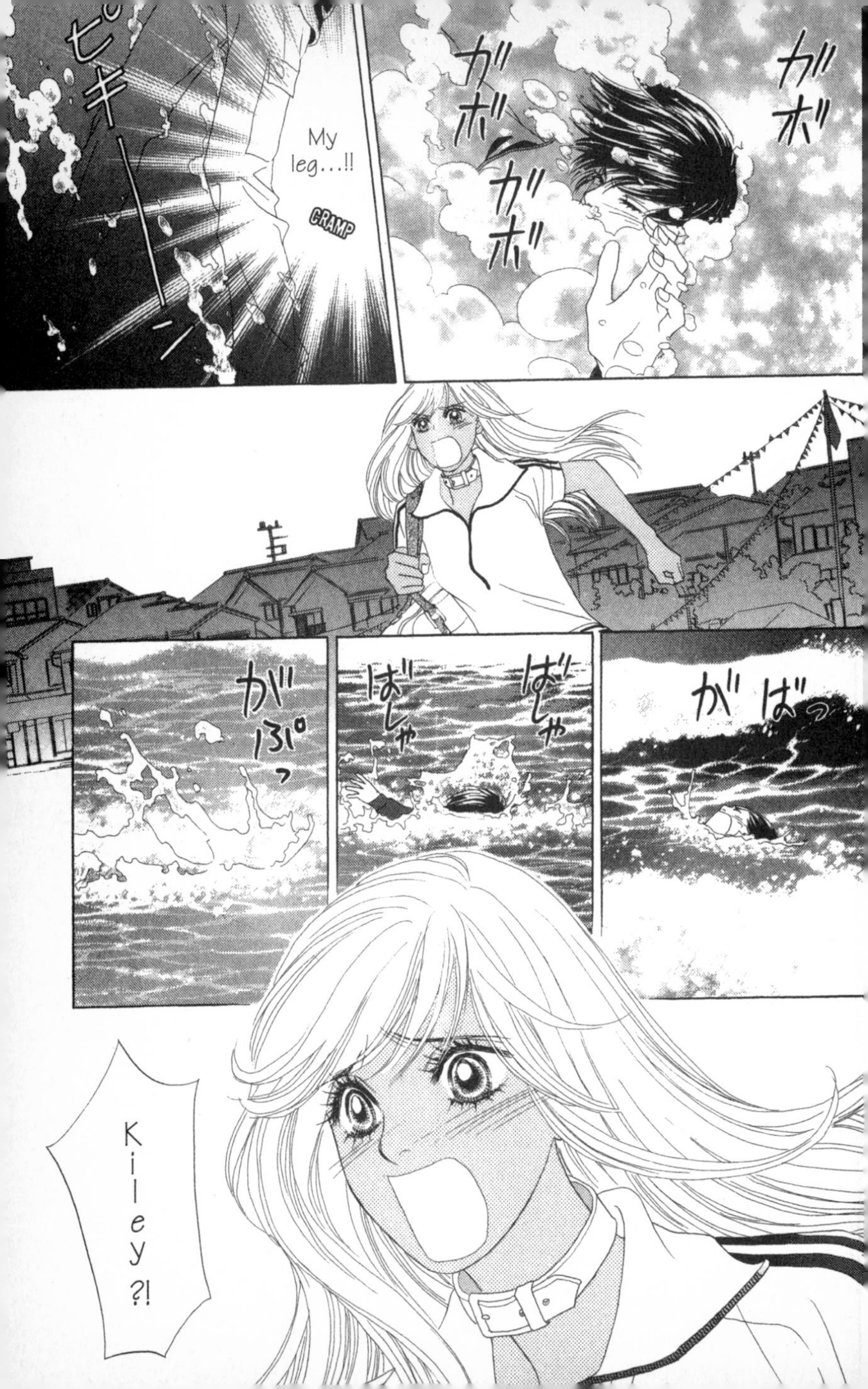

ガボ
ガボ
ガボ
ピキーン
My leg...!!
CRAMP
がばっ
ばしゃ
ばしゃ
がぷっ
Kiley?!

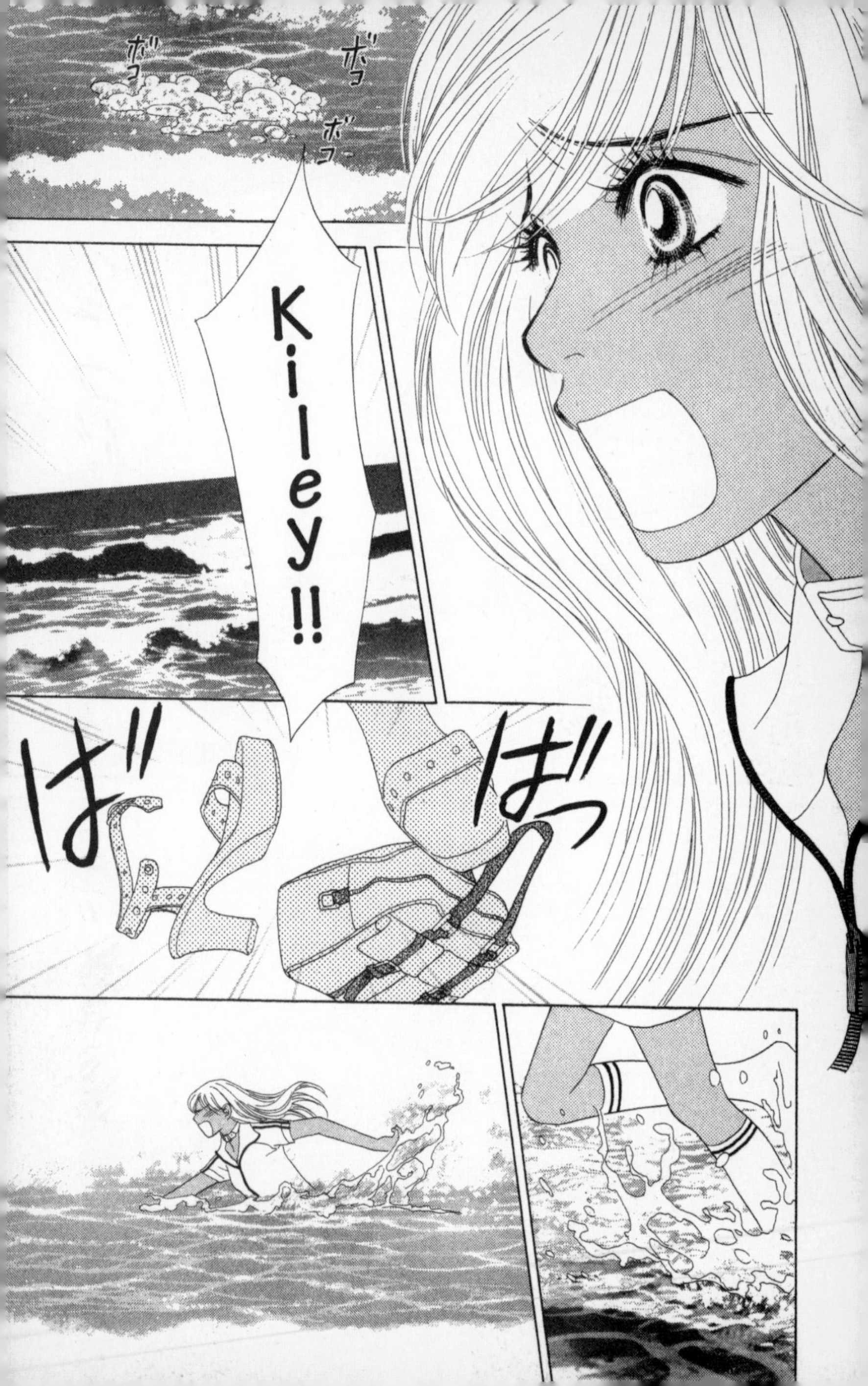
ゴボ
ゴボ
ゴボ
Kiley!!
ばっ
ばっ

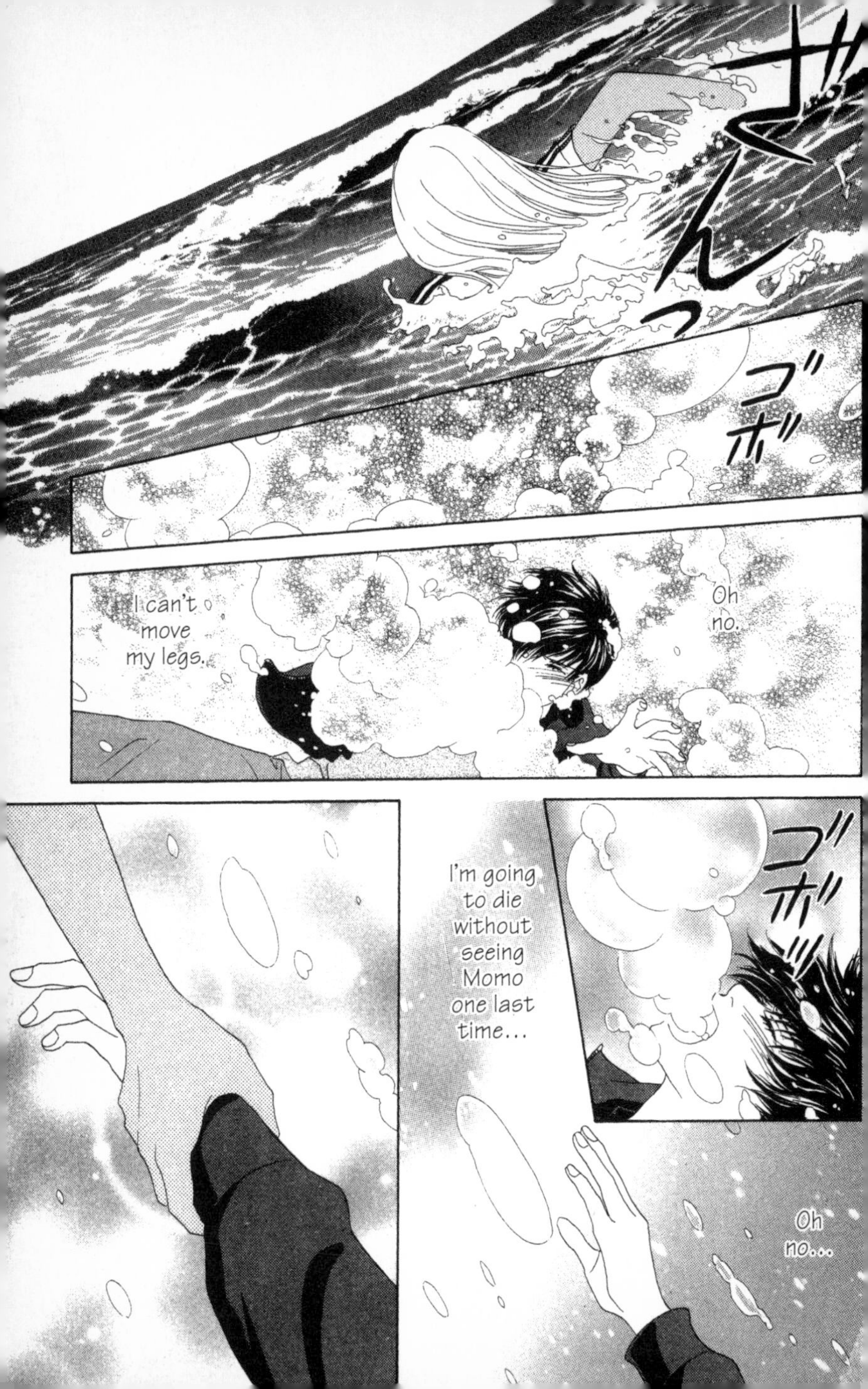
ざ!!ぶんっ
ゴボ
Oh no.
I can't move my legs.
ゴボボ
I'm going to die without seeing Momo one last time...
Oh no...

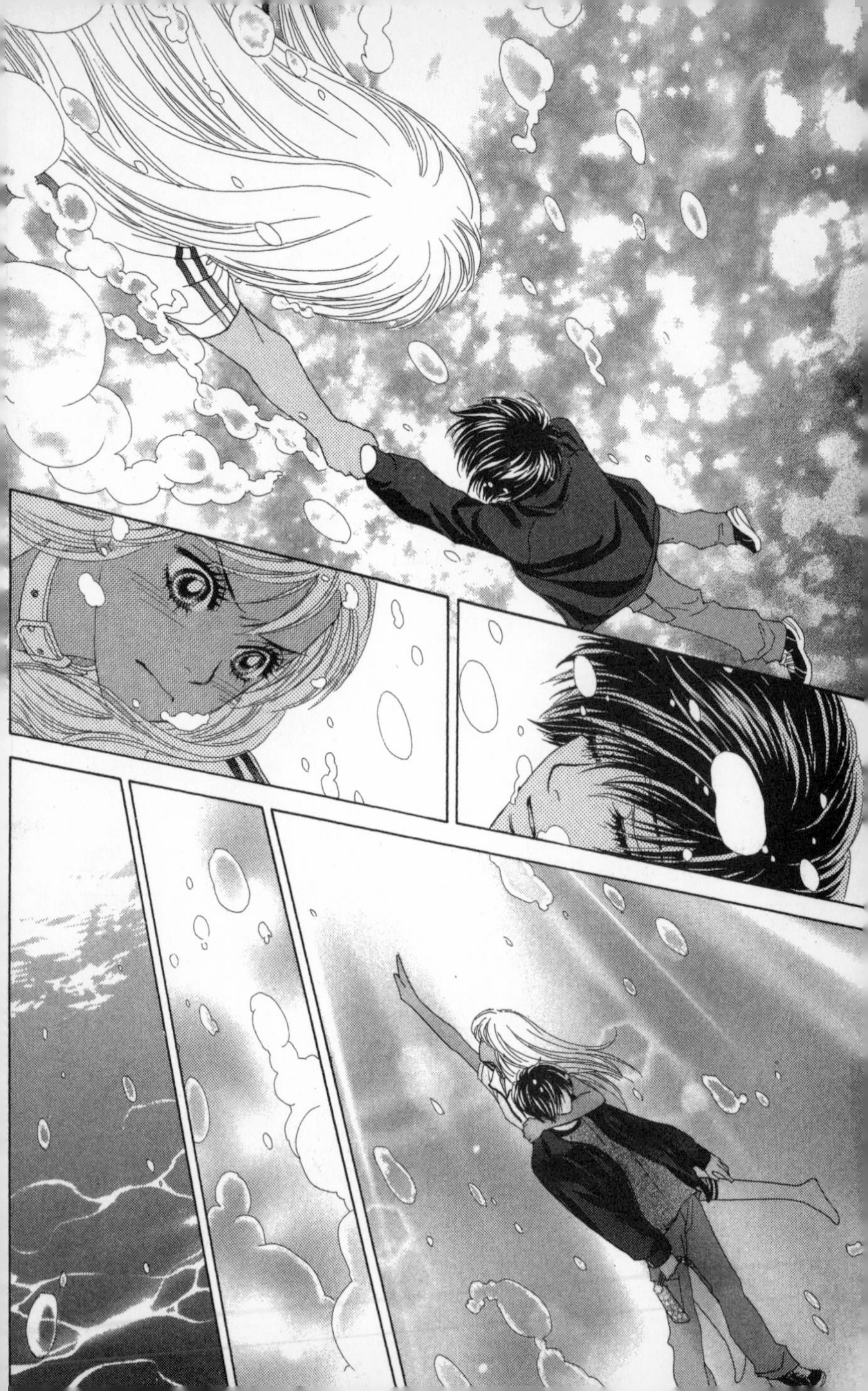

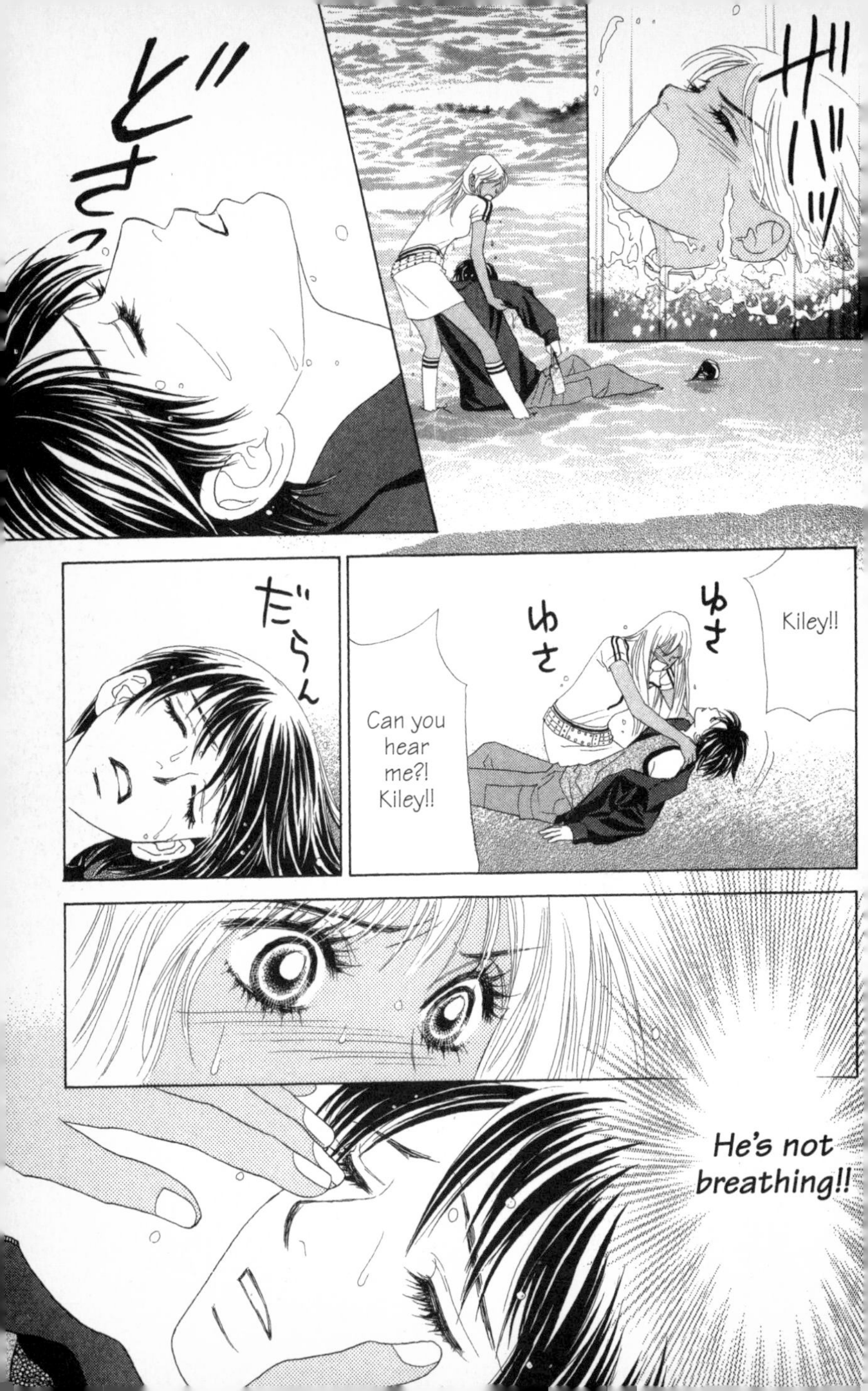
ザバッ
どさっ
Kiley!!
ゆさ
ゆさ
Can you hear me?! Kiley!!
だらん
He's not breathing!!

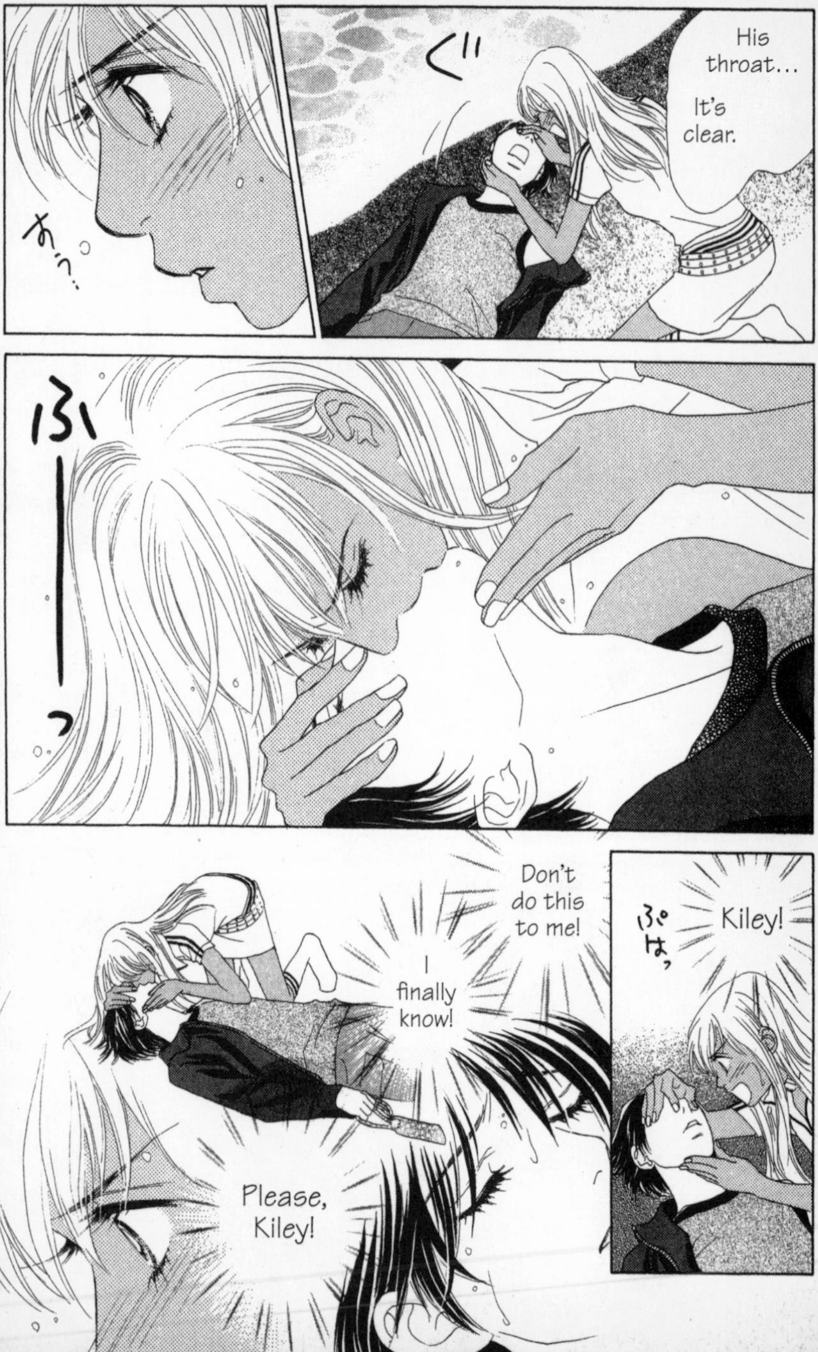
ぐい
His throat…
It's clear.
おっ…
ふーっ
ぷはっ
Kiley!
Don't do this to me!
I finally know!
Please, Kiley!

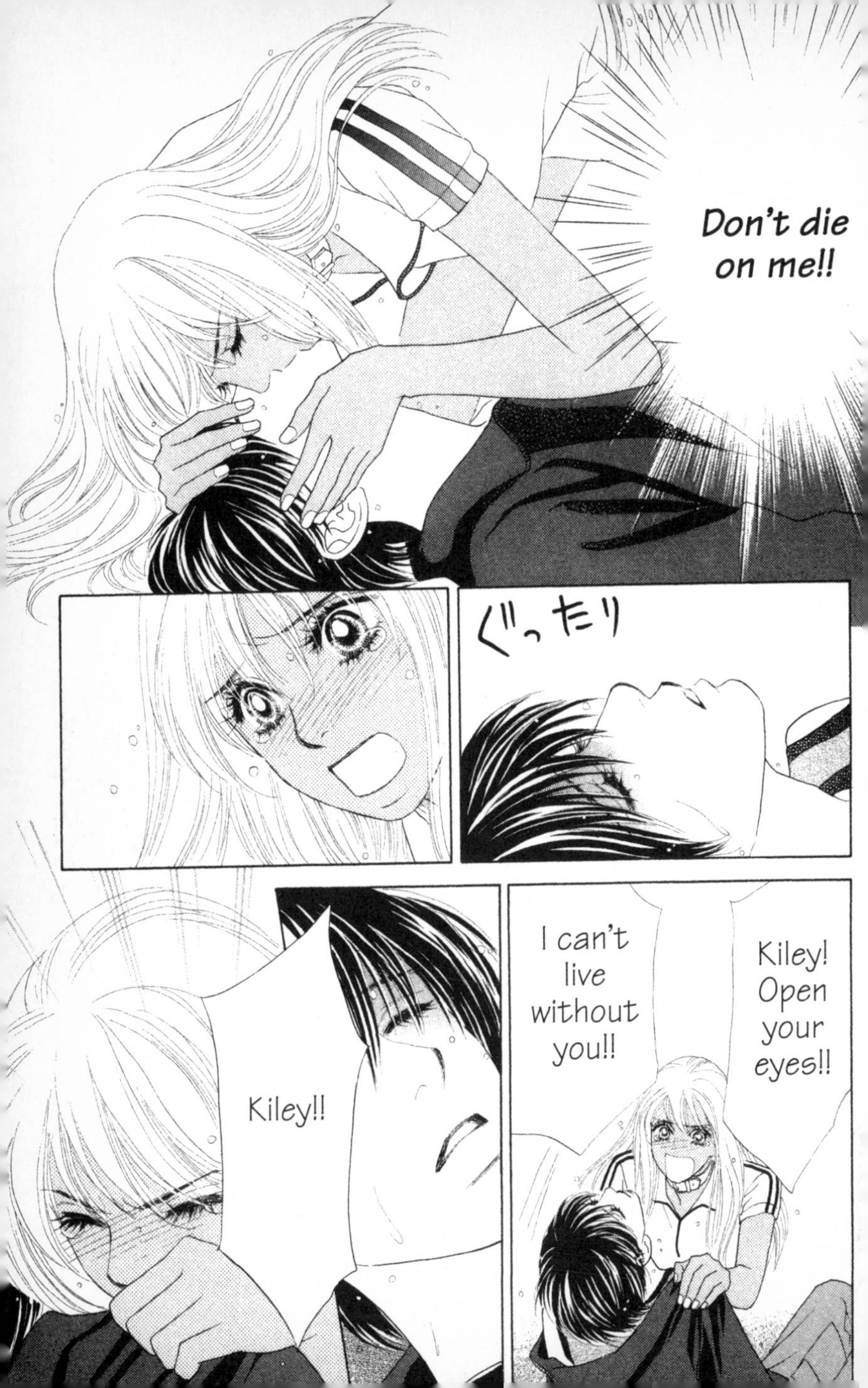
Don't die on me!!
ぐったり
Kiley! Open your eyes!!
I can't live without you!!
Kiley!!

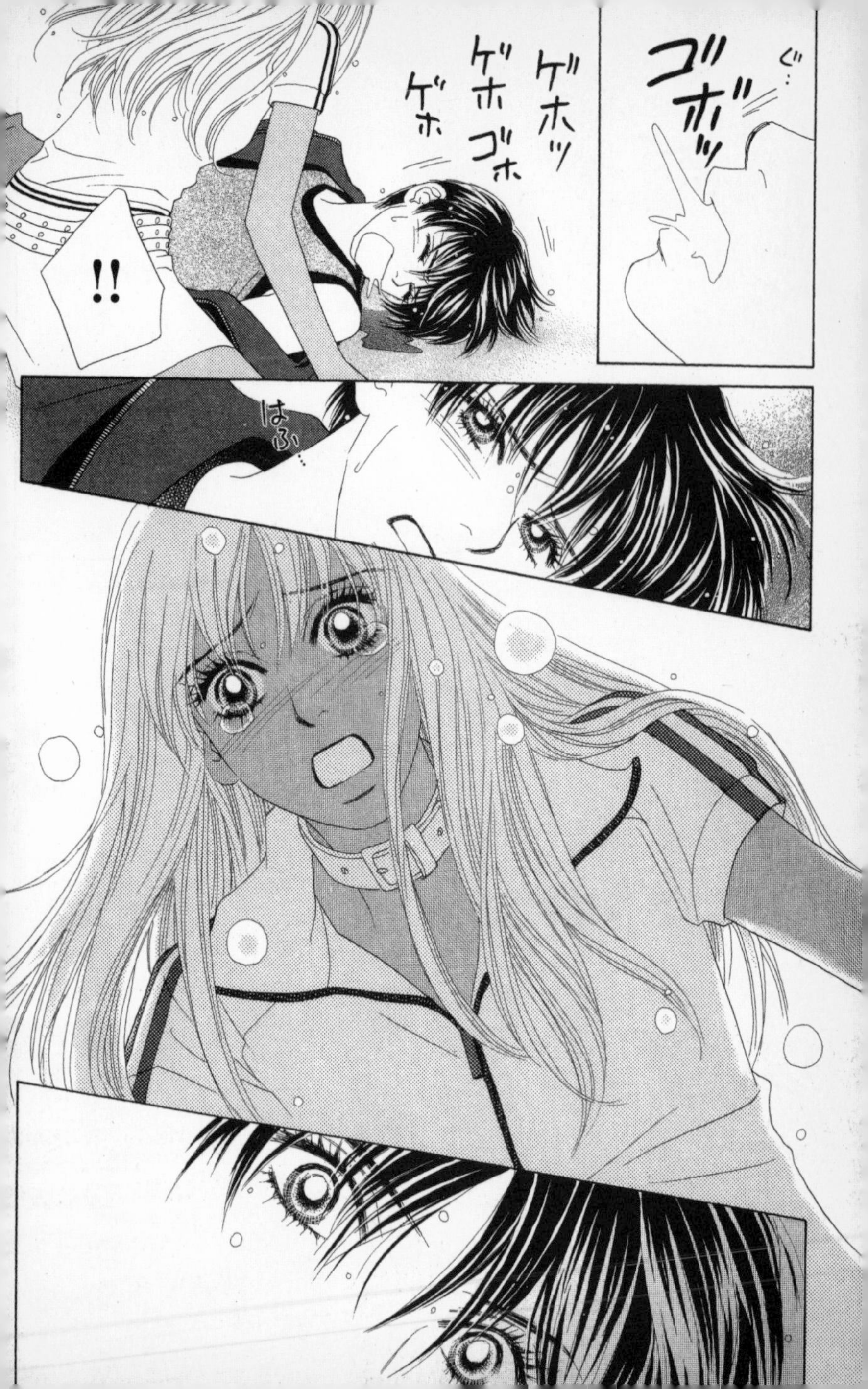
ぐ…
ゴボッ
ゲホッ
ゲホゴホ
ゲホ
!!
はふ…

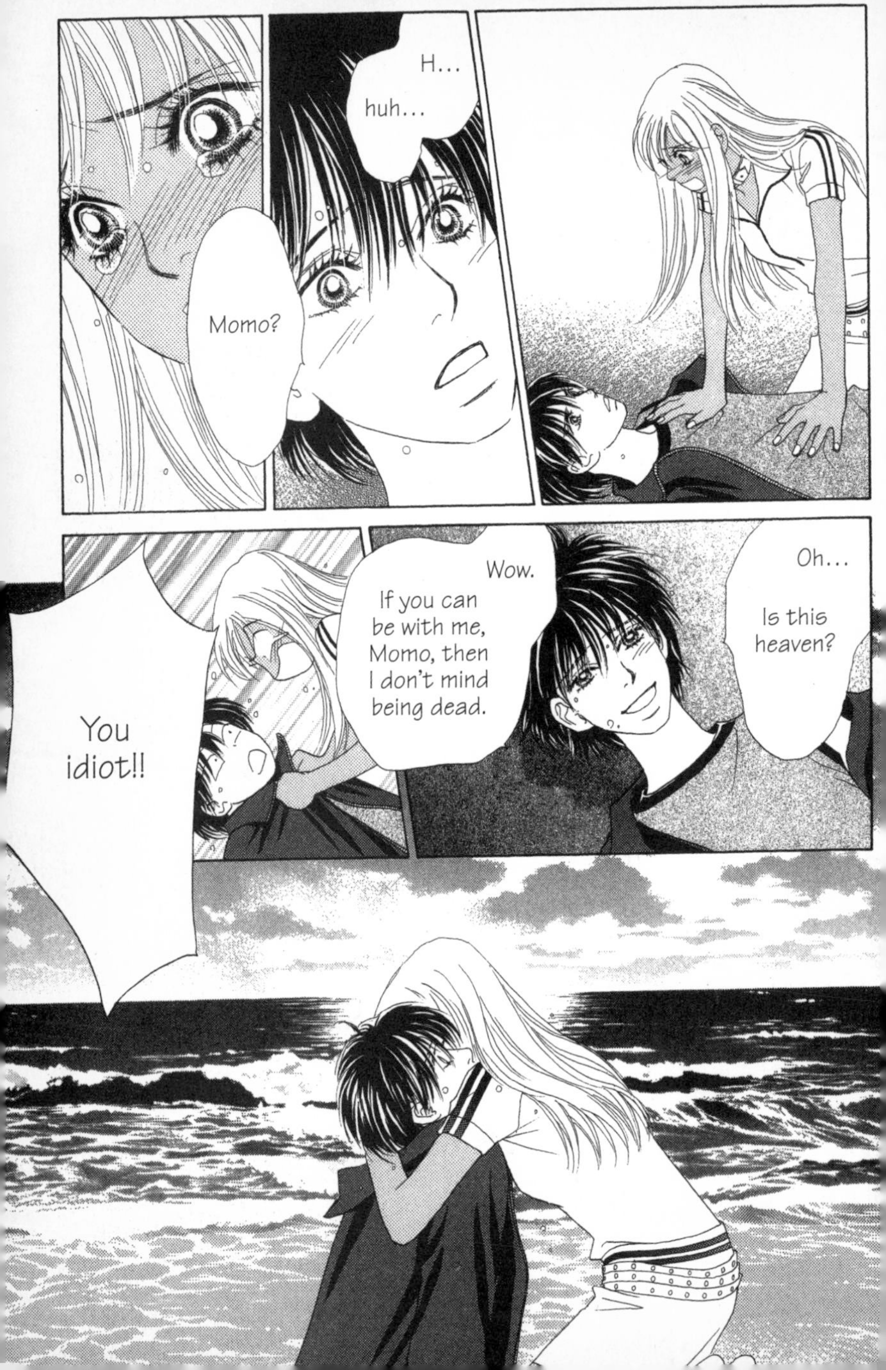
H... huh...
Momo?
Oh... Is this heaven?
Wow. If you can be with me, Momo, then I don't mind being dead.
You idiot!!

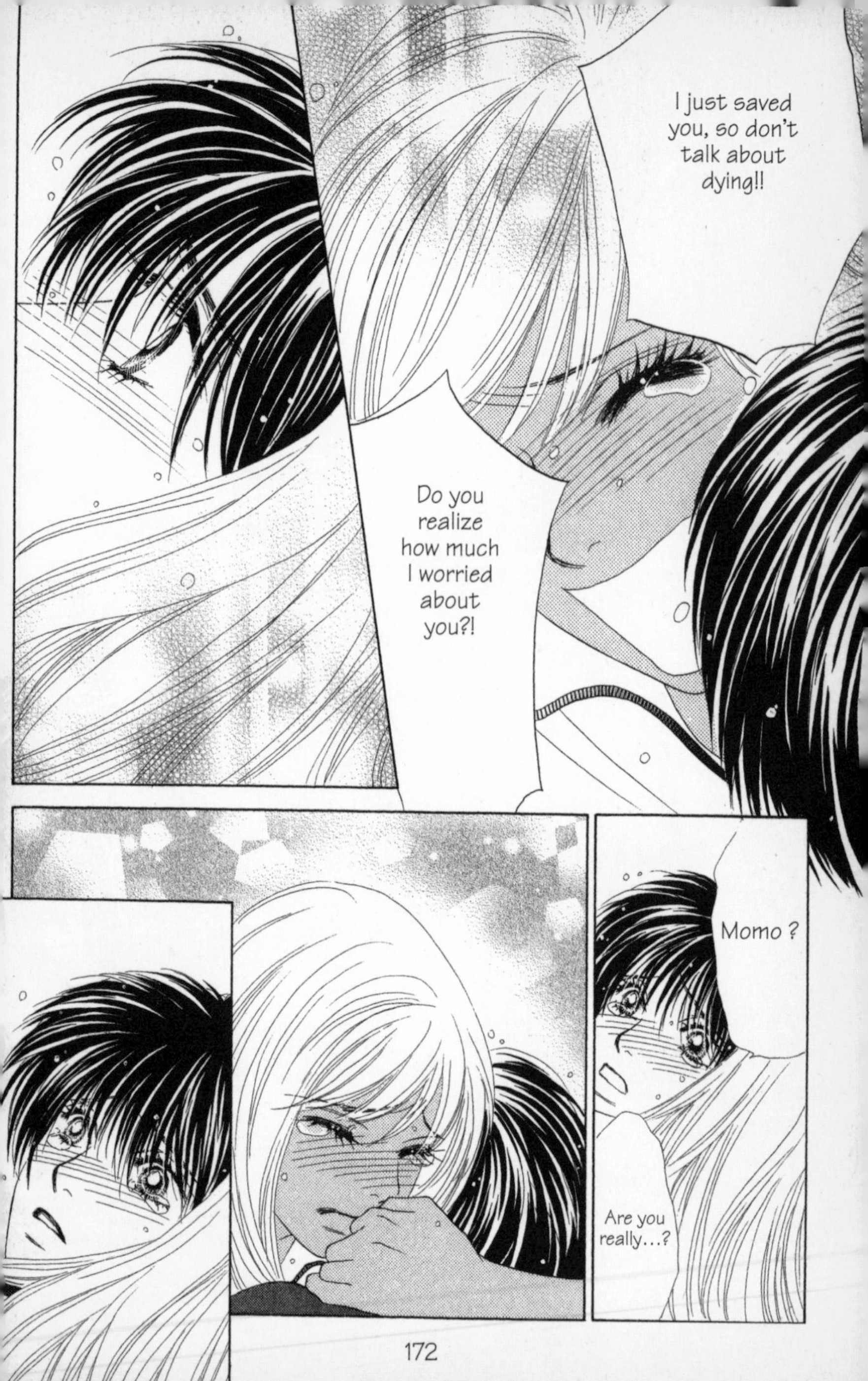
I just saved you, so don't talk about dying!!
Do you realize how much I worried about you?!
Momo ?
Are you really…?

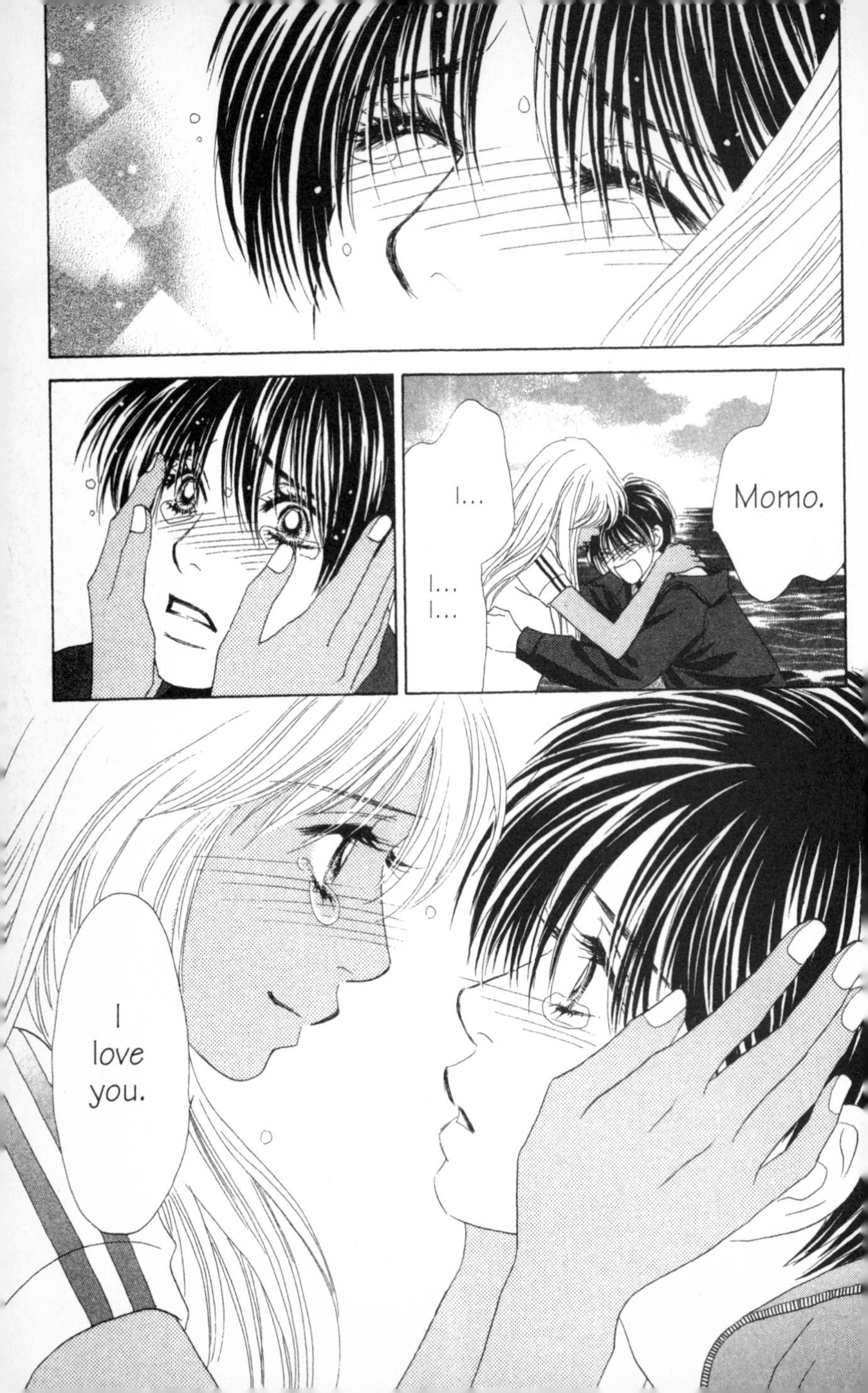
Momo.
I...
I...
I...
I love you.

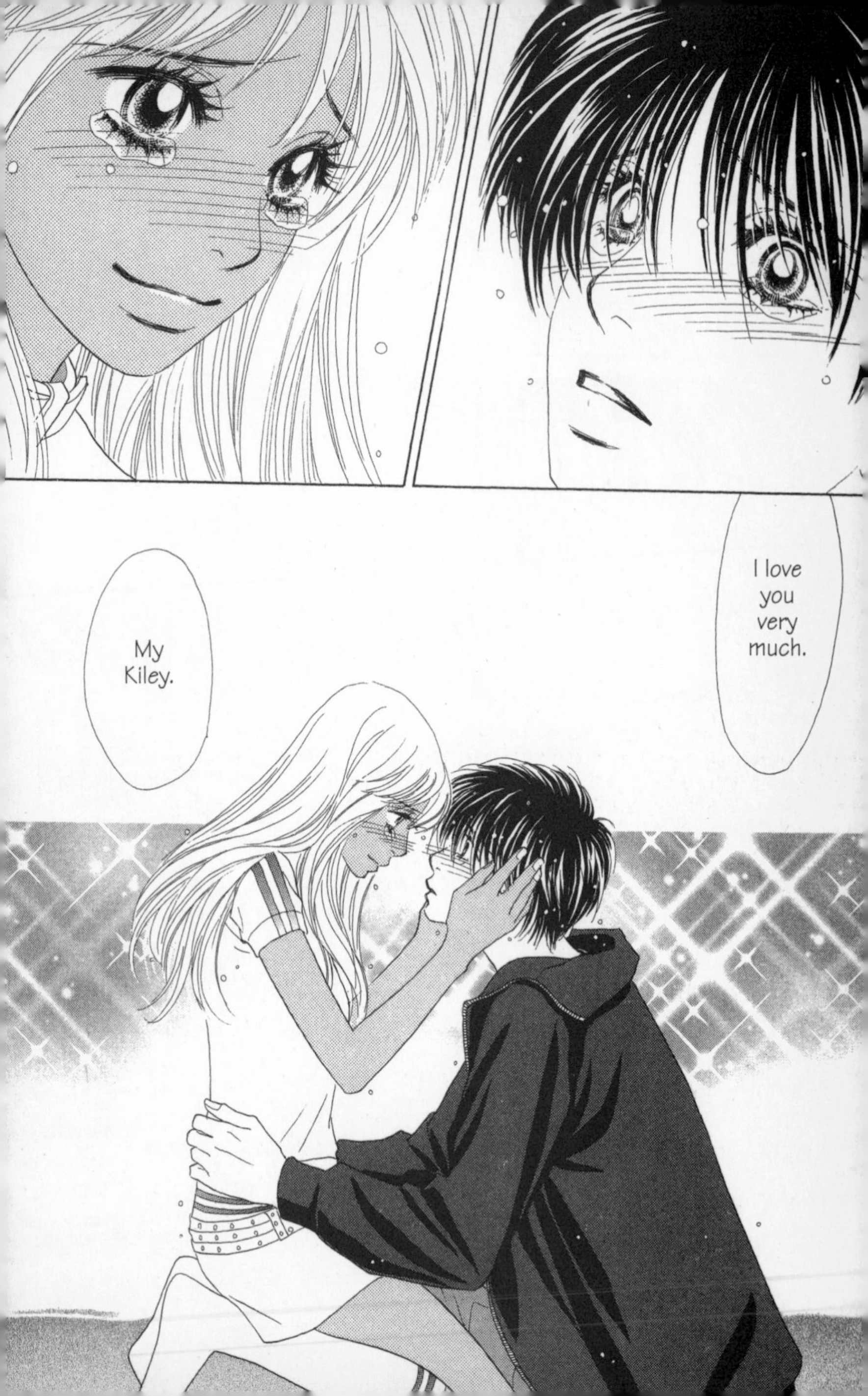
I love you very much.
My Kiley.

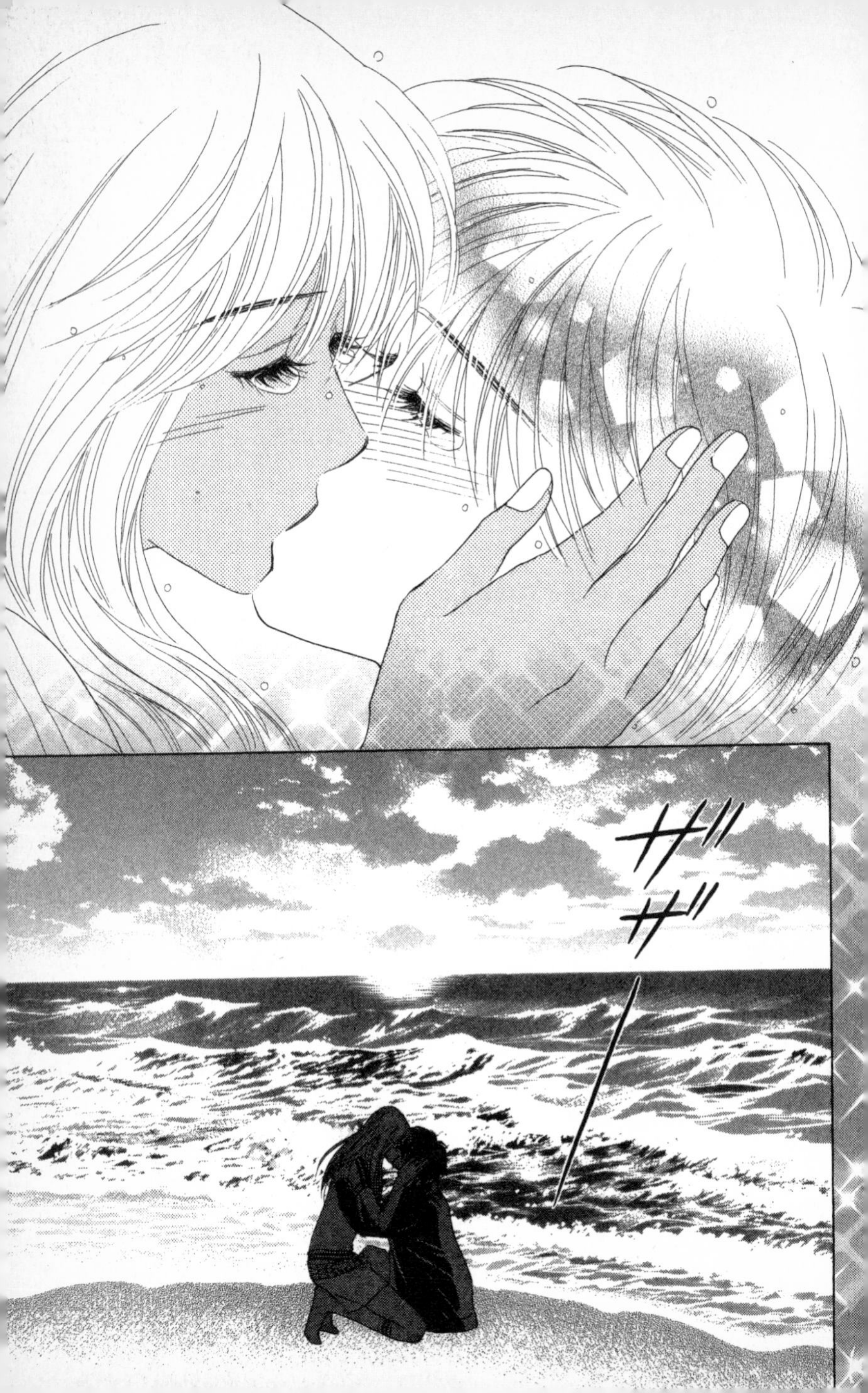
ザザ

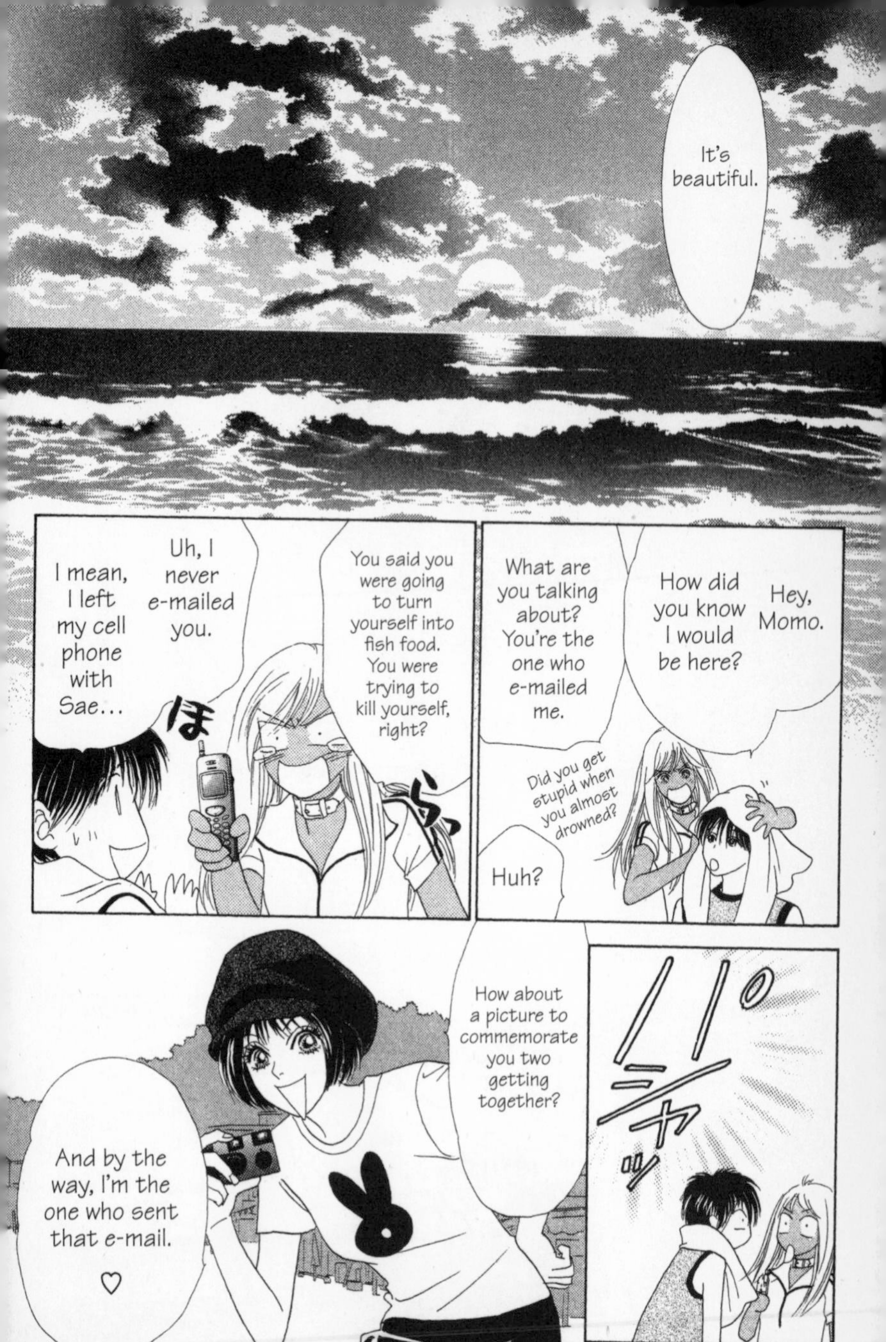

It's beautiful.
Hey, Momo.
How did you know I would be here?
What are you talking about? You're the one who e-mailed me.
Did you get stupid when you almost drowned?
Huh?
ふ
You said you were going to turn yourself into fish food. You were trying to kill yourself, right?
Uh, I never e-mailed you.
I mean, I left my cell phone with Sae…
ほ
パシャッ
How about a picture to commemorate you two getting together?
And by the way, I'm the one who sent that e-mail. ♡

Published in Bessatsu Friend, 2003, October—December issues, 2004 January issue.

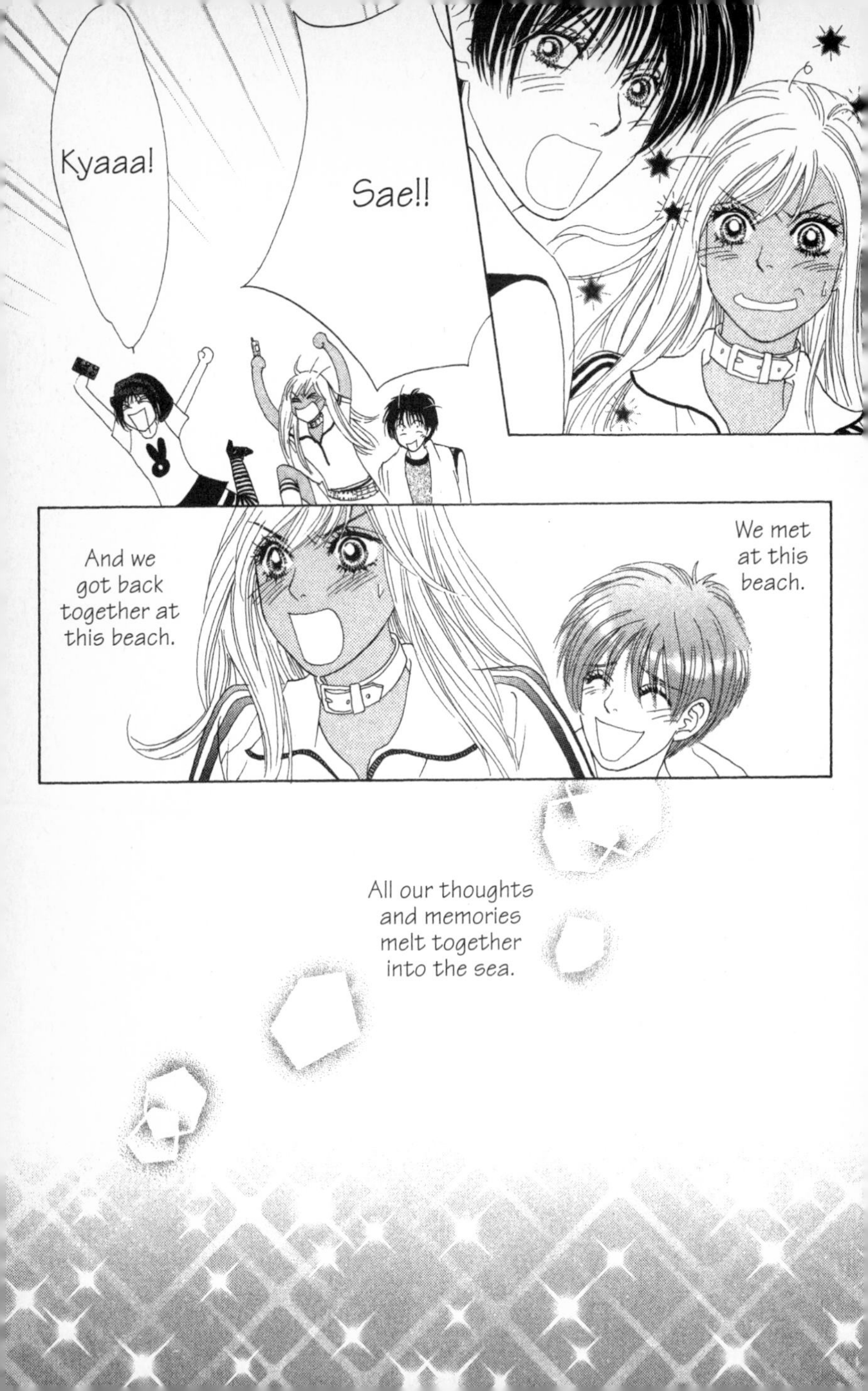
Sae!!
Kyaaa!
We met at this beach.
And we got back together at this beach.
All our thoughts and memories melt together into the sea.

I will never again lose what I cherish the most.

I'm making a promise today, a promise to the sea.

Peach Girl : Change of Heart
The End

Staff

Aiko   Amemori
Tomomi   Kasue
Satsuki   Furukawa
Akiko   Kawashima
Ayumi   Yoshida

Editor
Toshiyuki   Tanaka

2003. 12. 23

Miwa   Ueda

"Peach Girl: Why is it coming to an end?!" Special Interview

Miwa Ueda vs. Sonin

After 6 years, *Peach Girl* finally has come to an end with last month's episode. Here, we bring to you an interview between the author Miwa Ueda and a big Peach fan, Sonin (so big that she even named her cat Momo). You'll find a lot of secret *Peach* episodes here! This must-read interview is about to start!!

Was it fate?
My encounter with Peach Girl.

Sonin: How do you do. I never thought I would ever get to meet you, so I'm really excited today. First of all, I know this is sudden, but can I tell you how long I've been a fan? (laughs) When I was in my second year of junior high, I read *Oh! My Darling* and became a fan of your work, Ueda-sensei. When I learned that you were being published in *Bessatsu Friend*, I decided to buy it. And as it happened, that issue contained the first episode of *Peach Girl*.
Ueda: Really?
Sonin: The first episode was so much fun, I even wrote a fan letter. I wrote, "Please keep it going until you complete book no. 20!" (laughs) I was afraid, since *Oh! My Darling* ended after only 8 books…
Ueda: At first, I didn't intend on continuing it for that long. I had never done a manga that was as character-driven as *Peach Girl* was, so I had my doubts.

Sonin: Oh really? But I really had a great time reading it for such a long time. But in last month's *Bessatsu Friend*, when I read that the next episode was going to be the last, I thought, "No way! It's going to end?!" I was really sad. (laughs) And when I read the final episode, I was really touched! When you first began drawing, did you always envision that ending?
Ueda: It was never a firm idea. At certain points, I started thinking, "Maybe she's gonna stay with Toji…"
Sonin: When I first started reading, I thought for sure that she would end up with Kiley, but at some point, I began to wonder, "Hey, is she going to stick with Toji?" I really did!
Ueda: Yeah, yeah. There were times when I began to think otherwise, but in the end, I decided that she would be with Kiley, and so I settled on this ending.
Sonin: Taking advantage of this interview, there's something I wanted to ask you—the story begins like this (see illustration 1 at left)...

The commemorative first scene of the first episode of *Peach Girl*. Sonin: When I first read this, I was certain that it held some deep meaning. I decided to remember this scene. No matter how heated Momo and Sae's battles became, I was determined to never forget this scene.

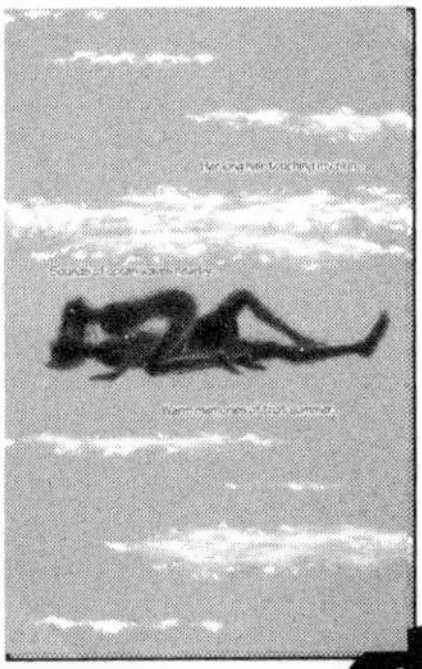

1

Ueda: There isn't any real deep meaning to this. I didn't have much time left before deadline, so I probably just winged it.
Sonin: Whaaaaat? I thought that you were trying to create a link to the very first scene, but that you were worried that you weren't able to maintain continuity with that first scene. That's what I thought.
Ueda: Oh, so you were worried about me. (laughs)

Sonin: So I guess there wasn't any particular meaning to it...

Ueda: But it did link up with the final episode, didn't it? I guess it was sort of a foreshadowing. Although it took 6 whole years. (laughs)

Sonin: I believe that readers were divided up into Toji factions and Kiley factions, but which camp would you say that you belong to?

Ueda: At first, I was a Toji supporter, but in the end I became a Kiley supporter. When I was mainly featuring Toji, I was a Toji supporter, and when I was featuring Kiley, I put a lot of emotion into Kiley.

Sonin: I believe that your emotions must have infected me, because at first I really liked Toji. But now it's Kiley. If they were real-life people, I'd probably have to go with Kiley also. I guess I'm kind of attracted to players. I guess in that sense I belong to the Kiley faction.

Ueda: Toji is a straight arrow, and doesn't reveal too much of himself as a character.

. . . .

Sonin: I think that the characters in *Peach Girl* feel really natural, and I wouldn't be surprised if they really existed. Were they modeled after any actual people?

Ueda: They weren't modeled after anybody. Neither Momo, nor Kiley nor Toji. I didn't even model them after celebrities or expand upon them either.

Sonin: So they were completely imaginary. I think that's amazing! I think that I relate a lot Momo's character. Even if people lie to me, I tend to just believe them. I guess I'm easy to fool. I think that part of me is just like Momo.

Ueda: Momo, unlike Sae, has certain values, and they tend to constrict her. I guess she has a strong sense of duty... So I suppose, for that reason, she has a hard time making decisions for herself, and in that sense I think that she's not really like most modern girls.

Sonin: And to top it all off, Toji and Kiley are such good guys that it's hard to choose. I could really understand how Momo would feel lost and unable to make a decision.

. . . .

If Sae weren't around, would Momo have chosen Toji?

Sonin: And the other character we can't forget is Sae. Or I should say, how could we forget? (laughs) Early on, Sae is really terrible, isn't she?

Ueda: Even now, sometimes when I read it over, I think to myself, "My goodness, how terrible she is." (laughs) I would get fan letters about "personal Sae sightings," which were pretty far out, and provoked me into thinking, "I guess I could take this a little farther" and so I suppose there was a time when I got a bit carried away.

Sonin: How did you come up with the concept of the "paper-thin Sae" who goes flat whenever she gets depressed?

Ueda: Well, usually I don't want to get into describing a supporting character's psychological state in the dialogue bubbles. And since Sae wasn't the main character anyway, I wanted to portray Sae's depressed state visually. I had several different ideas, (continued on p. 183)

(continued from p. 182)
... but in the end I decided that the paper-thin Sae was the most recognizable visual. I didn't think that I would continue to draw it for so long, but again, I guess I got carried away. (laughs)

Sonin: Oh, but I thought it was so much fun. Although I kept thinking, "There's no way, there's no way." (laughs) But that's the great thing about manga, isn't it? I thought it was so much fun how the paper-thin Sae would go back to normal, like *poof!*

Ueda: The backbone of Kiley and Sae's characters are pretty clearly defined, so they were easy to draw. But sometimes, when it came to Momo and Toji, I would stall and go in circles. The both of them are pretty passive, you know. If it were only Momo, Toji and Kiley, I wonder how things would have developed. The story might have ended around book four with Momo getting together with Toji, I guess.

Sonin: Not only are the characters in *Peach Girl* interesting, the story is very dramatic, and it's full of great dialogue too. I think it would make a great TV drama! And so, if that happened, I would love to play the part of Momo. I can still wear a school girl's uniform. (laughs)

· ·

This interview took place on December 2, 2003 at the Teikoku Hotel. (Published in 2004 February issue of *Bessatsu Friend*)

Who will be the main character for Miwa Ueda's Next Story...?!

Sonin: For my last question, this is something that I think all your readers are most anxious to find out, what are you thinking for your next story?

Ueda: I had this thought as I was drawing the last episode. I've always had "good girls" as my main characters up 'til now. So I was wondering if I couldn't have a "bad girl" be the main character next... But then again, I started thinking about a lot of other things too. So anyway, I haven't decided yet. (laughs)

She's so honest, hates lies, and is a very wonderful girl.

Sonin is so cute! Her face is so tiny, her skin is translucent, and her hair is so silky smooth.

LOVE (TRIANGLES)
CAN DRIVE A GIRL TO THE EDGE.
TOKYOPOP
Crazy Love Story™
T
TEEN
AGE 13+
©2004 Lee Vin, DAIWON C.I. INC. ©2004 TOKYOPOP Inc. All Rights Reserved.
www.TOKYOPOP.com

Snow Drop™

Like a fragile flower,
love often blooms in unlikely places.

TOKYOPOP
One
rocks to live.
One
lives to rock.
They've got nothing in common...except each other.
One™
T
TEEN
AGE 13+
©2003 Lee Vin / DAIWON C.I. Inc. ©2004 TOKYOPOP Inc. All rights reserved.
www.TOKYOPOP.com

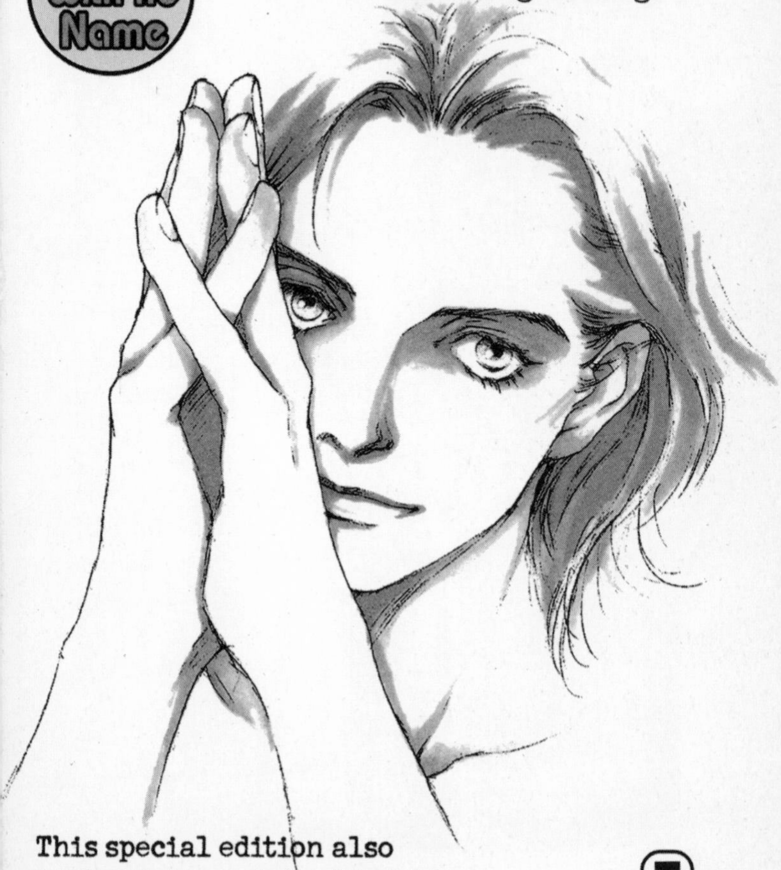

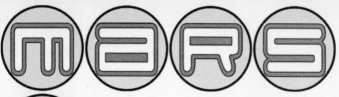

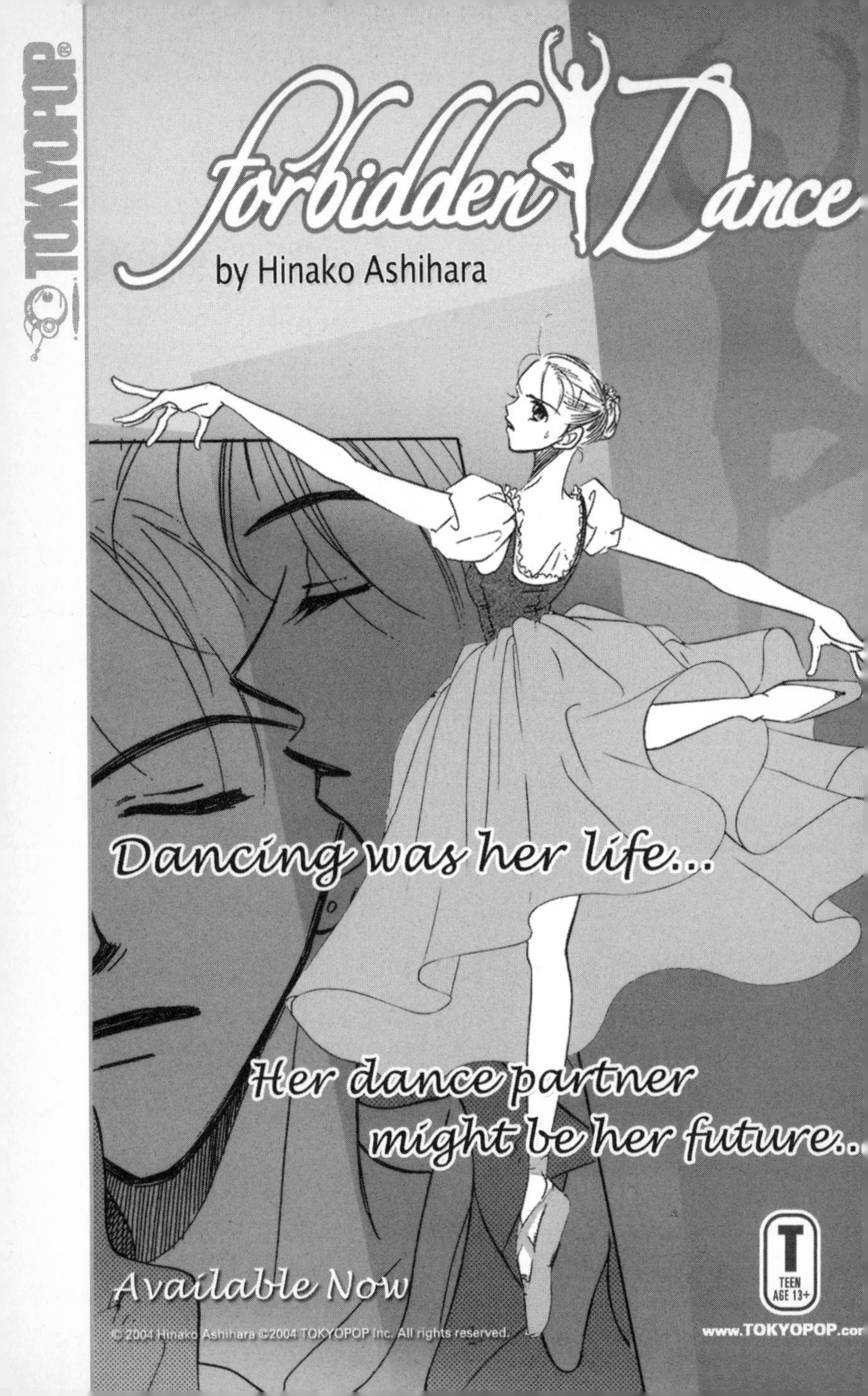
TOKYOPOP®
Forbidden Dance
by Hinako Ashihara
Dancing was her life...
Her dance partner
might be her future...
Available Now
T
TEEN
AGE 13+
© 2004 Hinako Ashihara ©2004 TOKYOPOP Inc. All rights reserved.
www.TOKYOPOP.com

ALSO AVAILABLE FROM  TOKYOPOP®

You want it? We got it!
A full range of TOKYOPOP
products are available now at:
www.TOKYOPOP.com/shop

07.15.04T

ALSO AVAILABLE FROM TOKYOPOP®

MANGA

.HACK//LEGEND OF THE TWILIGHT
@LARGE
ABENOBASHI: MAGICAL SHOPPING ARCADE
A.I. LOVE YOU
AI YORI AOSHI
ANGELIC LAYER
ARM OF KANNON
BABY BIRTH
BATTLE ROYALE
BATTLE VIXENS
BOYS BE...
BRAIN POWERED
BRIGADOON
B'TX
CANDIDATE FOR GODDESS, THE
CARDCAPTOR SAKURA
CARDCAPTOR SAKURA - MASTER OF THE CLOW
CHOBITS
CHRONICLES OF THE CURSED SWORD
CLAMP SCHOOL DETECTIVES
CLOVER
COMIC PARTY
CONFIDENTIAL CONFESSIONS
CORRECTOR YUI
COWBOY BEBOP
COWBOY BEBOP: SHOOTING STAR
CRAZY LOVE STORY
CRESCENT MOON
CROSS
CULDCEPT
CYBORG 009
D•N•ANGEL
DEMON DIARY
DEMON ORORON, THE
DEUS VITAE
DIABOLO
DIGIMON
DIGIMON TAMERS
DIGIMON ZERO TWO
DOLL
DRAGON HUNTER
DRAGON KNIGHTS
DRAGON VOICE
DREAM SAGA
DUKLYON: CLAMP SCHOOL DEFENDERS
EERIE QUEERIE!
ERICA SAKURAZAWA: COLLECTED WORKS
ET CETERA
ETERNITY
EVIL'S RETURN
FAERIES' LANDING
FAKE
FLCL
FLOWER OF THE DEEP SLEEP, THE
FORBIDDEN DANCE
FRUITS BASKET

G GUNDAM
GATEKEEPERS
GETBACKERS
GIRL GOT GAME
GRAVITATION
GTO
GUNDAM SEED ASTRAY
GUNDAM WING
GUNDAM WING: BATTLEFIELD OF PACIFISTS
GUNDAM WING: ENDLESS WALTZ
GUNDAM WING: THE LAST OUTPOST (G-UNIT)
HANDS OFF!
HAPPY MANIA
HARLEM BEAT
HYPER RUNE
I.N.V.U.
IMMORTAL RAIN
INITIAL D
INSTANT TEEN: JUST ADD NUTS
ISLAND
JING: KING OF BANDITS
JING: KING OF BANDITS - TWILIGHT TALES
JULINE
KARE KANO
KILL ME, KISS ME
KINDAICHI CASE FILES, THE
KING OF HELL
KODOCHA: SANA'S STAGE
LAMENT OF THE LAMB
LEGAL DRUG
LEGEND OF CHUN HYANG, THE
LES BIJOUX
LOVE HINA
LOVE OR MONEY
LUPIN III
LUPIN III: WORLD'S MOST WANTED
MAGIC KNIGHT RAYEARTH I
MAGIC KNIGHT RAYEARTH II
MAHOROMATIC: AUTOMATIC MAIDEN
MAN OF MANY FACES
MARMALADE BOY
MARS
MARS: HORSE WITH NO NAME
MINK
MIRACLE GIRLS
MIYUKI-CHAN IN WONDERLAND
MODEL
MOURYOU KIDEN: LEGEND OF THE NYMPHS
NECK AND NECK
ONE
ONE I LOVE, THE
PARADISE KISS
PARASYTE
PASSION FRUIT
PEACH GIRL
PEACH GIRL: CHANGE OF HEART
PET SHOP OF HORRORS
PITA-TEN

07.15.04T

WITHDRAWN

STOP!

This is the back of the book.
You wouldn't want to spoil a great ending

This book is printed "manga-style," in the authentic Japanese right-to-left format. Since none of the artwork has been flipped or altered, readers get to experience the story just as the creator intended. You've been asking for it, so TOKYOPOP® delivered: authentic, hot-off-the-press, and far more fun!

DIRECTIONS

If this is your first time reading manga-style, here's a quick guide to help you understand how it works.

It's easy... just start in the top right panel and follow the numbers. Have fun, and look for more 100% authentic manga from TOKYOPOP®!